UNIVERSITIES AND GLOBALIZATION

To Market, To Market

Sociocultural, Political, and Historical Studies in Education
Joel Spring, Editor

Spring • The Cultural Transformation of a Native American Family and Its Tribe 1763–1995

Peshkin • Places of Memory: Whiteman's Schools and Native American Communities

Nespor • Tangled Up in School: Politics, Space, Bodies, and Signs in the Educational Process

Weinberg • Asian-American Education: Historical Background and Current Realities

Lipka/Mohatt/The Ciulistet Group • Transforming the Culture of Schools: Yu'pik Eskimo Examples

Benham/Heck • Culture and Educational Policy in Hawai'i: The Silencing of Native Voices

Spring • Education and the Rise of the Global Economy

Pugach • On the Border of Opportunity: Education, Community, and Language at the U.S.-Mexico Line

Hones/Cha • Educating New Americans: Immigrant Lives and Learning

Gabbard, Ed. • Knowledge and Power in the Global Economy: Politics and The Rhetoric of School Reform

Glander • Origins of Mass Communications Research During the American Cold War: Educational Effects and Contemporary Implications

Nieto, Ed. • Puerto Rican Students in U.S. Schools

Benham/Cooper, Eds. • Indigenous Educational Models for Contemporary Practice: In Our Mother's Voice

Spring • The Universal Right to Education: Justification, Definition, and Guidelines

Peshkin • Permissible Advantage?: The Moral Consequences of Elite Schooling

DeCarvalho • Rethinking Family-School Relations: A Critique of Parental Involvement in Schooling

Borman/Stringfield/Slavin, Eds. • Title I: Compensatory Education at the Crossroads

Roberts • Remaining and Becoming: Cultural Crosscurrents in an Hispano School

Meyer/Boyd, Eds. • Education Between State, Markets, and Civil Society: Comparative Perspectives

Luke • Globalization and Women in Academics: North/West–South/East

Grant/Lei, Eds. • Global Constructions of Multicultural Education: Theories and Realities

Spring • Globalization and Educational Rights: An Intercivilizational Analysis

Spring • Political Agendas for Education: From the Religious Right to the Green Party, Second Edition

McCarty • A Place to Be Navajo: Rough Rock and The Struggle for Self-Determination in Indigenous Schooling

Hones, Ed. • American Dreams, Global Visions: Dialogic Teacher Research with Refugee and Immigrant Families

Benham/Stein, Eds. • The Renaissance of American Indian Higher Education: Capturing the Dream

Ogbu • Black American Students in an Affluent Suburb: A Study of Academic Disengagement

Books, Ed. • Invisible Children in the Society and Its Schools, Second Edition

Spring • Educating the Consumer-Citizen: A History of the Marriage of Schools, Advertising, and Media

Hemmings • Coming of Age in U.S. High Schools: Economic, Kinship, Religious, and Political Crosscurrents

Heck • Studying Educational and Social Policy: Theoretical Concepts and Research Methods

Lakes/Carter, Eds. • Globalizing Education for Work: Comparative Perspectives on Gender and the New Economy

Spring • How Educational Ideologies Are Shaping Global Society: Intergovernmental Organizations, NGOs, and the Decline of the Nation-State

Shapiro/Purpel, Eds. • Critical Social Issues in American Education: Democracy and Meaning in a Globalizing World, Third Edition

Books • Poverty and Schooling in the U.S.: Contexts and Consequences

Reagan • Non-Western Educational Traditions: Indigenous Approaches to Educational Thought and Practice, Third Edition

Bowers/Apffel-Marglin, Eds. • Rethinking Freire: Globalization and the Environmental Crisis

Butin, Ed. • Teaching Social Foundations of Education: Contexts, Theories, and Issues

Sidhu • Universities and Globalization: To Market, To Market

UNIVERSITIES AND GLOBALIZATION

To Market, To Market

Ravinder K. Sidhu

LEA LAWRENCE ERLBAUM ASSOCIATES, PUBLISHERS
2006   Mahwah, New Jersey   London

Lawrence Erlbaum Associates, Inc., Publishers
10 Industrial Avenue
Mahwah, New Jersey 07430
www.erlbaum.com

Cover design by Tomai Maridou

Library of Congress Cataloging-in-Publication Data

Sidhu, Ravinder Kaur.
    Universities and globalization : to market, to market / Ravinder Kaur Sidhu.
        p.   cm. — (Sociocultural, political, and historical studies in education)
    Includes bibliographical references and index.
    ISBN 0-8058-4965-3 (alk. paper)
    ISBN 0-8058-4966-1 (pbk. : alk. paper)
    1. Education, Higher—Economic aspects—Cross-cultural studies.   2. Education and
globalization—Cross-cultural studies.   3. International education—Cross-cultural studies.
i. Title: Universities and globalization.   II. Title.   III. Series.

LC67.6.S44   2005
338.4'3378—dc22
                                                                                2005047320
                                                                                       CIP

Books published by Lawrence Erlbaum Associates are printed on acid-free paper,
and their bindings are chosen for strength and durability.

Printed in the United States of America
10   9   8   7   6   5   4   3   2   1

Contents

Preface   vii

Acknowledgments   xiii

Prologue: Personal and Political Influences   xvii

1   Rethinking International Education: Place/Space
and Politics   1

2   Discursive Power and Subjectivity   26

3   Globalization: Ways of Knowing   42

4   "In America's Interest"   62

5   Education@UK   118

6   Australia: "Diversity" ma non troppo   177

7   Singapore: East Meets West   230

8   Brazil: "Priority Market"   270

9   To Market, To Market   296

References   318

Index   351

Preface

Education markets have been the object of much scholarly inquiry in recent times. Paradoxically, despite their critical slant, the net effect of studies into markets has been to create a taken for grantedness as to their very existence. In this vein, international education's conceptualization as a tradable commodity is viewed as an inevitable outcome of "globalization." However, the broad acceptance of both globalization and the desirability of international education markets raises wider questions about how we are governed, how we govern ourselves, and most important, how we govern others located in vastly different geographies. Education markets intrude into broader social fields of power and interrogate our perceptions of the normative role of universities in our societies, the "right" balance in state–market relations, and ultimately, what it means to be an educated subject in the 21st century.

This book seeks to answer the question: "How is the international student and the international university perceived and constructed at this historical moment when the term *globalization* has acquired currency in the language of government?" It explores this question by identifying the authorities and social practices that define international education in three countries: the United States, Australia, and the United Kingdom. It analyzes how marketing practices shape particular expressions of the international university while generating particular understandings of the international student. At the same time, the study that is the basis of this book is also concerned with exploring the operations of power, knowledge, and desire that generate the demand for an overseas education in two sites: Brazil and Singapore.

Simply put, this book brings an alternative discourse into discussions about international education. It recasts international education as a set of geopolitical and geoeconomic engagements with colonial roots and interrogates the conceptual relationship between international education and globalization.

To this end, the book investigates how the contemporary international university assumes and perpetuates particular global imaginaries. Global imaginaries throw light on the operations of power, knowledge, and desire in constituting personhood in a marketized, globalized world. How the global is imagined and translated into the social and cultural practices that define international education tells us something about the perceptions of otherness and the organization of relations of difference at this historical moment.

This book should not, therefore, be read as a definitive account of international education. It is motivated by a desire to problematize the phenomenon of international education markets and to interrogate the skewed distribution of international education networks, which sees a largely unidimensional flow of students travel from the South and East to seek tutelage in the First World. It also seeks to problematize globalization and its rationale in driving the broader international education agenda.

To bring greater analytical reflexivity into the study of international education, this book uses a multidisciplinary theoretical and methodological framework with insights from Foucault's methodologies, cultural studies, sociology, and cultural geography. The field of international education has largely been dominated by studies that focus on the recruitment and trade-related dimensions of international education, issues of cultural adjustment, and the learning problems of international students. The Foucauldian approach, which centers on visibilities ("what is visible and sayable") and power relations, is not likely to impress the traditional social science researcher for whom "proper" research centers around statistical analyses, with all else making one a prisoner of subjective illusion. However, Foucault's work offers valuable conceptual tools to understand the influence of social practices and cultural narratives in shaping personhood.

Having outlined what this book seeks to do, it is useful also to outline what it does not do. It does not take a conventional approach to the international education industry. It does not offer hints on strategies that universities may use to increase their recruitment statistics. It is not concerned with investigating strategic marketing models and inquiring into the efficacies of country-specific brands. It is similarly unconcerned, except in a peripheral sense, in understanding how international students choose study destinations. I am interested instead in how power relations shape international education networks, and how these relations shape and sustain the desire for a Westernized template of international education in the postcolonial world.

In preparing this book for a primary audience of faculty and administrators, I have tried to bring complexity, skepticism, and nuance to this work.

This is not an uncritical celebration of education markets, but I have tried not to lapse into zero sum thinking—that markets are all bad and impoverish many at the expense of making some wealthy. Instead, I make the point that the competitive logic of markets and market-like subjectivities are not sufficient if we are to solve the challenges of the 21st century for greater security, equity, and sustainability.

The book focuses on a number of distinctive themes. All are concentrated around the nexus of power, knowledge, and subjectivity. I explore the topic of international education in three ways. First, through an analysis of education brands and branding practices, I outline the ways in which market-driven, marketized universities in the Anglo-American world perceive and construct understandings of international students in and through their marketing and promotional narratives. My interest here is on the operations of power and knowledge within the international university. I explore the economic, political, and cultural influences in each of the producer countries—the United Kingdom, United States, and Australia— and analyze how these forces have consolidated Anglo-American dominance in global education markets. I then bring together this macro-level analysis of international education markets with an analysis of micropractices by specific universities in the Anglo-American world. Second, I look at how the contemporary international university is both influenced by and actively contributes toward the globalization of education markets. Third, I explore the desire for overseas credentials in the postcolonial world, a desire that continues to sustain the largely First World education export industry.

Foucault's work is discussed in detail in chapter 2. For now, there are three analytical themes within Foucault's work that have framed the objectives and scope of this study. The first is a concern with the relations between power and knowledge. For Foucault, knowledge is caught up in relations of power—it is neither neutral nor impartial; power and knowledge implicate each other. The conjoint relations between power and knowledge mean that they are best described by a single term, *power–knowledge.*

Power–knowledge relations shape our commonsense understandings of international education; they influence what is researched in international education, and what is written about international students and international universities. In other words, power–knowledge relations effectively discipline academic disciplines by establishing the parameters of knowledge through a series of "rules" about what are acceptable and legitimate modes of knowing. Thus, where researchers from the discipline of business have turned their investigatory gaze onto issues such as ways of increasing market share, education researchers have focused on the learning problems of international students. A power–knowledge lens is also useful in understanding how international education markets are associated with globalization.

Related to Foucault's conceptualization of power and knowledge as inseparable is the second analytical theme that has influenced this study: the use of discursive power to govern. Thus, the statements of political authorities, the promotional narratives of international universities, their Web sites, speeches by their executives, and newspaper reportings all shape our collective common sense of what constitutes international education, how the education of students should proceed and the role of the nation-state in producing, shaping, and steering international education markets. Discursive power also shapes how we understand globalization, including its pitfalls and the productive possibilities that it holds out.

A third analytic theme concerns Foucault's theorization of the human subject, which I use to understand the type of educated subject on which international education is premised and seeks to perpetuate. Whereas Western philosophy conceptualized the self as having an 'essence', Foucault's work showed that the subject is a product of historical developments, shaped by official knowledges and institutionalized practices (O'Farrell, 1989, pp. 29–40). Rationales such as individual choice and consumer autonomy that figure in the public discourse, that inform and constitute the utility-maximizing, self-sufficient individualized subject are historically specific and are not by any measure natural or inevitable. In this way, the desire for Western education credentials from the South and East can be related to the broader historical events and geopolitical rationalities, which I discuss in detail throughout the book.

This is not to suggest the existence of a top-down schema of power that freezes us in a historical frame while determining all of our choices, tastes, sensibilities, and political persuasions. Foucault argues that through practices that he dubbed 'technologies of the self' we are capable of assuming or rejecting particular subjectivities ahead of others. Our words and deeds in everyday life are opportunities to choose and to overcome particular expressions of personhood. Foucault also suggests that there can be a contingent dimension to the subjectivities that we inhabit and, furthermore, that the subject positions available to us are not fixed but ever shifting as circumstances change.

OVERVIEW OF CONTENTS

The structure of this book is as follows. The first chapter explores the multiple meanings surrounding the term *international education*. A broad historical sweep describes earlier educational exchanges including those that informed the imperial and colonial states. This is followed by a description and discussion of two major educational aid programs: the Fulbright Program and the Colombo Plan. The chapter concludes with an overview of national and global trends in the demand for international education.

Chapter 2 describes the theoretical and methodological tools used in this study. I introduce Foucault's work on power, knowledge and subjectivity, along with the work of governmentality theorists. A theory chapter is included because some theoretical tools are essential to decipher the claims and counterclaims contained in marketing and promotional narratives within international education. Chapter 3 illustrates how Foucault's theoretical tools can be used to unsettle normative understandings of globalization as an inevitable and evolutionary phase in human development.

Chapters 4 to 8 establish the basis for understanding the interrelationships between international education and globalization via the education–economy prism. Chapter 4 begins the analysis of selling practices by Anglo-American producers of international education. I start with a focus on the United States as a production site of international education, examining policies and practices in the macrocontextual terrain, as well as the micropractices that shape the public face of the international university. The focus on the textual practices of two American universities illustrates how they represent themselves and their international students. A similar approach informs chapter 5, which examines the United Kingdom and chapter 6, which focuses on Australia.

Chapters 7 and 8 shift the research gaze to the two "priority markets" of Singapore and Brazil. The historical and sociopolitical profiles of both countries are outlined as a basis for understanding the 'mentalities, arts, and regimes' of government in both countries. How nation-states manage globalization is a function of their histories and here some attention is given to discussing the roles of their governing elites. These snapshots provide a basis for understanding the spatial and historical basis of contemporary power–knowledge relations. They reveal how international education markets are implicated in the governance of countries and citizens.

Chapter 9 concludes with a discussion of how existing power–knowledge constructions shape international education, and the appropriateness of contemporary expressions of international education for an interdependent, global world. I also suggest ways of broadening the academic imagination and the place of *parrhesia* (fearless speech) in bringing about reform.

Acknowledgments

This book is a testimony to the collective efforts of many people without whose help it would not have materialized. It began life as a doctoral thesis and has since been reworked to make it more palatable for a wider readership. The research underpinning this book is interdisciplinary and required that I leave a familiar intellectual terrain, and engage with disciplines and epistemologies outside of my comfort zone. This task was made easier by Dr. Clare O'Farrell who introduced me to Foucault's work, easily one of the best contexts from which to approach interdisciplinary research. Clare's uncompromising commitment to excellence and intellectual generosity has been inspiring and I thank her for this. Dr. Julie Matthews and Professor Carmen Luke supervised my doctoral work and also helped to shape the interdisciplinary approach that I took. Julie's commitment to her students and genuine enthusiasm for their work deserves special mention. She challenged and helped to refine my ideas while providing much needed support to complete what often seemed like a never-ending task. Carmen's capacity to push boundaries and not to be hemmed in by convention helped instill in me two very important qualities: independence and a measure of self-sufficiency. Naturally, everyone that I have thanked for intellectual guidance does not have any responsibility for my analysis and any associated inaccuracies in this book for which I take full responsibility.

For the material sustenance to carry out this research, I was assisted by a Postgraduate Award from the Australian government. A travel stipend from the University of Queensland helped to offset the considerable costs of undertaking transnational, multisite fieldwork. More recently, I have been the recipient of a Postdoctoral Fellowship from the University of Queensland

and this has helped provide the resources in converting the dissertation to a book. At the School of Education, I thank Associate Professor Pam Christie who offered all kinds of practical and intellectual assistance in making the often-difficult transition from doctoral student to early career researcher. I also wish to thank Professor Bob Lingard who as Head of School helped to secure a research fellowship. As is the case with all learning, it is the informal understandings gained in unanticipated ways in an atmosphere of humor and friendliness that crystallizes thinking and grounds pulsating ideas into something concrete. For this, I thank my many friends in the postgraduate student community at the School of Education.

I thank Professor Allan Luke who first put forward the idea that my dissertation could be translated into a book, and thereafter helped to facilitate the process. Thanks also to the generous assessments of the examination triumvirate, Professors Fazal Rizvi, Simon Marginson, and Allan Luke whose feedback and enthusiasm along with those of two anonymous reviewers provided valuable guidance. In 2000, as a second-year PhD student, I met Dr. Wendy Larner who, thereafter, kindly responded to pestering e-mails for her papers. Since then I have continued to be inspired from knowing and using Wendy's work.

Lawrence Erlbaum Associates has been an encouraging publisher and provided many helpful suggestions for a first author. Pat Kelly's uncompromising courage and blunt egalitarian voice helped me to find my own voice and assisted in the last critical days of finishing the manuscript. The chapter on Brazil would not have been possible without Cecilia Torres who put aside her own formidable workload to conduct interviews and contribute rich insights into the workings of international education in the Brazilian context. I also want to record my appreciation to the people who agreed to be interviewed for this study.

I sincerely thank my friends and family in Britain, America, and Singapore for warmth and hospitality during my fieldwork: in the UK, Hannah Marquand, Kris Sen, and Lata Vadgama; in America, Rakesh and Jyoti Kapoor and Satinder Sidhu; and in Singapore, my cousins Puteh, Anil, Mohan, and Ladi and also Lydia, not only for the many wonderful meals but also for the useful insights on what it means to be other in a global city.

Lisa Ehrich, Gloria Dall'Alba, Pam Christie, and Dawn Butler continue to remind me there is space for generosity and nurturance in the competitive excellence of scholarly work. A shared dream with Annette Woods to bring the sea into our lives helped to break the monotonous grind of drafts and re-writes. Rhyll Vallis's acerbic wit, Ivana's reminders of the inextricability of spirit, soul, and intellect, and Simone's bubbling enthusiasm helped me complete this work.

Like so much of academic labor, writing a book cuts deeply into family life and friendships. It extracts a high price from those closest and dearest.

To special old friends who resumed our friendships without disappoint-ment and rancor at the one-sidedness of our relationship, particularly, Donata Rossi, Toni Pizzica, and Goh Bee Chen, I thank you. My parents, Balwant and Manjit, my brother, Raj, and cousins Pinder, Michael, and Chamkaur along with other members of my extended family have been pa-tient and stoic in the face of limited attention and contact.

Last but most important, I thank the love of my life, my husband Renato.

Prologue: Personal and Political Influences

This book could have been written in many ways. The question of why this approach and not some other rests on a series of connections, some personal and others intellectual, some past and others enduringly present. At one level, this is simply a study of intercultural flows and exchanges. But its reference point or supporting base is more complex and straddles the strategic relations interweaving markets, states, and cultures. The book provides an intellectual context and space to think about the cultural politics of knowledge—the power politics which influence the making, sharing, and exchanging of knowledges. As I argue throughout, the resolution of these power relations are crucial to uncovering epistemological solutions to the vexing moral and ethical questions of the 21st century: growing inequality, loss of human security, loss of biodiversity, fragmented social relations, and diminishing civic freedoms.

Many factors have influenced the theoretical positions and "analytics" that I use to understand the politics of making, sharing, and exchanging knowledges. These factors include my personal ethnic origins as one of a long line of migrants who moved countries in search for "a better life," and a childhood spent in Southeast Asia at a particular historical juncture, in the aftermath of political independence for the colonies and during the Cold War.

This book explores the operations of power and knowledge in the global education market (international education) and the desire in the postcolonial South for an overseas education. I examine the kinds of exchanges that are captured in the project of international education at this historical moment, characterized by globalization. How is international education being assembled through state–market relations and how do these developments influence our personal and professional identities; how we practice ethics, our politics, our understandings of citizenship; and how we imagine and enact the future?

Decades of feminist research have raised awareness that generating a research problem, investigating it using particular methodologies, and analyzing and resolving it, cannot be a disinterested undertaking. How researchers receive, interpret, and transmit the findings of their work is mediated by individual histories and positionings. These include class, gender, and ethnicity, as well as geography, profession, and discipline. On this basis, feminist researchers tend to acknowledge and make explicit their positioning and politics—their standpoint. However, knowing and stating one's standpoint is not simple. When we provide a life story, an autobiographical reflection, we include some things and leave out others; we emphasize some themes and subordinate others. The precariousness of self-knowledge, our limited capacities to be reflexive and the multiple subjectivities that we inhabit challenge the notion of a unitary, coherent standpoint. The story I offer next is intended to create a point of reference for the politics of my scholarship. It is not a life history. If there is a consistent theme, it is an attempt to understand how "context" with its myriad tensions and contradictions, shapes people and their capacities to act, think, and become moral agents.

JOURNEYS AND "HOMES"

Like the turbulent and disruptive movement of people from the Old World of Europe to the New World who were escaping war, internal displacement and poverty, my family left the Indian subcontinent looking for a better, safer life. They were part of the exodus from the Punjab region, in India, at the turn of the 20th century. People from the Indian subcontinent traveled to Africa, Fiji, Hong Kong, and, in the case of my family, Singapore and Malaya. For at least 100 years before my birth, members of my Sikh family had worked for the colonial authorities. My maternal great grandfather, Ritdaman Singh, was a surveyor employed by the British to work in the North-West Frontier Province, in Pakistan, during their attempts to expand their colonization efforts into Afghanistan in the 19th century. On my father's side, they were the empire's soldiers and policemen, like many Sikhs. They settled in Malaya at the start of the 20th century.

The family's interactions with colonial culture were marked by a pointed complexity and ambivalence. The men, extending back to my maternal great-grandfather in the mid-19th century, were fluent English speakers, skills acquired through their work. At the same time, they were fervent supporters of India's independence from the British. In colonial Singapore and Malaya they lived within a prewar system of apartheid where urban spaces were racialized and entire areas declared out of bounds to persons of color. This changed with the fall of "Fortress Singapore" and Malaya to the bicycle-borne Japanese Imperial Army. The fortress fell in just over 2 months. This, and the 3½-year Japanese occupation had a politicizing effect on many colonial and dominion "subjects" like my family. It showed them that White people were not invincible. The special privileges that White people had enjoyed before the war were no longer acceptable to them when the British returned to Singapore and Malaya after the occupation.

For the women of the family, the impulse and momentum of their daily lives were centered around Punjabi culture—their food, language, and religion were constants in what was an unfamiliar and vividly cosmopolitan world. They were surrounded by many different ethnicities: Hokkien, Cantonese and Hainanese Chinese, Arabs, Malays, and from the Indian subcontinent, Tamils, Sindhis, and Gujeratis. Neither of my grandmothers spoke any English. Their daily lives were largely untouched by things colonial and their involvement with White people in colonial Singapore and Malaya was limited to occasional sightings from a distance.

My parents' childhood was marked by the privations of World War II. As young adults, they witnessed the seismic events of decolonization, the Malayan Emergency, bloody race riots, curfews, and religious and ethnic communalisms. Like so many people of their generation, they experienced first hand the turbulence and tensions arising from the gladiatorial contests between capitalism and communism. The effect of these life experiences created a need in them to protect their children from what they had endured. They steered us toward choices that were framed around the goals of having a First World passport, a "good" (English-speaking) education, and enough wealth to insulate ourselves from danger, poverty, and racism. Their decisions facilitated a successful, if painful, assimilation for their children.

FOREIGNERS TO OURSELVES

The complex and contradictory politics of transcultural learnings, and identity building, surrounding the political independence of the colonies played out in our family home. Decisions as to what language we children should speak at home, how we should dress, how much we should know of our religion, how many people of our race we should mix with were part of a struggle between my parents. My father carried the flag for a Westernized, modernized set of sensibilities. An officer in the Malayan Army, trained by the British and Australian armed forces, he decided that we would speak English at home although this was not his first language. My mother, who was 19 when her marriage was arranged to my father, had completed a college education in India, spoke fluent Punjabi and Hindi, and had a good knowledge of Indian philosophy, music, and history was discouraged from speaking to her children in Punjabi, her mother tongue. As my father was absent from home life for most of our waking day, there would have been many opportunities for her to teach us Punjabi. That she adhered to his wishes suggests that she had internalized his perceptions that English was the language of opportunity, the "superior" language.

My father was extraordinarily disparaging of Indian people from India. He referred to them frequently as the "*Babu*" and regarded them to be smooth talking and dishonest. Much later I discovered that the term *Babu* was widely used by the colonial authorities as a term of derision for sections of the Indian anticolonial movement, the Bengali intellectuals. We grew up knowing little about our traditions and language, which made it difficult to cement close relationships with our grandmothers and our extended family in India. It was to be a convenient detachment. Not knowing them in a deeper sense, not having access to their worlds would make it easier to forget our responsibilities to care for them as we set off to make the most of our First World opportunities. The cultural contradictions and confusions my parents bequeathed to their children were significant, although these unfolded quietly. There was nothing dramatic about these tensions as they worked themselves into our lives. It was only later that we began to realize what had been given away, what we had lost.

My father was also full of contradictions. He remained turbaned and bearded, like most practicing Sikhs. His appearance marked him out significantly as "the other." He would not allow us to anglicize our names. He did not support cross-cultural marriages in the family. He took to manufacturing a repertoire of stories to warn us against transgressing ethnocultural and religious boundaries. An excessive mimicry of things Western was frowned on and ridiculed. Yet at the same time, we were encouraged to have friends from every religious and ethnocultural group. My parents' close and intimate friends were similarly drawn from different communities. As children, we moved in and out of each other's homes, enjoying an easy intimacy around shared meals and sleepovers. Selective dimensions of intercultural borrowings were clearly acceptable. A university degree from an English or Australian university was a good thing because it meant decent and stable employment, as was the ability to speak fluent English. It was all about having the right balance between East and West, although no one ever made it clear just what the formula was. They probably did not know themselves.

Looking back, a few things stand out. The stark poverty engulfing the marginal elements of society, seen everyday in the faces of beggars, child workers, the old who were abandoned by family or without family to care for them, and people with disabilities who had no labor to sell. We felt overwhelmed, dehumanized, and paralyzed into inertia, aware that little separated us from them. There were also large numbers of the working poor. In the Malaysia of my childhood some of the poorest people were the descendants of Tamil indentured laborers. The Tamils were brought out by the British to work in Malayan rubber plantations run by British multinationals, such as Guthrie's and Sime Darby, after slavery was officially abolished in the British empire. Estate workers were paid very poorly and lived in appalling housing provided by multinationals, usually a long way from services and amenities. They were so poor that they let their daughters, some of whom were barely out of childhood, work as domestics for the aspiring middle classes of Malaya like my family. Nearly all of the maids that worked in our home were named after goddesses—Devi, Lakshmi, Saraswati, Meenakshi, Jayarani, Janaki—perhaps a sign of the hope their parents may have held for them.

Another significant memory was the drive and desire of people around me, family, friends, and neighbors to get an English-speaking education. In 1970, when I was 7 years old, educational indigenization policies were being introduced into all Malaysian schools. Bahasa Malaysia replaced English as a medium of instruction. We were not happy with this postcolonial statement. The asymmetrical relations between the West and Southeast Asia meant that Bahasa Malaysia had no currency in the international world. It also meant little to Malaysians from the immigrant Chinese and Indian diaspora. In the Malaysian context of the 1970s, indigenization was perceived to have a covert goal, reflecting a political agenda aimed at shifting the balance of power in favor of the dominant group, the Malays (*bumiputera*).

My parents were not unusual in making sacrifices to give their children a good English-speaking education. Some people emigrated to the First World solely to give their children access to education; others borrowed heavily to send their children overseas. People bought costly English books for their children. Their actions brought foreign parables and metaphors into our imagination, and at the same time they squeezed out the local memories that had been part of our parents' childhoods. Little wonder that for my generation, Punjabi effectively become marginalized. Nurtured by two generations and resilient enough to survive colonial rule, it unraveled following independence. Yet, our entry and subsequent embeddedness in the Anglophone world occurred in an untheatrical, unremarkable way.

The emotional costs that accompanied these experiences and expectations were considerable, although it was some years before we allowed ourselves to become fully aware of it. We grew up with few role models for ethical, cultural, and intellectual guidance, a problem that was especially acute in smaller, settler societies with colonized histories. It is harder to erase a history, to stamp out dissenting views and opinions in a large country with hundreds, thousands, perhaps millions of intellectuals, artists, and professionals. It is easier for governments with coercive dispositions to mold a settler society.

Every engagement that features power relations has a productive dimension. This is one of the ironies of life. All that English speaking and reading eventually "paid off," especially once we emigrated to Australia. Comfortable in our monolinguistic superiority, we children were able to adjust to schooling with less difficulty than my Hong Kong friends, for example. It was a trade-off that many children of my generation accepted with few questions. You mechanically took on the linguistic and defacto cultural identity that would give you the best chance for the future. The best chance meant having a First World passport, as it would enable you to live somewhere relatively safe.

My other childhood memory is of considerable social pressure to have better material things. There were so many "must-haves" that it became increasingly difficult for my parents to keep up with our material aspirations. We were bombarded with consumer goods from the West: Tupperware, Corningware, Levis jeans, imported cars, Coca-Cola. We were bombarded by them but we also desired them because they marked us as having status, of being modern. Our media entertainment was dominated by American TV programming, a steady stream of movies about cowboys and Indians; Charlie's Angels, Starsky and Hutch, endless blockbusters and B-grade Hollywood movies. And as children we did regard the "Indians" as the "baddies" in the cowboy films. We were less exposed to the Bollywood movie culture from India because of my father's disparaging view of local programming. We were similarly unexposed to Malay romantic dramas and Indonesian horror (*pontianak*) movies, the two other film genres available to us.

In the public space, there was little in the way of multiple comments, opinions, and discourses. There was a paucity of spaces in which to talk about democratic politics. Lots of things were termed "sensitive," a euphemism for anything deemed politically contentious. We could not talk about things such as communism in schools aside from acknowledging it was "bad." These injunctions were also present in the foreign media accessible to us. Looking back, I don't recall any stories on the antiwar movements or American military atrocities in Indochina. Still closer in geography and history, we heard little about the loss of life that took place in Indonesia following the failed "communist coup," where with the connivance of the "free world," some half a million people were killed. A society, still fragile as it felt its way toward recovery from its disengagement from colonial rule, was robbed of some of its brightest citizens. I knew a lot more about the collective pathologies of the German people and Nazism, Hitler's monstrous evil, and the horrors perpetrated against the Jewish people.

There was also little space in the sanctum of family life to discuss difficult issues. My father's family background as one of the empire's soldiers meant more tensions and confusions than resolutions. He was, after all, a soldier fighting to prevent the domino theory from becoming a catastrophic reality. His schooling and socialization was built on the assumption of British (Western) moral and cultural superiority. I think he believed that they would surely do the right thing by everybody.

WHEN THE COLD WAR CAME TO A WARM CLIMATE

Like many people living in the newly independent, postwar Southeast Asia, we were acutely aware of the awesome ideological collisions between capitalism, communism, and imperialism[1] taking place in our midst. These confrontations occasionally produced peaceful and productive synergies, and at other times they generated profoundly destructive and dysfunctional outcomes. The Manichean struggle between the superpowers had consequences for countries in the region, their societies, families, and individuals. These were not random. Yet at the same time, it would not be accurate to write a story of all-powerful monoliths and inevitable, apocalyptic histories. As the impulses of modernization, nationalism, and communalism pushed and pulled against each other in the flow of everyday life, some people found the will and the imagination to inhabit different spaces and to practice a different ethics, admittedly sometimes at great personal cost.

Once every few months, we received a glossy magazine from the United States Information Service. It featured all sorts of glamorous stories—the tragic Kennedys, Christmas in Iowa, potato farmers in Idaho, the Nixons' trip to China, and so on. Through publications such as *Reader's Digest*, which was one of the cheapest and most accessible foreign magazines around, we gained a snapshot of the Western world and its values. We imported new forms of "othering." Hippies, for example, were reviled, noted for their drug experimentations, promiscuity, and engagement with crime. The irrational fear and dislike for hippies and what they represented was manifested in big and small ways. The Singaporean government would not allow males with long hair into the country. These simplicities, crude, even laughable, were also highly effective. Local men who insisted on keeping their hair long were considered to have criminal persuasions and were more likely to be arrested by the police. Official posters in government departments announced that "men with hair-length below their collars will be served last." Our own strongly hierarchical cultures, and our societies that now featured huge disparities of wealth, made it difficult to challenge the persistent cruelties that pervaded daily life.

---

[1]Imperialism is the political and economic domination of one or several countries by another power. For Lenin, imperialism was an inherent feature of economic development in advanced capitalist countries. Some theorists have argued that imperialism ended with political independence from colonial rule, whereas others argue that indirect control has increased with the end of colonial rule through economic domination (Jary & Jary, 1995, p. 309).

In this Manichean moral environment, things were uniformly portrayed as either right or wrong, good or bad. The lived effects of these discourses meant that it was tremendously difficult to know how and what to resist because everything was constructed in binary terms; even civil action to resist the petty micropractices of officialdom could result in one being labeled 'subversive'. In the rough and tumble of Cold War geopolitics, the sovereignties of small countries in geographically strategic areas such as Southeast Asia were shaped by the authority of the superpowers. Everyone knew this.

Of course, we were under no illusions about the powers of our own postcolonial governments. The police, military, judiciary—officialdom in general—were able to exercise considerable power over the lives of ordinary citizens. We learned how the newly independent states violated their people's rights with a practiced ease, usually under the aegis of maintaining national security. Freedoms were articulated within state-defined parameters and bolstered by the state's formidable capacity to monitor and regulate the activities of their citizens and institutions. There was an unspoken rule against crossing certain boundaries. A compliant press, intellectuals who heeded official warnings to keep out of politics, ambitious professionals and bureaucrats, agile careerists who were rewarded handsomely for maintaining the official line—all of these factors militated against civic freedoms. Aside from a few heroic, 'foolish' hotheads who may have pushed the limits, most people fell quietly into a routine of getting on with earning a living and raising families. We knew that all aspiring university students were routinely screened by the Central Intelligence Department to ensure that they were of 'good character' before being allocated university places. People altered their behavior accordingly. Student activism in both Malaysia and Singapore continued to be carefully controlled up to the end of the 1970s. Being caught with any 'subversive' texts, the works of Karl Marx for example, carried the risk of a prison sentence. Conversely, within the same period, the late 1960s and early 1970s, in a different geographical space, the West—the former colonial powers of Britain and France come to mind here—it was impossible to be considered an intellectual of any worth without engagement with the works of Marx. Today, the crudely overt practices of surveillance have been muted and in some cases discontinued, although in a climate marked by concerns about terrorism, some of these practices are being resurrected.

CHOICES AND IRONIES

Having witnessed the difficult circumstances that surrounded people's lives in the lead up to political independence, the enduring legacy of Cold War power politics, the minimalist models of democracy in the postcolonial colonies, my parents made certain choices—to live in the 'First World' and to raise their children to fit in as best as we could. We were caught in a complex web of contradictions, which featured rewards and reprisals. In the case of my family, we gave up our language, assumed decultured lives, and all but severed links with extended family to succeed in the 'First World'. Was this voluntary assimilation a bona fide choice? We felt fortunate to be cherry picked out of a disruptive region that was convulsing under the pressures of inequality, conflict, and poverty. Could there have been other options?

In this light, this book is personal in several senses. It is my attempt to introduce an alternative vocabulary to the study of, and understanding about, international education. It reflects my attempts to move away from an introverted and instrumental, pragmatic approach to the topic toward considering and integrating a range of concerns—ethical, economic, social, cultural, material. To this end, this book reflects my own journey to engage in reflexivity and to think and write outside the box after a lifetime spent acculturating myself to the dominant paradigms of the day.

The patterns and motifs in each chapter are different but throughout is a central theme: how we make sense of self–other relations, whether in the context of state–market relations or East–West–North–South relations, and what this means for our ability to engage in ethical practices. I wrestle with these issues, engaging the readers in a dialogue about the complexities of crossing boundaries and what this might mean for the self–other relation. These appear in selective chapters in italicized text.

Some of the questions I explore is how boundaries are crossed, by whom, and to what effect, and what this might mean for the academy. For instance, what does it mean to do scholarly work in a liberal, prosperous, First World society about issues that impinges on the other—globalization and international education? And how do the contexts in which we work shape our inquiries, our methods, and our theoretical frameworks? Finally, this book is an exploration of what it means to address the excesses of neoliberalism in the academy today.

Rethinking International Education: Place/Space and Politics

WHAT IS INTERNATIONAL EDUCATION?

In the aftermath of the terrorist attacks of September 11, 2001, international education has acquired a varied set of meanings. The U.S.-based Institute of International Education (IIE) linked international education with a "safer and more secure world" and with a certain type of understanding:

> The aim of the terrorists who attacked this country on September 11 is not to change American foreign policy but to close our markets, minds and doors. ... When more international students are given the chance for meaningful study and opportunities to gain an appreciation of our society, there will be less hatred of America and misunderstanding of our values and way of life. (Kaufman & Goodman, 2001)

In contrast, Australian-based education broker IDP Education charged international education with the responsibility of "making a critical contribution in developing global peace and understanding" (IDP, 2001). Echoing this view, a Vice-Chancellor[1] of an Australian university declared:

> I can think of no better antidote to international terrorism to international education. It helps us to develop the international perspective and cross cultural sensitivity that are essential attributes of the effective citizen of the 21st

---

[1]A Vice-Chancellor occupies a similar role to a president and is the preferred term to describe the chief executive of the university in the United Kingdom, Australia, and several Commonwealth countries.

century, and which gives us the skills and personal capacity to respond positively to globalization. (Yerbury, 2001; see also Yerbury, 2004)

Who has membership in this group, who is the collective "we" and "us"?
What constitutes "our values" and "our society"? This introductory snapshot
draws attention to the arresting complexities and contradictions surrounding the discursive realm of international education. Reflected in terms as
diverse as *export services, national income,* and *global peace,* international education is associated with such processes and outcomes such as "opening
markets, minds, and doors," producing "effective 21st-century citizenship,"
while creating "less hatred and more understanding of our values."

There is no consensus about what an international education means.
Neither is there a commonly agreed set of criteria for what makes a university international. How international education is defined and imagined,
what is thinkable and sayable about both international education and the
international university, is ultimately shaped by relations of power and
knowledge as evident in both of the preceding sets of quotes.

It is obvious, too, from a review of the literature that international education is defined in contradictory ways. International education is most commonly associated with the recruitment and enrollment of international students (Bennell & Pearce, 1998, p. 2). International education is also used to
refer to transnational education, the broad range of educational activities
that cross national borders (Clyne, Marginson, & Woock, 2001, p. 111).
When used interchangeably with global education, international education
includes any number of fields from peace studies to studies on ecological
sustainability. During the 'dot.com' boom, international education was also
used to refer to various online education initiatives (Farquhar, 1999, p. 6).

The term *internationalization,* on the other hand, usually appears in institutional mission statements and policies. The Australian Vice-Chancellor's
Committee (AVCC)[2] offered this vague definition in its International Relations Strategic Plan, "Internationalisation is the complex of processes that
gives universities an international dimension" (Hamilton, 1998). Within
the context of Australian higher education, the Organization for Economic
Cooperation and Development (OECD) definition of internationalization
has been widely adopted: "the process of integrating an international/
intercultural dimension in the teaching, research and service of the institution" (Knight & de Wit, 1995, p. 15).

On its surface, the OECD definition appears adequate: It is open-ended
and conceptualizes internationalization as a process that is unfinished and

---

[2]The AVCC is a major stakeholder in the Australian higher education field. It describes its
role as "advancing higher education through voluntary, cooperative and coordinated action"
(AVCC, 2002).

ongoing rather than having a discernible endpoint (de Wit, 1999). However, its weaknesses lie in its inherent generality and ambiguity. It is unclear just what constitutes an international/intercultural dimension, which is as likely to include the trite and superficial as the profound and complex. It does not, for example, preclude a largely one-way transmission of knowledge from West–North to East–South. Similarly, European calls for an internationalization at home are informed by a service approach to education and the desire to position European higher education "to survive and succeed in international competition" (Wachter, 2000, p. 11).

A more comprehensive definition of internationalization is offered by Francis (1993), "Internationalization is a process where education prepares the community for successful participation in an increasingly interdependent world . . . fosters global understanding and develops skills for effective living and working in a diverse world." Here, too, our understandings of what might constitute "effective living and working in a diverse world" impinges on our needs and aspirations, and our ethical, political, social, and cultural values.

As Patrick (1997) cautions, if universities view other expanding economies and societies largely as markets for their knowledge and their graduates, they establish the potential for a market-driven internationalization, which stands to resurrect the links between neoimperialism and internationalization. Internationalization, according to Patrick, requires engagement with interdisciplinarity in the teaching and research mission, but most important, it requires universities to develop in their graduates the capacity to "solve problems in a variety of locations with cultural and environmental sensitivity" (Aulakh, as cited in Patrick, 1997). Sadiki (2001) offers a similar understanding of internationalization: It must prepare recipients for 'global community' and it must feature 'curricular plurality', which he translates as engagement with non-Western epistemologies.

What is the history underlying international education, and how does this history shape the normative expressions of international education? What problems are institutions and governments hoping to solve through the international education market? Given that earlier expressions of what we now call international education were forged in spatialized relations of power, a brief overview of the enterprise of empire in education, and its successors the Cold War–inspired educational aid schemes, is useful.

EDUCATING FOR "EMPIRE"

A historical analysis of the movement of scholars and students would show that cross-cultural and interregional exchanges are neither a novel nor a recent phenomenon. As empires and civilizations have risen and fallen, the locations of teaching and learning centers have shifted accordingly. Today, with the centers of teaching and research clustered around the North Atlantic Rim, it is almost inconceivable for many to imagine an era when the Arabic centers of Baghdad, Damascus, Cordoba, and Byzantium attracted Western European scholar students (see La Goff, 1993, as cited in Ma Rhea, 2002). These premodern educational exchanges were arguably different in quality from those that took place during modernity. Their scope and diffusion were limited by the absence of sophisticated disseminating technologies such as the Internet and networks of academic journals. However, some similarities can also be assumed with contemporary educational exchanges: They produced hybrid outcomes. Said's (1993) salutary comment on the permeability of cultures and the inevitability of cross-cultural exchanges is worth keeping in mind:

> Far from being unitary or monolithic or autonomous things, cultures actually assume more foreign elements, differences . . . than they consciously exclude. (p. 15)

Intercultural education exchanges in the early and late modern eras took place against a background of colonization and imperialism, first and predominantly by the European states and from the 19th century onward by the United States.[3] Where the first wave of colonization in the 16th and 17th centuries—the era of "bandit kings"—had involved unfettered economic and human exploitation, the second wave of colonization, dubbed the era of philosopher kings, which extended for most of the 19th and early 20th centuries, oversaw the use of a set of altogether different tactics that were intended to create the conditions for a "colonization of the educated mind" (Nandy, 1983, pp. x–xi). Education was regarded as an investment to consolidate colonial power and subsequently exported by colonial centers to their colonies. The expectations underpinning these early education exchanges were captured in pronouncements such as the celebrated Macaulay Minute: "to create a class of persons Indian in looks and colour but English in tastes and opinions, in morals and intellects" (Macaulay, as cited in Loombia, 1998, p. 85; see also Willinsky, 1998, p. 89).

The colonial universities in the British colonies were developed to provide a Western training for native administrators. They were not expected

---

[3]While recognizing that the national and individual desire for a modern education is not limited to those countries occupied by Western colonial powers, I restrict my discussions to such countries. However, I acknowledge that colonization is not a wholly West versus East phenomenon. Examples of East–East colonization include Korea, which was a colony of Japan from 1910 to 1945. For much of 18th and 19th centuries the northern parts of peninsular Malaya were colonies of Siam (Thailand). Presently, the Free Tibet movement would consider Tibet to be colonized by China. Similar analogies can be drawn about Indonesia's annexation of East Timor and Irian Jaya.

to be academically prestigious; "the colonial state produced a colonial university which did not have the psychological, economic, social or legal potential to confront the powers that be" (Rahman, 2000, p. 127). The legislation that established the University of Calcutta, the first university in India, installed a governing structure that was politicized at the onset—the Governor General would be the Chancellor and the Chief Justice of the Supreme Court would be the Vice-Chancellor.

Similarly, Brazil's colonial relationship with Portugal delayed the development of a vibrant Brazilian university sector until the 20th century. Requests to develop a university in the 17th and 18th centuries were made by the local governments of Bahia and Minas Gerais to Portugal, but these were refused, and local aspirants traveled to the Portuguese metropolis (Figueiredo-Cowen, 2002, p. 471). By contrast, the Spanish crown was aware of the important role universities might play, not only in transferring Spanish culture and Catholicism from the imperial center to the colonies but also in instituting an appropriate political order. It established the University of Cordoba in Argentina in 1613 and by the 19th century there were 26 universities in Spanish-speaking Latin America (Figueiredo-Cowen, 2002).

The tenacious hold of a colonial imagination in education was sustained by a desire on the parts of postindependence politicians and intellectuals to modernize and to "beat the West at its own game" (Nandy, 1983, pp. xi–xiii). On achieving political independence, they steered education institutions to reproduce, disseminate, and legitimate key ideas of colonial modernity, under the aegis of modernization.[4] Universities became silent partners in relentless drives by postcolonial governments to modernize, in some cases, at the cost of violating civil liberties, and subjugating local knowledge systems while entrenching the privileges of local elites (Davies, Nandy, & Sardar, 1993, pp. 83–84; Nandy, 2000, pp. 118–120; Rahman, 2000, pp. 126–127). The influence of political and economic elites in Brazilian society, for example, laid the foundation for a higher education system that would stay aloof of radical sociocultural and political changes in the country (Figueiredo-Cowen, 2002, p. 475). They were first and foremost institutions run by and for the elite. The same observations can be made of the predecessors of the Commonwealth universities in the Indian subcontinent, Africa, and Southeast Asia.

Foremost in postcolonial theory is the injunction against reproducing the discursive logic of the colonial project, with its ritualized binaries and its essentialization of difference (see Pieterse & Parekh, 1995). It is more productive to accept contradiction and disjuncture as pervasive elements of the

---

[4]*Modernization* is a general term that is used to describe the socioeconomic changes generated by scientific and technological discoveries, industrialization, population movements, urbanization, and modern nation-state formation (Sarup, 1993, p. 131).

transcultural, transnational encounter. From a postcolonial perspective, then, various forms of postcolonial education were responsible for perpetuating a faulty politicoeconomic template premised on an insatiable demand for growth, an uncritical engagement with science and technology, and a privileging of the hypermasculine subject (Nandy, 1983, p. xv). The educated subject was not a "gullible, simple-hearted victim" but as a participant in the profoundly complex "moral and cognitive venture" that underpinned direct and indirect colonization efforts (p. xv).

The continuing hold of the colonial imagination, expressed in a collective desire for colonial education forms, cannot be understood as a form of brute domination imposed by the North/West. Western-style education provided a symbolism of nationhood, while postcolonial education systems harnessed modernity's ideas and ideals in a bid to prove their nation's intellectual, economic, and technological capacities (see Loombia, 1998; Nandy, 1983; Pieterse & Parekh, 1995; Tikly, 1999; Tuhiwai-Smith, 1999; Venn, 2002; Willinsky, 1998).

Today, the power relations of *realpolitik* continue to shape the desire for a 'First World' university education from non-Western countries. The standard conceptualization of the global education market as a level playing field, featuring the business-savvy, 'First World' international university that is simply responding to demand from other markets is the story we all know. In contrast, this study is concerned with understanding how the spatialities of power—the relations between power and space—shape international student flows. In the non-English-speaking world, the acquisition of a higher education credential from an English-speaking country has assumed greater and greater importance with the dominance of Atlantic capitalism ('Anglo-Globalization'). What does this mean for self–other relations as they are lived out through the production, transmission, and use of knowledge systems at this historical moment?

**The Fulbright Program: Establishing
A "Democratic Empire"**

From the start of the 20th century, the United States began a series of educational aid programs, which officially were intended to assist other countries to modernize. The United States contrasted its intentions and engagements from European imperialism, which it argued was based on outright exploitation and premised on an explicit racial ideology of superiority, with its own commitment to provide other nations with resources to progress through modernization (C. Klein, 2003; N. Singh, 1998). To this end, the United States refracted its own expansionist persuasions by providing opportunities for economic development through free trade and supporting political liberalization.

The exercise of military, political and economic power is always more productive if hinged onto cultural mechanisms (see C. Klein, 2003; Saunders, 1999). Educational aid schemes provided one of the best mediums for building influence. After the Boxer Rebellion of 1900, America set up a scholarship fund to educate the Chinese using money from reparations that had been forced from the Imperial Chinese government. In the Philippines, which became an American colony after 1898, a universal public schooling system premised on the U.S. education system was introduced (C. Klein, 2003, pp. 198–200). Between 1898 and 1901, American evangelists built some 90 schools in predominantly Catholic Cuba, and in 1900, 1,300 Cuban teachers traveled to Harvard to learn about American teaching models (Slater, 1998, p. 91). Non-state actors such as private philanthropists and religious bodies initially dominated the aid scene where they focused on health and population control. Nation-state involvement in aid really grew with the Cold War (Rojas, 2004, pp. 99–100).

The Cold War's superpower rivalries renewed interest and momentum in winning hearts and minds through educational aid schemes. The Fulbright Program was established in 1946 and today operates in 140 countries. Since its inception, approximately 255,000 people have participated in the Program. Of these, 96,400 were from the United States and 158,000 were from other countries. Funding for the Program is derived primarily from an appropriation from the U.S. Congress, and for the 2003 fiscal year, this amounted to US$122.9 million. Foreign governments also make direct contributions to the Fulbright Program, and for the 2001 fiscal year, these contributions totaled US$28 million.[5]

Conventional readings of the Fulbright Program attribute its impetus to the personal convictions of its founder, Senator J. William Fulbright, a former Rhodes scholar, who regarded educational exchanges between countries as the means to "erode the culturally rooted mistrust that sets nations against one another" (Fulbright, 1989, p. 218). He describes the Program's aims as follows:

> to bring a little more knowledge, a little more reason and a little more compassion into world affairs and thereby to increase the chance that nations will learn at last to live in peace and friendship. (Fulbright, as cited in U.S. Department of State, 2003)

The Fulbright Program embodied a complex set of forces that expressed and responded to the harmonies and dissonances of various political, economic, national, and ideological interests. Although some scholars, and

---

[5]In 2001, the individual contributions of 12 countries to the binational commissions that administer the Fulbright Program exceeded the allocations made by the U.S. government, suggesting a strong commitment to the Program by non-U.S. governments.

Fulbright himself, associate the inception of the Fulbright Program with an internationalist resurgence in the United States intended to counteract American nationalism and parochialism after World War II, other scholars link the Program with a broader American foreign policy platform to reduce the influence of socialism in the postcolonial world. Williams (1988) goes farther back in history to propose an economic frontier thesis. From the 19th century onward, overseas economic expansion was adopted as a strategy for offsetting domestic problems in the United States. The national desire to extend America's economic frontier was visible in Jefferson's 'empire for liberty', the Monroe Doctrine, and the brutal war against the Philippines (Kaplan, 2004).

However, the large-scale expansion of U.S. power really began in earnest after World War II. It coincided with the drive to decolonize in Asia and Africa. To offset the inevitable tensions between these movements—decolonization and the development of an integrated economic system—required a sustained program to 'win minds'. The Fulbright Program emerges as part of a broader policy ensemble aimed at persuading elites from other nations to regard the United States as a friendly authority with whom they shared common interests as members of a 'free world'. The free world would be defined as an integrated space, "a place where people, commodities, resources and products of intellectual activity could move easily across national boundaries" (C. Klein, 2003, p. 48). Considerable discursive effort was and continues to be invested in the constructing these exchanges as "fluid," "Although the US benefited from these flows, their fluid nature implied that the US neither controlled them nor used them to dominate others" (p. 48).

A series of sophisticated impression management strategies were subsequently deployed to identify the United States as the first postcolonial nation, a nation that was vehemently opposed to colonialism of any form (C. Klein, 2003, p. 39). Educational aid programs like the Fulbright were proof of an American benevolence and commitment to progress through modernization (p. 200). The American public was assiduously courted through a series of cultural narratives, which collectively formed a "middlebrow culture" to challenge isolationist sentiments and to "train up" Americans to accept their new role as citizens of a world leader (p. 21).

The theme of a moral leadership to govern the other is reiterated in Saunders' (1999) work, which maps the power-knowledge circuits in the Cold War era. Saunders' archival research is a fascinating exposition of how the U.S. government cultivated and financed the work of intelligentsia both in and outside of the United States. The outcomes of these diverse pedagogical impulses included the production of journals, books, conferences, seminars, art exhibitions, concerts, awards, and sister city programs. Educational institutions such as universities and their intellectuals were drawn into a grand foreign policy campaign, sometimes knowingly and other times unwittingly, to win hearts and minds to defeat the influence of communism.

If read against American exceptionalism and its "economic frontier thesis," an eerie parallel emerges between the educational aid programs of the 'free' and 'not-so-free' worlds. The benchmarks used to assess the Fulbright Program's outcomes must therefore be considered against America's paradoxical history of market-driven "imperial anticolonialism" and "imperializing idealism" (Williams, 1988, pp. 18–89).

But there are other influences that shape America's imperializing persuasions, and these can be located in its foundational doctrine of Manifest Destiny. Blessed by God, America is conferred with moral and ideological superiority and invested with the responsibility to lead the world (Williams, 1998, pp. 59–60). Starting from the founding fathers and upheld by presidents of every political persuasion, the notion of America as exceptional, a divine project ('God's own country'), guided by a divine process, has driven the rhetoric of American domestic and foreign policy and its self-imposed responsibility to provide both religious and secular leadership for the rest of the world (Monbiot, 2003a, p. 13; Younge, 2003, p. 11; see also Frank, 2002, pp. 3–4).

To a non-American, the reopening of the New York Stock Exchange (NYSE) after the terrorist attacks of 2001 captures this unyielding belief in America's divinity and its ability to triumph over all forms of adversity, terrorism included. In newsreels flashed all over the world, the chosen nation's "triumph over terror" was depicted through a moving rendition of "God Bless America." The cohesion between state and market, nowhere more evident than in the assembled line of dignitaries and the deployment of patriotic symbols—a huge American flag draping the NYSE façade and the stirring opening words of the Exchange's chairman, "Welcome back to the greatest market in the world" (see Milmo, 2001). The national self-image of divinity confirmed in this instance, is symptomatic of a broader momentum in discharging the project of national divinity (see Longley, 2002). God, America, and the market are increasingly being conflated in mainstream discourse:

> The Market, like Yahweh, may lose a skirmish, but in a war of attrition it will always win in the end. . . . Like Calvin's inscrutable deity, The Market may work in mysterious ways, "hid from our eyes," but ultimately it knows best. . . . There is, however, one contradiction between the religion of The Market and the traditional religions that seems to be insurmountable. All of the traditional religions teach that human beings are finite creatures and that there are limits to any earthly enterprise. A Japanese Zen master once said to his disciples as he was dying, "I have learned only one thing in life: how much is enough." He would find no niche in the chapel of The Market, for whom the

First Commandment is "There is never enough." Like the proverbial shark that stops moving, The Market that stops expanding dies. (Cox, 1999)

The Colombo Plan

Similar in its focus to foster regional stability and curtail the spread of communism among the newly independent Asian countries was the Colombo Plan, an educational aid program initiated by seven Commonwealth[6] donors. The Plan's donor countries also extended to a number of non-Commonwealth donors (e.g., Japan and the United States). Like the Fulbright Program, the Colombo Plan assumed that successful students would return home to constitute a technological and administrative elite, effectively a Westernized middle-class intelligentsia, who would be supportive of their Western benefactors (Alexander & Rizvi, 1993, pp. 9–10; Auletta, 2000, pp. 48–49; Rizvi, 1997, pp. 16–17; Wicks, 1972, pp. 10–13). By 1963, some sections of the Australian bureaucracy were moving to link aid with "free" access to regional markets (Auletta, 2000). Put simply, the Plan was part of a broader ethnocentric and instrumentalist discursive machinery aimed primarily at securing political and diplomatic policy goals. These goals took precedence over the educational needs of the region (Alexander & Rizvi, 1993; Rizvi, 1998, pp. 5–6).

By the time the Plan was subsumed into the present development cooperation ("aid") programs, an estimated 300,000 students from 26 countries had been educated under its aegis (Brown, 1993). The outcomes that emerged were typically ambivalent, with a mix of benefits and costs. Although official accounts espoused the success of the Colombo Plan, there was some disquiet about the extent of its success in contributing to the economic development of recipient countries. Its critics pointed to the availability of cheap labor rather than to the presence of a Western-educated middle and professional class as the cause of national economic success (Taylor, 1965, and Drakakis-Smith, 1992, as cited in Brown, 1993, pp. 126–127; Alexander & Rizvi, 1993, pp. 18–19).

Concerns about the appropriateness of the educational programs offered under the aegis of the Plan were raised fairly early on. The Colombo Plan was also held responsible for a 'brain drain' by reducing the critical mass of skilled professionals in the newly independent countries. This was not a unanimous view, as others pointed to a "brain overflow" whereby qualified returnees left their home countries after failing to find jobs suited to their qualifications (Rao, 1979). These debates reflected a tension between

---

[6]The Commonwealth is a multilateral organization made up of 54 member countries, all of which were former colonies of the United Kingdom. The countries are supposed to share common values of democracy, rule of law, good governance, and human rights.

notions of private and public good; individual aspirations and ambitions were pitted against commitments to national or regional goals. The outflow of professionals, back to the 'First World', also established the basis for spatializing power-knowledge networks and contributed to strengthening the status of First World intellectual centers.

Although constructed as a gift, the Colombo Plan, like the Fulbright Program, was fueled by complex and conflicting rationales, some of which continue to influence present-day aid schemes. The Plan sought to educate the "other" in an Australian image. By providing a gift of education to its neighbors, the implicit hope was of subverting hostilities including territorial ambitions from the 'communist North'. To the extent that the Plan was motivated by a national anxiety of the "other," it was discursively allied to a xenophobic and racist discourse (see Alexander & Rizvi, 1993, p. 17; Rizvi, 1997, pp. 14–15). Here, it reflected continuities with classic nation-building discourses that were premised on ethnocultural superiority and enemy stereotypes (see Castles & Miller, 1998; Fiske, Hodge, & Turner, 1987; Hodge & Mishra, 1991; Turner, 1994). I discuss the resurgence of this national anxiety of the other in chapter 6 when I canvas public discourses (public common sense) on international students.

The Colombo Plan's recent resurrection as the Virtual Colombo Plan in Australia suggests, on the one hand, a national desire to recapture the objectification of education as a gift.[7] On the other hand, it exemplifies the close commercial connections among governments, universities, and various business multinationals in the enterprise of knowledge capitalism (see Thrift, 1999, 2001).

Events such as colonization and the Cold War refracted the production of knowledge by influencing what could be thought, written, and researched. They helped sustain the modernist imaginary, a powerful force in the colonial project, in national education systems (Alexander & Rizvi, 1993; see also Venn, 2002). In the former colonies, the desire to engage with modernization was grounded in the broader goals of recovering and retaining national sovereignty (Loombia, 1998, pp. 57–69; see also Nandy, 1983). Although engagements with the project of colonial modernity have yielded some productive outcomes, the question now is whether this vision is appropriate for this historical period, under present conditions of globalization. For education, the significant challenge is how to decolonize the imagination in preparation for a democratic, equitable, and humane globalization (see Nandy, 1983; Pieterse & Parekh, 1995; Tikly, 2001).

To sum up, the ostensible function of colonial education and the post-independence educational exchanges that followed was to serve as a politi-

---

[7]See "Reaching Out Virtually" (2002), "Plan to Throw Net Over Poverty" (2001), "Aid Goes to Cyberspace" (2001), and "Industry Benefits in Virtual Aid Plan" (2001).

cal and economic investment. Discursively packaged as a gift to be transmitted from educated, civilized colonizer to culturally and educationally deficient colonized subject, the consequences for both giver and receiver were unanticipated and ambiguous, resulting in political independence on the one hand, and facilitating the continuation of a colonized imagination in the ongoing drive to modernize on the other hand. The boundaries between colonized and colonizer today are even more complex:

> Ultimately, modern oppression as opposed to the traditional oppression, is not an encounter between the self and the enemy, the rulers and the ruled. . . . It is a battle between the dehumanized self and objectified enemy. . . . The White Sahib may turn out to be defined not by skin colour but by political and social choice. (Nandy, 1983, pp. xv–xvi)

Having outlined the influence of the colonial encounter on early expressions of international education, and the influence of modernization both in Cold War educational aid programs and in the symbolism of postcolonial nationhood, I now examine a second mode of thinking about international education, the discourse of markets. The markets discourse is composed of two broad sets of views. One perspective equates international education with bold innovation, institutional revenue, and export profits for the state. It rests on the assumption that markets provide the space for innovation and creativity as they respond to a new discerning international student who cannot be 'duped' into purchasing a tired colonial template. The argument is that the educational products sold in the global marketplace offer a vast improvement on the limp colonial pedagogy offered to the colonized elites in the "aid" era of international education. Accordingly, educational markets are noted to have facilitated a clean break from the neo-colonial impulses of modernity. Where its predecessor, the modern university, was noted for its service to the ideological and imperializing imperatives of the nation-state, the contemporary international university is represented as a dynamic agent of a postcolonial form of globalization (Scott, 1998, pp. 123, 126–127). And here, university staff and recruitment agents point to rising enrollment statistics as proof of success of the contemporary international university.

A less optimistic perspective associates international education markets with the multinationalization of education, where the profit motive is noted to subordinate attempts to challenge the neocolonialism of existing educational products (Altbach, 1999b). The international education market is criticized for valuing a Westernized educational template while failing to consider how education addresses the needs and concerns of different geographies of consumers and spatialities (including places and nations). A commodity approach to education privileges exchange values and perpetua^tes an educational imagination that appears fixed in both space and time.[8] Furthermore, aside from a nodding reference to historical factors, the emphasis is on short-term goals at the expense of longer term considerations. It is this preoccupation with the short term that is partly responsible for the growing influence of English as the language of instruction in education markets, a trend that is posing risks to linguistic diversity (Marginson, 2003a).

Given the divergence in views, a brief discussion of education markets is warranted to establish a foundation for later questions as to whether international education markets, through their conceptualization of international students as customers, have succeeded in introducing alternative discursive practices to earlier neocolonial, nation-centered practices.

TRADE IN EDUCATION

How has a university education been redefined to a tradable commodity? There are no simple answers to this question, although two sets of factors can be identified as having influenced the trend toward the market. In the first instance, the reconceptualization of education as a tradable commodity has been influenced by the rise of market liberalism (neoliberalism), which has witnessed a proliferation of trust in markets, most evident in their objectification to an almost sage-like status by politicians, policymakers, and institutional leaders. Not only is the market portrayed as having emotions and feelings—"the market is nervous, excited, bullish, energetic" (Henry, Lingard, Rizvi, & Taylor, 1999, p. 87)—markets are also discursively constructed as mediators and managers. It is not uncommon for financial journalists, for example, to pepper their commentary with phrases such as 'the markets will reward/punish this move' as a way of explaining the movement of national currencies or the efficacy of business decisions by companies.

This stance ignores the fact that markets "are neither natural nor neutral phenomena, [but] are socially and politically constructed" (Ball, 1994, p. 111). How markets are conceptualized and analyzed is very much a function of the disciplinary and ideological paradigms used to understand them. It is with this in mind that Marginson (1997) observes that markets are best understood as a set of behavioral relations, which are embedded in the sociocultural and political fabrics of nations and communities, rather than as concrete structures with predictable processes and outcomes (pp. 29–30). How these behavioral relations play out in different geographical spaces, and the assumptions of human subjectivity on which they are premised and subsequently generate, is an area of interest to this study.

---

[8]I discuss this in chapter 2 when I examine the select interactions between space-bound notions of education and globalizing processes and forces.

A second contributing factor to the commodification of knowledge is related to the prominence of ideas about a "new" phase of human development, labeled variously as postindustrialism, postFordism, and the 'New Economy'. Social theorists such as Bell, Touraine, and Castells, along with business gurus such as Drucker and Reich, heralded the arrival of a new role for knowledge, skills, and creativity—they were now regarded as factors of production, not unlike the role of land and capital (see Jessop, 2000). This argument, when taken further, associates the competitiveness of nation-states with their capacities in knowledge production, creativity, and innovation. Given that the university is a key actor in the knowledge-production enterprise, and given the growing pressure on individuals to retrain and to reskill to acquire competitive advantage in the labor force, the university emerged as a major actor in the 'New Economy' (Larner & Le Heron, 2003; Peters, 2004).

The 'New Economy' provided the impetus for the rise of the business-centered university, committed to preparing "job-ready" graduates and developing and strengthening its market-friendly disciplines. The international university came to be understood as an institution with spatial reach, able to draw income from a variety of international sources including international student fees, franchises, branch campuses, development assistance (aid) consultancies, and donations from overseas alumni and students. Being international meant having staff who traversed selected parts of the globe to recruit new students, undertake consultancies, and deliver training programs along with "just-in-time," "any place, any time" academic courses. Some universities also jumped onto the e-learning bandwagon and complemented their income by selling 'dot.edu' digitized and virtualized courses.

The 'New Economy', so clearly a grand narrative, yet born in an era described by many social theorists as postmodern, was premised on, and promised, not plural new economies but singularity: the New Economy. Constituted by buzzwords—information society, network society, knowledge-based society, globalization, virtual capitalism—this new phase of human development was marked out as one which had clearly broken with the old economy. It promised the end of boundaries, sluggish bureaucracies, and hierarchies; these would be replaced with speed and the porosity of flows and networks. In this 'New Economy', organizations would take on flatter and more democratic structures, technology would enhance mobilities and choices, work would mirror the flexibility of the times and function as an avenue for creativity. Work would be fun (Lofgren, 2003; Thrift, 2002). The era of this 'New Economy' saw economic forms and activities being given distinctly cultural expressions, exemplified in the branding of places and the production of images, symbols, icons, and events as commodities or services for sale. Creating mixes, synergies, and melange was the order of the day. A preoccupation with design, performance, and style

(imagineering) entrenched aestheticization and fetishization as important
dimensions of new economy processes (Lofgren, 2003).

The culturalization of production that characterized the 'New Economy'
drew universities into an increasingly commodified world. The enterprising, entrepreneurial university embraced melange and imagineering, offering a suite of market-friendly courses and degrees programs in new fields
such as e-commerce. These were usually promoted through elaborate marketing "roadshows." The business-centered international university was an
active participant in the romance of the 'New Economy'; it helped formal-
ize and rhetorically stabilize the new economy.

The discourse of the 'New Economy' emphasized the fleet-footed,
weightless dimensions of this new stage of human development while ob-
scuring its less heroic, more mundane dimensions including the fact that
many of the production and consumption activities were grounded in real
places and involved armies of old economy workers, many who were increasingly disadvantaged by the flexibilization of production and consumption (Lofgren, 2003):

> Looking back at those millennium years, the important thing is not the ques-
> tion of whether or not the new economy was fact or fiction, a managment phi-
> losophy, a generation war, a marketing trick, a piece of magic, a corporate
> strategy or a constant revolution—it could well have been all this and much
> more—but to discuss how this world of production and consumption was pro-
> moted and developed, lived and experienced. . . . There are lessons to be
> learned . . . how does the new have a deep and lasting effect on people's lives.
> (p. 241)

Although the implosion of the dot.com bubble has removed some of the
gloss from the promised 'New Economy', the deeper issues concerning the
commodification of knowledge, its association with competitive advantage,
and its uneven distribution across geographies merit more attention than
that afforded by standard writings on global education markets.

Educational Benefits as "Goods"

Fully grasping the outputs and benefits of a university education is a profoundly complex undertaking. Even theorists who recognize higher education's wide-ranging contributions and advocate a recognition of its more
varied outputs are hemmed in by the discursive tools at their disposal. The
extensive use of terms such as *capital, value, services,* and *goods,* and a prevailing instrumental logic are indicative of the tenacious hold of the language
of the market on the academic imagination. Framing the debate in language and concepts that acknowledge the complexity of human existence

is not simply about a nostalgic yearning to capture the romance, innocence, and poetry of the human spirit. A vital function of the university is to strive in imagination and practice to provide its graduates and society with alternatives that they may use to re-organize systems of production and exchange, social institutions, social relations, and interactions with the environment.

The scholarly imperative, to critically analyze structures and systems of thought, requires reason, but in addition, an ethics of care. Scholarly work requires a certain fearlessness to both serve and challenge the interests of the state, industry, and commerce. Attaining the right balance between service and critique is critical for the well-being of these institutions and broader society (O'Farrell, 1996). A globalizing context also requires universities to strive to go beyond the implicit architecture of the nation-state in their educational visions. It means enabling faculty to explore alternative epistemologies and methodologies, models, and techniques that transcend the familiar container of the nation-state (see Appadurai, 2004, for a discussion of the challenges for social sciences). It means a firm commitment to building transnational, cross-regional relations that exceed the largely symbolic and ceremonial, such as formal visits by senior university executives to exchange signatures and establish the obligatory 'memoranda of understanding'.

At the top of the hierarchy of market-friendly discursive taxonomies is the classical economics framework, which privileges exchange values at the expense of use values in measuring educational outputs (Marginson, 1997, pp. 27–36). Where exchange values are signified by money, use values are associated with more complex outputs. For example, use values may be associated with such outputs as vital social capital for the development of a civil society, embodied knowledge in the form of intercultural awareness and goodwill, and the range of ancillary services provided by educational institutions to their local and national constituencies.

Use values are not quantifiable by conventional accounting instruments such as cost–benefit analyses and productivity measurements (Marginson 1997, pp. 27–28; see also Baker, McCreedy, & Johnson, 1996).[9] In its more extreme forms, positivist logic suggests that what cannot be measured does not merit a place in the academic and scientific canon. Unmeasurable phe-

---

[9]Baker et al. (1996) attempt to quantify the benefits to Australia of having an international education export industry. They find that international education's nonpecuniary benefits could not be measured by using a cost–benefit conceptual tool. A counterfactual was required to assess what should occur without international students. This proved too difficult as "it required prohibitively large amounts of information [and] many approximations and assumptions." In an institutional climate where performance, funding, and management are increasingly dominated by measurement, "objects" that don't lend themselves to measurement can find themselves assigned to the category of subordinate knowledges.

nomena either cease to matter or exist only as subjugated knowledges. As the following discussion shows, even research that criticizes marketization and seeks to incorporate greater complexity into understandings of educational outputs is restricted by the markets discourse.

According to Marginson (1997), educational outputs fall into two broad categories: student goods and knowledge goods. Student goods include self goods and training goods, which are purchased by employers to value add to their employees' skills and potential (pp. 46–47). Knowledge goods, which are regarded as having a greater profile in a 'New Economy', take the forms of tradable intellectual property (e.g., software, microchips, pharmaceuticals, vaccines, income from international aid consultancies, etc.). The production of knowledge goods is expected to assume a bigger profile in institutional life (pp. 48–49). As I discuss later, universities seek to embellish their status within the highly competitive international education market by highlighting the types of knowledge goods they generate.

Self goods[10] are often regarded by marketing personnel as being particularly relevant to international students as they represent *positional goods*, or the means to social advantage (Marginson, 1997, p. 38). Positional goods assume particular importance in more stratified societies where education is a means to socioeconomic mobility. Presently, the most coveted positional goods in the global education market are credentials from the Ivy League and Oxbridge universities, in those disciplines and fields considered "market-friendly," such as Law, Medicine, Business, and the techno-scientific fields. In this consumer context, positional goods represent an investment not only for the individual but also other family members.[11] Also included in the self goods category are education credentials and other goods of self-improvement, such as relationships, confidence, particular tastes, and sensibilities (Marginson, 1997). Education marketing narratives tend to promote the desire for these self goods in their promotional brochures and videos.

The preceding discussion is revealing of two important points. First, the importance of exchange values and the concomitant normalization of education as a private good, paid for by the individual procurer, who is anticipated to reap extraordinary benefits from their investment. Such a commodity approach to international education fails to acknowledge fully public good considerations and ignores the needs of those on the fringes who cannot pay for an education. Second, a discursive logic that distills human relationships, dreams, visions, and aspirations into the language of value is indicative of the tenacious hold of a market-based instrumentalism

---

[10]Bourdieu (2003) uses the term *habitus* to capture the multidimensionality of self goods.

[11]Funding for overseas studies is often kin related, with several family members involved in paying for a student's education.

on the intellectual imagination. Breaking this hold presents significant challenges for the 21st-century university.

INTERNATIONAL STUDENT FLOWS: NATIONAL AND GLOBAL TRENDS

In 2001, the OECD estimated that 1.65 million students worldwide were undertaking tertiary studies outside their countries of origin (OECD, 2003). Some 94%, or 1.54 million, of these students were enrolled in institutions in OECD countries with five countries—Australia, France, Germany, the United Kingdom, and the United States—playing host to the majority (71%) of these students (OECD, 2003). By 2010, it is predicted that some 2.8 million students will be studying abroad[12] (Van Damme, 2001, p. 418). Exports of international education are estimated to exceed the 1998 estimates of US$30 billion (OECD, 2003).

The biggest exporter of international education is the United States, which had 572,509 foreign students studying in its higher education institutions in 2003/2004. This represents earnings of US$12 billion to the American national economy.[13] Collectively, India, China, Korea, and Japan are the source countries of 41% of America's international students (see Table 1.1). The most popular fields of study are Business and Management, followed by Engineering, Mathematics, and Computer Science. In 2003/2004, there was a 2.4% decrease in international students in the United States.

International students make up 4.6% of total enrollments in American higher education, a proportion that is smaller than that in the United Kingdom and Australia where international students constitute 10.9% and 13.9% of total student numbers, respectively (Table 1.2).

Whereas two decades ago it was the student supported by country-based aid who was the identified customer targeted for attention by university marketing and recruitment divisions, today the target is the self-funded individual (Van Damme, 2001, pp. 420–421). A total of 81.8% of all international undergraduates finance their education in the United States from

---

[12]Accurate and current data on global flows of international students are difficult to procure. United Nations Educational, Scientific, and Cultural Organization (UNESCO) *Statistical Yearbook* provides total numbers of students who are studying in a country other than their own. However, it is not always able to provide up-to-date information. In the United States, IIE's *Open Doors* publication provides information on international student numbers in the United States, and in Australia, the Department of Education, Science, and Training (DEST), and International Development Plan (IDP) are good sources of statistical data. The British Council's Education Counselling Service (ECS) and the Higher Education Statistics Agency (HESA) are an important source of information on international students in Britain.

[13]From *Open Doors* (2004).

TABLE 1.1
International Students in the United States
by Leading Places of Origin

Rank	Place of Origin	2002–2003	2003–2004	2003–2004 % Change	% of US Int'l. Student Total
1	India	74,603	79,736	6.9	13.9
2	China	64,757	61,765	−4.6	10.8
3	Korea, Republic of	51,519	52,484	1.9	9.2
4	Japan	45,960	40,835	−11.2	7.1
5	Canada	26,513	27,017	1.9	4.7
6	Taiwan	28,017	26,178	−6.6	4.6
7	Mexico	12,801	13,329	4.1	2.3
8	Turkey	11,601	11,398	−1.7	2.0
9	Thailand	9,982	8,937	−10.5	1.6
10	Indonesia	10,432	8,880	−14.9	1.6
11	Germany	9,302	8,745	−6.0	1.5
12	United Kingdom	8,326	8,439	1.4	1.5
13	Brazil	8,388	7,799	−7.0	1.4
14	Colombia	7,771	7,533	−3.1	1.3
15	Kenya	7,862	7,381	−6.1	1.3
16	Hong Kong	8,076	7,353	−9.0	1.3
17	Pakistan	8,123	7,325	−9.8	1.3
18	France	7,223	6,818	−5.6	1.2
19	Malaysia	6,595	6,483	−1.7	1.1
20	Nigeria	5,816	6,140	5.6	1.1
	World Total	586,323	572,509	−2.4	

TABLE 1.2
Foreign Students and Total U.S. Enrollment 2003–2004

Year	Students	Change	Enrollment	Foreign
1989–1990	386,851	5.6	13,824,592	2.8
1990–1991	407,529	5.3	13,975,408	2.9
1991–1992	419,585	3.0	14,360,965	2.9
1992–1993	438,618	4.5	14,422,975	3.0
1993–1994	449,749	2.5	14,473,106	3.1
1994–1995	452,653	0.6	14,554,016	3.1
1995–1996	453,787	0.3	14,419,252	3.1
1996–1997	457,984	0.9	14,286,478	3.1
1997–1998	481,280	5.1	13,294,221	3.6
1998–1999	490,933	2.0	13,391,401	3.6
1999–2000	514,723	4.8	13,584,998	3.8
2000–2001	547,867	6.4	14,046,659	3.9
2001–2002	582,996	6.4	13,511,149	4.3
2002–2003	586,323	0.6	12,853,627	4.6
2003–2004	572,509	−2.4	13,383,553	4.3

TABLE 1.3
Primary Source of Funding for International
Students in the United States, 2003–2004

Primary Source of Funds	% Undergraduate	% Graduate	% Other
Personal and family	81.8	51.6	69.7
U.S. college or university	10.1	40.4	7.8
Home government or university	2.0	2.2	4.1
U.S. government	0.3	0.7	0.3
Private U.S. sponsor	2.8	1.5	2.0
Foreign private sponsor	2.6	1.7	1.3
Current employment	0.3	0.4	13.9
International organization	0.2	1.4	0.8
Other sources	0.0	0.0	0.0
Total	100.0	100.0	100.0

personal and family sources. Educational aid scholarships from the American government support only 0.7% of international students. Graduate students are more successful in securing scholarships, with nearly 40.4% obtaining financial assistance from American universities and colleges (Table 1.3; IIE, 2004).

In 2002–2003, 184,685 international students were studying onshore in British universities.[14] They were largely enrolled in the Business and Economics streams, followed by Engineering and Technology. The British Council has predicted that by 2025 there will be 1 million international students enrolled in British universities (MacLeod, 2004a).

In 2003, there were 136,252 international students enrolled at Australian universities; 114,680 were onshore students and 60,052 were transnational (offshore) students (Fig. 1.1; IDP Education Australia, 2004). For the 2003 calendar year, the total value of Australia's education exports was estimated at $4.281 billion. This figure includes the tuition revenues earned by education institutions and expenditure on goods and services by students (IDP, 2004). The main source countries were China, Hong Kong, South Korea, Indonesia, Malaysia, and Japan (Table 1.4). Korean and Japanese nationals are more likely to be undertaking English language courses, whereas students from countries such as Malaysia, Singapore, and India tend to undertake full degree programs.

What is significant about these flows is that the producers of higher education are mainly from the industrialized, Western nations of the world, the North, whereas students are overwhelmingly from the South and East of de-

---

[14]This number does not include students from the European Union who are entitled to study in British universities under the same conditions as those available to local students.

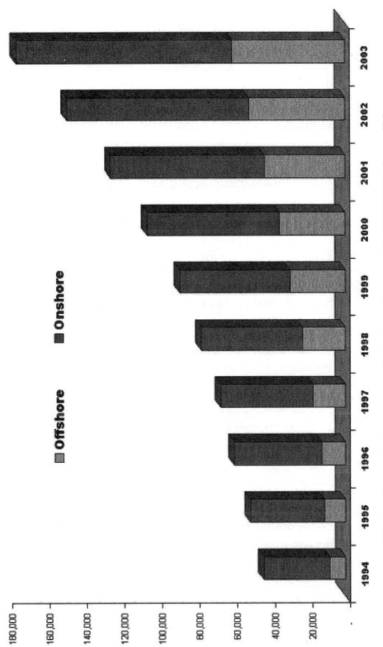

FIG. 1.1. International students enrolled in Australian universities (1994–2003). Source: IDP Education Australia (2004).

TABLE 1.4
International Students in the United Kingdom (2002/2003): Areas of Study

Discipline or Subject Area	Student Numbers
Agriculture	580
Economics	6,660
Business studies	21,275
Health/allied to medicine	9,640
Biological sciences	5,515
Physical sciences	4,470
Engineering and technology	23,410
Law	10,820
Education	8,185

veloping and newly industrializing nations. Prospective students select as study destinations countries that are perceived to be economically dynamic and that offer credentials that are internationally recognized. The volume of economic exchanges between nations is an important factor in shaping these student flows (Chen & Barnett, 2000). America's popularity as a study destination in Southeast and East Asia commenced in the 1980s, and can be attributed to the rapid and significant increase in investment by U.S. firms in these regions. Figure 1.1 outlines the regions of origin of international students studying in America—55% come from Asia. Australia's international higher education students come from Malaysia, Indonesia, Singapore, China (Mainland and Hong Kong), India, and the United States.[15]

'First World' to 'First World' movement also takes place but at a smaller scale: American and European students frequently undertake a study abroad semester in Australia; European Union students are studying in both the United Kingdom and the United States. As a general observation, there are fewer Americans studying in Australia and Europe (Haug, 1996, as cited in Van Damme, 2001, p. 419) compared with the nationals of both of these regions studying in the United States. Female Americans are more likely than males choose to go on an exchange or study abroad sojourn. When Americans do study overseas, they prefer shorter stays, a summer semester being the most popular length of the sojourn (Green, 2002).

A popular interpretation of the patterns of student flows is that they are no longer driven by colonial or postcolonial links. Instead, market factors are noted for facilitating discernible shifts in student mobility:

> Flows are no longer about developed countries such as Britain importing students and developing countries in Asia and Africa exporting them. . . . Increasingly universities from developed countries are reaching out to students

---

[15]IDP Education Fast Facts (2004).

TABLE 1.5
Australia's Top 15 Source Markets, Semester 2, 2003 Versus 2004
(Full Degree Onshore Students)

Source Country	2003	2004	Growth
India	8,476	12,932	53%
China	16,733	24,003	43%
Bangladesh	1,935	2,493	29%
Canada	1,477	1,666	15%
Japan	2,309	2,491	8%
Korea	3,032	3,243	7%
Vietnam	1,936	2,035	5%
USA	1,622	1,732	4%
Hong Kong	9,407	9,631	2%
Taiwan	2,808	2,828	1%
Malaysia	12,141	12,167	0%
Thailand	4,131	4,115	0%
Indonesia	8,839	8,191	−7%
Singapore	8,617	7,786	−10%
Norway	2,941	2,438	−17%
Total	106,274	118,369	11%

in developing countries by setting up local campuses, franchising the early years of their degrees to local colleges, devising collaborative programmes with indigenous universities and so on. (Scott, 1998, p. 118)

A clever choice of words is used to create a rupture from the era where Britain "imported" students from developing countries to this era where universities "reach out" to students by establishing offshore (local) campuses. The implicit message here is that the market offers an improvement from an earlier era. Market-driven factors are also held to be responsible for the growing profile of consumers from newly industrialized countries and transitional economies, a development attributed to the vastly improved economic circumstances of the middle classes in these settings. Here, patterns of consumption are linked to national affluence in sending countries. Consumption is also shaped by the capacity of local producers to meet demand. Simply put, both push and pull factors shape consumption. The push factors are the reduced national capacity of universities in the sending countries, and the pull factors include the marketing and promotional activities of universities in producer countries that help stimulate demand in an affluent middle class to consume a Western commodity (Chen & Barnett, 2000). The growing importance attributed to English for participation in global community, by "those with a vested interest in the promotion of English" is another pull factor that works to increase demand for international education (Pegrum, 2004, p. 3).

As a general observation, discussions about demand for international education invest considerable power in the student-consumer while depoliticizing the terrain of international education. In the politically neutral language of the market, agency is seen to reside firmly in the sending countries and autonomous choosing consumers. The distinctions between push and pull factors are diluted and choice is delinked from historical and geopolitical factors. Yet, a closer look at the supply-and-demand equation reveals that economic pressures together with political, ethnic, and racial tensions are central factors in shaping student flows. The affirmative action policies of the Indonesian and Malaysian governments that discriminate against ethnic minorities have been responsible for the flows of significant numbers of students to the three producer countries examined in this study: the United Kingdom, Australia, and the United States. In these cases, a set of push factors, the cultural politics surrounding national higher education systems in demand (sending) countries, has been responsible for students' decisions to choose an overseas education. In other national spaces, the robustly interventionist roles of the International Monetary Fund (IMF) and the World Bank and the globalization of neoliberal economics have influenced educational policies, often leading to a reduction in state funding for higher education. The cumulative effect of these policies has been to deprive national universities of much-needed resources, eroding their capacity to engage with and respond to international developments and standards and, in the case of institutions in developing and transitional economies, making them less attractive to the brightest and best of their citizens (Jones, 1997; Tomasevski, 2003).

Discussions about the choices of study destinations often refer to factors such as the "absorptive capacities" of higher education systems of "receiving countries" (Cummings, 1991, p. 118). These expressions occlude the hard-nosed commercialism of governments and universities to recruit international students. One could be forgiven for visualizing higher education institutions as blotting paper (or worse, toilet tissue), capable only of absorbing international students, and lacking in agency to educate and inspire entire generations of professionals. Such terms of reference minimize the close links among state, market, and university, including the role of power politics in national settings that aim to keep national borders impermeable to less desirable others through the use of various technologies of surveillance and exclusion. These extend to cumbersome screening processes for visas for international students from the South. Post 9-11, official anxiety has seen greater screening of prospective students by 'First World' governments, particularly the United States (Swarns, 2004; Zhao, 2004). In the overwhelming majority of instances, it is 'First World' identity markers that differentiate the desirable from the undesirable student.

National politics play a part in defining and setting limits for international student recruitment. The neoliberal policies of the UK and Australian governments have steered universities in both countries to bolster their efforts to raise revenue from overseas students. Local contingencies such as demand by domestic students and a perceived institutional capacity to satisfy this demand can culminate in a less welcoming environment for particular categories of international students. Similarly, references to sending countries and countries that export their students may shift the emphasis away from push factors in these consumer sites. Political imperatives also surround the reduced domestic capacity in consumer sites, which forces individuals to seek an overseas education at significant personal cost. These complexities are diluted by market language.

When read as part of an unproblematic panoply of choices, opportunities and desires of individuals that are set against a background of greater accessibility to technology, transport, booming home economies, and the disposable income of a burgeoning middle class, the trends and flows of international students become no different from the flows of tourists, business expatriates, and cosmopolitan academics. However, this book shows how these conventional orthodoxies can be problematized by mapping the relations that define and underpin flows.

Chapter 2

Discursive Power and Subjectivity

This chapter provides an overview of the theoretical and methodological tools used in this study. It introduces the concepts of discourse, discursive power, and governmentality, and explores their uses in analyzing the organization and operations of international education markets. The chapter establishes the context for analyzing the construction of understandings, social vocabularies, and imaginations that make up international education. It provides the instruments to investigate the discursive practices that are shaped and mobilized by nation-states, individual universities, and the faculty to constitute the industry known as international education. It is, by and through, a set of differentially powerful discursive practices that the international university materializes and the international student is constructed as an object, to be recruited, educated and enlisted for a range of endeavors: the generation of revenue through tuition fees, donations, endowments, and lifelong learning professional development courses; the construction of alumni networks and the creation of associations with professional communities.

A FOUCAULDIAN APPROACH

Foucault is credited with introducing a new sensibility to doing research. His work seeks to unsettle humanist assumptions by arguing against the idea of a free, rational, self-sufficient, autonomous subject who is the orginator of meaning, discourse, and knowledge. The subject, according to Foucault, can be compromised by the effects of power in the world

(O'Farrell, 1989, pp. 121–124). At the same time, the subject is also a vehicle of power and thus capable of exercising will and choice. A second informing principle within Foucault's work is a recognition of the limitations of discipline-bound knowledges, including their role in constituting the very reality they purport to be studying (Foucault, 1980c; see also Miller & Rose, 1997). Knowledge is caught up in relations of power, and therefore it is neither neutral nor impartial.

Thus, not everything is visible or sayable; rather, a set of rules determines what can be said, written, communicated, and legitimated as institutional practice, knowledge, and 'truth' about international education, global education markets, and globalization. Notably, Foucault sees a 'positive unconscious' dimension to the production of discourse and, by extension, the production of knowledge. He argues that the rules that shape discourses can elude the consciousness of those who use them (McNay, 1994, p. 52).

In the next section I discuss discourse and discursive power. I then examine how a Foucauldian conceptual scheme can be used to unsettle naturalized understandings of international education. I follow this up with discussions of the role of discursive power in governmentality—the government of others and the government of ourselves.

POWER-KNOWLEDGE AND DISCOURSE

Foucault's interpretation of the term *discourse* is broad and not restricted to texts, vocabularies, sets of thoughts, or sayings. Discourse is more than just language and more than just signs (signifiers) that reflect reality. Discourses can take textual forms, but texts are only a small part of what constitutes discourse. Instead, discourse refers to *practices* that are rule governed and that shape what can be said, written, and transmitted. Inevitably, discursive practices are informed by social practices and political governance, which prescribes what is selected and excluded to form discourse (McNay, 1994, p. 27). Discourse does not just represent reality. It enables and constrains the imagination and social practices; it is constitutive of reality. This means discourses can be used as technologies to govern. In this capacity, discursive practices are instruments of power (Foucault, 1984, p. 12). However, discourse is not only an instrument of power, it is also an effect of power—it is produced by authorities and interests that exercise power.

A broader definition of discourse also includes *spatial texts*—the interactions among people, places, and materialities (see Law & Hetherington, 2000). The spaces occupied by international education offices in universities and the layout of international education exhibitions (roadshows) offer clues not just on how international education is assembled, ordered, and financed but also on the power relations that constitute international education markets. Similarly, the experiences of international students in places—cities, towns, and countries—throws some light on how they are regarded and how they experience the overseas sojourn. Spatial scripts, then, offer an opportunity to analyze power relations within the discursive field of international education.

At any one time, there is a multiplicity of discourses, some competing or in tension with each other and others in relationships that are broadly reinforcing. It is this multiplicity that opens spaces for resistance (Foucault, 1978, p. 101). Furthermore, its capacity to be transformed means that discourse should not be conceptualized as a fixed, essentialized entity but rather as a window to a partial and situated reality that is changeable across space and time (Foucault, 1994, pp. 10–12). From this perspective of multiplicity, a field such as international education can be understood as a plurality of competing discourses, spanning different disciplines, featuring different actors, and producing different meanings that are just as likely to change over time and across geographical spaces. The underpinning rules that subject discourse also monitor and regulate the disciplines, seeking to eject any interlopers that might contaminate the 'purity' of their conceptual and theoretical arsenals (see Hall, 1988).

A discourse that originates from a discipline such as Business or Economics may prioritize the following topics or objects for investigation: priority markets, new and emerging markets, recruitment targets, market intelligence, customers, and competitor analysis. Within this lexicon of terms, considerations of human subjectivity are marginalized. An Education discourse, on the other hand, may make references to: language proficiencies, academic skills, critical analysis, deep learning, plagiarism, and contribution to original scholarship. An Education discourse places the international student in the position of a learner who is willing to be educated into the norms of a Western academic culture. A Tourism discourse, by contrast, may construct the human subject variously to be a visitor with interest in natural attractions or heritage icons, or a discerning shopper who seeks flexible shopping hours and home country cuisine, and who deserves recognition because of the economic contributions made to the retail industry, local businesses, or national tourist revenue. Finally, scholars' writing in the field of Development Studies may identify the following as objects of discourse: uneven development, the uneven distribution of professional skills overseas, and the risk of a 'Third World' to 'First World' 'brain drain' (Altbach, 1998, pp. 197–200; Chitnis, 1999, pp. 22–23; Eshiwani, 1999, p. 35).

Different discourses, then, provide sets of naming practices, together with new types of knowledges and techniques to manage the subject of these different discourses. The question of which discourses are institutionalized and which assume dominance for national and local governments, for university administrators and academics, or for different groups of international students implies ever-shifting and uneven power relations.

Discursive constructions of the international university can also vary across spatialities. Many British and Australian universities discursively construct themselves as public institutions, committed to the public good within Australia. Many within universities argue that their involvement within the higher education export industry is intended to support this public good role. However, the public good role changes with the university's engagement with other geographies of consumers, resulting in its metamorphosis into a private sector organization, as a senior university administrator noted, "[The university] is predominantly a private institution with government subsidy."[1] How different discourses simultaneously pull and push against each other to generate particular expressions of international education and subject positions for students forms the basis of the next section.

THEORIZING POWER

Foucault was keen to distance himself from providing a theory of power. He argues that the notion of theory implied a context-free and ahistorical view of power's exercise, effects, and outcomes. In place of theory, he provides an *analytic* of power that is able to accommodate the situatedness of power: its historical contingencies and its variable expressions across time, spaces, and places, across institutions including academic disciplines, and across cultures (Foucault, 1982, p. 184). His work extends understandings of power beyond commonplace notions of top-down, repressive, impositional models (a 'descending analysis'). In the Foucauldian scheme, power is diffused and operationalized through a series of mundane and routine practices (micropractices). The deployment of power thus involves a heterogeneous ensemble of political rationalities, expert knowledges, and strategies. Power, according to Foucault, also has a productive quality; it yields positive outcomes: "induces pleasure, forms knowledge," meets the aspirations of particular individuals and institutions, and so on.

Foucault argues against focusing entirely on the conscious intentions and motivations of individuals. Questions such as who has power and their aims are redundant. The more important question is how power installs itself, how power acquires the status of truth, and importantly, how power induces truth regimes that collaborate to produce particular subject positions and both dominant and subjugated knowledges.

---

[1]Interview conducted with marketing director November 2001.

There are two characteristic features of Foucault's theorization on power that are useful for understanding the power regimes that constitute international education markets. First, that power's distribution to the 'capillaries', or peripheries, point to the fruitfulness of analyzing the peripheral and inconsequential realms (micropractices)—in this case promotional materials—to uncover the exercise of power in international education markets. Second, its productive qualities must be acknowledged as this feature allows power to be self-sustaining. Even if international education is embedded in neocolonial constructs, it should be recognized as still capable of delivering potentially positive outcomes for some of its recipients. The desire for international education within the postcolonial world rests on this productivity of power relations. A Western credential has cultural capital within the global labor market and increases employability. This is a major influence in sustaining the demand for international education. Equally, a heightened insight and awareness on the part of students about the links between power and knowledge could translate into an ability to refuse particular subject positions and increase their capacity to produce transgressive knowledges.

How can Foucault's theorizations be put to work to understand the organization and operations of international education markets? A descending (top-down) analysis of power would deem the corresponding peripheries within international education markets—the East/South, universities, or international students—to be relatively powerless, with their objectives and ambitions dictated by a powerful center. By contrast, an ascending analysis of power means conceptualizing international education as a diffusion of networks with multiple sites or nodes such as universities, cities, towns, and countries, along with other educational spaces that feature brokers, marketing instrumentalities, and consumer markets. Power is diffused within the circuits of these networks and is best studied by examining the various scales that encompass the broader network—from transnational and national to the local, from the locus of institutions to the individual, and from macrocontextual forces to mundane micropractices.

POWER AND GOVERNMENT: GOVERNMENTALITY

In Foucauldian usage, government and governmentality refer to a heterogeneous ensemble of political rationalities and organized practices aimed at "the conduct of conduct" (Foucault, 1982, pp. 220–221; see also Miller & Rose, 1990, p. 3). The concept of governmentality provides a theoretical map to understand how the aspirations of government are connected to the actions of organizations, and the ambitions, desires, and beliefs of human subjects. In other words, governmentality is a model of governance that aims not to crush the capacities of individuals but to harnesses their productive capacities as a way to govern entire populations. Individuals internalize the effects of power and regulate themselves toward ends that are congruent with the forms and effects of power deployed by both state and non-state actors (Foucault, 1991a, pp. 91–94; Miller & Rose, 1990, p. 2). This government of the self often takes place in and against a backdrop of self-betterment and self-improvement and includes a belief that the well-being of the individual is linked with the health and strength of the state. Rose (1999a, p. 145) puts it succinctly: "[There is] no longer a conflict between the self interest of the . . . subject and the patriotic duty of the citizen." At its simplest, governmentality is premised on a looser form of power where the cooperation of individuals is directly or indirectly harnessed by the nation-state toward particular ends, which Foucault refers to as "convenient ends" (Foucault, 1980d, p. 58, 1991a, pp. 102–104; see also Dean, 1999, pp. 205–206; Rose, 1999a, pp. 1–14).

The exercise of power to shape particular subjectivities in and through discourse is a salient feature of the Information Age. Discourse—the sets of embedded and naturalized frameworks of understandings—helps shape what is socially imaginable, acceptable, and desirable. The use of political discourse to create popular understandings about the inevitability of globalization, what citizens can expect from their governments, and what is expected of them as ideal citizens—in short, the types of citizen subject positions valued by the state and social institutions—reduces the necessity for stringent rules or laws. Individuals will steer themselves, using an array of strategies and beliefs that Foucault denotes as 'technologies of the self' or ways of governing the self (Foucault, 1982). Besides identifying political rationalities, governmentality offers the means of understanding governance as "the self acting on the self."

Technologies of the self can be deployed to engage in resistance to particular norms. Foucault observes that they allow individuals to transform themselves to attain a certain state of happiness or wisdom. Technologies of the self can also be used by individuals and groups to refuse ascriptions (subject positions), to push the limits of parameters of freedom, and to explore the 'other'. When informed by the principles of ethical self-formation, technologies of the self can offer a series of potentially liberating opportunities for human agency (Foucault, 1996). Equally, they can be used to support existing norms including those that are detrimental to democratic futures.

However, technologies of the self can be co-opted not only by disciplinary knowledge but also by, and through, particular political rationalities. Neoliberal forms of government are noted for blurring all distinctions between the economic and noneconomic spheres of life. Neoliberal governance is premised on a political rationality that seeks to develop a congru-

ence between the economic subject—the rational, utility-maximizing individual—and the responsible, self-sufficient, moral individual (see Burchell,
1993, pp. 324–325; Lemke, 2001, pp. 201–203; Marshall, 1995; Miller &
Rose, 1990, 1997; Rose, 1999a, pp. 230–232). Through a series of nuanced,
processes of normalization, autonomization, and responsibilization, the
moral individual is constructed as one who works on himself or herself to
be self-sufficient. This helps establish the conditions for enabling political
government to relinquish its responsibilities for providing security, health
care, education, and so on for its citizens.

In drawing together his theorizations on the human subject, Foucault's
work can be said to unsettle notions of an authentic, unitary subject.
Whereas Western philosophy conceptualized the self as having an essence,
Foucault's work shows that the subject is a product of historical developments shaped by official knowledges and institutionalized practices. In this
way, his work problematizes the long-held liberal notion that knowledge is
power (Gordon, 1980, pp. 233–234). Furthermore, Foucault argues against
imposing a singular reading on the subject, something he associated as being 'a dangerous act of power'.

In his earlier works, which include *Archaeology of Knowledge* (1972),
Foucault understands the subject to be largely scripted by social forces such
as institutions and discursive formations (disciplinary knowledges). He was
criticized for taking a deterministic perspective of the subject. In response
to some of this criticism that accused him of skepticism and nihilism,
Foucault takes the view that the subject is both object and vehicle of power.
It is by recognizing the subject as historically constituted, and, thus, shifting, that we are prompted toward greater self-scrutiny and greater accountability. In place of declarations of an autonomous and authentic subject,
Foucault's position is to demand *how* the subject practices autonomy and
authenticity. Foucault's later work on technologies of the self outlines ways
in which subjects could negotiate and craft their identities, and engage in
practices of freedom (Mansfield, 2000, pp. 54–59).

Having introduced the key dimensions of governmentality—government by others (including the state) and government by the self—I turn to
how knowledge and intellectual work in general are implicated in governing international education.

THE GOVERNMENT OF EDUCATION

As noted earlier, a complex assemblage of know-how including a proliferation of apparatuses, bodies of knowledge, strategies, and techniques, is
used to govern what can be said, written, and transmitted. Only certain objects are talked about and then only in certain ways within disciplinary para-

digms. Historically, the discourses of women, indigenous people, and many non-Western people, along with other minorities, have been constructed as irrational, and their knowledges subsequently subordinated. Overall, the rules of discourse contribute toward a tendency by disciplines to remain fixed in time and space. Disciplines, therefore, are more likely than not to privilege First World spaces while ignoring regional power geometries (Massey, 1999, pp. 28–29). Many disciplines also neglect an engagement with time, most evident in their failure to engage with the future and historical pasts. It is highly unusual for theorists, particularly those working from a single discipline, to ask themselves: What image of the future does this theorization construct? Which social actors and issues are taken into account and which are marginalized or absent? How is the human subject and human society understood by this theoretical exposition?

Expert Systems in Constructing Student Subjectivity

Although researchers from the discipline of Business concentrate their research efforts on educational markets and ways of increasing market share, Education researchers focus on the learning and psychosocial adjustment problems of international students. The topics of their research are varied and include: bridging the expectation gaps between tutors and international students (Ridley, 2004), learning to write the U.S. way (Angelova & Riazantseva, 1999), issues of sociocultural adjustment (Hellstein, 2003; Volet & Ang, 1998), teaching international students intercultural skills (Jacobsen, Sleicher, & Burke, 1999; Volet, Smart, & Ang, 2000; Volet & Ang, 1998), identifying impediments to successful international student learning (Scheyvens, Wild, & Overton, 2003) and exploring gender and the experience of international study (Kenway & Bullen, 2003). Studies that undertake comparative analyses between the learning approaches of domestic (host country) and international students are relatively rare (see Ramburuth & McCormick, 2001, for one such study). A dominant theme to emerge from these Education studies is the overall complexity of intercultural learning and the potential for clashes in values between cultures. International students are often portrayed as holding instrumental attitudes toward learning, and education in general. Keenly aware of the significant costs and expectations surrounding the overseas study sojourn, and the difficulties of learning in a second or third language, many choose to highlight a pragmatic, academically serious subjectivity (see Kenway & Bullen, 2003). The macrocontextual issues surrounding international student learning, however, are often given less attention, and here, research could potentially benefit from using a postcolonial analytic.

One of the most cited work in discussions about international student learning in Australia is *Study Abroad: A Manual for Asian Students* (Ballard &

Clancy, 1984). *Study Abroad* is directed at the individual student from Asia who is planning to or who has already embarked on a study abroad sojourn. To this end, *Study Abroad* describes itself as offering prospective and actual students assistance in developing skills in critical learning. It is also directed at teachers of international students and, as I discuss later, has been elevated to the position of an authoritative text by the practices of citation.

Throughout the book Ballard and Clancy (1984) make explicit their view that cultural variations exist in thinking and learning. They suggest that Asian students are likely to bring an uncritical and reproductive approach to learning compared with Western students. These students are preoccupied with conserving knowledge, rote learning, and the uncritical acceptance of written texts and teachers' authority. A different attitude to knowledge, authority, and learning is held responsible for a disjunction between the goals of an Australian university education and the education expectations of the overseas students. Ballard's (1987) paper, *Academic Adjustment: The Other Side of the Export Dollar,* and her two books coauthored with Clancy, *Study Abroad* (1984) and *Teaching International Students* (1997), construct an Asian subjectivity that is passive, dependent, and uncritical in learning. Through the practices of citation, this deficit subjectivity as constituted in these texts has assumed significance, perhaps even dominance among university staff.

Academic Adjustment: The Other Side of the Export Dollar makes much of an Asian culture where the authority of the teacher means that students have little curiosity and will follow their explanations unquestioningly. Ballard draws comparisons between a monochromatic Western and an equally singular and essentialized Asian culture. "In Western education . . . the ideal model of the teacher is Socrates, and the Socratic method the ideal teaching style." By contrast, "in Asia, knowledge is not open to challenge and extension . . . the Zen master is no argumentative Socrates. . . . Questioning analysis, criticism are not part of the learning process, nor are they allowed for in the teaching style" (p. 114).

Although acknowledging that developing countries face significant material and economic problems, Ballard (1987) is firm that the cause of the problem is "these cultural attitudes to the process of teaching and learning" (pp. 113–114). Quoting from a 1960 text that describes the relations between teacher and student in a Burmese village school, Ballard discusses the "reciprocal expectations and obligations" between teachers and their students in Asian culture:

> If the student has worked diligently, learned thoroughly the materials presented in class, and followed the teacher's explanations unquestioningly, then that student has the right to expect to pass. If the student fails, it must be the fault of the teacher who in some way has misled the students and not pro-

vided clearly and adequately, the correct material and the correct ways of answering the questions. At postgraduate level overseas students may see the responsibility of their supervisors in much the same light. Such a view, however,
may not be shared by the Australian teacher. In fact, even the small courtesies
offered by overseas students to their teacher—small presents, politeness, un-
failing smiles and assurances that everything is going well . . . may be misread
as "crawling," "bribery" or "blackmail" by an insular and democratic Australian lecturer. (pp. 113–114)

Two points can be drawn from this paragraph. First, that the cultural expectations held by Asian students of their teachers absolves them of accepting responsibility for their learning and academic performance. The attributes we expect this Asian learner to have are passivity, dependence, and
irresponsibility. It is hard to avoid arriving at a notion of subjecthood that is
of a child-like and intellectually inferior native. Second, references to alien
courtesies are suggestive of a set of sinister motives by a subject who is dishonest, greedy, and rapacious. The "insular and democratic Australian lecturer" has few options but to "misread" these courtesies as "bribery," "crawling," or "blackmail" (Ballard, 1987). Both statements reflect a discursive
continuity with colonial ideologies and function to position the other as intellectually inferior and duplicitous.

Elsewhere, Ballard (1987) refers to "long suffering supervisors," noting
that "most teachers, no matter how well disposed they feel towards overseas
students resent spending time . . . editing the English of written assign-
ments and coping with inarticulate tutorial participants" (p. 116). Here, the
international student emerges as an "oppressor" who causes suffering and
dissipates the goodwill of teachers by virtue of having poor English language and academic skills. Ballard fails to reflect on or to challenge the hegemony of the English language, or the linguistic challenges and achievements associated with bi- and multi-lingual study.

Although providing some useful suggestions for institutional changes,
including ways to support both academic staff and international students,
Ballard's (1987) text nevertheless reproduces a discursive logic that is anchored in classic colonial discourse. Premised on 'othering' and simple
essentializations between Asian and Western, she offers few insights into
the multiplicities contained within these very categories.

Teaching International Students: A Brief Guide for Learners and Supervisors, a
later publication by Ballard and Clancy (1997), takes a less simplistic approach to the challenges of teaching of bilingual and multi-lingual international students. However, the old truisms have been retained. As with their
earlier work, a binary is constructed between the Western and Asian attitudes to knowledge. Asian cultures have a conserving orientation, whereas
Western educational traditions are premised on an extending approach to

knowledge. Thus, a reproductive style that is associated with Asian learners is also identified with primary school education in the West. A discursive link between the Asian attitude to knowledge and that of primary school children is almost inevitable. How has this discourse remained so resilient given the progressive impulses of internationalization and what does its dissemination tell us about power–knowledge relations in international education?

Put simply, many of the studies on the learning needs of international students share similarities in that they operate on essentialisms and binary thinking. The role of other variables of the educational environment such as language difficulties, the hegemonic status of English language, different pedagogies, and methods of assessment between home and provider countries is acknowledged, but the overall preoccupation is with proving that there are more deep-seated issues at the foundation of Asian students' learning difficulties, namely, cultural differences in attitudes to knowledge, learning, and teaching. Researcher introspection is missing, and the small sample size of students studied casts further doubt on the generalizability of this research. This 'common sense' regards Asian students as passive, uncritical, and superficial learners. The discourse of the Asian learner has an intertextual resonance with the civilizing imperatives of colonial modernity and legitimates the need for the developed Western world to provide tutelage to underdeveloped Asia. But it is also a discourse that helps legitimate the intellectually passive other who can have no claim in the rough-and-tumble negotiation about intellectual property rights. I argue in the course of this book, using promotional narratives, that this discourse remains within the international university.

By the 1990s, some studies into the learning approaches of international students were challenging the stereotype of the passive, surface-learning Asian student (Biggs & Watkins, 1996; Niles, 1995; Volet & Renshaw, 1995; Volet, Renshaw, & Tietzel, 1994). A number of these were longitudinal studies, and they focused on problematizing the institutional context, and its impact on student learning behaviors. A significant finding to emerge from these studies was the incidence of surface learning behaviors among Australian students as well as international students.

The institutional context was further problematized for the types of academic acculturation universities sought to instill in international students. Nines' (1999) study of the learning needs and styles of Indian MBA students found that Australian universities used a variety of technologies to maintain hegemonic knowledge relations, namely, a dominant knowledge system that serves the interests of international business and capitalism. This discursive structure is presumed also to be in the interest of choice-exercising and autonomous clients—international students. The business text had little interest in incorporating other epistemologies. Thus, students learned that project presentations demanded particular modes of dress and particular styles of speaking. Engaging in appropriate communication by "speaking up in tutorials" and "using Powerpoint" presentations was imperative; otherwise, "if you don't ask, you don't speak, that's it. Your MBA is gone" (p. 31). Like Benesch's (1999) study of academic practices in American universities, Nines found that, for the greater part, students acquiesced into the course-determined, normative styles of learning and communication to achieve the desired results of good marks. In most cases, students expressed their conviction that the course represented training in the real world of international business (Nines, 1999, p. 37). Both Benesch (1999) and Nines (1999) concluded that student resistance was rare, taking place mainly in those situations where there were poor levels of interpersonal synchrony with teaching staff.

In the Australian context, there has been much criticism about the type of education that is promoted as international but is resolutely monocultural and nationalist in focus, raising questions about the capacity of such education to educate for a globally oriented citizenship. (Cadman, 2000; Kelly, 1998, 2000; Morris & Hudson, 1995; Nines, 1999). Here, the argument is for a way forward that goes beyond interculturalism and instead strives for transculturalism, where the emphasis is on creating a third culture—different from the original cultures of both international students and the normative culture of nation-centered universities (Cadman, 2000; Kelly, 1998, 2000).

What I attempted to do in this section was to provide a selective historical snapshot of what has been visible and sayable about international students by the discipline of Education. The studies discussed are not by any measure representative of *all* that has been said about international students. Rather, it is an example of some of utterances that key authorities have made and as such is a useful exercise in mapping the types of subjectivities attributed to the international student. This snapshot of the literature provides a historical grid against which to assess contemporary subject positions of international students. However, the power relations that underpin the disciplinary discourses about international students should not be regarded as fixed in time or across spaces, places, cultures, institutions, and practices. They are amenable to change and are likely to be reinscribed to suit social and institutional needs.

Expert Systems and Calculative Technologies

Experts, their knowledges, and the regimes of truth they propagate are now a well-established feature in the government of education. Experts not only generate new ideas, they also exercise influence through their interpretations about the true meaning of primary texts, what Foucault refers to as "commentary." Through commentary, experts build a textual hierarchy about what can be said or thought about a particular topic or theme. A particularly powerful expression of commentary is the citational network, which is based on the practices of citing the works of particular authors to support or alternatively dismiss their standpoints. This mass of commentary also has the potential to produce new discourse. The academic commentary on the Asian learner, discussed earlier, has installed particular regimes of truth about the learning abilities and subject positions of the international student. But academic speakers and writers are themselves subject to discourse. They are influenced by national trends, the cultures of individual institutions, and the political economy of the academy, all of which also affect governance in universities.

Few would dispute the trends within universities to promote collaborations with industry and to push for the development of market-relevant knowledges. The influence of 'calculative technologies', imposed by managerial modes of accountability, is particularly noteworthy. Certain types of academic outputs receive greater recognition than others, for example, publishing in high-status refereed journals and earning consultancy income. These outputs now assume greater significance than teaching students. There has been much criticism about the rise of performative practices in the academy whereby the productivity of individual faculty and the quality of their work and that of their institution is influenced by performances ahead of substance (see Ball, 2000, 2003a; Broadhead & Howard, 1998; Marginson & Considine, 2000; Marginson & Mollis, 2001; Ozga, 1998; Rhoades, 1998; Slaughter & Leslie, 1997; Vidovich & Currie, 1998; Vidovich & Slee, 2001). This is not to suggest that the political economy of the academy exerts a totalizing power over individual faculty, who retain the ability to resist performative knowledges and practices. I return to this theme in subsequent chapters.

Calculative technologies such as theorizations, procedures of examination and assessment; the development of surveys, audits, and league tables; and techniques of notation, computation, and calculation are technologies of government and all are informed by knowledge regimes (Broadhead & Howard, 1998; Lemke, 2001; Rose & Miller, 1992). The use of the discourse of quality assurance to govern higher education and international education is one example of how market-based accountability, and managerial accountability systems, shape institutional practices in international education. In Britain and Australia, instrumentalities such as the Australian Universities Quality Agency, and the British-based Quality Assurance Agency (QAA) occupy a prolific role in monitoring institutional practices, procedures and standards through institutional audits. The Unite States lacks a federal body that investigates quality assurance issues in international education. Organizations such as the Center for Quality Assurance in International Education (CQAHE) appear to be supported by private-sector corporations with a vested interest in facilitating trade in education and play an important role in instilling an audit culture in international education markets.

Perhaps one of the most important technologies of government within higher education is the funding mechanisms employed by the state. These are comprised of a set of highly influential calculative technologies that steer institutions toward particular ends (Rose & Miller, 1992, p. 185). They involve competitive funding models that feature defined bidding criteria and performance-related outcomes (Polster & Newsom, 1998). They are a form of governance based on "steering from a distance," aimed at producing a culture of compliance with the state's goal to inculcate an entrepreneurial rationality within universities (see Berman, 1998, pp. 216–224; Johnson, 2002; Lingard & Blackmore, 1997; Marginson, 1997, pp. 229–230; 246–247; Marginson & Considine, 2000, pp. 236–243; Meek & Wood, 1997, pp. 264–270; Preston, 2001, pp. 355–360; Shore & Wright, 2000).

League tables are a more recent but increasingly powerful technology in the governance of education. In the United States, the choice of league table publications is endless. *America's Best Colleges by U.S. News & World Report*, *Princeton Review: The 300 Best American Colleges, Barron's Profiles, The Insider's Guide to Colleges*, the *Fiske Guide to Colleges*, and *Peterson's Best College Picks* are just a few examples of the plethora of league tables that govern the American higher education market. The widespread use of sporting metaphors—league tables—is a discursive marker of the extent to which the ethos of competitiveness is embedded in the culture of higher education. Ehrenberg (2000, pp. 50–53) observes that American universities play close attention to these rankings while criticizing them. Given that nearly all of the data used in the rankings are provided by universities and colleges themselves, league tables cannot be considered objective measures by any standard. Not only are the criteria highly selective, but the weight attached to individual criteria is arbitrary, often changing from year to year.[2] It is their quest for prestige that prompts universities to try to get the best rankings (p. 50), the assumption being that this prestige translates into a reputation for quality whether in terms of staff and students recruited or endowments garnered from high-flying alumni.

Until its demise, *Asia's Best Universities Guide* was one of the most well-regarded by Australian marketeers of international education, because "it

---

[2]Thus, "Institution A may rank higher than Institution B in one year but because the weight given to a particular criterion changes, B may outrank A in the next year" (Ehrenberg, 2000, p. 53). Ehrenberg (2000) poses the question of whether academic quality can change dramatically in the space of a single year by providing an overview of Cornell's changed ranking over 3 years from 14th to 6th to 11th place (p. 61).

comes from Asia and is trusted by Asians."[3] Run by *Asiaweek*, a magazine from AOL Time Warner Inc's empire of print and electronic media, it offered a 'benchmarking by media' service, which was rapidly accepted by the marketing divisions of Australian universities. Typically, a university receiving a favorable rating from *Asiaweek*, would feature its rating on its webpages or in promotional brochures destined for the overseas market.

Asiaweek (*Asia's Best Universities*, 2000) claimed that its objective was "to help Asia's schools celebrate their strengths and correct their weaknesses." Curiously, in this discursive domain, the inclusion of Australia as part of Asia is unproblematic. The magazine's practice of publishing a list of universities that declined to participate in its surveys worked as an implicit disciplining mechanism. By default, nonparticipant universities were positioned as shirking from their responsibility to be accountable to their constituents. The subterranean question—what have they got to hide?—was woven within the factual listing of nonparticipants.

Asiaweek (*Asia's Best Universities*, 2000) thus constructs itself to be an expert and positions its survey as a public service. It observes sagely that "universities need an outsider to celebrate their strengths—and point out their weaknesses." The well-publicized Australian University of the Year competition, together with the league tables instituted by "quality" broadsheet British newspapers, such as *The Times Good Universities Guide, The Guardian University Guide,* and *The Independent A-Z of Universities,* are other examples of governing technologies that use systems of expertise, calculation, and comparison (see Berry, 1999).

Although expert systems within higher education purport to embody neutrality, authority, and skill, the large numbers of fee-based consultancies and tied grants point to the emergence of new forms of knowledge capitalism. In the domain of international education, educational brokers such as Australia's IDP, the U.S.-based IIE, and the British Council's ECS are increasingly being cast in the role of neutral experts, despite being governed by strongly nation-centered agendas. They are able to establish and stabilize their networks of influence through the inauguration of yearly conferences, and the commissioning of selective studies.

The theoretical tools introduced in this chapter are used in later chapters to map and analyze what is visible and sayable about international education. Briefly, this chapter outlines how the reciprocal relationship between power and knowledge produces, sustains, disseminates, and institutionalizes discourse. It examines how particular sociocultural and historically situated

---

[3]Interview with manager, International Education, Group of 8 University. The Group of 8 Universities in the Australian context refer to the research-intensive universities. They include: Universities of Sydney, New South Wales, Queensland, Monash, Melbourne, Adelaide, Western Australia, and the Australian National University.

power–knowledge constellations attribute to commonsense understandings about the passive, uncritical Asian learner. In subsequent chapters, I discuss how power–knowledge constellations have been responsible for generating particular 'truths' about the international student and the international university. From this basis of identifying regimes of truth about international education, the international university, and the international student, this study outlines how international education is assembled under conditions of globalization.

Chapter 3

Globalization: Ways of Knowing

Despite its hold on the imaginations of academics, policymakers, politicians, and the popular press, there is no agreed-on definition of globalization. It is broadly acknowledged by researchers that globalization's diffuse and chaotic use has significantly reduced its analytical utility (Robertson & Khondaker, 1998, p. 6). Its critics point to the conceptual imprecision, historical illiteracy and empirical shallowness of much of the writings and research into globalization (see Dicken, 2004; Scholte, 2000; Therborn, 2000; Urry, 1998). When subjected to careful empirical scrutiny, the tendency to view globalization as a causal factor, and a basis for explaining what is going on in the world is unsettled (Dicken, 2004, Hay & Smith, 2005).

> Globalisation's real power may lie in its discursive (rather than its material) role. In acting as if globalisation is true, policy makers create the outcomes they attribute to globalisation itself. (Hay & Smith, 2005, p. 125)

This chapter explores the power-knowledge relations that shape representations of globalization. It poses the following question: given the multiple possibilities of what can be written or said at any particular time about globalization, how have particular themes and interpretations emerged? How have particular thematic mappings of globalization assumed dominance, with others relegated to the status of subordinate knowledges? Bartelson's (2000) careful observation that "practices of definition and usage are never innocent" (p. 182) is a good starting point for this chapter, which seeks to establish the context for understanding the conceptual links between globalization and international education. These links merit a closer examination because policymakers and academic commentary frequently deploy globalization as the rationale for the internationalization of universities. It is argued that globalization creates pressures on universities to become internationally competitive and world class. It is in this context that the recruitment of fee-paying overseas students emerges as the most rational response toward acquiring world-class status.

The aim of this chapter is to introduce globalization as a form of governmental power. It draws on Foucault's work on thought and governance, knowledge and power, to explore the production of certain truths about globalization and their uses in governing ourselves, our societies, other subjects and other geographies. Globalization is taken as a *dispositif,* a heterogeneous assemblage that privileges particular topics and objects of knowledge, and normalizes particular understandings of the human subject and social relations ahead of others. Methodologically, treating globalization as a governmentality creates the opportunity to study the global and globalizing through "peripheral places and marginal others"; in other words, using the Foucauldian historical technique of *genealogy* (Larner & Walters, 2004b)'. It also prompts analysis into the 'mentalities, arts and regimes' of practices used to assemble globalization. Simply put, a genealogy of globalization asks the following questions: How is the global imagined, based on what types of rationalities and emanating from which spaces? What understandings of the human subject (subjectivities) are implied by conventional globalization talk? How are nation states, individuals, and populations understood through these discourses? In short, it is by revealing the discourses and practices used to describe, construct, and assemble globalization that the politics of globalization can be made visible (Schirato & Web, 2003).

The use of governmentality as an analytic unsettles the conventional story of globalization as an inevitable, external economic compulsion. Globalization is taken "not as a pre-discursive phenomenon and objective reality with particular causes and consequences but as a discursive 'event' which emerged at a particular historical moment" (Larner & Walters, 2004b). Regarding globalization as a collection of discourses—ways of knowing—that are deployed toward convenient ends by its various subjects creates a discursive space for social action. Individuals, institutions, and nation-states are able to intervene to shape contemporary social and economic events rather than assuming the role of objects who are acted on by global forces (Kayatekin & Ruccio, 1998, p. 80). Governmentality problematizes conventional readings of globalization as a 'natural' set of processes in the evolution of humankind ("the next phase of human development") or a macro-level set of external forces, resting on an imaginary of an unstoppable juggernaut. Instead, a governmentality analytic inquires how globalization became to be seen as both a problem and a solution for nation-states, institutions, and individuals.

However, a caveat is necessary here: By acknowledging globalization's discursive dimension, the intention is not to deny the existence of a rubric of material processes and forces that have a global reach. The position taken in this chapter is not similar to those theorists labeled by Held, McGrew, Goldblatt, and Perraton (2000) as 'skeptics'.[1] Rather, the intention here is to establish how the use of discursive power shapes debates and governs understandings of globalization's risks and opportunities. It is the terms of these debates that shape policy and individual responses about the disjunctures arising from globalization, namely, those that produce the "fundamental problems of livelihood, equity, justice, suffering and governance" (Appadurai, 2001, p. 5).

The chapter proceeds in the following way. It outlines the possibilities that arise by taking globalization as an "assemblage" or dispositif that is used to govern ourselves and others. Specifically, it argues that globalization research could benefit by engaging with space, time, positionality, and subjectivity. The chapter then discusses two regimes of truth to emerge from writings on globalization—hybridization and deterritorialization— that have been used as normative discourse in international education. The chapter ends by discussing the politics of globalization, with reference to two broad areas: the role of the nation-state and the power relations underpinning transcultural–transnational flows.

GLOBALIZATION AS A WAY OF KNOWING

The commentary on globalization is dominated by epochal transformation, largely depicted in such terms as mobility, speed, reach (extensivity), and the compression or annihilation of space, and time (Giddens, 1990; Harvey, 1989; Jameson, 1991). As a general observation, flows and networks have emerged as definitive tropes in theorizations of the global (see Appadurai, 1996; Held et al., 2000; Castells, 1996). The types of metaphors used to capture transformatory dimensions of globalization are also instructive of how globalization is assembled. For example, discussions about flows tend to subordinate or render invisible notions of asymmetries, boundaries, and hierarchies. Instead, the geographical spaces that make up the world are conceived as sets of horizontal spatial relations that are located in the same latitudes of power. Yet, considerations of power relations are paramount in understanding the interactions between geographies and globalizing forces. A preoccupation with mapping globalization's transformatory dimensions has also limited the discussions about the essence or quality of the transformations invoked by globalization (Brown, 1999; Hay & Watson, 1999; Larner & Walters, 2004b).

---

[1]For example, Hirst and Thompson (1999) would be likely to place themselves in this category.

A radically different way of conceptualizing globalization is by identifying globalization with epistemology—a particular way of knowing (Larner & Le Heron, 2002; Larner & Walters, 2002). Rather than trying to locate the origins of globalization, in a particular epoch or in association with particular events such as the collapse of communism or the rise of sophisticated information and communication technologies, globalization is seen as a *dispositif.* Foucault (1977) defines *dispositif* as "a thoroughly heterogeneous ensemble consisting of discourses, institutions, architectural forms, regulatory decisions, laws, administrative measures, scientific statements, philosophical, moral and philanthropic propositions—in short, the said as much as the unsaid" (p. 194). In Larner and Walters' (2002) words:

> Globalisation did not exist in a strong sense until, at a certain point, governments, international agencies, corporate actors began to name 'globalisation', coupled it with a series of measures to harness it, govern it and channel it. (p. 10)

Taken as a dispositif, globalization ceases to be a monolithic, unitary force. Instead, it begins to encompass myriad human and nonhuman actors and institutions. Its elements and effects are heterogeneous and as such have an unpredictability or contingency about them. That stated, globalization as a dispositif ontologizes, and therein lies its function as a specific project of governance (Larner & Walters, 2002, p. 16).

An important insight into the discursive effects of globalization is gained through the use of genealogy, that is, studying it through "peripheral places and marginal others" (Foucault, 1980b). Taking Foucault's description of genealogy as "a historical knowledge of struggles"; a "union of erudite knowledge and local memories" (p. 83), a genealogy of globalization would involve tracing and mapping how and when practices of the global acquired currency. A useful line of inquiry might be to ask how a phenomenon such as the global trade in education services came to be regarded in extraterritorial terms, where previously the movement of students was analyzed using a territorial lens? Genealogy analyzes how space, time, and positionality are played out in our imaginations and performances of the global (Hesse, 1999; Massey, 1999; Shephard, 2002; Tikly, 1999, 2001).

A genealogy of globalization with its focus on both the mundane and erudite problematizes interpretations of globalization as a universal narrative of change that offers progress and development. A genealogy of globalization takes Foucault's injunction against a "heroization" of the present, an attitude that Foucault regarded as intrinsically modernist (see Foucault, 1984a, p. 32). Importantly, it interrogates the notion that we are living in a unique era, unsurpassed by earlier periods. Genealogy establishes the basis for reexamining the teleological reasoning underpinning the logic of inevitability (Foucault, 1980a).

GLOBALIZATION AS SITUATED: SPACE OR TIME
AND POSITIONALITY

How then should globalization be studied and understood? One way of un-settling the thesis of globalization as a First World story is to *spatialize global-ization* (Massey, 1999). In short, where the academic imagination has tended to subordinate other geographical spaces while privileging EuroAmerican spaces as reference points from which to theorize, a spatial analytic introduces considerations of the geopolitical into how the global is imagined and experienced, and the risks and opportunities associated with transformations (Hesse, 1999; Massey, 1999; Shephard, 2002; Slater, 2002; Tikly, 2001). The global is not imagined or studied through placeless spaces and subjectless processes but as practices and events that are situated in place and in time (Sassen, 2001). Spatialized readings of globalization do not treat the local, national, and global as ontologically separate but as im-plicating and constituting each other (see also Foucault, 1980a).

Critical globalization theorists have cautioned about conceptualizing space as free and unbounded, suggesting that this is a view that resonates with the impulses of free trade (Massey, 1999). Similarly problematic is the tendency of convening different spatialities under the aegis of progress and development, which reinforces the globalization-as-modernity narrative (Massey, 1999, pp. 33–35; see also Shephard, 2002, pp. 11–14). In this last instance, spaces such as Mali and Chad are appreciated as being different but, as Massey (1999) notes wryly, "Don't worry, they soon will be like us" (p. 34). The potential of these spaces to compose a different narrative of globalization and to follow different paths is effectively removed.

When space and positionality are brought into the theoretical and meth-odological framing of globalization, its construction as a teleological pro-gression to an improved future is brought into question. Taking a spatial and temporal analytic to study globalization enables engagement with past and existing "power geometries," including the historical legacies of colo-nialism that continue to deliver vastly different material consequences for places, countries, groups, and individuals (Hay & Watson, 1999; Massey, 1994, 1999; Slater, 2002).

GLOBALIZATION AS EMBODIED

Focusing empirical work on investigating how the global manifests at the level of the body is another means of shifting the debate away from notions of a singular and external force (Hay & Watson, 1999; Larner & Walters, 2002, 2004b). This opens up several lines of inquiry, including how differ-ent versions of globality are embodied and who the subjects of globalization are (Larner & Walters, 2004b). As subjects of globalization, how do the experiences of entrepreneurs, expatriate executives, First World university academics, refugees and asylum seekers, diasporic intellectuals, international students, and migrants differ from, and resemble, each other? Are particular performances and embodiments of the global more common than others (Larner & Walters, 2004b)? For example, can it be argued that the subject position of consumer in a global market of commodities and services eclipses the subject as a planetary citizen of an interconnected, interdependent global life force and ecosystem? Alternatively, is the global embodied as a 'flexible', mobile labor force, or as a cosmopolitan subject with a heightened commitment to the civic freedoms of people wherever they may live?

It is also worth considering how understandings and practices of the global are played out in gender relations and family dynamics. Here, Appadurai (1996) poses a vitally important question: "How do small groups, especially families, the classical loci of socialisation, deal with these new global realities?" (p. 43). He goes on to argue that the spatial and cultural displacements associated with global flows are potentially destabilizing on family relations, including marriages. The smooth, unmediated quality of flows can obscure the significant burdens faced by families in meeting their transgenerational responsibilities and the tasks of cultural reproduction. Taking globalization as embodiment also raises the question of how self–other relations are played out, whether a discursive space exists in narratives of globalization for cultural difference, or whether masculinist and capital-centered subjectivities dominate.

Two regimes of truth to emerge from writings on and about globalization are: globalization as cultural hybridization, and globalization as deterritorialization. Both have exerted a significant influence on how international education is understood and enacted in policies and practices.

Problematizing Flows and Hybridities

In postmodern analysis, notions such as hybridity, creolization, "glocalization," cultural syncretism, and "third cultures" have emerged as the definitive tropes of globalization. Third cultures, defined as "sets of practices, bodies of knowledge, conventions and lifestyles which have developed in ways which have become increasingly independent of nation-states" (Featherstone, 1996, p. 60) are used to support the argument for complex and diverse circuits of cultural flows. The argument is that these flows cannot be read using the simplistic logic of binary opposites such as local versus global, or Eastern versus Western. The third culture argument has helped elevate the globalization as hybridization thesis to its current metanarrative status.

The conceptual language of glocalization, third cultures, and boundary crossing draws heavily from the postmodernist concepts of melange, pastiche, and transformation. Although intercultural mixing and synthesis have a very long history, indeed predating modernity, globalization is noted as accelerating interconnections and interdependencies. Accordingly, flows of people, ideas, media, technology, and capital are said to drive the production of new hybrid knowledge practices and create expanded possibilities for cosmopolitan identities (pp. 88–89).

Pieterse (2004) poses the question, "How do we come to terms with the phenomena of Thai boxing by Moroccan girls in Amsterdam, Asian rap in London . . . Peter Brook directing the Mahabaratha?" (p. 69). He locates his answer in the long history of hybridization and the resilience of people and cultures toward cultural standardization and uniformity. Although Pieterse acknowledges that processes of hybridization can be asymmetrical and uneven, he argues that the productive possibilities of hybridization offered by globalization exceed its limitations (pp. 52–58). Hybridities have significant potential to denaturalize and disarm entire sets of essentialisms and fundamentalisms, including those that are cultural, political, and epistemological.

Hybridity's critics, on the other hand, are of the view that there are substantive and conceptual difficulties in understanding globalization as hybridization (see Friedman, 2000). The basis of their criticism is the tendency of theorists to disarticulate understandings of flows and hybridities from power geometries, including those inspired by political economy and geography (see Anthias, 2001; Mitchell, 1997, 2001; Larner & Walters, 2002). Pointing to a dearth of empirical work to investigate performances and embodiments of hybridities, Mitchell (1997) argues that the perpetual abstraction of these and other terms such as *spaces, networks, flows, rootlessness,* and *transience* have worked as discursive strategies to dematerialize and depoliticize these concepts. The direction of flows and the nodal points of networks are obscured, giving the impression that history and geography no longer matter. These terms are thus highly susceptible to appropriation and reinsertion (albeit in new forms) into 'old' geographies of power.

In their criticisms about hybridization, neo-Marxists have argued against the manifest material and promotional power of Western capitalism, which generates and sustains skewed and uneven transcultural exchanges. A shrewd rebranding of capitalism into postmodern forms sees it incorporating local tastes, sensibilities, idioms, and sensitivities, while retaining an unswerving loyalty to the bottom line. The emergence of aesthetic cosmopolitanisms, featuring hybrid music, fashion, and dance, all of which are reputed to pay little heed to national and cultural boundaries, have been well documented (Urry, 1996). However, the neo-Marxist perspective argues that such aesthetic cosmopolitanisms are being harnessed into the cultural circuit of capital while their transformatory effects are blunted; the result involves tinkering with a flawed status quo. Although the neo-Marxist perspective could be criticized for its notion of passive and uncritical consuming subjects, its strength lies in its recognition of the influence of power geometries in transcultural flows and processes. Pieterse (2004, p. 73) proposes a taxonomy of hybridities, ranging from the assimilationist, which mimics hegemony, to radical forms of hybridity, which destabilize dominant paradigms. Pieterse's rudimentary taxonomy opens possibilities for mapping the types of hybridities that are being standardized, commoditized, and institutionalized in the field of international education, including how such hybrids create access to alternative knowledges that sit outside the reigning epistemes of rationalism and commodity capitalism.

The advertisement described in the following is typical of examples that are used to support the view of globalization as profoundly differentiating and not homogenizing. Here, a tactical use of culturally sensitive marketing sees the engagement of nostalgia and local imagination for the goal of profit maximization. A hybrid product is created—a Singaporeanized version of McDonald's—that fits with consumer desires and a state ideology that is selective in its borrowings of American cultural and ideological products (Chua, 2000):

> One of the repeatedly used TV advertisments especially during the run-up to National Day begins with a morning assembly of primary school boys in a flag-raising ceremony . . . this is followed by a frame of two eggs frying and piping hot coffee suggesting that it is breakfast time, it then cuts to a Chinese old lady in a shophouse, symbol of old Singapore architecture opening a window to let in the sunshine . . . the next frame is of a young man driving a red convertible sports-car . . . singing to himself the McDonald's song in Mandarin . . . the final shot is of an old Chinese gentleman in traditional clothes . . . sitting stiffly in a rosewood chair, playing the McDonald's refrain on a Chinese string musical instrument, the *erhu*. (pp. 195–196)

How does this imagery destabilize the universalizing and hegemonizing impulses of globalization? What sort of subject positions does it imply and perpetuate? At one level, this advertisement works to reinforce the universal appeal of McDonald's while instilling a common sense that the peripheries once disconnected from the center now have direct access to the same commodities and cultural texts as those in the center. Thus, "geography and history are simply dissolved by flows of commodities, capital, people and information" (Hay & Watson, 1999, p. 420). Singaporeanizing McDonald's implies subject positions of discerning, autonomous consumers who are able to retain their traditions (singing in Mandarin, playing the *erhu*) while partaking of the joys of a McDonald's breakfast (see Friedman, 2000, p. 140).

At another level, the transgressive potential surrounding this and other contemporary understandings of hybridity, diaspora, and cosmopolitanism appears overstated. Anthias (2001) argues, "The litmus test of hybridity lies in the response of culturally dominant groups not only in terms of incorporating cultural products of marginal or subordinate groups, but being open to transforming and abandoning some of their own central cultural symbols and practices of hegemony" (p. 630). Furthermore, interstitial spaces and subject positions are produced in the context of economic as well as cultural processes and thus must be theorized in tandem (see also Ahmad, 1995; Dirlik, 1996).

Pieterse (2004, pp. 74–77) acknowledges that not all constellations of hybridity have been accommodated, nor can all expressions of hybridity be considered progressive or desirable. Hybridity across modes of production—through combinations of pastoralism, agriculture, industry, craft, hunting, and gathering—remain outside of mainstream discourses of governance (pp. 101–102). Hybrid practices and identifications may just as well include ethnocultural fundamentalisms, long-distance nationalisms, or ethical cosmopolitanisms (Anthias, 2001, pp. 628–630). Hybrid imaginaries that are premised on rewarded acculturation, for example, can give rise to technologies of the self that do little to address the 'disjunctures of living', evocatively described by Appadurai (2001). Kramer's (2003a) and Bhatt's (2003) studies of highly successful immigrants in the United States—the 'model minorities'—is a case in point. Bhatt (2003) and Kramer (2003a) observe that the days of wholesale and totalizing assimilation and homogenization are over. In their place are carefully crafted, nuanced practices, some couched in the language of global connectivity. But the cumulative effects of these surface hybridizations could well contribute to a general shrinkage in the varieties of languages, values, expectations, and ways of living that are valued:

> Indian computer companies are offering extensive training programs to teach new employees how to interact with Western clients. . . . Lessons include how to speak during conference call and how to sip wine properly. . . . *It is particularly imperative for employees of software companies to appear culturally seamless with Americans* . . . [as] . . . American clients account for more than two-thirds of India's software and services export revenues. (Rai, 2003, p. W1, italics added)

Turning to the discipline of Education, earlier optimism that the globalizing imperatives of new information and communication technologies and a host of culturally diverse, market-savvy customers would nurture a diversification in educational curricula and pedagogy has not been realized. Mason's (1998, pp. 45–46) study into the uses of information and communication technologies in education suggests that global education providers have not been particularly successful or vigilant in accommodating cultural differences in their pedagogical approaches (Evans, 1995, as cited in Mason, 1998, p. 45). Online executive MBA programs provided a forum for greater sharing of cultural information among participant students. However, the scope of these exchanges was, and continues to be, framed by a market-liberalist and instrumentalist text in place of a genuinely pluralistic and transformative discourse (pp. 47–49).

Instilling a Metanarrative

How have concepts such as hybridity, liminality, boundary crossings, glocal, and the cultural third space acquired currency in globalization debates? How has globalization as hybridization become a regime of truth? And what implications do they have for our understandings of social relations and subject formation? The Foucauldian schema of power argues that power is immanent in all social relations and this raises questions about the discursive invisibility of power relations in conceptualizations of flows and networks (Hay & Watson, 2003). Foucault's prescient observations on commentary in the academy implicate citation practices in building a textual hierarchy about what can be said or thought about a particular topic or theme. Power/knowledge relations in the academy and discourse communities have produced a repertoire of defining objects, concepts, and issues on globalization, for example, deterritorialization, hybridization, Westernization, McDonaldization, neoliberalism, and so forth. These constellations provide ways of understanding globalization as mobilities, flows, weightless economies, or networks. In much the same way, power and knowledge come together in discourse to construct particular understandings of global subjectivities: as elite cosmopolitans, consumers of world music, practitioners of "fusion" cuisine, intercultural brokers, diasporic intellectuals, Internet surfers, or shoppers in a giant global supermarket of goods.

Put simply, power's invisibility in discussions of global flows have influenced theorists to discuss and represent flows and networks as sets of horizontal spatial relationships, while subordinating notions of asymmetries, boundaries and hierarchies (Shephard, 2002). How did power become invisible in the academy's ruminations? How did a grand theory, globalization, arise amid postmodern pronouncements about the end of metanarratives?

A partial explanation is also offered by Thrift (1999, 2001) who uses his studies into the global dissemination of managerial knowledge as a reference point to explain the rapid embedding and embodiment of particular metaphors. He identifies the following factors: the receptivity of academic disciplines, the influence of intellectuals and practitioners, the impact of technology that allows for the easy transfer of ideas, and the influence of the "cultural circuit of capitalism" that needs a constant flow of new ideas and metaphors. A more cynical inference from Thrift (1999) is that "flexible" metaphors produce less friction and subsequently travel fast because they "become almost completely meaningless" (p. 39).

Two other points merit reflection and exploration to understand how power relations have been invisiblized in discussions about globalization. First, O'Tuathail's (1999) prescient observation that the basis of neoliberalism's appeal rests on keeping geopolitics out of sight and out of mind. Second, Said's (1981) analysis of "Travelling Theory" throws some light on the conditions of acceptance of ideas and knowledges over spatial and temporal distances.

In the education literature, the globalization as hybridization thesis is usually supported by references to Appadurai's (1996) scapes framework. Appadurai's work is very well cited, and the archive of secondary narratives emerging from these interpretations has normalized the idea of flows as smooth, unproblematic and unmediated by power relations, while refuting any suggestion that globalization creates the conditions of possibility for Americanization/Westernization. Appadurai's observation that *if* a world culture is emerging it is "full of idiosyncrasies and inconsistencies . . . ironies and resistances" (p. 47) has been hastily translated to mean that flows are unavoidably contingent and random. Such notions of radical indeterminacy then can "be turned to all manners of ends, not all of which are pleasant" (Thrift, 1999, p. 60).

Furthermore, Appadurai's (1996) call for the development of more sophisticated theoretical and methodological tools to study global flows has largely gone unheeded. He highlights the importance of engaging with situatedness in a fuller sense—a multilevel situatedness. Although acknowledging the individual's agency, he argues that "the individual actor is the last locus of the perspectival landscape" (p. 33). He proposes that studies of flows engage with the situatedness of its myriad actors: nation-states, multinationals, diasporic communities, subnational groupings, families, and individuals. Yet, many studies purporting to examine the relations between globalization and education fail to consider situatedness in its complexity by using the narratives of individual actors or subjects as the only locus of the perspectival landscape and leaving scale and positionality absent from their analyses (see Slater, 2002; Tikly, 2001).

Transcultural exchanges have always taken place, and the indigenization of imports is a historical and contemporary reality. It is arguably a highly desirable reality and one that has probably been pivotal to the survival of human societies over time. What is problematic is the limited scope and possibilities for *reciprocal* exchanges between cultures and nations. Without these exchanges the unevenness that characterizes global processes will remain in place. The challenge "to arrest the relations of disjuncture between flows, particularly those disjunctures which produce the fundamental problems of livelihood, equity, justice, suffering and governance" (Appadurai, 2001, p. 5), requires a simultaneous globalization of knowledge and knowledge of globalization (Appadurai, 2001; see also Stromquist & Monkman, 2000).

Postcolonial theorists and feminists have been vociferous in their criticism of the uniform and universalizing formulae imposed by transnational institutions, national governments, donor agencies, and educational institutions. They use these as examples of the superficiality of hybridization within structures. The result is wholesale compression of vastly different spaces with different needs into the trite imaginary of a global community. Postcolonial theorists point out that prolific globalization theorists such as Robertson (1992) and Giddens (1990) have been able to declare that globalization cannot lead to an outcome of imperialism or Westernization because their analytics for studying globalization are aspatialized and ahistorical (Hesse, 1999; Sum, 1999; Tikly, 2001; see also Hay & Watson, 1999; Massey, 1999). This dominant discourse—that globalization is not leading to Westernization—has been promoted to the point that it has achieved the status of common sense. A more important omission concerns the issue of uneven globalization, which is largely left out of out of debates (Halliday, 2000; Hay & Watson, 1999). In drawing attention to the struggles for livelihood faced by an increasing proportion of the world's population, Slater (2003, p. 85) challenges the agents of knowledge in the academy to explore the *limits* of their inquiries, and to question the extent to which the *locations* of their thought give priority to issues and agendas that are inimical to the lives of so many.

Despite access to significant information and communication technologies that claim to reduce the phenomenological distance between nations, culture, communities, and individuals, there are indicators that fears and fantasies of "the other" have continued to proliferate, contrary to claims of greater desire for, and acceptance of, hybridization and hybridities. A pervasive ethnocultural and national anxiety about the eclipse of cultural particularities (e.g., losing the American, Australian, or English identity) has contributed to a rising tide of fascism, racism, and various forms of religious fundamentalism. All of these developments pose significant challenges for civic freedoms (Bauman, 1998, p. 3; Hall, 1997, pp. 21–26; Waters, 2001, pp. 187–196). In their study of extreme right politics in the United States, Flint (2004) and his colleagues uncovered widespread popular support and desire for the notion of place as sealed, enclosed and resistant to the flows of capital and people considered "other." Emplacement—constructing places as isolated containers that are fortified by strong borders—is a response to the unsettling deterritorializations associated with globalization. Flint et al. (2004) conclude that the social and the spatial demand theoretical attention as both are implicated in creating fundamentalisms.

It is not sufficient, then, to merely talk of hybridities. We need to ask how
the hybrid is implicated as governmental project, how it is assembled,
through which knowledges, from which spaces, and based on what types of
social relations between self and other? We also need to ask about the direction of flows and the quality of the transformations associated with globalizing processes. And most important, we need to ask how these self–other relations contribute to arresting the disjunctures that produce inequity and
injustice. And here, feminist and postcolonial contributions have much to
offer to challenge existing power-knowledge considerations by asking new
questions, proposing new practices and methodologies, and introducing
reflexivity into studies of the global (Larner & Walters, 2004b).

Problematizing Deterritorialization

Much of the writing on globalization has characterized its extraterritorial
character, which is captured in the concept of deterritorialization: "the
problematic of territory losing its significance and power in everyday life"
(O'Tuathail, 1999). Discourses of deterritorialization construct the global
as a borderless world, which features speed, informationalization, reduced
importance of the nation-state, and greater identification with a global
community. These discourses also work to create a rupture from 20th-
century understandings of geography, power, and identity, in other words,
by constructing a civilizational epoch that is deemed to be unprecedented
in history.

In problematizing the discourses of deterritorialization, O' Tuathail
(1999) offers three observations: First, rather than transcending national
identity, territoriality, and statism, deterritorialization involves a rearrang-
ing of sociocultural, economic, and political relations, which produces a simultaneous reterritorialization. Second, de- and re-territorialization are
producing the conditions of possibility for a new geopolitical rationality
and geoeconomic relations, which are marked by uneven development:

> While transformations in markets and telecommunications are creating a
> global village, this village is characterized by a functional global apartheid
> that separates and segregates. (O'Tuathail, 1999)

O'Tuathail poses an old political economy question starkly: For whom is
the world borderless? Who benefits? Third, many of the discourses of
deterritorialization are criticized for their abstractions—they do not describe or reflect a set of actualities. Instead, they end up with a discursive
construction of space as being beyond statist control. As a discursive formation, then, deterritorialization has an ideological effect. It combines elements from a Western humanistic discourse such as human freedom, liber-

ation, and fulfillment to construct globalization as an inevitable and positive development in a global free-market society (O'Tuathail, 1999).

In different ways, in different national and political contexts, discourses of deterritorialization are being used to reinforce the hegemony of a neoliberal globalization. Thus, in response to criticisms by transnational advocacy movements, such as the antipoverty NGO, Oxfam, and following violent protests at international economic forums such as the 1999 WTO meetings in Seattle and Cancun, globalization is being reframed by the mainstream media. Globalization as the deterritorialization of markets—trade liberalization ("free trade")—is increasingly being represented as the only means toward universal economic security and well being (Hay & Smith, 2005, pp. 132–135). In other words, globalization as trade liberalization is constructed as the "only feasible cure for poverty." Having succeeded in giving globalization a moral gloss, these discursive practices are redeployed to convince readers, viewers, and citizens that the best thing to do is to "keep on track" with the free trade agenda (Starr, 2004). Those who align themselves with free trade and minimal regulation, and those who promote the historical naturalness of globalization are portrayed as contributing to the interests of humankind, especially the developing world's poor (p. 393). Neoliberal globalization thus emerges as mutually beneficial for the First and Third Worlds. By contrast to this subject position of "enlightened global decision maker," those who question globalization and free trade are labeled as "illogical, ill-informed, short-sighted, and unable to think through their arguments" (p. 388). People in developing countries are portrayed as objects of sympathy who inspire compassion. Significantly, in discourse, they are represented as having neither knowledge nor voice worthy of mention (p. 387).

NATION-STATES AND THE POLITICS OF GLOBALIZATION

Foucault's work invites the unsettling of the self-evident and prompts taken-for-granted categories to be reconsidered in a historical light. Accordingly, the nation-state, which is theoretically treated as a unified and natural category, emerges as a historical entity, which is made of up conflicting interests, identifiable in discourses and practices. This raises another issue: moving beyond zero-sum thinking about the nation state and globalization (Jessop, 2000). Globalization does not mean the end of the nation-state but a reconstitution and reconfiguration of the nation-state. Because nation-states exist in myriad forms and operate in radically different contexts, the very notion of the nation-state should not be associated with one teleology.

A historical analysis quickly unsettles assumptions of the primordial status of the nation-state. The European nation-state emerged as a political entity at the time of the Enlightenment in the 17th and 18th centuries. Where rulers had drawn their right to govern from divine power by claiming to be God's representatives in the world, the nationalization of the masses during the Enlightenment saw the nation replace God as the center of political authority. Many religious ceremonies were subsequently adapted to become ceremonies of the nation. For example, the practice of singing national anthems emerged from the singing of hymns. Where saints' images were once displayed with fervor, the images of heads of states were now accorded prominence. The national flag replaced the saints' banner as a mystical and revered icon (Mosse, 1988, pp. 65–68). The modern nation-state's history in the non-West is even more recent, nationhood having arrived at political independence from colonial authorities.[2]

Total state laissez-faire is a historical fiction, as revealed by the work of the Marxist historian Eric Hobsbawn. It is the *character* of state intervention and the extent to which it manages capitalism that merits debate and analysis. Historical variants of state intervention span mercantilism, Keynesian, neoliberalism, and the developmentalist Asian state, to name a few examples. Writing about the rise of the British modern nation-state, Hobsbawn (1984) argues that British economic triumphs in the 18th and 19th centuries were the result of the readiness of numerous British governments to "back their businessmen by ruthless and aggressive economic discrimination and open war against all possible rivals" (p. 232). Much of this economic war was conducted in Britain's colonies. Overseas empire meant power, prestige, and profit. But British commercial interests and colonial incursions came at a price of considerable human suffering. Empire is hardly benign (Colley, 2002).

From a neoliberal perspective, the desired subjectivity for the nation-state is one exemplified by economic openness and responsibility. Theorists writing from this school argue that globalization has mediated disorderly and disjunctive flows of people, information, ideas, and commodities, which reduce the state's regulatory capacity and the scope for fiscal and social protection. The discursive framing of capital in this discourse sees its construction as fleet footed, hypermobile, able to exit on whim, and likely to raid national currencies of 'undisciplined' states. Today, the success of a nation-state rides on its emulation of business sector practices and its will to restrict welfare provision to its citizens (the constrained state). In discourse,

---

[2]There has been little research by political scientists into the ethnocultural, religious, and linguistic affiliations of the anticolonial elites that led the push for political independence from colonial authorities, although historical works abound. The impact of their collective memberships on subsequent nation-building strategies may cast light on the multiple forms of states that have arisen in the South and East.

the neoliberal state is constructed as lean and disciplined, in contrast to the use of bloated metaphors to describe the Keynesian state (Weiss, 2003).

A governmentality analytic poses the question of how the nation-state became the problem having once been regarded as the solution to political and economic difficulties. Taking this further means investigating the discursive framing of good governance, economic openness, and international competitiveness. It also raises such questions as how global subjects are constituted in, and by, these discourses. What and who is left out or invisibilized? What attributes and capacities do these concepts impose on, or assume of, industries, firms, universities, professors, and ordinary citizens (Larner & Walters, 2004b)?

The constrained state has not only emerged as an ideal type, in discourse and practice, but is increasingly regarded as the *only* type of state. Yet, within the locus of other domains and spaces, the United Nations (UN) Security Council being a case in point, the enduring power of (selective) nation-states to influence events in the global forum dispels the end of the nation-state thesis that so dominated earlier writings on globalization.

Other multilateral initiatives that have been defeated by neoliberal nation-states include the UN's proposed Human Rights Code, which seeks to make multinational corporations legally liable for human rights abuses (Gow, 2004). The catalogue of failures for multilateralism are too numerous to discuss here, but they recast the roles of nation-states onto a more complex terrain than earlier discussions by 'First World' globalization theorists that focused on whether the nation-state exercised the sovereign power to provide welfare protection to its citizens. As Weiss (2003) argues, there is an urgent need to reintroduce notions of enabling states, which are premised on other global imaginaries—not just a global market.

The neoliberal order of things is not entrenched; it is reversible. To arrest the financial lifelines of global terrorism, an earlier subject position implied of capital, as unmanageable and beyond state control, was overturned, and the PATRIOT legislation expanded the state's powers to control capital flows (Marcuse, 2002, p. 634). Similarly, the federalization of security in American airports, an effective deprivatization of public service, illustrates how a pillar of neoliberal policy can be reversed for convenient ends by the state (p. 636).

An Alternative Politics?

A different politics of globalization can be authored by nation-states. Pettifor and Greenhill (2003, pp. 211–212) suggest a set of *first principles* to guide the development of a new politics of globalization. First, tame financial markets through measures such as capital controls. Second, upsize the state in ways that enable the government to respond to a *democratic mandate* as well as a mandate for environmental protection. Notably, the state expansion proposed here is manifestly different from roll-out neoliberalism, which has seen huge state expenditures on militarization, prisons, and various forms of corporate welfare (Peck & Tickell, 2002). There are a plethora of examples of how roll-out neoliberalism contributes to wealth polarization across the world. I offer one, the bizarre reversal of geography that places Europe in the position of the world's largest exporter of white sugar, produced at twice the cost by sugar-growing countries in the South because of its generous agricultural subsidies to agri-business. In 2000, developing countries received $50 billion dollars in overseas aid but lost about $65 billion because protective subsidies in agriculture and textiles imposed by the North (Mathiason, 2004). Third, downsize the single global market by acknowledging the issue of appropriate scale in trade engagements. It is entirely appropriate for certain industries and countries to engage in nation-centered, localized, protectionist practices for cultural and ecological reasons.

The World Social Forum's proposals for an alternative globalization are similar and include multilateral economic justice (production for people, not profit), environmental protection including the preservation of biodiversity, promotion of cultural diversity, and social equity by introducing a democratic mandate at local, national, and global levels (Fisher & Ponniah, 2003). Finally, if we accept that "our world is a world of overlapping communities of fate" (Held, as cited in Paehlke, 2003, p. 275), achieving a more humane globalization requires us to exercise democratic rights at subnational, national, and global levels. In effect, it requires us to imagine and practice "multilevel citizenships" (Held, as cited in Paehlke, 2003) or globally oriented citizenships (Parekh, 2003).

RETERRITORIALIZATION THE SUBJECT

Of interest to governmentality theorists is how nation-states reterritorialize subjectivities through manipulations of community and nation, as ways of responding to the challenges of globalization. For the greater part, reterritorialization strategies have aimed at inculcating a banal nationalism (Billig, 1995). Premised on an (imagined) heroic and uncomplicated past, its most common expressions are through seemingly "harmless" nationalist liturgies such as flag raising, anthem singing, and the reciting of various pledges. Many of these practices have a historical resonance with religious and military symbolism.

More recently, there are indicators that social dislocations arising from market fundamentalist policies are being managed by more pernicious strategies of reterritorialization, more precisely through the politics of fear and exclusion. National identity is thus reterritorialized through a kind of "paranoid nationalism" (see Hage, 2003), or "resentment politics" (McCarthy & Dimitriades, 2000). In countries such as the United States, and increasingly Australia and the United Kingdom, considerable discursive effort is invested in reasserting a national identity that is premised on an essentialized Whiteness. Reterritorialization efforts thus seek to dilute antagonisms and divisions, such as class, gender and ethnicity, by projecting them onto overt ethnocultural and religious differences. The culture wars in the United States, which position cultural differences as the dominant source of conflict, exemplify these governing technologies.

As projects of governance, paranoid nationalism and the resentment politics that exemplify the culture wars harness popular support by denying moral worth to those on the margins of the nation-state. A critical question that merits further exploration is what impact resentment politics has on the processes of culture borrowing. More precisely, to what extent is the synthesis of cultural elements that might inform a progressive and humane global imaginary stifled in the face of threat—whether real, manufactured, or imagined?

Crafting the national subject can take more productive forms, such as furthering the nation-state's economic interests. In the 1990s, the success of the Asian Tigers (Singapore, Korea, Hong Kong) was widely attributed to Confucian values, which was officially translated by their governments and many First World economists to mean collective sacrifice by a diligent workforce prepared to defer wage demands for long-term economic and social benefits. The appropriation of ethnocultural myths (some of which rested on orientalist codes) by governing elites led to the presentation of a series of favorable national images. An East versus West discourse positioned a decadent, undisciplined, and individualistic West against a hardworking, thrifty, and community-minded East. This was used as a governmental project aimed at attracting international investment and securing economic prosperity (see Cheung & Sidhu, 2003; Coe & Kelly, 2002).

Reterritorializing the citizen-subject through ethnocultural and religious nationalism is also a governmental project outside First World countries. In India, the Bharatiya Janata Party supported religious fundamentalism, an expression of identity localization, while steering the country toward trade liberalization:

> The two arms of government work in synergy—while one arm is busy selling the nation off in chunks, the other to divert attention, is orchestrating a baying, howling, deranged chorus of cultural nationalism . . . ordinary people march around and learn that amassing nuclear weapons, religious bigotry, misogyny, homophobia, book burning and outright hatred are the ways in which to retrieve the nation's lost dignity. (Roy, 2001, p. 85)

The rise of ethnocultural nationalisms and religious fundamentalisms, and their impacts on the nation-state, have been the source of much academic commentary. Typically, the theoretical treatment of Kurds in Iraq and Turkey, Basques in Spain, Tamils in Sri Lanka, Muslim separatists in the Philippines, West Papuans and Achenese in Indonesia, and Albanians in Macedonia is centered on a culturalist argument; whereby cultural factors form the basis of their rejection or marginalization by the nation-state. Much has been written about how these groups use sophisticated composites of mediascapes, technoscapes, and the funds and lobbying power of their diasporic communities to press their case (see Appadurai, 1996, pp. 37–38).

A culturalist argument fixes these separatisms into a primordial frame instead of regarding them as historically specific assemblages that are linked to the webs and networks of colonial and postcolonial power relations (Mamdani, 2001). Analytics such as governmentality, postcolonial theory, and actor network theory quickly reveal that the networks of long-distance nationalism, and ethnocultural separatisms embrace not only the nodal points of ethnocultural diasporas but also the foreign policy centers of the Northern and Western democracies of the United States, United Kingdom, Germany, France, and Italy.[3] The global arms trade, estimated in 1998 to be worth some US$30 billion, enjoys considerable in-country political support in these democracies (see Bauman, 1998, p. 61; Levine, Sen, & Smith, 1999).[4] The networks of finance and investment that constitute the global arms trade are so well-dispersed into First World political economies that they include numerous public bodies, universities, trade unions, hospital trusts, and charities. Although committed to beneficial and ethical goals, pragmatic considerations about returns on their investments have linked these organizations into the enterprise circuits of the arms trade (Campaign against the Arms Trade, 2004).

THE GLOBAL SUBJECT

The intention of this chapter is to raise more questions than answers. It seeks to stimulate debate on how regimes of truth such as deterritorialization and hybridization are deployed in practices of government and to investigate the constructions of personhood they imply and assume. Both deterritorialization and hybridization are informed by largely apolitical notions of subjectivity, space, and time. Both construct understanding of geographical and cultural spaces within the one latitude. Subsequently, flows between spaces are considered to be unconstrained by historical and geopolitical forces. The subject emerges as fluid, strategically fragmented, un-

---

[3]A growing number of industrializing countries such as Brazil, China, and India are increasing their profile as arms suppliers.

[4]This was the estimated worth of the arms trade in 1998 as reported by Levine, Sen, and Smith (1999).

constrained by boundaries or hierarchies, and unencumbered by histories and geographies.

In the neoliberal state, governmental power normalizes and deploys such a free-moving, eclectic subject toward convenient ends. The logic of a deterritorialized and hybrid subjectivity encourages self-reliance and self-sufficiency in citizens. Nation-states and institutions wishing to manage the uncertainties stemming from market fundamentalism may use the free-moving subject toward convenient ends: Citizens have a responsibility to be flexible and mobile—to reconfigure themselves to meet changing economic and political demands—rather than demanding particular rights as situated citizens of a nation-state.

However, these expressions of global subjectivity are not inevitable. Other possibilities exist including the ethical cosmopolitan subject whose concern for civic freedoms is not restricted by territorial affinities, or the subject who is a citizen in a planetary ecosystem. As Foucault's work has demonstrated, power/knowledge relations mediate whether individuals create coercive, dominating, or ethical relations with others and with themselves. An "ontological" politics underpins what we understand as globalization. Concepts such as globalization, trade liberalization, and knowledge economies do not merely describe a reality but help to constitute and construct social realities and social worlds (Dicken, 2004; Hay & Smith, 2004; Peters, 2004). In other words, "theory has effect and methods are performative—they enact realities; they bring into being what they discover" (Law & Urry, 2004, pp. 393–393). What realities then might educators wish to enact?

> Neoclassical ones? Ameliorist agendas? Revolutionary realities? Anti-patriarchal or postcolonial worlds? Realities composed of post-structuralist partialities and shifting identities? Cyborg-like and materially heterogeneous worlds? (p. 396)

For many first world educators and including researchers in the field of international education, some realities have been easier to enact than others. It has been easier to go with an intellectual vision dominated by the perspectives of the richest countries in the world, which ignores the geopolitics of intellectual practices and their effects on other geographies, other people, and other cultures.

The subjectivities perpetuated by the international education industry forms the basis of the next chapters. Beginning with the United States, these chapters examine how international education is assembled by the interactions between nation-states and markets, and how these interactions create particular institutional subjectivities for universities as agents of globalization (globalizers). The focus is on marketing narratives used in the recruitment of international students rather than on curricular and pedagogical initiatives, although these are also referred to in the course of analysis.

"In America's Interest"

The American higher education system is not only one of the biggest mass systems of higher education in the world,[1] it is also highly differentiated in terms of quality, featuring both high-profile research and teaching universities as well as some less impressive institutions (de Wit, 1995). America is home to the largest private sector; 58% of its higher education institutions are private (American Council on Education [ACE], 2001, p. 1). The private sector, once dominated by nonprofit institutions, has seen further differentiation with the rise of the for-profit (proprietary) higher education institutions. In general, there is a steep reputational gradient between private and state universities. Private universities are regarded as offering programs of greater academic rigor and being more selective in their choice of students. The exceptions to this generalization are the large research-oriented public universities. American higher education is highly decentralized compared with Australia and the United Kingdom. It features a large number of external constituencies noted for having a significant impact on institutional autonomy and direction (Harcleroad, 1999).[2]

---

[1]In 1999, 66% of the American population had some level of college or university education.

[2]The external constituencies include private foundations (e.g., Carnegie and Rockefeller foundations), institutionally based associations (e.g., Association of American Colleges and Universities, ACE), professional associations (e.g., the American Medical Association), voluntary accreditation organizations, and regional compacts (Harcleroad, 1999).

STATE–MARKET RELATIONS

Despite liberal exhortations about the natural separation of states and markets, the U.S. higher education system is not a fully fledged free market but is best described as a quasi-market. Both federal and state governments have a long history of involvement in shaping the higher education's political economy.[3] The American federal government may not have direct responsibility for the direct management of education,[4] a sanction imposed by the American Constitution, but it retains significant influence through its role as provider of loans, merit scholarships, tax credits, and grants (Marginson & Rhoades, 2002; Rhoades, 1998; see also de Wit, 1995, p. 5; Dill, 1997, pp. 172–179; Gade, 1991, pp. 1084–1085; Gladieux & King, 1999, pp. 151–155). Federal government policy does not distinguish between public and nonpublic higher education in its distribution of funds so long as national interest objectives are met. Federal government loans are now available to students in proprietary (for-profit) institutions, a move anticipated to produce greater institutional isomorphism between nonprofit, public universities and their for-profit counterparts (Pusser, 2000, pp. 26–31).

By the end of the 1980s, a broad-based policy shift by the U.S. government saw economic competition replacing military competition as the driving force behind much of American national economic planning and foreign policy. A number of legislative acts were enacted by the federal government to steer science and technology research within universities toward commercial ends. The Bayh–Dole Act (1980), the National Cooperative Research Act (1984), the Orphan Drug Act (1983), and the Small Business Innovation Development Act all helped facilitate closer links between universities and both industry and small business interests.[5] A series of other acts increased protection of intellectual property. The net effect of

---

[3]The portability of student funds has played a significant part in changing the political economy of American education (Pusser, 2000, pp. 27–30). This has been significant in strengthening the role of the private providers (Gladieux & King, 1999, p. 155). In 1972 the government's role changed from that of a direct provider of education to the provider of subsidies following the introduction of higher education amendments. Students were able to use their state and federal funds (either as loans or grants) at state institutions or at private institutions, both those that were not-for-profit and for-profit. The federal government has played an active role in fostering the creation, development, and financing of both private and public universities at particular historical junctures. The Morrill-Land College Grant Act (1867) established agricultural universities, and after World War II, the Serviceman's Readjustment Act of 1944 (GI Bill) established the precedent for student financial aid and the advent of a mass system (Gladieux & King, 1999, p. 162).

[4]The exception is the direct management of federal institutes such as military academies, Howard University, and 28 tribal colleges (see de Wit, 1995, p. 34).

[5]Slaughter and Leslie (1997, pp. 45–48) provide detailed descriptions of the outcomes of these policies for the commercialization of research. The Bayh–Dole Act (1989) permitted universities to retain title to inventions developed with federal R&D money. It also allowed cor-

these acts was to institutionalize further knowledge as a commodity and to steer American universities toward "academic capitalism" (Slaughter & Leslie, 1997, pp. 45–48). However, the drive toward the market preceded these acts as American universities have a long history of collaborating with industry, in research and development (R&D), particularly in the agriculture, engineering, and applied sciences. In the 1970s, following developments in the biomedical sciences and biotechnology, major American research universities began to increase their patenting and licensing activities (Mowery, Nelson, Sampat, & Ziedonis, 2001, pp. 99–101). Federally sponsored research to support America's military objectives helps to place American research in its preeminent position. Defense-related science and technology continue to be the best funded domains, particularly in light of the war on terror. The research budget aids national economic competitiveness through the prioritization of projects with commercial value such as technology transfer initiatives (Barrow, Didou-Aupetit, & Mallea, 2003, pp. 43–50, 58–60; Gladieux & King, 1999, p. 158). Federal funds are not always awarded in accordance with competitive tenders and concerns have arisen in the past about financing of "pork barrel science" (p. 159).[6]

The most comprehensive role in American education, however, is occupied not by the federal government but by state governments. There is no constitutional protection for the autonomy of universities, and in recent times some state governments have deployed a range of disciplinary techniques to get more value from universities using the logic of quality.[7] The

---

porations exclusive access to government-funded research performed at universities. The Small Business Innovation Development Act required federally funded agencies with annual expenditures above $100 million to devote 1.25% of their budget to research needs of small businesses. The Orphan Drug Act (1983) offered major incentives to companies including tax advantages and market monopolies which led to the growth of the biotechnology industry. The National Cooperative Research Act (1984) extended anti-trust status to R&D ventures and encouraged greater inter-industry collaboration. A series of other acts, the Drug Export Amendments Act (1986), the Omnibus Trade and Competitiveness Act (1988), North American Free Trade Agreement (NAFTA; 1993), and General Agreement on Tariffs and Trade (GATT; 1994) were also aimed at enforcing global intellectual property rights.

[6]In the past, these earmarked research grants have favored universities in the home states of ruling congressmen.

[7]Ensuring the provision of quality education services falls under this ambit of proper use of state money. In some states, legislatively mandated program evaluations allow state government finance officers to undertake broad-ranging institutional audits including auditing academic programs. Mandated faculty teaching loads have also been mooted (Berdahl & McConnell, 1999, pp. 75–78; McGuiness, 1999, p. 189). By using various outcomes-based mechanisms, state governments are able to make inter-institutional comparisons about academic quality, which is seen to reside in such indicators as the learning outcomes of students, faculty teaching workload, and degree completion times. The influence exercised by state governments on university governing boards is often considerable depending on the state's political culture (McGuiness, 1999, pp. 191–192).

regional differentiation in the United States means that education–state relations are shaped by the diverse political cultures of individual states, including their economic and historical particularities (Alexander, 2000; Berdahl & McConnell, 1999; McGuiness, 1999). State government involvement in education can also have the effect of normalizing particular types of university models. The establishment of the Western Governors University (WGU), a virtual degree-granting and accredited university, is one such example.[8] State governments also act as regulators by licensing education institutions. However, having the legal authority (license) to operate as an educational institution and to offer degrees and diplomas should not be confused with academic legitimacy. State-licensed "colleges" or "universities" may just as well be "diploma mills," business operations that issue bogus degrees (ACE, 2001, p. 6). Unlike the United Kingdom and Australia, there are no legislative controls in America over the use of the term *university*, and the academic legitimacy of an institution is decided by the process of accreditation, which is carried out by voluntary organizations. Seeking accreditation is entirely voluntary, as there are no legislative requirements for a university to be accredited to promote and provide an educational service.[9] Given that enrollment in an accredited institution is a requirement for any domestic student seeking financial aid from the government, obtaining accreditation remains an important aspect of ensuring institutional viability (ACE, 2001, p. 3).

American universities are staffed by significant numbers of talented foreign-born and -trained scientists, entrepreneurs, artists, researchers, theoreticians, educators, and administrators. Universities and the country in general are adept at managing diversity in ways that help further the American political and economic enterprise. The desired subjects are enterprising model minorities (Bhatt, 2003; Kramer, 2003a). Managing diversity the American way helps facilitate a nuanced reconfiguration between race and

---

[8]The WGU draws its rationale from the for-profit sector, which has focused on high-demand, profitable and highly vocationalized courses. It views technological teaching as increasing efficiency (doing more with less), improving access (reach more students), and ensuring quality (increasing job preparedness of graduates). WGU does not provide instruction but brokers instruction from a network of affiliated colleges, universities, and private corporations. As such, it personifies the institutional type recommended by Chipman (1998). It also favors competency-based assessment, which involves granting students academic credit for skills and knowledge acquired through work.

[9]In recent times, the integrity of the accreditation processes has also been called into questions (see American Association of University Professors [AAUP], 1999). The 1998 accreditation of Jones International University (JIU), an online university, by the North Central Association of Colleges and Universities is a case in point. Despite limited staffing (only 4% of the staff of JIU were noted to be full-time employees, of whom only two were full-time academic staff) and the brevity of its courses (1 hour per week for 8 weeks), it received accreditation status (see AAUP, 1999).

statehood, but only within accepted parameters. The racializing logic that defined Black–White relations in America and which continues to disadvantage poorer African Americans has not changed greatly (Walters, 2004, p. 27).

The Rise of the Corporate University

Market logic plays a fundamental role in shaping American higher education. Market-inspired notions of quality impose two types of subjectivities onto faculty: education service provider and entrepreneur (see Altbach, 1999a, 2001; Barrow, Didou-Aupetit, & Mallea, 2003, pp. 53–58; McGuiness, 1999; Rhoades, 1998; Slaughter, 1998, 2001a, 2001b; Slaughter & Leslie, 1997). One of the most visible expressions of university corporatization involves the recruitment of 'trophy professors'—academic staff who are offered generous salaries, light teaching loads, and extensive research funding (Ehrenberg, 2000; see also Walters, 2003). Educational marketing, another expression of higher education marketization, emerged in 1980s following government cuts to university funding (Dill, 1997; Hite & Yearwood, 2001; Slaughter & Leslie, 1997). The wealthy and intellectually elite universities, such as the Ivy League universities and Stanford University, tend to eschew full-blown marketing practices, as they are assured of students. By contrast, universities at the other end of the prestige spectrum compete fiercely for students.

Educational marketing is now institutionalized in the American higher education field, evident in a panoply of promotion and marketing materials, personnel, journals, books, and companies—aimed at advising prospective consumers on ways of selecting the 'right' institution and assisting universities (providers) in attracting the 'right' students (see Dill, 1997). It is commonplace for individual students to call on the services of private guidance counselors for help in deciding which university to select (Ardolino, 2002). Some university admissions departments function primarily as market analysts and enrollment specialists. Positions such as provost of university enrollment, unheard of in other national systems of higher education, are found in the United States. The success of these departments hinges on the collection, ordering, and analysis of data using sophisticated geographical information systems, as well as better communication technologies to identify and persuade the desired customer. A new kaleidoscope of phraseology, with terms such as *recruiting funnels, marketing mixes, message strategies, branding,* and *building name recognition,* characterizes this discursive formation (see Sevier, 2000). Where once persuading technologies were put to work when prospective students applied to universities, increasingly the trend is for many non-elite American universities to define the preferred student and clarify the recruiting geography, which usually translates into identifying desired zip codes and feeder schools (see Hite & Yearwood, 2001; Sevier, 2000). As a general rule, these elaborate marketing strategies target domestic rather than international students.[10]

American universities have access to diverse funding sources, and on the positive side, these varied funding sources—fees for teaching both domestic and international students, specific purpose contracts for undertaking research, donations, various gifts and endowments—mean that the American university is not beholden to any single master. On the negative side, significant institutional resources are spent on fund-raising activities, which dilute the university's institutional mission and role in society. Furthermore, given that the education market is not an even terrain, private institutions in remote and less prosperous areas such as the Rocky Mountain states and the West are less likely to do as well as a public institution in California. The market's uncertainty was reflected in the mixed fortunes of online ventures by universities. The circumstances surrounding the emergence and closure of the California Virtual University and New York University Online (NYU Online) is instructive (see Hira, 2003, pp. 922–924).[11]

Phoenix University, a for-profit university, is often used as a benchmark for the successful proprietary university for the 21st century. In part, Phoenix's success lies in its capacity to embrace the principle of convenience. It offers classes outside of normal working hours, in the evenings and weekends, in venues that offer plentiful parking facilities, such as malls and industrial parks. It is customer centered in the strictest sense of the word. However, a more significant contribution to its success lies in its access to indirect state subsidies through student financial aid (Fairweather, 2000, p. 84). But Phoenix's use of market logic in student recruitment also sees it applying fairly restrictive principles, for example, stipulating students' minimum age (23 years) and requiring them to be in employment (Palatella, 2001, p. 34; see also Hira, 2003, p. 923). Phoenix should not be considered normative nor as a benchmark free-market university.

---

[10]With the exception of a few state universities that levy higher fees for international students, on the whole there are no immediate financial advantages to American universities in recruiting international students. International students pay the same fees as domestic students in private universities and the same rate as out-of-state students in state universities.

[11]Begun in 1998 as a for-profit company owned by the private, not-for-profit NYU, NYU Online ceased trading in 2001 (Carnevale, 2001). Princeton University's recent departure from The Alliance for Lifelong Learning, a partnership established in 2000 with Yale, Stanford, and Oxford universities suggests that all may not be well on the digital front. Cardean University, initiated by Mike Miliken, who gained fame and notoriety as a Wall Street junk bonds dealer is another online for-profit university. It describes itself and its mission as "an online learning community for working professionals" and sees its mission as "providing superior online business education for individuals and businesses around the world" (Cardean University, 2002). It has secured partnerships with several prestigious universities such Columbia University, The Chicago Graduate School of Business, Stanford University, and the London School of Economics.

As a general observation, a more marketized system does not protect universities from financial difficulties. The exception is the Ivy League and West Coast private institutions that are assured of students, research funds, and donations, and whose prestige is legendary (Walters, 2003). However, it is erroneous to take these universities as mainstream although their prestige and wealth means they tend to be considered normative (Leslie & Slaughter, 1997, p. 241).

The Cultural Circuit of Capital and E-Education

In the years surrounding the dot.com boom, online education (e-education) was embraced by both proprietary institutions and traditional universities to increase their market share and improve their earning potential (Honan & Teferra, 2001, p. 190). The emergence of e-education was part of the push toward the 'New Economy', a phenomenon discussed in some detail in chapter 1. Associated with stakeholders with access to extraordinary levels of money and authority, it was a world where the fast and furious circulation of money, ideas, and power worked to order relations such that people, institutions, and entire countries were either winners or losers. Entities that were local carried connotations of old-fashioned insularity, whereas the global, placeless, and free floating were privileged and rarefied (Lofgren, 2003; Thrift, 2002). E-education rode on the crest of the infinite possibilities created by collapsing space and time.

Buoyed by estimates by the U.S. brokerage house Merrill Lynch that global spending on education and training stood at US$3 trillion in 1999, there was explosion of media commentary on the possibilities offered by virtual or online education (Lyon, 2000, p. 32). A trinity of consultants, information technology (IT) companies and faculty worked to produce a new imaginary—the virtual university, which offered flexible, cost-effective, and convenient online degrees. Much of the commentary was commissioned by supporters of for-profit education who were seeking investment by business and industry interests (Lyon, 2000). Some institutions and scholars were predictably wary of the pedagogical benefits of online education but joined the virtual bandwagon out of concern that they might be left behind. The story of the new economy featured the art of "cairology"—the art of catching the right movement. Significantly, it drew its influence from the constant fear of being too late and missing out (Lofgren, 2003, p. 247).

The discursive watchwords used to promote online education were progress, opportunity, and social equity. Arguments for technologically mediated education were premised on several factors including "there are about to be too many students and not enough classrooms" (Huffstutter & Fields, 2000) and the obsolescence of facilities-based education as it is deemed to be too costly to operate on a world scale (Huffstutter & Fields, 2000). Online education was thus constructed as the means to the democratization of educational opportunities for the global community:

> If China were to achieve the college participation rate of the United States, it would need to build 40,000 average US-sized colleges. . . . This level of investment is surely absurd given the alternative and vastly less expensive technology. . . . We are building a company that gives people all over the world instantanous access to "world-class" educational services. (Rosenfield, 1999)

At the same time, online education was constructed as being demand driven: "People want to learn what they need to know, not what the professor wants them to know. You can only do that on the Internet"(Rosenfield, as quoted in Huffstutter & Fields, 2000). What was invisibilized was the elaborate marketing machinery—the cultural circuit of capital—put in place to drive this demand (see Thrift, 2002). Key authorities, many with illustrious academic qualifications, sold the message that e-learning was the next frontier. For example, Gary Becker who won a Nobel prize in Economics in 1992 for his work in developing human capital theory, promoted Unext. com, an education company that runs the online Cardean University. UNext.com is part of a collection of education companies owned by former Wall Street trader Mike Miliken and includes Knowledge Universe, Children's Discovery Centers, Bookman Testing Services, Pyramid Imaging Inc., Nobel Education Dynamics, and Leapfrog (see McLaren & Farahmandpur, 2001). The symbiotic relations among government, investors, business consultants, and the media helped normalize e-education as the next stage of educational progress.

CHALLENGES

There are a number of pressing challenges facing American universities. The main ones are the rising cost of education, which is affecting its affordability (Budd, 2002, pp. 14–16; Ehrenberg, 2000; see also Walters, 2003, p. 25). In the 1990s, there was a 51% increase in tuition fees for public colleges and a 35% increase for private institutions (ACE, 2001, p. 39). Student indebtedness has increased significantly as government and institutional grants have not kept pace with the rocketing costs of higher education (Budd, 2002, p. 14; "Help Students," 2004; Leonhardt, 2004). Presently, Pell Grants are estimated to cover 40% of tuition costs, where in the past they covered more than 80% of tuition costs[12] ("Help Students," 2004).

---

[12]There have been calls to redirect funds from the Federal Family Education Loan Program (FFEP) as a solution to increasing support for American students. Under the FFEP, private banks receive federal subsidies to make student loans. These loans are guaranteed by the taxpayer. The costs of the FFEP has been estimated to be in the vicinity of US$3 billion ("Help Students," 2004).

Some public sector and small private universities are also facing financial problems, which they have tackled by a series of strategies including greater collaborations with industry, establishing for-profit technology transfer units, outsourcing various academic functions, and concentrating academic programs in profitable disciplines (see Barrow, Didou-Aupetit, & Mallea, 2003, pp. 60–63; Leslie & Slaughter, 1997, pp. 241–245; Zusman, 1999).

Reduced state funding in the face of growing student numbers also brings challenges for access and quality in education. American graduate students, long the source of cheap academic labor, have begun to unionize to obtain better salaries, access to professional development, health benefits, and fee waivers (Leonard, 2001, p. 28; Westheimer, 2002).

Another challenge facing higher education is providing access to equity groups, those traditionally underrepresented in higher education (ACE, 2001, pp. 41–42; Budd, 2003, p. 15). Because financial aid is increasingly veering toward loans instead of grants, fewer low-income students are prepared to incur high debt levels and are rejecting university education as an option. Recent statistics released by the Higher Education Research Institute point to declining numbers of students from low- and middle-income families in America's prestigious universities. In the 2003 academic year, some 40% of freshman in the top 42 state universities were drawn from higher income families, those who earned in excess of US$100,000 annually. The Institute estimates that less than 20% of American families fall into this category of earnings (Leonhardt, 2004).

Compared with other electorates, the American public has shown itself to be remarkably trusting of government priorities when it comes to military spending and corporate welfare. American society is thus prepared to tolerate the diversion of taxpayer funds to defense and business instead of demanding universal, high-quality health care and education. Negative public opinion about the rising costs of education is more likely to be harbored against universities (McGuiness, 1999, p. 184) than against a social structure that enables military and corporate Keynesian policies ahead of social spending.

State universities will continue to face fiscal constraints as they compete with other state priorities such as burgeoning health care costs and the establishment and maintenance of prisons (McGuiness, 1999, p. 188). Fiscal constraints will also continue to have an impact on university governance, where tensions are already being played out among the vision, goals, and values of managerialists and academic staff (Honan & Teferra, 2001; Rhoades, 1998; Westheimer, 2002). Another significant challenge facing American universities is how to encourage innovation in research and teaching in a climate that promotes educational instrumentalism.

The United States is often portrayed as an example of hands-off governance. However, this brief snapshot of the financing and organization of

U.S. education illustrates the profoundly powerful role that the nation-state exercises in higher education. As a general rule, this governance is indirect, for example, through the use of performance-based systems that allow both state and federal governments to steer the American university sector toward national interest goals such as economic and military dominance. Quality and value for money are other rationalities used to justify governmental use of disciplining instruments such as achievement tests, measures of faculty performance, and interinstitutional benchmarks to ascertain institutional worth.

Turning to the international education sphere, the main drivers of international education in the United States have been national security and national interest. As Gillespie (2001) astutely observes, "The biggest leaps in international education in the United States have occurred in response to war" (p. 80). Institutions and initiatives such as the IIE and the Fulbright Program emerged in the aftermath of the First and Second World Wars. Before moving onto a discussion of how international education is ordered and institutionalized in the United States, the next section explores the political rationalities that have influenced the development of international education within the United States. By using insights from critical geopolitics, the state's involvement in international education can be understood as expressions of geopolitical and geoeconomic rationalities. These insights also provide a historical framework for understanding how international education has influenced the existing world order.

AMERICAN GOVERNANCE: EXCEPTIONALISM, TRIUMPHALISM, AND MARKET POPULISM

A pivotal force behind the push to offer educational aid was the Cold War rivalry with the communist world. Aid has always been an instrument of foreign policy, and during the Cold War educational aid was used to establish a network of intellectuals and professionals, cultural texts—in effect, an entire imaginative community who would advance the ideas of the free world. The strong didactic element associated with fighting and winning the Cold War established the basis for federal government investment in Area Studies and foreign language study in the 1958 National Defense Education Act and the 1965 Higher Education Act Title VI (Green, 2002).

From the 1940s to the 1960s, international education in the United States rested on two pillars—educating overseas students in the United States to ensure their allegiances and educating Americans to take a greater interest in international affairs, to prepare them for America's 'manifest destiny' to lead the world. As a population, Americans are noted for their disinterest in what happens outside the United States, preferring instead to focus on internal issues, what happens to them within. Their historical resistance to defense expenditure and war casualties is a case in point (Hobsbawn, 2003). Challenging these isolationist sentiments had to be an ongoing project. American foreign policy after World War II was guided by a particular global imaginary—an internationally integrated free-market economic order:

> [The United States] perceived that any effort on the part of decolonizing nations to remain outside of this integrated system—by pursuing nationalist economic policies for instance—as a threat to the economic and political stability of the capitalist "free world." The creation of this integrated global economy—and its preservation through military and economic means—became along with the containment of the Soviet Union, . . . [a] fundamental goal of postwar US policy makers. (C. Klein, 2003, p. 23)

At the same time, policymakers faced a political and cultural problem that they tried to resolve through education of the other and the American people: "How can we define our nation as a nonimperial world power in the age of decolonization? How can we transform our sense of ourselves from narrow provincials into cosmopolitan citizens of the world?" (C. Klein, 2003, p. 9). In other words, there was a strongly pedagogical impulse to the Cold War, and this was translated into a contest between the free world and the communist governments to win the hearts and minds of people (see NAFSA, 2003b, 2003c). International education became a matter of national security (C. Klein, 2003, pp. 62–63). It was drawn into a broader American foreign policy goal to prepare the nation, its people, and other nations for the United States's new position as a global power in the decolonizing world. International education was thus shaped by American foreign and economic policies, and heavily imbricated in American exceptionalism (Pieterse, 2004, pp. 123–125).

The term *cultural propaganda* has been used to describe the vast network of activities and programs funded by the United States to "nudge the intelligentsia of western Europe . . . away from its lingering fascination with Marxism and Communism" (Saunders, 1999, p. 1). A more nuanced analysis using Foucauldian theory is preferable and argues against such a passive construction of the individual subject. Accordingly, the dispositif deployed to steer people toward a more accommodating view of the American way was embraced by individuals, institutions, and countries partly because Pax Americana offered certain productive possibilities for self advancement.

Pax Americana was represented both domestically and internationally as modernization. It was constructed as a chance for the former colonies to break free from the tyrannies of European imperialism. Pax Americana was *the* most rational response, and those opposing these modernist sensibilities and by extension, the American way, were deemed to be irrational (N. P. Singh, 1998). The United States thus exercised 'soft power' through these discourses of modernization, and in doing so effectively distanced itself from European colonialism and the totalitarian persuasions of communism (Kaplan, 2004; N. P. Singh, 1998). It succeeded in establishing itself as a moral authority that would bring to the world the civilizing imperatives of the American way (C. Klein, 2003; N. P. Singh, 1998). The legitimacy of American power was sealed by linking the American way to democracy and modernization. The 20th century was to be the American century.

All of this is not to minimize the deployment of oppressive instruments to advance the American way. Some of America's allies in Southeast Asia, Africa, and Latin America embarked on a range of oppressive measures including brutal labor control regimes, punitive policing, and the suppression of public debate to stem opposition to their policies. Within America, too, the dangerous other of communism worked as a rationality to justify the need for harsh policies aimed at uncovering subversives at home. The workings of the House Un-American Activities Committee reanimated the nationalist game. Dissenters were duly dubbed 'anti-American'.

If America was to be the world's exemplary nation-state, and bearer of universal democracy, it had to create for itself an image of an internal democracy. A national narrative celebrating immigration with its tenuous links to inclusion of the other was taken to new heights. It was also necessary for the United States to invisibilize its race politics. Black protests for civil rights, labor unrest, and the continuing existence of Jim Crow were initially managed and deflected through 'red scare' tactics. These strategies had some success in marginalizing more radical Black leaders such as Paul Robeson and W. E. B. DuBois. Both had long stressed the need to resolve the issue of political rights for colonized people and minorities in the EuroAmerican world and the danger of the United States presiding over a new empire. DuBois observed that the Black people of the United States were "a nation without a polity, nationals without citizenship" (DuBois, as cited in N. P. Singh, 1998). The heterogeneous, strategic and contingent dimensions of power were reworked toward productive ends, and by the 1960s, concerted efforts were under way to delink American anticommunism from associations with White supremacy and xenophobia (N. P. Singh, 1998).

The 1970s and 1980s were marked by a national anxiety that the American century was ending. Political and popular discourse cast America as a victim of circumstances, whose external enemies were numerous: OPEC, Japanese industry and communism (Buell, 1998; N. P. Singh, 1998). America's "losses" in Indochina, Nicaragua, and the oil crises propagated a narrative of the nation at risk whose national foundations were under threat. What emerged thereafter were a series of defensive fundamentalisms, some with domestic expressions, such as the culture wars, and others directed outward, such as the aggressive unilateralism in America's foreign and trade policies (N. P. Singh, 1998; see also Kaplan, 2004).

The turn toward fundamentalism was externally reflected in the emergence of a new Cold War policy involving the privatization of resistance against procommunist client states. Having faced popular protests against military involvement in Vietnam, the United States began clandestine funding of a series of proto-terrorist movements in Latin America, Afghanistan, and Africa. These movements deployed the services of numerous secular and religious warlords, and in many respects they reflected the privatization of conflict and counterinsurgency efforts by a democratic nation-state[13] (Mamdani, 2001).

In the domestic sphere, these defensive fundamentalisms were reworked into a governmentality that drew insight and inspiration from neoliberalism and populism. Market populism emerged as a powerful political technology. A highly divisive neofundamentalist rhetoric was used to roll back the social contract, or national bargain, achieved in the 1930s among organized labor, business, and the U.S. government. Reaganites valorized populism, which featured criticisms of political correctness and multiculturalism (N. P. Singh, 1998). Where Cold War liberals had advocated a variant of cosmopolitan universalism, market populism (neoliberal populism) was based on two governing rationalities: belief in the market and suspicion of multiculturalism. Market populism drew its support by attacking the liberal left, which it accused of eroding American family values while pandering to ethnic separatists and cultural relativists values (Buell, 1998; Frank, 2002, pp. 23–39). Diminishing the credibility of the left also involved recycling the trope of the Cold War to galvanize support for the American way, a tactic perfected to an art form by the Reagan presidency. Together, the imminent threat of the evil empire and the culture wars succeeded in drawing attention away from how neoliberal policies were taking wealth polarization to levels previously unknown. Casual comparisons with the red menace would continue into the 1990s, fueled by sections of the media who fiercely

---

[13]With the collapse of the Soviet Union and the end of the era of proxy warfare, some U.S.-backed terrorist movements, such as Renamo in Mozambique, remained territorialist; others regrouped, reorganized, and extended into extraterritorial networks, such as al-Quaida (Mamdani, 2001). What is often missing in analyses of terrorist movements such as al-Quaida, then, is a recognition that the political rationalities, technologies of governance, knowledges, and strategies they deploy are not primordial nor premodern (Mamdani, 2001). A sober analysis of their associations would reveal the extent to which they are linked by a complex web of informal circuits to democratic nation-states such as the United States. A particularly serious unanticipated consequence of the clandestine nature of U.S. support for these shadowy groups was their implication in gross human rights abuses.

criticized labor dissent and any skepticism about the glories of the new economy (Frank, 2002, pp. 23–44).

The loss of jobs that accompanied the 'New Economy' was lexically transformed, described variously as downsizing, rightsizing, and outsourcing. Job losses were regarded as entirely rational, a precursor to greater wealth and opportunity. In the spirit of market populism, the democratization of finance, information, and technology was widely celebrated. The stock market was discursively constructed as the people's market and entrepreneurs were identified as the salt of the earth—portrayed as a hard-working underclass that had to battle against liberal elites, bureaucrats, and liberal intellectuals to realize their dreams (Frank, 2002). Books such as the *Lexus and Olive Tree* portrayed globalization as "the end object of human civilization," which would "make us rich, set us free and elevate everyone everywhere" (p. 65). Financial democracy also entered the lexicon of journalism and expert commentary by professionals, its circulation facilitated by the cultural circuit of capital (Thrift, 1999). Regular people could win in the people's market. A series of investment fables provided real-life examples of how the democratic virtues of the market reached all. The Beardstown Ladies, a group of grandmas from a small town who succeeded using their small town wisdom, was a case in point (Frank, 2002, pp. 128–131).

Suspicions that a small and rapacious minority was accumulating wealth at the expense of ordinary people were diluted by a well-resourced imagineering machinery. Bill Gates' public persona as generous philanthropist and geek were augmented while the predatory instincts of his company, Microsoft, disarmed. The celebration of an uber-capitalist philanthropy successfully rehabilitated the corporate image. Imagineering took the public's attention away from the widespread corporate self-enrichment that was so widespread that at the height of the boom, from 1996 to 2000, almost two thirds of American businesses paid no tax (Teather, 2004, p. 14). The governing rationalities that informed market populism and market fundamentalism drew a veil around the deep-seated structural problems surrounding U.S. corporate culture.

The 1990s, also saw the emergence of a new set of political rationalities, premised on the clash of civilizations thesis. Its proponents predicted that the great divisions among humankind and the dominant source of conflict in the 21st century would be cultural difference. Putting aside its misantropic impulses, what is noteworthy about this thesis is its use of a paradoxically binary logic that separates East from West while essentializing what constitutes the East and the West. The conflict and tensions between East and West were anchored in a primordial logic, rather than being regarded as having historical underpinnings.

With the end of the Cold War, an era and ethos of triumphalism began. The most immediate consequences for international education was a reduced commitment by the state to supporting structures and initiatives such as educational aid and foreign language programs. Educational aid programs, once regarded as significant instruments of political persuasion, lost their importance.

In recent times, the exercise of global power by the United States has raised the issue of whether the United States presides over an empire. Denial of empire may once have served as a counternarrative to charges of U.S. imperialism during the Cold War, but it is increasingly part of mainstream discourse (Ferguson, 2003; Pieterse, 2004). There are several narratives of empire, although two are particularly salient: a neoconservative interpretation of manifest destiny and a liberal interventionist narrative that sees the United States as a reluctant imperialist forced to intervene in the face of threats to liberty by various totalitarianisms (Ferguson, 2003; Kaplan, 2004). However, as Hobsbawn (2003) points out, both camps are affected by universalist reason, noting that "Few things are more dangerous than empires pursuing their own interest in the belief that they are doing humanity a favour."

Whether the geoeconomic and geopolitical rationalities surrounding U.S. governance can be considered in terms of empire is a moot point. The more relevant question is how an ethos of exceptionalism and triumphalism plays out in governing technologies by the state and technologies of the self by citizen-subjects. Because American exceptionalism declares America and the American subject to be uniquely blessed and free, an outstanding issue is how solidarities can be formed with the other, and how alternative technologies of the self can be instilled, chosen, and normalized.

INTERNATIONAL EDUCATION IN THE UNITED STATES

The United States remains the most popular study destination for international students despite a 2.4% decrease in student numbers in the 2003–2004 academic year. The decline has been attributed to a number of factors: real and perceived difficulties in obtaining student visas, especially in scientific and technical fields, robust recruitment efforts by other Anglophone nations, rising tuition costs in the United States and a general perception overseas that international students are not welcome in the United States (Holman, 2004; IIE, 2004). Despite the fall in numbers, international education still contributed U.S. $12 billion to the national economy.

Aside from its international student program where international students reside in America for the duration of their studies, American private universities, many of which are accredited liberal arts colleges, are found throughout the world.[14] Additionally, American universities are involved in

---

[14]The American University in Paris, Beirut, Cairo, and Bulgaria are examples.

numerous offshore initiatives in partnership with local institutions,[15] although there have been long-ranging concerns about the academic integrity of some of these programs (see Gillespie, 2001; Yee & Lim, 1995; see also Morrow & Torres, 2000).[16]

The recruitment of international students is not driven by export considerations to the extent that it is in either Australia or the United Kingdom, although various American interest groups have flagged loss of market share as an issue demanding policy intervention. As a general observation, American universities are motivated to enroll international students for two major reasons: as a form of cheap academic labor and as a strategy for maintaining enrollments in disciplines such as science and engineering where domestic interest is waning:

> It's a sad reality that relatively small numbers of American students pursue graduate degrees in engineering and science. As a result the research efforts at many American universities depend on international graduate students. They do much of the laboratory work that leads to new discoveries. (Gates, 2004, p. 23; see also Leslie & Slaughter, 1997, p. 25; Miller, 1999, pp. 71–72; NAFSA, 2003a, pp. 6–7)

In 1999 following extensive lobbying by interest groups[17] concerned about relative loss of market share by the American higher education sector to Britain and Australia,[18] a federal International Education Policy was announced. Although praised by interest groups such as NAFSA for its comprehensive scope, it was not accompanied by funding increases, resulting in

---

[15]The American university abroad is not a recent phenomenon. Yenching University in Beijing, China and St. John's University in Shanghai were just two examples of American universities overseas. Most of these early institutions were driven by philanthropy with a strong missionary representation in the administration and teaching staff. In this respect, the early universities differed significantly from American offshore institutions today, which are largely organized along business lines and motivated by profit (Yee & Lim, 1995, pp. 181–183).

[16]American–Japanese tertiary partnerships, for example, are considered to be shameless diploma mills. Although efforts have been made to ensure standards by developing accreditation criteria for American offshore initiatives, resource constraints have affected the monitoring function by organizations such as the Centre for Quality Assurance in International Education (Yee & Lim, 1995, pp. 182–184).

[17]NAFSA, IIE, and commercial stakeholders such as the Alliance for International Educational and Cultural Exchange and the Educational Testing Service (ETS), which administers the English language proficiency test, TOEFL, were part of a diverse coalition that called for increased recruitment by American institutions to recapture lost market share. A conference was convened in 1998 titled "U.S. Leadership in International Education; The Lost Edge."

[18]The key elements in the U.S. International Education Policy include: international student recruitment, study abroad schemes to encourage Americans to study abroad, the inclusion of foreign language study and regional or area studies as an integral part of the higher education experience, and the promotion of citizen and scholar exchanges between Americans and scholars from abroad (NAFSA, 2000).

its failure to have much impact. Inevitably, the noneconomic aspects of internationalization initiatives were relegated to the margins of priority, in the face of competing priorities such as campus computerization, regulatory compliance costs, and inflationary pressures (see Altbach & MacGill Peterson, 1998; Chandler, 1999; Dunnett, 1998; Mestenhauser, 1998). It is not surprising that the policy was framed by national interest considerations, which in some regard were not dissimilar to Cold War discourses—educating and knowing the other was deemed necessary to safeguard American interests. Governing from a distance required the United States to build ties with business, political, and professional elites:

> To continue to compete successfully in the global economy and to maintain our role as a world leader, the United States needs to ensure that its citizens develop a broad understanding of the world, proficiency in other languages, and knowledge of other cultures. America's leadership also depends on building ties with those who will guide the political, cultural, and economic development of their countries in the future. (Clinton, 2000)

How does the Policy perceive and construct the international student. While the Policy frames national interest in terms of the immediate economic gains brought by the international student, the international student is also regarded as a member of a pliable elite class with similar interests to those of the United States. This subjectivity—of U.S. ally—has assumed renewed importance following the attacks on the World Trade Center:

> To defeat terrorism, our global military, law enforcement and intelligence capacities must be complemented with positive initiatives and programs aimed at the young people in developing nations who will guide their countries in the future. No policy has proved more successfully in making friends for the United States, during the cold war and since, than educating students from abroad at our colleges and universities. . . . Protecting our security requires more than defensive measures; we have to win the war of ideas, too. (Gates, 2004, p. 23)

In several respects, the ethos of the Policy hearkens back to the era of colonization where elite formation was pivotal to governing from a distance.

The Brave New World of International Education

Despite elaborate claims by various institutions about "doing" international education, the internationalization of curricula remains a poorly conceptualized and insufficiently funded area. This deficit leaves American graduates with the unchallenged view that all knowledge is universal and universally transferable (Mestenhauser, 1998, p. 2). Internationalization of the curricula is a vital component of generating a deep and intellectually sophisticated paradigm of international education, but it requires universities to first unsettle existing power–knowledge relations in the academy. What does this mean? Simply put, it means unhinging the dominance of American exceptionalism, triumphalism, and market liberalism. It also means committing faculty and graduates to develop the competencies, ethics, values, and responsibilities to be globally oriented citizens (see Ellingboe, 1997; Johnston & Edelstein, 1993; Morrow & Torres, 1998; Rhoades, 1998; Tierney, 2001). An additional complication arises because of the profoundly privatized and individualized dimensions of international education. As Barrow, Didou-Aupetit, and Mallea (2003, pp. 166–167) observe: "Internationalized higher education is not a public good to be provided by government at prices affordable to all who can benefit from it, but a private good to be financed by individuals (students) and institutions (transnational corporations and post secondary institutions)."

Internationalization of the university cannot progress on the basis of economic nor national security rationales, which may well end up being "counterproductive and dangerous" (Mestenhauser, 1998, p. 1). For two decades now, market models have been vested with the hope of facilitating the internationalization of knowledge. What has emerged from the market is an internationalization that is inclined toward educational instrumentalism:

> In the United States, internationalization of the curriculum tends to mean the development of applied master's degree programs in business and engineering designed to enable the United States to exploit international markets, more than it means the development of educational experiences designed to promote cooperation among countries, even within regional trading blocs. (Rhoades, 1998)

Internationalization can only succeed in American higher education if engagements with the other are able to transcend American exceptionalism. At the very least, this will require American educators to interrogate the deep-seated belief held by so many internationalist Americans of their country's destiny to be a trustee of the world's welfare. This popular viewpoint that theirs is a benign brand of empire that does nothing more than exporting democracy and consumer goods to the rest of the world, prevents many Americans from seeing their nation through the eyes of its critics: The United States is the author of a malign imperialism in an increasing number of situations (Colley, 2002).

After 9-11 there has been a renewed emphasis on internationalizing American higher education. ACE's (2003) initiative, *Promising Practices*, is a blueprint for American institutions wishing to internationalize. It documents good practice in internationalization by using case studies of institutions who have successfully internationalized. *Promising Practices* describes a range of strategies from infusing non-American content into curricula, requiring all students to undertake one or two courses in multicultural education, providing professional development opportunities for faculty, and facilitating study abroad programs for students, to setting up student residences with quotas of American and international students (ACE, 2003). It is a start; however, the challenge is to move beyond the instrumental and to engage with the relations of power and knowledge that shape internationalization initiatives.

In the aftermath of the terrorist attacks on the World Trade Center and riding on the crest of populist xenophobia, the federal government has intensified measures to monitor international students under the pretext of "homeland security." The Patriot Act (2001) extends wide-ranging powers to government instrumentalities (e.g., U.S. Citizenship and Immigration Services, Justice Department, FBI). Together with the Homeland Security Act (2002), it obliges universities to provide detailed information about all their international students to the U.S. government (AAUP, 2003; NAFSA, 2003c, 2003d; Sutherland, 2003). An electronic reporting system, SEVIS (Student and Exchange Visitor Information Service), is able to facilitate the seamless transfer of information about international students and foreign nationals between various state and non-state institutions. Although some universities have expressed concern about their surveillance role, others see few contradictions between their role as centers of scholarship and instruments of national security: "Universities are willing partners in strengthening homeland security. This is not the 1960s. We are working with the government to keep track of international students" (Gates, 2004, p. 23).

National interest considerations also saw the federal government reauthorize Title VI (International Studies in Higher Education) of the 1965 Higher Education Act in 2003, with one significant change—the establishment of an International Education Advisory Board whose role it is to advise Congress and the Federal Department of Education on issues of international education (H.R. 3077; Committee on Education and the Workforce, 2003).

Title VI resurrects the Cold War ethos of seeking international knowledge to govern the other:

> [It] provides support for a critically important group of programs at colleges and universties ... to advance knowledge of world regions ... and train Americans to have the international expertise and understanding to fulfill pressing national security needs. (Boehner, 2003)

Although Title VI prohibits the International Education Advisory Board from "directing programs, curricula and instructional methods" (see Committee on Education and the Workforce, 2003) and restricts it to an advisory role, concerns about academic freedom remain in some quarters (AAUP, 2003).

Part A of Title VI notes that "the security, stability and economic vitality of the United States in a complex global era depend upon American experts in and citizens knowledgeable about world regions, foreign languages and international affairs" (U.S. Department of Education, 2003). The educated American subject is conferred with the role of global policeman who protects the nation-state and its interests. The institutional subjectivity assumed of the American university by Title VI is as producer of human resources for the nation-state, except in this instance, it is human resources that "fulfill pressing security needs" of the nation-state that are required. At about the same time as Title VI's reauthorization was taking place, concerns were being raised that American universities were running programs that reflected an anti-American bias (see Kurtz, 2003).[19] Within this discourse, the American university emerges as a subversive institution, staffed by faculty who are unpatriotic.

"Superpowers deploy the rules of practical advantage. They are not bound by moral imperatives but strategic ones which ultimately aim to advance their self interests" (Monbiot, 2003b). The spirit of American exceptionalism—the assumption that America is a redeemer nation with a manifest destiny to bring to the world the benefits of peace and prosperity, capitalism and democracy, liberty and the pursuit of happiness—is strongly evident in the documents and debates that frame international education in America (Hodgson, 1996, 2001; Kaplan, 2004; Madsen, 1998; Pieterse, 2004; Williams, 1988; see also NAFSA, 2003a, 2003c).

The 1999 International Education Policy, the 2003 NAFSA Report on International Student Access, In America's Interest (2003b), and various pronouncements by higher education leaders (see IIE, 2001) reflect a self-absorbed ethos that is untroubled by self-consciousness or nuance. The foreign policy objectives of various initiatives have been to expose future leaders to American values so that they could be relied on to serve Ameri-

---

[19]The criticisms have charged that area studies curricula are dominated by the "extremist postcolonial theory of Dr. Edward Said." American universities have also been accused of discouraging their students from working for the American government (see Kurtz, 2003). The criticisms have been refuted by the AAUP (see AAUP, 2003) and ACE (see ACE, 2002). The allegations used a University of California Santa Barbara course titled "Why Do They Hate Us" as a basis of their claims of anti-American bias. The course featured individuals noted for their criticism of American foreign policy such as Said, Robert Fisk, Tariq Ali, and Arundhati Roy. Kurtz (2003) argues that the course should have included alternative speakers as well.

can foreign policy objectives (see also NAFSA, 2003a). Naturally, future leaders are not passive beings who are content to be pawns in an American empire. French President Jacques Chirac, who was once an international student in the United States, defied American attempts to elicit French support for the war against Iraq in 2003. That stated, a leader from a G-8 nation such as France will necessarily have more room to maneuver and dissent than smaller nations that are heavily reliant on American trade and investment.

THE OTHER IN THE AMERICAN ENTERPRISE: MEDIA DISCOURSES

Until the 2001 attacks on the World Trade Center, media reporting of international education focused largely on America's loss of market share in the global education market. The article "Wasted Opportunity" (Moreno, 2000) constructs the international student as human capital for America's multinationals and a custodian of American values and interests:

> The US is losing its edge in attracting foreign students. Other countries count up the gains. . . . In the process, the US may miss out on connections to the next generation of billionaires. . . . Even lesser-heeled foreign students can pay dividends after they return home, either by working for the host country's multinationals or starting businesses with ties to that nation. (Moreno, 2000, p. 129)

The international student as valued human capital is also present in the global talent race, a new discourse refashioned from the discourse of the new (knowledge-based) economy. The high-achieving international student is identified as a prospective immigrant who will contribute to America's preeminent position in the world. Media reports such as "How America Can Gain," "The New Global Job Shift," and "The Challenge From India" conflate the issues surrounding international student immigration and American economic dominance to author a win–win fairy tale.

These e-mail responses, which formed part of a discussion facilitated by a business magazine[20] on the role of foreign students and immigrants in the global talent race, are depressingly unidimensional in their understandings of the human subject:

> As a founder of a software company, I believe . . . Indian programmers have internalized a principle that American workers seem to have forgotten. If I

---

[20]These are excerpts from a *Business Week* article, which appeared on December 29, 2003, titled, "How America Could Gain."

ask them to add a small but unforseen feature to our software they do not protest. . . . They stay up all night and make it happen. They work 10 to 18 hours
a day; they work every other weekend. (Person A)

The highly educated entrepreneurs and innovators from India have fully embraced American-style capitalism. As an added bonus they are bringing millions of dollars of revenue and cost savings to American shareholders each
year. (Person B)

In these vignettes, the other is identified as a willing subject of capitalism, appearing in manifest forms as a pliable, hard-working employee and
entrepreneur cum innovator. A masculinist discourse of individualism and
First Worldism perpetuates a divisiveness between the American and non-
American subject. This is a win–win tale that is centered on rewarded acculturation by a model minority, the Indians. This discourse makes no mention of the effects of brain drain on the developing world and ignores the
noneconomic spheres of human existence and the unrealistic demands
placed by employers on the worker. Should labor be required to work a 10-
to 18-hour working day? How do such labor practices affect the health and
well-being of individuals, families, and communities?
A futurist, high-tech imaginary is the object of discourse, however, it is
largely ineffectual in producing a discursive separation from the feudal working conditions that remain in force in a distinctly 21st-century occupational
field—the technomanagerial sphere ("they work 10 to 18 hours a day").
More significant though is the construction of Indians as subjects whose role
it is to serve American-style capitalism. Ultimately, it is a discourse that "rewards behaviours and attitudes that support an elite (white) minority" and
functions to reinforce a neocolonial system (Bhatt, 2003, p. 205).
The inevitable global job shift is presently being formalized, both materially and discursively, by American universities, many of which now offer
outsourcing as an elective in their MBA curriculum (Stewart, 2004). American media reports also normalize the global shift in jobs by depicting
outsourcing in win–win terms. Thus, a mutual symbiosis links American
boardrooms and Indian backrooms. Everyone is a winner: American consumers, shareholders, and workers, along with the workers, middle-class
professionals, and entrepreneurs in developing countries (Friedman,
2004a). Among the more brazen claims is that outsourcing plays a part in
the war against terror (see Klein, 2003 for a critique). It does so by creating
jobs in countries and places where restive natives without work or hope
might otherwise resort to terrorism.
Thus Friedman (2004) argues:

[There are] two basic responses to globalization: Infosys and al-Qaida. . . .
Infosys, an Indian software company, uses the Internet, fiber optic telecom-

munications and e-mail to get superempowered and compete anywhere. [It becomes] part of a global supply chain that produces profit for Indians, Americans and Asians. al-Qaida uses the same instruments to develop a global supply chain of angry people that will hit back at the Western civilization.

At first blush, such "commonsense" logic cannot be faulted on economic or humanitarian grounds, until one investigates what happens in the backrooms. Practices such as accent neutralization training programs, which aim to teach call center workers in India to speak in American accents, is outsourcing's least troubling dimension (Roy, 2001, pp. 83–84). More troubling are concerns that First World multinational companies are engaging in highly exploitative labor practices overseas, undeterred by the scrutiny of investigative journalists, civil libertarians, and labor rights legislation. When fast capitalism meets a highly stratified social system, it creates previously unimagined possibilities for human exploitation (N. Klein, 2003). The discursive logics of productivity, efficiency, and staying on top of the competition do more than merely prescribing and codifying outputs, targets, and deadlines. The combination of elaborate accounting mechanisms and high-tech tools of surveillance also help create labor practices that are detrimental to the capacity of individuals to work and live in safety and dignity (N. Klein, 2001, chap. 9).

American news coverage has also focused on the visa and immigration problems encountered by international students, a topic that has assumed greater and greater salience after 9-11.

- "U.S. to Mandate Fingerprinting and Photos of More Foreigners" (Swarns, 2004)
- "Keeping Intellectual Borders Open" (2004)
- "The Visa Trap" (Zhao, 2004)
- "New Security Plan in Place, U.S. Halts Foreigner Registry" (Hall, 2003)
- "Student Scrutiny: Universities Cringe as Foreign Enrollees Face a Visa Crackdown" (Lord, 2001)
- "INS Arrests 10 in Hunt for Student-Visa Violators" (2001)
- "Knock, Knock: The FBI's Here: Interviews of Muslim Students Create Tensions on Campuses" (Marklein, 2001)
- "Eager for Foreign Students, Universities Persuade Senator to Drop Plan to Limit Visas" (Schemo, 2001)

The need to win hearts and minds remains a salient discourse even in the more liberal sections of the media. "Keeping Intellectual Borders

Open" (2004), an opinion piece in the *New York Times*, for example, criticizes current American government policy restricting publishers from editing works from countries subject to American economic sanctions, such as Cuba, Sudan, Libya, and Iran. The report argues that government policy is "diminishing America's role as a central exchange in the marketplace of ideas" (p. 20). It counsels, "There are many weapons in the war against terrorism. One of the most powerful is the enlightened, rational values that America has come to stand for" (p. 20). American exceptionalism remains a major influence on the national self-image.

I conclude this section with an analysis of an "advertorial" on international education, "A Global Liberal Arts Education" (2000), which appeared in the *New York Times*. Two themes form the basis of this advertorial. First, the rationale for international education is used to sponsor and consolidate a discourse of American exceptionalism: "For America to continue to be a world leader, American education must be more international." Second, a series of discursive maneuvers seek to other non-Americans and in doing so confirm American hegemony:

> Most [American students] go to English-speaking countries or Western Europe, never experiencing the poverty of a developing society, the deep faith of an Islamic society, the dynamic Asian economy or the variable status of women around the world. . .There is tremendous value in learning about another culture first-hand.

A singular Asia is constructed that ignores the region's enormous diversity. A series of binaries are discursively created between America and the "deep faith of an Islamic society" and "the poverty of a developing society." There is no acknowledgment that these "problems" along with their internal others exist within America's geographical boundaries, for example, the poverty of working Americans, so well documented in Ehrenreich's (2001) work *Nickel and Dimed* (see also Ehrenreich & Hochschild, 2002). The binary also ignores the fact that tensions between the fiercely secular and the aggressively religious are played out in every society—America is no exception.

The country's faith-based presidency and the electoral influence exercised by the country's evangelical Christians is a case in point (Stanley, 2004). Non-Americans reading about the display of the 2½-ton granite cast of the Ten Commandments in the Alabama courthouse and the chief justice's determination to "keep God in the public domain" could also be forgiven for considering the country's politics to be driven by the "deep faith of fundamentalist" Christian communities (Apple, 1998; Apple & Oliver, 1998; Younge, 2003, p. 11). Because it is a superpower, America's internal contradictions are also played out in the global stage, leading to concerns about the presence of strong fundamentalist instincts in its foreign policy (Monbiot, 2003a; Younge, 2003). President Bush's reelection in 2004 has secured the influence of a triumphalist sectarian Christianity in U.S. foreign policy. A virtuous empire that has God's approval has the right to strike preemptively against any threat, real or imaginary (Ryn, 2003, pp. 138–139).

The advertorial attempts to inject complexity and depth into the meaning of international education, for example, by emphasizing its interdisciplinary programs, internationalized curricula, and language fluency. It also raises global human rights issues. However, a strongly othering discourse runs through and overrides attempts made to build common ground. The result is that it succeeds in perpetuating the exceptionalism of American values and leadership:

> To explore a culture where women's roles are not what she already knows, to read newspapers where there is no free speech, to be in a place which is truly "other" and discover common ground—this will inspire her leadership. . . . If women are to be leaders—if they are, in fact to change the world—they must know the world. ("A Global Liberal Arts," 2000)

Here, a narrative of difference and threat to the American way by external others is used to justify the need to know the world. This is depicted by references to 'other' contexts where "there is no free speech" and where, by implication, women have fewer rights. Using the other as a grid against which to compare the American way sets the context for a justification of policy and pedagogical impulses to support an ethnocentric expansionism. The overriding message from this advertorial reads as follows: "We need knowledge about others so that we can strategically position ourselves to retain our position as a world leader." The advertorial manages to reinforce the moral and intellectual exceptionalism of America by its myopia to the existence of the identified problems within the United States.

The attacks on the World Trade Center have led to a resurgence of internal fundamentalisms. In the mainland, homeland security has been deployed as a disciplining device. Its racializing logic and anti-immigrant sentiments enable arbitrary detentions and deportations of the visibly foreign other (Burbach & Tarbell, 2004, pp. 139–142; Kaplan, 2004). In the ambiguous borderland of Guantanamo, a site where "the many narratives about the Americas intersect," 'enemy combatants' are subjected to solitary confinement and indefinite detention while the Defense Department publicizes its multicultural sensibilities by providing halal food (Kaplan, 2004).

(UN)KNOWING LOCATIONS

After nearly 20 hours of travel from my home in Australia, I arrive in San Francisco. As I move into another spatiality, which is by most rational indices similar to the place where I live—English speaking, Western, and "democratic"—I experience quite profound culture shock. Clearly, I have made too many assumptions of similarities. The shock starts at the airport at Los Angeles (LAX), ostensible gateway to the United States for visitors from the Pacific Rim. Approached by two beggars in the American Airlines lounge while I wait for a delayed connecting flight to San Francisco, I am struck by the visibilities of poverty in this very public space, a veritable Third World in this very first of First World nations. One man gives me a barely legible pamphlet in very poor English describing the plight of a group of Korean orphans in Los Angeles. Another addresses me in Spanish. I am too afraid to reach for my wallet and look away. Two seats away, a physically disabled Caucasian man in a wheelchair, surrounded by plastic bags, is engaged in a loud and abusive conversation with his mother. Exhaustion overtakes me and I doze and wake in fits and starts, feeling to see if my luggage is still there. I wonder if this picture confronts international students when they arrive to start their education in America. Do they see the Third World in the First World as I do?

The tensions and contradictions of traveling into a space that is both similar and different continues, made worse by my body's physiology that is unconvinced that the constraints of geography have receded. Because of last-minute stresses in preparing for fieldwork, I haven't spent sufficient time, prearrival, to investigate accommodation options. In San Francisco, I manage to end up in SOMA (South of Market Area), an area known as the 'tenderloin' quarter. The metaphor is unambiguous for denoting vice and crime. My room is incredibly filthy and I am reminded of my backpacking holidays off the beaten track in Southeast Asia, except the cost of a room then was more like 60c, not US$60 I have just paid. I collect my bags and manage to negotiate a departure without penalty. The Irish receptionist is sympathetic as I mumble something about being at the wrong place, "I haven't entered your details in yet. So, it's OK." The fetid stench of the shabby street hits me as I try to hail a cab. Yet this is a crow's flight away from Silicon Valley, the nexus of capitalist enterprise and wealth.

The cab driver who stops is a Palestinian. In between phone calls (he is trying to sell a restaurant), he tells me that he came to the United States in 1976 as a refugee. It is not too bad living here but he doesn't like the government's double standards of appeasing Israel while punishing the Iraqis. I am deposited at a youth hostel in Union Square, which thankfully has retained its basic cleanliness since my last visit. My roommates are two other travelers: Hazel, a Malaysian-Chinese, and Karen, a Norwegian who works as an au pair in London. I start to feel a bit more connected; I am linked to both places by friendships, family ties, nostalgia, and affection. We make arrangements to go out together the next day.

The next morning, I head for Stanford University where I have an appointment with staff at the Bechtel International Center. I end up walking to the train station through SOMA's streets, passing many homeless people wrapped in blankets to ward off the first chilly signs of autumn. I try to connect with "my" spatial world through the San Francisco Chronicle *newspaper during the train journey to Palo Alto. It takes thumbing through pages of advertisements—autumn sales, Halloween sales, opening sales, closing down sales—to finally find* The World *squeezed into two pages in an obscure part of the paper. Arriving at Palo Alto station, I board the Marguerite bus, a free service to Stanford University. I find myself next to a Thai doctor who has come to Stanford on a government training program to specialize in ophthalmology. Does he like it here, I ask. "It is very competitive." His smile betrays the anxiety in his eyes. He gets off at the Stanford Medical Center and the bus drives on for several kilometers. I have to get off and catch a connecting Marguerite bus to get to the Bechtel International Center. I am no stranger to universities, having at various times visited friends and family at the elites, but even so, I am unprepared for the size of Stanford, which brings a new meaning to the term* greenfields *campus.*

For the savvy practitioners of consumer brand names, universities such as Stanford are highly desirable places in which to study. For international students, this is a perception also fueled by government policy. Singapore's romance with the American mindset in education means that Stanford receives the recipients of both private sector and Singapore government scholarships—a good sign of quality in the eyes of many Singaporeans. Stanford also retains its positional status, as it is not frequented by the average Singaporean. No chance of encountering "Ah Bengs"[21] *out here. However, what I do see are numerous people of Asian Indian extraction, the most recent representatives of the model minority in the American race matrix.*

For a novice researcher like me, with limited time and worse, a limited budget, the sheer size and complexity of Stanford presents several problems in identifying whom to speak to. I eventually end up at the Bechtel International Center. The Center was built by donations from the Bechtel Corporation, an engineering-construction firm that has telecommunication interests and significant investments in developing countries.[22] *The center is described as a place that "provides opportunities for direct international experiences" by way of facilitating interactions between the international and domestic student and scholar communities at Stanford (Bechtel International Center, 2001, p. 4).*

It is a handsome white building located near the Staff Club and close to the student amenities area with its cluster of cafes, the sports center, and bookshop. The center's foyer opens to a handsome, bright, and airy drawing room. In one corner, there is

---

[21]An Ah Beng is usually a Hokkien-Chinese, a working-class Singaporean who is thought to lack finesse.

[22]The Bechtel Corporation was established in 1898. It is a fourth-generation family business with an annual turnover in 2000 of US$14.5 billion (Bechtel Corporation, 2002). It is the U.S. government's preferred contractor for much of the reconstruction work in Iraq.

a beautiful grand piano; at the end closest to the foyer are two well-appointed sofas.
There are no artifacts that may suggest the non-Western world adorning the walls or
coffee tables. However, I later find out that the clock that shows the times in various
cities around the world (I note Sydney) was a present from the Japanese Student Asso-
ciation in the early 1980s. Also due to Japanese largesse is a large-screen TV and
VCR, which is connected to the university cable system to allow international news
shows to be viewed and recorded at the center. The rest of the ground floor is occupied
by meeting rooms for student use. At one end of the ground floor a set of doors connects
to a paved courtyard, which leads to a hall. An elderly American woman, immacu-
lately groomed, with well-coiffured hair, sits behind a beautifully crafted antique-
looking table in the foyer. She directs me to the staff offices upstairs, a warren of rooms
that are less impressive and staff who are friendly, although obviously overwhelmed
with work.

International education is more than the production and consumption of infor-
mation, knowledge, and credentials. It also presents rich possibilities to develop net-
works of human relationships, although the complexities and ambiguities of spatial
and cultural displacements can act as deterrents. At 10:30 a.m., I join the spouses
group—all women—for morning tea. They are wives of postgraduate (graduate) in-
ternational students and visiting fellows. The room and its multicultural, interna-
tional occupants represent a warehouse of cross-cultural scenarios. There are a large
number of Japanese and German wives, some from Sweden and Finland, Morocco,
Portugal, and Korea. This is the first meeting for the new academic year, to welcome
the new arrivals. A program of activities for the semester is announced. To an out-
sider like me, the activities appear extraordinarily old-fashioned, hearkening back to
another era where gender roles were fixed, with women lives centered around the
home. It is not what I would have associated with an intellectual center. The first
workshop for spouses will focus on Christmas wreath making. A future workshop will
be belly dancing, to be conducted by one of the wives from Morocco. A 'potlatch' has
also been organized where the visitors will be matched with an American family for
Thanksgiving dinner. The announcer, an elderly volunteer, with just the faintest
hint of disapproval in her voice tells the "ladies" that "this is a nice opportunity but
no one took it up last year." They must "bring a plate of food to share" and must regis-
ter no later than Monday. I am surprised that the announcer does not make any at-
tempt to historically, and culturally, contextualize 'potlatch' and 'Thanksgiving' for
the visitors. Perhaps, their meanings have eclipsed for Americans too, or perhaps the
assumption is that everyone has these celebrations.

A children's playgroup, organized by some of the German wives, is running at one
end of the hall. The Japanese women cluster together, speaking to each other in Japa-
nese. They have to be reminded by discreet coughs from the International Student Ad-
visor not to speak to each other while she is addressing the group. By contrast, the Eu-
ropean women in the group are much more confident. They all speak fluent English
and in conversation with them, I find that most are professionals in their home coun-

try. For some, it is their second trip to Stanford, having first accompanied their hus-
bands when they were undertaking doctoral studies. It has not been easy to establish
friends with the Americans: "They are not friendly. They will say, 'hi.' But they are
not interested in making friendships." They are mystified about why Americans have
such an aversion to paying taxes. This seems to be an ideological point of contention
and several other nationalities join in as well. The tea ends after about an hour and
a half, with some women lingering on to chat.

STANFORD UNIVERSITY

Established in 1891 by Leland Stanford, in memory of his deceased son,
Stanford University was intended to be:

> a great university, one that, from the outset, was untraditional: co-educa-
> tional, in a time when most were all-male; non-denominational, when most
> were associated with a religious organization; avowedly practical, producing
> "cultured and useful citizens." (Stanford University, 2002)

Stanford was part of a group of 19th-century American industrialists,
along with J. P. Morgan, Carnegie, Rockefeller, and Vanderbilt, who were
described as robber barons. Altenberg (1990) makes this observation of the
barons,

> After a lifetime of accumulating untold sums of money, many came to be phi-
> lanthropists. . . . This certainly softened the image of the Robber Baron, and
> these exercises of noblesse oblige had the effect of demonstrating that the
> Robber Baron might promote the general welfare as well as appropriating it
> for himself.

Names such as Carnegie and Rockefeller continue to be associated with
higher education philanthropy today.[23] This long historical association between higher education and the largesse of entrepreneurs is notable in normalizing the links between American universities and the business community. As the robber barons demonstrated, entrepreneurial appropriations
no matter how duplicitous, can still deliver productive possibilities for the
recipients of their largesse.

---

[23]For example, the Carnegie Foundation for the Advancement of Teaching is a national
and international center for research and policy studies about teaching. The Carnegie Institute of Washington funds and is engaged in basic research and advanced science education,
particularly in biology, astronomy, and the earth sciences. The Rockefeller Foundation funds
various overseas development projects.

In 2003–2004, there were 3,007 international students at Stanford (*Open Doors*, 2004) out of a total student population of 15,104.[24] In 2003, 58% of the university's foreign students were from Asian countries (Stanford University, 2003).

Persuading Without Promotion: Elite Marketing

Stanford stands aloof from American universities that strive for competitive advantage by aggressive marketing. Its promotional materials take a relatively low-key approach. Earlier versions of its promotional and marketing materials were largely devoid of student images, preferring instead a largely nonhuman semiotic materiality to showcase the institution.[25] The 2004 Web site departs from this tradition and features a greater number of student and staff images, more pictures of its buildings and grounds, and a new logo (Stanford University, 2004). The spirit of interdisciplinary inquiry, captured in Stanford's motto, "the wind of freedom blows" (Stanford University, 2004) is promoted along with its culture of innovation. "Stanford ideas that changed the world" carries black-and-white images that create a long history of innovation and enterprise. There are no student testimonials or personal endorsements but there are numerous references to the university's illustrious alumni such as the Father of Silicon Valley (Bill Terman); various entrepreneurs (e.g., Jerry Yang of Yahoo fame); 17 Nobel laureates, 4 Pulitzer Prize winners; and Supreme Court justices. The 2004 Web site actively promotes the university's community, a shift from an earlier version that depicted a more remote institution with only incidental images of its students (see Stanford University, 2004).

A hard sell and strongly persuasive 'why choose Stanford' message is absent, suggesting that its promotional materials speak to a selective group with certain desires and ambitions. It is possible, too, that Stanford's primary target is not the first-generation customer, and certainly not the average young person. As with many elite institutions, it seeks to reproduce itself through a series of discreet recruitment and promotional activities, for example, through its network of alumni and benefactors. Thus, whereas an ordinary place-based university might focus on the local high school, Stanford's international recruitment involves linking up with clusters of geographically dispersed feeder schools, such as the overseas American schools that cater to the educational needs of American expatriates. Stanford's re-

---

[24]In 2003, Stanford had 6,500 undergraduates and 7,700 graduate students.

[25]The marketing dictum that service marketers are noted for extravagant use of physical imagery in their advertising whereas product marketers tend to use abstract ideas offers some hints on the discursive constructions of this university. The university does not perceive itself as part of a service industry. Stanford is secure in the knowledge that it offers a particular educational product, the benefits of which need no promotion or public explanation.

cruiting geography is an elite constituency that has the means to pay the yearly charges of US$35,000 to attend Stanford.

In a discursive field noted for enrollment consultants, recruitment specialists, and college marketing companies, where the use of geodemographic data, personality inventories, and statistical tools are commonplace (see Sevier, 2000; Hite & Yearwood, 2001), a more subtle form of education marketing is taking place at Stanford. Where publications such as the *Journal of College Admission* and the *Journal of Higher Education Marketing* work to produce an art and science of marketing, Stanford authors a more traditional type of marketing that is centered around using its alumni, showcasing its trophy professors and promoting its research entrepreneurialism.

A Universal Education for Enterprise

The Stanford Business School's Web site is instructive in revealing how the educated subject is understood and molded by this high-status institution, and further, how the university constructs itself (see Fig. 4.1):

> Stanford Business School students come from all over the world. They have done every type of job and activity imaginable. Students are competitive, but they benefit from a supportive, cooperative environment. The Business School community provides ample opportunities for students to share and learn from one another, as well as work closely with a superb faculty. (Stanford University Graduate School of Business [GSB], 2003)

The lexical devices in this text are unambiguously clear about the importance of competitiveness, and its universal importance: "Students come from all over the world. . . . Students are competitive." Presumably, competitiveness has its limits and this is where the "superb" Business School faculty step in to facilitate the creation of opportunities for "students to share and learn from one another." The GSB is constructed as having global appeal. It attracts students who are geographically and occupationally dispersed: "They come from all over the world" and "have done every job and activity imaginable." The intended audience of prospective applicants is thus not only those working within the business, economics, and commerce fields, but in any other imaginable domain. At work here is a discursive logic that seeks to reproduce and consolidate the dispersion of business rationalities into social relations and practices in every geographical and occupational discursive domain. It is an overwhelmingly neoliberal vision.

The core values of the GSB reside in risk taking—complacency is not an option—continuous learning, collaboration, and integrity. Much is made

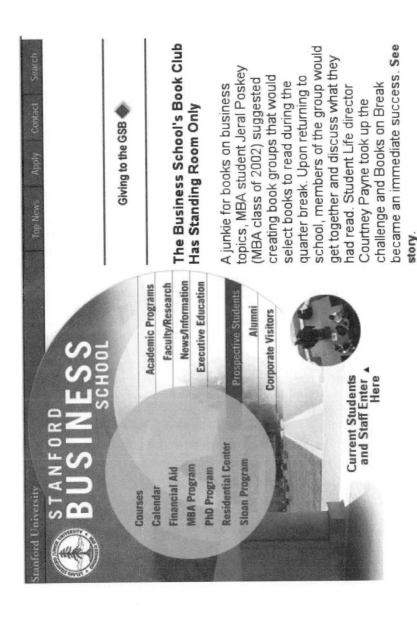

FIG. 4.1. Stanford Business School Web site.

of the curriculum that is described as "world class, dynamic, forward looking, and innovative . . . enriched constantly . . . each year about one-fifth of
our course offerings are new." GSB graduates are talented, well rounded,
future leaders who can "manage change and meet the unknown and the
unforeseeable." At the same time, the GSB claims to "promote an enduring
style of thinking" (Stanford University, GSB, 2003). These narratives are
less contradictory than they first appear. Dynamism, continuous learning,
and forward thinking are permissible within defined and enduring parameters only. We can expect the graduate then to be subject to a set of fixed
truths, and one who is unwavering in his or her convictions.

Living With the Other in the International University

Although the university appears to be encouraging diversity in its student
body, it is not very clear from official textual materials why this is a desirable
outcome. This statement extracted from the Web site link titled *Campus Life*
embodies this ambivalence:

> [The university] believes in the value of diversity and seeks a graduate student
> body that is both highly qualified and diverse in terms of culture, class, ethnic-
> ity, background, work and life experiences, skills and interests . . . African
> Americans, Mexican Americans, Native Americans, and Puerto Ricans as well
> as others whose backgrounds and experience provide additional dimensions
> to the University's programs. (Stanford University Registrar's Office, 2002)

An institutional desire for a graduate student body that is *both* highly
qualified and diverse implies clear limits to affirmative action initiatives:
The desired subjectivity is the elite other who has the right qualities to assimilate into Stanford's sociocultural and academic milieu. A clearer rationale for engagement with diversity is provided in this description of the university's liberal education programs:

> an education that broadens the student's knowledge and awareness in each of
> the major areas of human knowledge . . . to understand the important "ways
> of knowing" to assess their strengths and limitations, their uniqueness, and no
> less important, what they have in common with others. (Stanford University,
> 2000, p. 21)

There are hints here of an institutional acceptance and promotion of
multiple ways of knowing, although a closer reading reveals less discursive
space for alternative ontologies and epistemologies. It is power and its myriad relations that will ascertain what are the *important* ways of knowing.
There is a definitiveness in Stanford's references to "*the* major areas of human knowledge," which suggests the superiority of a singular, universal
knowledge.

Less veiled in admitting to the tensions arising from self-other differences is Stanford University's 2000 *Orientation Handbook for International Graduate Students*. The handbook warns of culture shock:

> You may start to feel homesick, miss your family and friends, idealize your life back home while being highly critical of life in the US. . . . Some term this as culture shock and it can include frustration, anxiety, anger, minor health problems, difficulty in forming new friendships, lack of motivation, disruptions in eating and sleeping patterns. . . . These are natural reactions to living in a new culture. (Bechtel International Center, 2000, p. 10)

By alerting students to the emotional and physical health problems arising from entry into a new cultural space, the turbulence of the intercultural encounter is medicalized. The stranger, in this instance, the international student, is also warned about emotional-cognitive dissonance, which includes frustration, anxiety, and a tendency to "idealize your life back home while being highly critical of life in the US" (Bechtel International Center, 2000). A series of suggestions, framed in the imperative, instructs students to "take responsibility to get through this period":

- Make contact with students and scholars from your home country.
- Ask questions. Most US students are very willing to answer questions.
- Try not to evaluate and judge.
- Show openness and curiosity; be open to new experiences.
- Show a sense of humor. If you can laugh at your mistakes it will ease your anxiety (Bechtel International Center, 2000).

A subsequent section titled "American Values and Assumptions" purports to offer advice on American sociocultural norms as a means of promoting adjustment: "To help you adjust, we have compiled a brief explanation of why Americans behave as they do." A list of American values follows: individualism and privacy, equality, achievement, informality, and attitudes to the future, change, and progress:

> The most important thing to understand about Americans is probably their devotion to "individualism." They have been trained since early in their lives to consider themselves as separate individuals who are responsible for their situations in life and their own destinies. They have not been trained to see themselves as members of a close-knit family, tribe, religious group, nation or other collectivity. (Bechtel International Center, 2000, p. 12)

The American subject emerges as a responsible, independent-minded individual who exercises agency over his or her destiny. These statements do not acknowledge the tenacious hold of American exceptionalism on the national psyche. It is beyond the scope of this study to undertake a deconstruction of American nation-building and citizen-formation technologies, aside from noting that this statement celebrating the rugged American individual clearly neutralizes any assumptions that others may hold about American nationalism and its military, political, and economic hegemony.

Not all constructions of the American subject in the handbook are positive. This is evident, for example, in references to their "superficial friendliness," and a tendency to: "sometimes violate the ideal of equality in their daily lives, particularly in matters of interracial relationships" (Bechtel International Center, 2000, p. 12). However, such violations are constructed as occasional transgressions ("sometimes") rather than a reflection of a systemic and institutionalized culture of violating the other. By far and large though, the nation and its people are discursively constructed as progressive and dynamic: "They look ahead. They have the idea that what happens in the future is within their control. They believe that people can change most aspects of their physical and social environment" (p. 13). The future is not problematized, the assumption being that there is only one future.

The statements in the handbook also construct Americans as honest and hard working by using a collage of lexical items such as: "achievement centered," "hard workers," "approach a task conscientiously and persistently through to successful conclusion." They are noted for inspiring awe from foreigners: "Foreign visitors commonly remark that Americans work harder than I expected them to." Americans are "frank, open, direct in their dealings with other people" (Bechtel International Center, 2000, p. 13). A number of statements work to consolidate the American subjectivity by contrasting it with a less favorable other who is not as wise as Americans in the use of time and not as authentic in the communication of emotions, a hint that the inscrutable "Oriental" is unwelcome: "Americans are not taught as people in many Asian countries are, that they should mask their emotional responses." Moreover,

> In their efforts to use their time wisely, Americans are sometimes seen by foreign visitors as automatons, inhuman creatures who are so tied to their clocks and their schedules that they cannot particiate in or enjoy the human interactions that are the truly important in life. "They are like little machines running around," one foreign visitor said. For Americans, time is a "resource" that can be used well or poorly. . . . The future will not be better than the past or the present . . . unless people use their time for constructive, future oriented tasks . . . One of the most difficult things many foreign busines people and students must adjust to is the notion that time must be saved whenever possible and used wisely every day. (Bechtel International Center, 2000, p. 14)

These statements indicate a persistent rationalism with its attendant beliefs of individualism and instrumentalism, depicted here in American understandings of time. In all, an American subjectivity emerges that is wise, dynamic, and achievement centered. American values are denoted as culturally exceptional, and a series of warnings and admonitions to the foreign student construct foreign values as problematic. American exceptionalism functions as a governmentality that seeks to reinforce the uniqueness of American norms.

As an expression of globalization, international education can reasonably be read as altering the experiences of proximity and social connectedness. Waters (2001) typifies the stance taken by many theorists who associate globalization with transnational and transcultural social relations: "Relationships between people in disparate locations will be formed as easily as people in proximate ones" (p. 5). Hence, we could reasonably expect that in an international university like Stanford, with its seemingly cosmopolitan, intellectually elite individuals who are consumers of global symbols, signs, and norms, that territorially defined boundaries between people will be removed. People who speak a common language and who have shared aspirations would surely find territorially constructed distinctions of self and other unsatisfactory. However, there appears to be a conflict between what social theorists are saying about the impact of globalization on supraterritorial social relations and student narratives that point to the enduring symbolisms of national identities and powerful asymmetries framed by broader political and economic factors.

Even though geographical distances are obliterated by on-campus living and studying arrangements, spatial barriers manage to reassert themselves into the social spaces of this international university. International students attribute this to a general American disinterest in the non-American world, a strongly insular orientation that they perceived as "extreme ignorance" of the global, including their cultures and their countries.[26]

> It was orientation day. . . . Because international students arrived first and I pretty much knew where things are . . . they were looking for the bookstore and I overheard them. went and told them and she is, like, "you speak Eng-

---

[26]The students I interviewed for this study included three Chinese-Singaporeans, of whom two were female (Mei-ling and Yoke Lan) and one was male (Michael); a Malay-Malaysian female student (Salmah); and a Hong Kong Chinese female student who was born in Indonesia and completed a large part of her education in Toronto, Canada (Moira). All names have been changed. Michael, Mei-ling, Yoke Lan, and Salmah were recipients of private sector scholarships. Salmah, Yoke Lan, and Moira could reasonably be classified cosmopolitan. They were well traveled and multilingual, had attended school in different countries, and counted themselves as being part of several different spatial communities.

lish?" "Yes." "You speak good English! Where are you from?" I [said] am from Hong Kong. . . . "Oh, Hong Kong! I have been to Hiroshima and Tokyo too." . . . They didn't even know. . . . Just because I look Chinese. (Moira, Hong Kong and Canadian nationality, born in Indonesia)

Although many international students are motivated to acquire exposure to different worlds, ideas, and people, it cannot be assumed that their American peers hold the same expectations. When read against the othering statements of the handbook, these student narratives suggest that the nation-state (America) continues to shape commonsense understandings of outsiders or strangers from other territorial spaces. The discourse of American exceptionalism (America's manifest destiny as world leader) can assert itself in the social spaces of this international university where it reaffirms boundaries between the American nation-state and others.

> In an era of globalisation it is very important to be aware what is going on in the world. Even if it is Pakistan or Cambodia. I find it fascinating how uninterested they are in international affairs. . . . They are so insular. It really baffles me completely. . . . I think the whole insularity and the inward-lookingness is just not healthy. (Mei-Ling, Singaporean female)

The students' critical views do not suggest a passive, compliant, and inert subjectivity that is entirely accepting of broader geopolitical power relations. Living and studying in America had demystified the country, its people, and the ideals associated with it. This was evident in the terms and phrases used to describe America: protectionist, glorified, propaganda. At the same time, a set of contradictory impulses were evident in the students' keen appreciation of American economic achievements along with their desire to emulate these achievements despite their reservations about American values and ideologies:

> If you look at the Internet boom and all these entrepreneurial things . . . "we are going to achieve the world" . . . and amazon dot com . . . and even how their country started . . . I think that is something that Asia can do with. And it is something that you can't do by giving a billion dollars and a technopreneur fund, or 10 million dollars and a life science fund. . . . So . . . that is very interesting. (Yoke Lan, Singaporean female)

The rationalities that delivered the "Internet boom" and "entrepreneurial things" are accorded the status of received wisdom: "That is something that Asia can do with." In their entirety, these narratives raise the possibility that self–other identifications are still being defined by territoriality, despite the considerable mobility enjoyed by people, including this intellectually elite group of international students. Even in universities that espouse to be international institutions, foreign students are discursively constructed as others from a less developed spatiality, through comparisons with 'achievement-centered', 'responsible', 'independent-minded', 'hard working', efficient Americans. It is against this backdrop that a remolding of student subjectivities takes place.

It is possible in some cases for this remolding to take the form of a renationalization (reterritorialization) of student subjectivities. For this group of students, though, a critical and reflexive subjectivity emerges that questions the market-like subjectivities and political passivity that predominates in the hypercompetitive, commercially oriented societies of Hong Kong and Singapore:

> That is something I would like to change about Singapore. I would like young people to make a difference. That they would go out and distribute flyers and put out notices on the internet. Like we want to save the spotted salamander. . . . That would be cool. Instead of saying I want to make . . . a five figure salary! (Mei-Ling, Singaporean female)

> In very local Hong Kong culture, . . . they go along with *whatever* is popular! Let's say in Japan, whatever is popular, whatever is popular in the US . . . and . . . people won't open up to other alternatives . . . like . . . "people are going to do that . . . let's do that!" I want them to think for themselves . . . what is right for them. . . . I want them to be more individual. (Moira, Hong Kong, female)

The experience of studying overseas also creates possibilities for the development of a new student subjectivity that is critical of norms encountered in both home and host countries—insularity, conformism, hyperconsumption, and authoritarianism. The intercultural encounters that emerge from student ethnoscapes do not necessarily enable ideational synergies, particularly not on the parts of hegemons, nations, cultures, and ethnicities that are secure in their positions of relative dominance. Broader social, cultural, historical, and geographical contexts continue to influence how international students are perceived on campus. On the parts of American hosts, indifference can function to reinforce the American position of relative dominance. For international students, the same indifference enables them to manage the turbulence of the intercultural encounter, to retain their core values, and to resist ethnocentric stereotyping.

In spite of official pronouncements on the value of diversity within the university, the dominance of a discourse of American exceptionalism reinforces binaries between them and us. This limits the possibilities of reconstituting subjectivities to those that express and engage with globally oriented citizenships. Therefore, although both globalization and international education are rhetorically framed as contributing to a dissolution of boundaries, institutional micropractices and student narratives suggest that geographies of differences remain and that these are profoundly influential on social relations. Transnational and transcultural flows can be impeded by discursive practices that fix international students into imagined spatial identities. Such fixing can take myriad forms—being categorized as Chinese and by extension as a non-English speaking person, for example. Furthermore, phrases such as *foreign student,* which abound in official terminology, reinforce this subject position of outsider. The alien subjectivity has assumed new importance after 9-11 as suggested by this directive to Stanford's students:

> Immigration law requires that this university verify the presence of each new international student. In order for your physical presence to be verified, you must appear at the Registrar's Office with your passport (picture ID). A registration block has been placed on your enrollment until you appear at the Registrar's Office so that your physical presence can be verified. (Stanford University, 2004)

The paradoxes and contradictions of transcultural and transnational exchanges that Appadurai (1996) describes so elegantly are also mirrored in the students' desires for an American education. They are critical of American insularity but they are impelled to study in a high-status American university. They regard the Stanford University credential to be an immutable mobile: It is sufficiently stable and robust to move through multiple contexts without losing its legitimacy and authority. It retains its exchange value and as such continues to offer access to positional goods as it moves across spatialities. These productive dimensions to the overseas study sojourn retain their attractiveness to students, despite the phenomenological disjunctions they experience.

I miss the train (Long Island Railroad) because I am waiting at the wrong platform in Penn Station. Secure in the knowledge that there are nearly 3 hours before my interview, and laboring under the illusion that a major public university close to one of the world's largest metropolises will surely be well serviced by public transport, I decide to wait for the next train only to find out that it runs bihourly. I will miss my 11:30 a.m. appointment. I ring the university to apologize and try to reschedule my appointments. "Oh, that train. Yes, I missed it too on my first day at work What about 1 p.m. then? You will be here by then." I locate the right platform, dose myself with caffeine, and prepare to wait.

This time I have more luck with rail staff and Eric, a White American, assures me that I am waiting at the right platform. "Born and raised in New York," he gives me his opinions of the oncoming election. "I think Hilary Clinton will lose. I don't like her. She should just go back to Arkansas because this is New York and we don't appreciate the likes of her." What about her policies? Isn't she campaigning for more affordable health care for working Americans? Eric is unimpressed and states that he will cast his vote for the Republican candidate who is a "real" New Yorker. He couldn't afford a college education but hopes that his children will be able to get the education he didn't.

The train passes through magnificent countryside; the trees dotting the landscape are shrouded in golden autumnal shades. Aesthetically, it is a long distance from the squalor of the tenderloin district of SOMA. Every house I see is tastefully large and surrounded by spacious grounds. Eric returns with some questions about working conditions in Australia, which he has heard are good. He also tells me that his father does not have health insurance coverage because he is a blue-collar worker.

THE STATE UNIVERSITY OF NEW YORK
AT STONY BROOK (SUNY)

SUNY is a state (public) university that is located in four sites: Richmond, Buffalo, Albany, and Stony Brook.[27] SUNY Stony Brook (hereforth referred to as Stony Brook) was established in 1957 and in 1962 moved to its present campus on Long Island. In the 2002–2003 academic year, the university enrolled 21,989 students, of which 2,233 were international students (*Open Doors*, 2003). The Carnegie Classification of Institutions of Higher Education has ranked Stony Brook 39 in its list of top 40 research institutions (*Open Doors*, 2003).

Not all the students classified as foreign students at Stony Brook are fee-paying students. A significant proportion of its doctoral students, particularly those in the technosciences and biomedical sciences, are scholarship recipients. In this respect, Stony Brook reflects the norm among American research universities: The recruitment of international students is not run along the commercial lines favored by British and Australian universities. International students are more likely to be regarded as furthering longer term American foreign policy and economic objectives than providing short-term cash injections for cash-strapped institutions.

HARVESTING KNOWLEDGE GOODS

Like many American universities, Stony Brook targets international graduates rather than undergraduates. This decision is governed by the university's academic priorities, as this comment from a senior staff member indicates:

---

[27]My case study of the university's Stony Brook campus is an accidental choice prompted by a minuscule fieldwork budget and the offer of free accommodation in New York. This deciding factor, coupled with the prompt response from staff at this university, led me to include SUNY Stony Brook in my study.

We find that the interest from domestic students in going into the physical and applied sciences is way down. They have halved. In those disciplines . . . they are only kept alive by international students.

The university's marketing strategy for international students is described as "arm chair marketing": "We have lots of international applicants without doing very much. Twenty years ago we had no Chinese students and now we have 500–600."[28] Advertising to attract international students is the exception rather than the rule because of the costs involved. When it does take place, careful attention is given to where advertisements should be placed. Graduate places may be advertised in discipline-specific journals and publications.

Postgraduate international students in market-attractive disciplines yield knowledge goods for the university and therein lies their attractiveness.[29] Although the higher education system in the United States is largely local or national in orientation and focus, it is not averse to overseas recruitment to acquire the requisite human capital for furthering the aims of a knowledge-based economy. To this end, a political rationality is at work that overrides local trends and idiosyncracies to ensure national and institutional competitiveness in the face of global forces:

> Much of the very best science gets done by graduate students, many of whom are from overseas. . . . A lot of these people are supported on federally funded research finance. . . . Some may say that our mission is primarily to train PhDs with particular emphasis on citizens in the USA. We don't think that that makes much sense because we are competing in a world system. (Dean, male)

The British-educated staffer compared American higher education policies with the rest of the Anglophone world, noting:

> It is a good deal for the US. I mean you get . . . all the way through the Bachelor's Degree at somebody's expense. And then you pick the very brightest in the world to do a PhD for 5 years and then they go on to start up a multimillion dollar company or some "dot com" or work in health care or work in universities. . . . So we are getting the very brightest people around.

In short, the political economy of R&D in the United States plays an influential part in the recruitment of international students. In this case, the recruitment of valued foreign human capital is prompted by a national de-

---

[28]Interview with university executive Dean, November, 2000.

[29]As discussed in chapter 1, the desirability of knowledge goods lies in their status as intellectual property with market value. Knowledge goods can include patents, copyrighted publications, software, and so on (see Marginson, 1997, p. 38).

sire to build a more competitive economy. America's research enterprise draws heavily from the intellectual labor of non-Americans because they are a readily accessible and presumably cheap pool of talent. Staying competitive in a world system is a primary consideration that overrides the responsibility to nurture and develop local talent. At the same time, an internal market operates in selective, market-desirable disciplines, which forces Stony Brook to compete with other American universities for talented graduate students (see Ehrenberg, 2000). Those students at the high end of human capital are in a position to benefit from the competitive dynamics of this internal market:

> It's market driven as much as anything else. Every other American school is offering the same thing. So, if you are going for the high end students, the students from the best university in China . . . whatever . . . they know that they are getting offered free tuition plus a stipend everywhere they apply in the US and . . . they compare how much they get offered. This year in Molecular Biology we pay $18,000 salary after we pay the tuition fees. That is income. I think that the rest of the Anglophone world will have a very tough time competing for those kind of students. (senior staff, male)

Unlike much of the Australian place-branding discourse that focuses on beaches and wildlife attractions, Stony Brook's drawcard is its proximity to a grid of intellectual capital. It markets itself as an intellectual hub that is part of a network that features renowned research institutions such as the Cold Springs Harbor Laboratory. Much is made of the rich and informal interactions assumed to occur with large concentrations of scholars in a small geographical area:

> East of Stony Brook is the Brookhaven National Laboratory, an internationally known center of research in physics, biology, chemistry, and other disciplines. . . . To the west . . . is Cold Springs Harbor Laboratory, well known for its excellence in the biomedical sciences. . . . Long Island region [where Stony Brook is based] is home to growing electronics and biotechnology companies. Many of these have been started by Stony Brook faculty and maintain close ties with the university. . . . Stony Brook is fortunate to be close to two New York cities which provide . . . countless opportunities for collaborations. (SUNY Stony Brook, 2001a, p. 6)

Statements within its promotional literature position Stony Brook as the center of R&D: "At a world-class research university such as Stony Brook, you expect to find world-class researchers and scholars" (SUNY Stony Brook, 2004b). Its leadership role in the international arena is celebrated: "We play leadership roles in the international search for the top quark in particle physics, the molecular basis for genetic forms of diabetes, the cause of Lyme disease, and the psychological causes of domestic violence" (SUNY Stony Brook, 2001b, p.3).

Like Stanford, Stony Brook uses its star-studded, award-winning faculty as a marketing tool:

> Our community of scholars, teachers and researchers includes a Nobel laureate, a Pulitzer Prize winner, five MacArthur Fellows, a Fields prize winner, recipients of the national Medal of Technology and the Benjamin Franklin Medal, 16 members of the National Academy of Sciences, 14 members of the American Academy of Arts and Sciences, and three members of the National Academy of Engineering. Stony Brook's faculty are also dedicated teachers, and include seventy-three recipients of the Chancellor's Awards for Excellence in Teaching. (SUNY Stony Brook, 2004a)

The university tries to bridge the teaching–research chasm, declaring firmly that:

> at a world-class research university such as Stony Brook, you expect to find world-class researchers and scholars. But many of our leading scholars and researchers are also inspiring teachers and they have the awards to prove it. At Stony Brook, we're committed to putting our best teachers into our undergraduate classes. (SUNY Stony Brook, 2004c)

Like most of the other universities examined in this study, the education–economy symbiosis is overwhelmingly present in repeated emphases on the instrumental dimensions of learning: "Stony Brook graduates find that their schooling has prepared them to find places in the world of work"; "Schools and divisions enjoy long-standing partnerships with local and regional businesses" (SUNY Stony Brook, 2001b, p. 4); "They're also in high demand in the workplace, with nearly 600 corporate organizations recruiting on campus" (SUNY Stony Brook, 2004a).

Frequent references to league table rankings in Stony Brook's promotional literature point to an institutional rationality that takes its market profile seriously:

- Stony Brook's faculty rank second in the nation in articles published in prestigious journals (SUNY Stony Brook, 2004d).
- A recent study ranks Stony Brook among the top three public research universities in the nation (SUNY Stony Brook, 2004d).
- Stony Brook is second only to University of California Berkeley in research productivity per faculty member, with 851 inventions and 363 patents issued since 1978 (SUNY Stony Brook, 2004d).
- In the Gourman Report, Stony Brook ranks 46th among all private and public colleges and universities in the nation (SUNY Stony Brook, 2004d).

- Stony Brook faculty rank 12th nationwide among their academic colleagues on citation impact—the frequency with which their work is cited by other scientists (SUNY Stony Brook, 2002).

These pronouncements suggest an institutional subjectivity that is competitive and market savvy, and claims membership in the club of elite American public universities. The use of market analogies to construct audit criteria and benchmarks work as technologies of government to shape the subjectivities of individual staff and to produce new institutional structures that are lean, fit, and flexible, while simultaneously producing epistemological shifts in the university's teaching and research activities (Lemke, 2001, pp. 202–203). The resultant governmentality is one that could marginalize the more abstract, albeit critical, functions of the international university, including those that impinge on its civic responsibilities (see Cooper, 2002, pp. 227–231; Halliday, 1999).

EXPAND YOUR UNIVERSE: ENGAGING
WITH THE OTHER

Expand Your Universe (SUNY Stony Brook, 2001b), a generic promotional brochure produced by the Office of Undergraduate Admissions, is intended to provide an overview of the disciplines taught and researched at Stony Brook. Its front cover carries the profile of a female student, with a constellation of stars projected onto her head (see Fig. 4.2). The describing text states:

> Swirling inside the head of Jennifer Jacobs, class of '97, is a photo of the most distant objects ever seen in space. Recently discovered by Stony Brook professors Kenneth Lanzetta and Amos Yahil and a colleague from Spain, the galaxies are so far away that they may have existed when the universe had been barely born. (SUNY Stony Brook, 2001b, p. 1)

An uneven positioning of the subjects of discourse emerges. "Jennifer Jacobs, a '97 student and two Stony Brook professors Kenneth Lanzetta and Amos Yahil" are given an identity but this legitimacy is not conferred to the Spanish researcher who remains nameless ("a colleague from Spain"). By default, the exceptional American effort is consolidated.

Expand Your Universe is packed with images of a diverse student body and diverse faculty. The phenotypically diverse Stony Brook faculty are described as "Stimulants of the First Rank" and are pictured along with a list of awards they have won (see Fig. 4.3). The captions accompanying the images

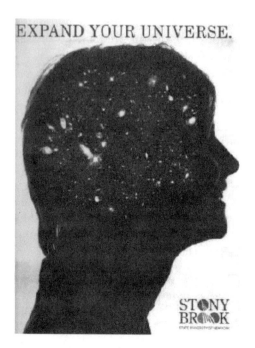

EXPAND YOUR UNIVERSE.

ST●NY
BR●●K

FIG. 4.2.   Promoting Stony Brook.

suggest a university keen to showcase its multidisciplinary and multicultural talent (SUNY Stony Brook, 2001b, pp. 4–5).

This bold institutional effort to link cultural diversity with excellence is less successful elsewhere in its web-based promotional materials that carry bland references to "a cosmopolitan student body" and "students hailing from 80 countries" (SUNY Stony Brook, 2004a; see also SUNY Stony Brook, 2001d, Fig. 4.4). The diversity on campus theme appears several times in numerous other sites, although like the Stanford prospectus, the rhetoric on diversity leaves more to the imagination than to elaboration. There is the merest of hints that the aim is to recruit a high-achieving other: high-achieving students from underrepresented groups rather than to institute a bold affirmative action program.

Stony Brook's Host Family Program, which is offered by the International Student Services office, offers additional insights into how self–other relations are understood by the university:[30]

---

[30]I have selected the Host Family Program which commenced about 25 years ago, for analysis as it is a program that has the potential to develop relationships (social capital networks) between international students and Americans. The program recruits families, single people, and couples from the community. The frequency of contact varies with the parties involved and can be anything from sporadic to regular.

JEROME Z. LIANG, Associate Professor
Departments of Radiology and Computer Sciences
Ph.D. 1987, City University of New York

Jerome Liang focuses his attention on the development of medical imaging hardware for single photon detection. This work includes creating a quantitative SPECT imaging modality as a cost-effective means for patient diagnosis as well as developing a high resolution PET as a functional research imaging modality. Liang is also striving to create a virtual colonoscopy as a cost-effective procedure for colon screening and to construct an automatic method for brain-tissue segmentation for diagnosis of disorders. In addition, he plans to build various models, in terms of physics, mathematics, and statistics, to simulate the practical problems above and then to validate the models by experiments. Liang has published his findings in journals such as *Magnetic Resonance Medicine.*

(631) 444-7837, JZL@clio.rad.sunysb.edu

FIG. 4.3. Multicultural excellence.

107

The majority of international students are in graduate programs with high academic aspirations and achievement. They are bright, talented young men and women from different countries who will generally be in positions of leadership upon return to their home country. (SUNY Stony Brook, 2000)

The international student is defined as a member of an intellectually elite group, a model minority ("bright, talented," "high aspirations and achievement") whereas the American host is constructed as diplomat, pastoral carer, and friend. The benefits of hosting an international student are described in reciprocal and largely noninstrumental terms (respect, friendships):

You can fulfil the mission of a private ambassador for a better future when international students experience your warmth, and acceptance in the community. . . . Long-time host families will tell you that some of their warmest memories are of times spent with their international student and of the rewarding experience of developing long-lasting friendships in the process. . . .

Children who have contacts with international students are more aware of the world around them and will be able to use such experiences to their advantage as they learn to respect and interact with people with different ideas, practices and values. (Interview with Stony Brook staff, November 2000)

The economic and political rationalities which underpin contemporary expressions of international education are perceived to be impediments to attempts to reconfigure self–other relations on campus:

What really drives it [international education] in this country . . . the strongest selling point for international education, [is] more about learning other people's customs so that we can continue to have the upper hand in the global economy. I mean, that is the bottom line and the harsher reality. If Congress for example, is going to call for an International Education Week, it would be, "Americans need to learn other languages so that they can compete in the global marketplace." It is not because they can make friends with other people. (staff, female)

A list of barriers to transcultural relations are noted including: workload demands on international students who have strict timelines for completing their studies, vastly different communication styles, a desire to remain within culturally comfortable groups where dissonance from the failed intercultural encounter is less likely ("a comfortable place to find folks from your country . . . make fewer mistakes"), and finally, different expectations of friendships ("a lot of students encounter false friendliness from Americans that doesn't have anything behind it"). There is also the matter of host students who may have been socialized to accept assimilation as the norm and thus bring this expectation to their intercultural interactions:

FIG. 4.4. Stony Brook's International Services Web site.

The American way is . . . that everybody will come here and learn English and learn our way. . . . So everyone will do things our way and everything will be our way. (staff, female)

The plural possibilities offered by the cultural dimensions of globalization are limited by an American-inspired homogeneity:

Globalization sounds like maybe, something that is OK. It is hard to be against something that is "world this" and "world that." But I think that it is more of a development of a pervasive one-culture . . . definitely the American culture. (senior staff, male)

Globalization? From my perspective it means exchanging ideas or goods across regional boundaries and cultural boundaries. So, it is like everything looking like plain vanilla in the end. (staff, female)

Dissenting views like the ones above coexist with a nuanced concession to American exceptionalism. It takes a crisis to bring out the more overt symbols of nationalism. Figure 4.5, which appeared on a university web page (*Messages Related to the Twin Towers Tragedy*) elicits the classic Foucauldian question: How has this particular statement appeared and not some other? The university's proximity to New York suggests that its community would have been affected by the Twin Towers tragedy and involved in the aftermath of recovery. However, there could have been any number of alternative images that could have been used to reflect the university's humanitarian sentiments instead of Capitol Hill (the shining city on the hill?) and the American flag, two potent symbols of American nationalism.

THE INSTITUTE OF INTERNATIONAL EDUCATION (IIE): OPENING MINDS

The IIE was developed in 1919. It administers a range of programs on behalf of both government and nongovernment organizations such as the U.S. Department of State, the U.S. Agency for International Development (USAID), various foundations (e.g., the right wing Freeman Foundation), multinational corporations, international organizations, and various development assistance agencies. It also organizes overseas educational exhibitions for member American universities seeking to recruit international students and administers the government sponsored Fulbright Program.

The diversity of education programs administered by the IIE are far greater than those run by either its British and Australian equivalents, the

FIG. 4.5. Flying the flag.

111

British Council and IDP Education Australia. A cursory mapping of the network of programs offered by the IIE, its sponsors, their interests, and their
links with circuits of power, influence, and capital is instructive, although the
matter-of-fact, instrumental tenor of the IIE narrative renders their politics
opaque. A significant proportion of the 250 programs the IIE administers are
backed by private sector sponsors, such as investment banker, Goldman
Sachs, which funds the Goldman Sachs Global Leaders Program. It aims to
"ensure visionary leadership for the new century by nurturing talented young
people from across the globe" (IIE, 2002). The IIE also runs the Freeman
Foundation–sponsored AsiaJobSearch, a web-based employment search service that links Asian graduates of U.S. colleges and universities with employers in East and Southeast Asia;[31] Global Partners, which matches American-
educated international employees with U.S. firms undertaking global operations; and Global Careers Service, which has the stated aim of "assisting
[IIE] fellowship recipients . . . to obtain leadership-track positions in their
home countries" (IIE, 2002). Also in place are a series of short-term Professional Exchange Programs that are aimed at providing "professional development for leaders and specialists from other nations."

   The IIE's motto, Opening Minds to the World, is strongly internationalist:

> Peace and prosperity in the 21st Century depend on increasing the capacity
> of people to think and work on a global and intercultural basis. As technology
> opens borders, educational and professional exchange opens minds. (IIE,
> 2002)

The theme of open borders, open minds is a recurrent one:

> IIE believes that the means for creating a better world community is investing
> in people through international education. Since our founding the Institute
> has fostered the free flow of knowledge and ideas across national boundaries,
> in the conviction that no nation can prosper economically, culturally, or intel-
> lectually in isolation from the rest of the world. (IIE, 2001)

   By discursively linking isolation with a failure to prosper, the suggestion
is that no country can prosper in isolation from American political, cultural, and economic enterprise. Elsewhere lexical links between prosperity,
enterprise, and the free flow of ideas have the effect of normalizing free
trade and knowledge capitalism. The numerous IIE programs that are
aimed at helping other countries open their markets are illustrative. The

---

[31]The Freeman Foundation is part of the Foundation for Economic Education (FEE). Established in 1946, it describes itself as a research and philanthropic organization aimed at promoting individual freedom, private property, limited government, and free trade (FEE, 2002).

Emerging Markets Development Advisors Program (EMDAP), for example, is described "as an opportunity for US graduate business students to provide management assistance to small- and medium-sized enterprises in developing countries" (IIE, 2002).

The Institute's espousal of internationalist goals, expressed as the "free flow of knowledge and ideas across national boundaries" says little about the need for reciprocity of these free flows. It obscures the issue of whose knowledge is able to cross boundaries. Instead, the tenacious discourse of governing and knowing reappears: "Asia is of increasing importance to America's economic well-being and global security, making knowledge of Asia increasingly vital to our future success" (IIE, 2001; see also IIE, 2003). Linking America's economic well-being with global security resurrects the Cold War discourse that established and sustained educational aid programs and the field of international education.

The nuanced language of phrases such as 'knowledge shared across borders' and 'free flows of knowledge' obscures the extent to which education, aid, and trade are used to consolidate U.S. political, cultural, and economic hegemony. The imagining of a humane hegemon renders invisible the roles played by successive U.S. governments and American corporations in driving the globalization of intellectual property regimes such as TRIPS (Trade Related Intellectual Property Rights). Regimes such as TRIPS escalate the costs of goods deemed 'knowledge rich' while biopiracy practices appropriate traditional foods and medicines only to deny adequate compensation to the poorest communities in the world (Africa News Service, 2003; Drahos & Braithwaite, 2002; Fisher & Ponniah, 2003; Parry, 2002, 2004; Sidley, 2003; Stiglitz, 2002).

Impact, another IIE publication goes further in consolidating a humanitarian and visionary subjectivity for both the IIE and the United States. Its language credits both entities with: "rescuing threatened scholars," "fostering understanding through Fulbright," "repairing a damaged earth," and so on (see IIE, 2003). What is not acknowledged is the strategic calculus of American economic and foreign policies in producing some of these problems.[32] Repairing a damaged earth, for example, rings hollow given the U.S. government's failure to endorse the Kyoto Agreement and its generally hostile position on environmental concerns. Although much discursive effort is directed at creating the notion of a green model of capitalism by a corporate-sponsored public relations machinery (in connivance with the

---

[32]For example, under the heading. "Helping rebuilding countries," *Impact* notes that East Timor attained independence "after five decades of bloody violence which claimed the lives of 200,000 people and saw the destruction of 75% of East Timor's schools." It does not acknowledge that American foreign policy supported Indonesia's decision to annex East Timor in 1975. Successive U.S. governments thwarted East Timor's attempts to secure independence as it did not suit the American geopolitical interests (George, 1985; Martinkus, 2001).

American nation-state), other indicators point to serious environmental transgressions by U.S. corporations[33] (Carroll, 2003; Denny, 2004; Engel, 2003; see also Vidal, 2003, for an overview of how practices by American mining multinationals such as Texaco-Chevron and Rio Tinto contribute to environmental destruction).

Under "Opening the American Mind," *Impact* states that

> IIE is helping US students and scholars study and teach abroad in a time when many Americans know little about the rest of the world, and many people overseas have few opportunities to confront the stereotypes they hold about Americans. (IIE, 2003)

Here, the largely unidirectional flow of international students to the United States is acknowledged (see IIE, 2002, 2003). IIE's initiatives to send Americans to Asia, Africa, and the Muslim world are surely commendable as there can be no dialogue without encounter. On close reading, the text attributes the underlying problem to ignorance and misunderstanding: "Many people overseas have few opportunities to confront the stereotypes they hold about Americans"; "Most Americans have never been to another country"; "87% of American college age students could not find Iraq on the map" (IIE, 2003). The text suggests that all that is required is interpersonal contact between Americans and non-Americans for animosity to be diluted. There is little instrospection that in their current forms, American structures and systems may be inimical to the interests of global others. The focus on the interpersonal is also reflected in the IIE's 2003 motto: Opening minds to make the world a less dangerous place. The international student is constructed as a subject to be educated about American values so that they will not lapse into misunderstanding. With America and Americans positioned as humanitarian educators and learners about other cultures, what is obscured is that their ultimate aim is to engage in a kind of human capacity building that reinforces American values and aspirations.

As discussed earlier, the quest to know the other is anchored in the national goal of consolidating America's geoeconomic and geopolitical interests. These ambitions and practices of state craft have historical resonances with America's Manifest Destiny and are linked to a desire to expand America's economic frontier. The purpose of knowing the other is to correct their anti-American stereotypical views and to build relationships that are critical to the success of U.S. diplomacy and business. A clever play of words reinforces the homogenizing imperatives of U.S. business and foreign policy by positing "America with the world." Thus, "the lasting ties that Ameri-

---

[33]Transparency International, the global corruption watchdog, has also implicated American oil multinationals for supporting repressive regimes by secret payments to corrupt officials (see Denny, 2004; Transparency International, 2003).

cans make during their sojourns abroad are important to our country and the rest of the world." The implicit suggestion here is that American ways and values *are* those of the world.

> In a world rapidly changing due to technological innovation, economic globalisation and national, ethnic and regional re-alignments, others [sic] problems were increasingly becoming our own. (IIE, 2001)

A recurrent subjectivity is implied of America—that of an innocent by-stander drawn into the maelstrom of others' problems by people who don't understand American values. America emerges as a victim of circumstances outside of its control.

A series of visual statements complement the textual statements in constructing the United States as educator and facilitator of free ideas. Figure 4.6 is fairly typical of the types of images found in IIE's promotional materials. In past annual reports, images of White Americans who were depicted as educators of the other predominated. Recent images have featured a few individuals from America's model minority—people of color who are pictured in positions of professional authority. In most cases, the images feature various icons of modernity that function as aspirational symbols for the underdeveloped world: a laboratory and a laptop and printer connected to the ultimate signifier of American life, the automobile. In nuanced ways, the images work to marginalize the other. Overtly foreign people of color are largely depicted as passive beings, absorbing the wisdom of a White or model minority expert; machines (e.g., the automobile, lap top) are usually foregrounded and nature is all but absent. These visual statements suggest a discursive continuity with the corpus of modernization theories. Their overall effect is to reinforce the message that the American way holds out the promise of modernity.

A cluster of statements within its promotional literature also reveals the IIE's mission to support capitalism, euphemistically described in terms such as *free trade* and *market economics*: "The IIE is initiating programs for leaders, managers, professors, and students in formerly Communist countries to learn about market economics and democratic institutions." The pairing together of the lexical items of *market economics* and *democratic institutions* deterritorializes American capitalism by promoting it as the means to democracy. Programs such as Ecolinks Partnership Grants are promoted to "build the capacity of businesses and municipalities in [Central and Eastern Europe] to develop market-based solutions to environmental problems." The power–knowledge relations here are aimed at consolidating the authority of market-produced and inspired knowledges and facilitating their dispersal into the physical, cultural, and social dimensions of life. The links with a neoliberal governmentality are all too obvious.

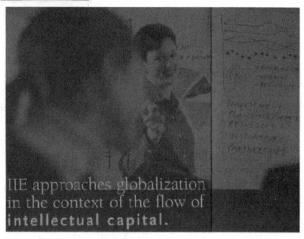

IIE approaches globalization in the context of the flow of intellectual capital.

FIG. 4.6.   Educating the other.

Statements that link the IIE and, by extension the United States, with the expertise and commitment to tackle global issues and problems are commonplace. Propositions like this one are bold to the point of audacity:

> Our work on energy and the environment is becoming increasingly important as developing countries grapple with energy shortfalls and the world seeks solutions to global climate change. (IIE, 2001)

Market solutions are manufactured as the answer to tackle the growing gap between rich and poor countries and to address the globalization of poverty and economic injustice, with scant consideration that an unregulated market may have helped produce these problems in the first place. The IIE's rhetoric seeks to emphasize its commitment to tackling issues of poverty and sustainability; however, the solutions it seems to be proposing appear painfully myopic and overwhelmingly cosmetic.

Its unabashed promotion of American exceptionalism suggests that the IIE's promotional materials are intended for a predominantly domestic audience. However, their accessibility through the Internet opens the Institute to a wider audience, including elements of the international community who may not agree with the U.S. doctrine of exceptionalism. "Opening minds to make the world a less dangerous place"—the IIE's 2003 motto—perceives international students as subjects to be educated about American values so that they will not lapse into misunderstanding. It positions America and Americans as humanitarian educators and learners about other cultures, and not the kind of country that "goes around looking for markets to raid and cities to bomb" (Lapham, 1998).

Education@UK

Despite claims of an ancient pedigree, British universities are by and large the product of the modern nation-state. There was little need for universities in preindustrial England, and the two institutions that existed were primarily responsible for training clergymen and teachers (Scott, 1995, pp. 11–12). The 19th-century universities—the Victorian civic age universities—were born in an imperial age and initiated to serve the nation-state. They were supported by the state and various industrial, commercial, and civic sponsors (p. 13). How has the British university, a modern and modernizing institution, changed to incorporate global and globalizing influences? How does it facilitate critical engagements with difference and otherness under conditions of globalization?

This chapter provides the discursive background to understand how power/knowledge relations produce and sustain particular expressions of international education in the UK. It does so through an analysis of the marketing narratives of two universities—the London School of Economics (LSE) and Oxford Brookes—and the promotional narratives of the British Council's Education Counselling Service (ECS). The chapter begins by describing the ensemble of legislation and policy introduced by the state which established the conditions for the UK's education export industry.

MAPPING THE POLICY TERRAIN: A BRIEF HISTORY

Government funding began only in the late 19th century and a mixed-funding model prevailed up to World War II. The universities received about one third of their operating expenses from the central government and the rest from tuition payments (approximately 30% of income), local government subsidies, and, in the case of the Oxbridge universities, from endowments from wealthy benefactors.

After the war, Keynesian economic management policies, together with a belief that the university had a vital role to play in producing human capital for postwar reconstruction, saw an accompanying increase in state funding for universities. British universities remained aloof and elite during this period of growth. The University Grants Committee (UGC) had direct access to the Treasury and its structural detachment from the Department of Education and Science (DES) was indicative of the power held by universities (Salter & Tapper, 2000, p. 69; Scott, 1995, p. 17).

The 1963 Robbins Committee established the basis for the massification of higher education, declaring that state provision should be made to enable all those who qualified for and desired a place in a college or university (Scott, 1995, p. 17). A new group of universities and polytechnics were progressively created from 1958 to 1970.[1] By 1970, the state had abolished fees and was meeting 90% of the operating costs of universities (Trow, 1994, p. 12; Williams, 1997, p. 285).

The 1980s heralded the start of major changes in the financing, operations, and governance of the British higher education sector. The higher education sector was to be transformed into a 'managed market' governed by the state using market mechanisms which were designed to achieve greater efficiency and 'value' for public investment (Broadhead & Howard, 1998; Salter & Tapper, 2000, p. 71). These changes were similar to those that took place in the various OECD member countries including Australia.

By the end of the decade, a number of 'truth regimes' had effectively been entrenched in the political and institutional imagination of governments and education bureaucrats. These included a belief in the market's ability to arbitrate supply and demand and a minimal role for the state in funding universities. A new governmentality emerged premised on the merits of managerialism ahead of collegial governance and the use of technologies of quality and accountability to ensure the 'performance' of universities (see Harley, 2002, pp. 188–189, 201–203; Preston, 2001, pp. 354–357; Watson & Bowden, 1999, pp. 243–244; Williams, 1997, pp. 276–281). As with Australia, the dramatic policy shifts within UK higher education were not informed by a coherent vision for higher education but reflected tensions, compromises and reworkings, although the initial impulse was simply to reduce public expenditure (Williams, 1997, pp. 276–278).

The 1985 Green Paper, *The Development of Higher Education in the 1990s* (DES, 1985); the Higher Education Reform Act (1988); the 1991 White Pa-

---

[1]This new group included the redbrick universities, technological universities, and the polytechnics, which themselves were amalgamated into the university system in 1992.

per, *Higher Education: A New Framework* (DES, 1991); and the 1992 Further
and Higher Education Acts of England, Scotland and Wales can be read as
part of a broader state-initiated discursive ensemble that institutionalized
economics as an organizing framework for education policy.[2] A protracted
struggle between government and higher education stakeholders ended
with a form of governance that strengthened the role of government. Government would set the standards, establish monitoring and evaluation technologies with the cooperation of universities, and intervene according to
the goalposts established by these standards[3] (Salter & Tapper, 2000, p. 72).

By the start of the 1990s, British universities were being exposed to a 'veritable panoptican of inspection' in the form of Academic Audits (AA), the
Research Assessment Exercise (RAE), and the Teaching Quality Assessment (TQA). These auditing technologies placed significant financial and
workload burdens on universities (Shore & Wright, 2000, p. 70). They
helped to transform norms of conduct and professional collegial and personal identities. The first Research Assessment Exercise (RAE), introduced
to modernize the research functions and financing of universities, profoundly influenced institutional structures, policies, departmental cultures—institutional subjectivities—and the individual subjectivities of staff.
Simply put, the RAE steered universities and their staff toward practices
that favored a culture of short-term instrumentalism and competition
(Harley, 2002, pp. 110–117; Henkel, 1999, pp. 110–113):

> It has forced many, including myself, to pursue multi-publications of dubious
> value. (psychologist from an old university, as quoted by Harley, 2002, p. 200)

> They have increased competition, jealousy. People are falsely rated on the ba-
> sis of certain types of publication. [The RAE] ranks individuals and depart-

---

[2]Commencing with the 1985 Jarrett Commission, which produced the Green Paper, there
was a successive shift toward greater managerial accountability. The 1988 Higher Education
Reform Act abolished academic tenure and replaced the UGC, an instrumentality that had
previously acted as a buffer between the university sector and the government, with the Universities Funding Council (see Slaughter, 1998, pp. 58–60; Williams, 1997, pp. 276–279). The
new council would also have a different composition from the UGC. Besides academics, it
would include those with "shown capacity in industrial, commercial or financial matters or the
practice of any profession" (see Trow, 1994).

[3]These attempts were broadly unsuccessful, as evidenced by the replacement of various instrumentalities that had previously been dominated by academics (e.g., UGC), with statutory
bodies that were dominated by nonsector stakeholders, many of whom were corporate identities (e.g., the University Funding Council and its successor, the Higher Education Funding
Council). The establishment of an external agency to monitor quality, the QAA, saw the displacement of the Higher Education Quality Council (HEQC), a progeny of the peak academic
interest group, the Committee of Vice-Chancellors and Principals (CVCP). Salter and Tapper's (2000) work on higher education governance in the United Kingdom points to a relatively protracted struggle between government and academic stakeholders. The struggle was
less pronounced in Australia.

ments in a crude and materialistic way and is psychologically destructive. (sociologist from old university, as quoted in Harley, 2002, p. 203)

The RAE's effectiveness as a technology of government lay, on the one hand, in its ability to co-opt traditional academic values, culture, and identity for managerial ends (Harley, 2002, pp. 203–204; see also Blaxter, Hughes, & Tight, 1998, pp. 307–308). A tradition of collegiality steered some individuals to submit to the RAE despite major misgivings about its effect on research quality, whereas others saw the competitive individualism fostered by the RAE as currency to further their careers (Harley, 2002; Willmott, 2003, pp. 137–138). On the other hand, the RAE violated the ethic of collegiality by using something of a name-and-shame strategy to identify which staff members were not research active (Willmott, 2003, p. 134). Further changes to the RAE are planned following the Roberts Review (2003) of research assessment practices. The Review's declared aims were to identify ways of accurately assessing research of international quality and ways of increasing emphasis of enterprise-based research. Its recommendations have been criticized for increasing bureaucratic complexity and for shifting funding toward the more elite institutions such as Oxford and Cambridge (Roberts, 2003; see also MacLeod, 2004b).[4]

A large body of academic discourse attributes the broad changes in British higher education to a neoliberal rationality that was anchored in minimal government expenditure in public services and widespread faith in the ability of the market to plan and arbitrate in all spheres of economic and social life. The drive to reform higher education was grounded in the view that productivity gains were required:

> British universities were [considered] backward, conservative, self-serving institutions and were responsible in part for Britain's poor performance in the international competition for markets. . . . [They] were incapable of reform from within but must be forced to shape their missions, roles . . . [and that] . . . the transformation of universities was to be achieved by radically cutting their budgets, forcing them to seek new funds from sources outside of government. (Trow, 1994, p. 12)

Universities were criticized for responding with an indecent haste to the first significant push toward the market by the government (Williams, 1997). By self-steering toward the policy outcomes dictated by government, they contributed to the subordination of their status as expert providers. As

---

[4]The proposed changes include giving greater weight to practice-based research and the inclusion of business and industry representatives in judging panels (MacLeod, 2004b), which were previously composed by peers. The Roberts Review criticizes institutional games playing, which it argues has been used to boost university RAE ratings and increase access to the funding cake (Roberts, 2003).

possessors of academic capital, universities should have been able to negotiate reasonable institutional conditions for teaching, research, professional development, and remuneration. The precedent was set for a radical reconfiguration of the provider–agency relationship between universities and the state (p. 276).[5]

The new governmentalities that came to exist in universities have been explained by resource-dependency theory, which reasons that individual universities will adopt the necessary behaviors to maintain revenue flows and to protect and maximize their institutional reputations (Slaughter & Leslie, 1997). In a neoliberal political terrain, a series of national higher education policies were formulated to promote academic capitalism (Slaughter & Leslie, 1997). Within universities, there was a greater emphasis on university–business interactions, a higher profile for market-friendly disciplines such as the technosciences, and greater emphasis on knowledge goods (pp. 26–37). The effect of marketization policies on the university sector is a point of contention between those who believe inculcating business principles into the operations and management of the public sector had improved services,[6] and those who argued that these policies had weakened the resource bases of universities.[7]

Instead of the promised productivity and efficiency, its critics argue that the tensions and contradictions between the different accountabilities created a performative culture.[8] At the apex of accountabilities was a manage-

---

[5]Here, Williams (1997) refers to two significant marketization initiatives: the loss of public subsidy for overseas students and the policy of accepting overenrollments at a reduced unit income from the government. The first initiative was normalized by the universities when they levied fees on overseas students, and the second by polytechnics that recruited more students to make up for the 15% shortfall imposed on the sector (pp. 275–276).

[6]The argument is that market accountabilities have forced elite academics to respond to their customers (students and the state) with better services (see Bosworth, 1992, pp. 106–108). Marketization initiatives are also credited with developing a more differentiated higher education sector in the United Kingdom with decided specialisms and strengths (Scott, 1995, 1998).

[7]Critics of economic rationalist or market liberalist policies argue that they gave rise to greater stratification both *within* and between individual institutions. Institutions and disciplines deemed to have market relevance subsequently have flourished whereas those with limited marketability have languished (see Harley, 2002; Henkel, 1999; Preston, 2001; Slaughter & Leslie, 1997; Trow, 1994; Trowler, 1998). Sustained research into instruments such as the Teaching Quality Assessment (TQA) and its managerial stablemate, the Research Assessment Exercise, conclude that they have done little to improve teaching and research outcomes (see Badley, 1998; Harley, 2002; Henkel, 1999; Middleton, 2000).

[8]Performativity, a construct that was first conceptualized by Lyotard (1984) in *The Postmodern Condition*, is used to signify an excessive belief in rational systems and objective knowledge, all of which are anticipated to produce efficiency and performance. Another useful definition of performativity is provided by Ball (2000) as "a technology, a culture that employs judgements, comparisons and displays as a means of control and change. The performances of individuals serve as measures of productivity, quality and output" (p. 1).

rial accountability (to government) instead of a professional accountability (to the discipline) and democratic accountability (to the general community). Talk of accountability to the customer established the discursive logic for education to be regarded as an investment and private good with instrumental value rather than as a right and public good (Middleton, 2000, p. 549).

Instruments such as the RAE and its managerial sibling, the TQA, function as political technologies to govern. Using the language of democracy, participation, and self-empowerment, these audit instruments claim to 'enable' individuals and institutions to ensure quality and improve performance. But like most political technologies, their effectiveness rests on disguising the workings of power. The relationship between the evaluator-examiner and those being evaluated remains hierarchical (Shore & Wright, 2000).

By the end of the 1990s, the emphasis on developing a knowledge-based society had moved British universities to the center stage of policy rhetoric. They were identified as having a role in responding to an inevitability—globalization. A highly educated citizenry was required to position the nation-state to compete globally—to keep up with the 'Joneses', in this case other countries that were establishing postindustrial, postFordist, and informational economies and attracting foreign investment (see Ahier & Beck, 2003, pp. 326–328).

The discourse of an inevitable and unstoppable globalization was deployed not only by the government but also by the university leadership who took the position that globalization gave them few choices. However, universities cannot be regarded as passive recipients of globalization (see Deem, 2001, pp. 15–18; Marginson & Rhoades, 2002, pp. 285–288). They are *both* agents and objects of global forces and mechanisms. The globalization of the neoliberal state would lead to the globalization of the market-driven university.

Third Way Fantasies

The election of New Labour into government in 1997 projected a new governing discourse, the Third Way, into public discussions. Described as new politics, the Third Way claimed to steer a course between neoliberalism and the old social democracy of the Keynesian Welfare State (Giddens, 1998, pp. 60–65). By stressing the reconciliation of opposites (e.g., rights *and* responsibilities, cutting corporate taxes *and* ensuring a minimum wage, etc.), the Third Way has been criticized for sloganizing rather than offering educational alternatives (see Hyland, 2002, p. 249; Power & Whitty, 1999, pp. 538–540). Its main pillar, modernization, gives primacy to economic considerations and echoes the ideologies of earlier conservative governments (see Cole, 1998; Power & Whitty, 1999). Its much publicized welfare-to-workfare ethic has been associated with a "nineteenth century puritan ethic but given a new ethical gloss" (Rose, 1999b, p. 488).[9] Simply put, the Third Way has been criticized for its similarities with the foundational principles of neoliberalism—that markets represent the natural order of things and are beyond government control; that the state's environmental, education, social, transport, fiscal, and monetary policies should be business friendly; and that "working people must fit in a market agenda by working harder, and shouldering the greater burden of adjustment" (Elliott, 2003, p. 12). According to the Third Way then, considerations of social justice must be subordinated to economic efficiency. References to globalization featured prominently in Third Way thinking and politics, an indicator that by the end of the 1990s, globalization had become a governmentality.

Notably, the discourses of globalization used by New Labour have mutated over time and across space. Globalization is framed differently depending on whether the intended audience is domestic or international. Over time, a discourse of an 'inexorable globalization' with non-negotiable outcomes was replaced by a new discursive framing of globalization as a contingent political project with countertendencies that could be mobilized for the benefit of all. Overwhelmingly, globalization is portrayed as having largely positive outcomes (Hay & Smith, 2005, pp. 126–131).

The 1,700-page Dearing Report, *Higher Education in the Learning Society*,[10] published in 1997, reflected the state's desire to steer higher education toward greater engagement with the global economy. The Dearing Report's recommendations were framed in the language of market and democracy, using signifiers such as the United Kingdom's economic competitiveness, new technology, user contribution, and value for money (Barnett, 1999). The state's commitment to new technology materialized in UKeU, a virtual university that was heralded as the first national e-learning initiative in the world. Operated by a consortium that featured UK universities, colleges, and the private sector, UKeU was expected to translate the fantasies of the dot.com boom into tangible benefits for universities. By March 2004, UKeU had folded with a loss of £62 million (MacLeod, 2004c).

Joining the ensemble of legislative acts, policies, reports, and commissions aimed at reforming higher education were the government's Competitiveness White Papers; the first of these appeared in 1994. In introducing

[9]The Third Way has been criticized for privileging the discourses of modernization, rationalism, and Eurocentrism. See Rose (1999b) and Hay and Smith (2005) for an incisive critique of the Third Way.

[10]The inquiry responsible for the Dearing Report was initiated against a backdrop of warnings from the Higher Education Funding Council (HEFC) that by 1999–2000 some 55% of universities in England would be in financial deficit. The inquiry was predictably preoccupied with the issue of finance (Bennett, 1997, p. 29).

the 1998 Competitiveness White Paper, *Our Competitive Future: Building the Knowledge Driven Economy* (Department of Trade and Industry, 1998), the British prime minister articulated the national vision, reserving special mention for universities. The 'public good' role of universities was linked to a mission of producing the entrepreneurial citizen-subject who would earn national income and secure Britain's prosperity and future:

> In Government, in business, in our universities and throughout society we must do much more to foster a new entrepreneurial spirit. . . . That is the route to commercial success and prosperity for all. We must put the future on Britain's side. (Blair, 1998)

"Strong universities which have creative partnerships with business" were to be a vital part of the equation to "put the future on Britain's side" (Blair, 1998). This construction of universities as productive nodes in driving economic prosperity reappears in the 2003 White Paper, *The Future of Higher Education* (Department of Education and Skills [DofES], 2003) and the Lambert Review of Business–University Collaboration[11] (2003). *The Future of Higher Education*, published 6 years after the Dearing Review, reexamined the issue of financing higher education. Acknowledging a 36% drop in funding per student from 1989 to 1997,[12] the White Paper promised a 6% increase in real funding for higher education. It proposed an income-contingent graduate repayment scheme that would allow students to defer repayment of university fees until employment. In this regard it resembles the Higher Education Contribution Scheme (HECS) in Australia. Although criticized for bringing little new money into teaching and for concentrating research funding in large institutions by using a big science model to inform its vision of research (Deem, 2003, p. 78; Garner, 2004; Kelly, 2003),[13] the paper was passed by the House of Commons by a narrow margin in 2004.

---

[11]The Lambert Review found that the biggest challenge to greater business–university collaboration was the short-sighted R&D vision of British businesses.

[12]Funding per student in higher education institutions is noted to have fallen from £7,916 in 1989 to £5,022 per student (Garner, 2003).

[13]Other criticisms directed at the White Paper include: its potential to increase the bureaucratization of university procedures, intensify government control over universities, and exacerbate the resource differentials between the established Russell Group and newer universities by removing opportunities for some of the smaller and newer institutions to do research (Deem, 2003, pp. 78–79). The nation's largest education trade union, the Association of University Teachers (AUT), also raised concerns about the paper's failure to acknowledge the need for improved working and pay conditions for academic staff (AUT, 2003) and a tendency to privilege the economic above the full range of contributions made by higher education to society. A general failure to acknowledge how the paper's vision sits with European initiatives, such as the Bologna agreement and the impact of 2-year degrees on the United Kingdom's reputation in the international education market, were other areas of concern raised by the AUT.

The White Paper's language is revealing of the governing discourses that are being used. Written in the language of crisis, the paper appeals to a national self-image of stoicism and sacrifice:

> There is no easy, painless way to put our universities and student finance system on a sustainable basis. If we duck the difficult decisions needed, the risk of decline will increase and the country at large will suffer. (DofES, 2003)

Media coverage of the white paper's proposals focused on the politics of charging fees for students who are variously conferred with such identities as elite, privileged (see "The Benefits," 2003), and unmotivated as this account suggests:

> Too many students have too much time on their hands . . . finding a job while a student makes sense. It brings in much needed cash, teaches students how to manage their time, and gives them a taste of the big wide world. When they come to looking for permanent work, it helps to show an employer that you have got out of bed and done something more than write essays and drink beer. ("Work Experience," 2003)

Media reports also focused on the poor salaries paid to faculty whose earnings were reported to have fallen by 40% in real terms (Cassidy, 2004). In summarizing the trajectory of developments within British higher education, higher education assumed a nation-building role in the first three postwar decades. However, by the end of the 1970s, a neoliberal state had emerged and universities were simultaneously pushed, and steered themselves, to respond to market forces. The discourse of the knowledge-based society, allied with Third Way thinking, has placed increasing emphasis on the capital accumulation role of education institutions. Marketization has not alleviated the financial pressures on British universities. A flurry of media reports on institutional deficits and departmental closures dominated the news in 2004. The financial problems of universities were attributed to a drop in overseas recruitment and a rise in general running costs (Curtis, 2004; MacLeod & Curtis, 2004).

Where previously senior academics combined management responsibilities with teaching, which exposed them to the concerns and situations of individual students, the trend now is to regard and engage with the students as a disembodied mass of student units who are to be recruited, retained, assessed, and credentialized in ways acceptable to funding bodies (Johnson & Deem, 2003). Government and institutional policies make rhetorical mention of the needs and rights of the student consumer-customer but the resource bases of higher education along with a managerialist ethos have diluted universities' responsiveness to the general community and to students.

REBUILDING BRITANNIA

The presence of international students in the United Kingdom predates the development of education markets. Educating colonial subjects was part of an imperial investment aimed at maintaining British influence in colonies and protectorates, and creating demand for British goods and services (see Altbach, 1998, pp. 54–58, 62–68, also 1999b; Parsons, 1987, p. 9; Spring, 1998, pp. 72–73; Willinsky, 1998, pp. 107–112). As a governing technology, education facilitated a unique form of 'steering from a distance'. It enabled a little island of about 125,000 square miles in area, and with an imperial army of about 150,000, to administer control over a quarter of the globe's surface, some 35 countries or colonies (Colley, 2002; Hobsbawn, 2003). Education emerged as a useful instrument to build and sustain popular support both in the imperial metropolis and the colonies. As Colley (2002) observes, Britons could separate themselves psychologically from the tyrannies of the Roman and Catholic empires by pointing to their readiness to take up the White Man's Burden: Providing education for their colonial subjects was one such example. Education thus helped to rehabilitate the British empire in the national psyche, from another typically exploitative enterprise to one with moral and ethical underpinnings (Colley, 2002).

Furthermore, the processes of educating subjects in accordance with colonial cultural norms in their protectorates and colonies assisted in developing and maintaining local elites and administrators who could be guaranteed to keep things in order. Education also created desires and aspirations among ordinary people in the colonies. An English-speaking education would provide access to material and cultural resources, which ultimately would lead to improved living standards and opportunities to leave behind poverty (Tikly, 2004; see also Hickling-Hudson, Matthews, & Woods, 2004, for an exposition of education's varied links with coloniality and postcoloniality). The creation of educational opportunities through the provision of educational scholarships continues to be used as a means of legitimizing British interests overseas.

Until 1979, the British government provided public subsidies to universities for the international students they enrolled. This subsidy was removed in 1979 as part of a wider policy to reduce government expenditure. British universities responded to this market mechanism with characteristic market-like behavior: They introduced fees for overseas students (Williams, 1997, p. 276). After a momentary decline in numbers, demand from international students grew steadily and by 1987 had exceeded pre-1979 enrollments.

In 1998, in response to greater competition in the global education market, the British government outlined the Prime Minister's Initiative (PMI), a policy platform intended to increase the United Kingdom's market share in the international education industry by 25% by 2005.[14] A close reading of the prime minister's speech is instructive in revealing the policy's rationalities:

> Wherever I travel I meet international leaders who have studied in Britain . . . dynamic, intelligent people. . . . This is good news for the UK. People who are educated here have a lasting tie to our country. They promote Britain around the world, helping our trade and our diplomacy. It is easier for our executives and our diplomats to do business with people familiar with Britain. . . . Our young people also benefit. They gain from the window to the world which contact with international students gives them . . . we can teach but we can also learn from others.
>
> In a world of lifelong learning, British education is a first class ticket for life. I want to see the benefits of . . . that ticket given to as many as possible across the world. It is in our interests and it is in their interests that we should. (Blair, 1999)

The Blair speech is a bold attempt to reinvent Britain's image by transforming it from a waning center of Empire to dynamic and knowledge driven. It is revealing of two long-standing texts, one economic and the other colonial. An economic referent, "doing business," provides a tacit link with Britain's contemporary geopolitical and geoeconomic interests: "It is easier for our executives and our diplomats to do business with people familiar with Britain." Here, Blair (1999) uses Britain's colonial history and an imperial text to set the context for a new Britannia that aspires to reclaim the colonial role of educating the international elite: dynamic and intelligent people. British education is also described as offering the means to gain entry into a socially stratified world, captured succinctly in Blair's claim that "it offers a first-class ticket for life." The torch of empire may have been passed to another power, but the nostalgia and desire to relive the imperial experience and to once again be 'Great' Britain is woven through the Blair speech.

Education's imbrication in the nation-state's economic and political rationales is accepted unabashedly as this Web site posting reveals:

> Those who experience UK education and training tend to become life-long friends of the UK. . . . Huge political, trade and economic benefits over the long term might therefore be gained by maximising the numbers and ensuring the quality of individual experiences. . . . UK institutions [also] gain in many other ways through extending their international outlook and welcoming talented students who make an important contribution to the UK's research effort. (British Council, 2001b)

---

[14]As part of this policy, the government introduced the Chevenning Scholarship program, 2-year undergraduate degrees, and a relaxation of work regulations for graduates of UK universities.

The subject, "the life-long friend of the UK," is the other who is able to provide access to "huge political, trade and economic benefits over the long term."

The Education UK Brand: Cool Britannia

Education branding is a practice borrowed from the advertising field. As with its advertising parent, educational branding practices work by building up particular sets of attributes as a means of establishing a brand loyalty for an education product or service (see Maguire, Ball, & MacCrae, 1999, 2001). Branding constitutes a broad impression management technology, which not only embraces individual universities, but the locales (places) in which they are located. It is now commonplace to brand entire countries (country branding) to construct them as desirable for capital investment (Harvey, 1993).

The Brand Report was commissioned by the British Council's ECS in 1998 with support from a number of government instrumentalities from Defence to Trade and Industry.[15] The report's declared aim was "to provide a competitive edge for the UK product within an increasingly crowded market place" (British Council, 1999a, p. 3). ECS engaged three firms with market research, public relations, and advertising expertise to revitalize the image of British education. Their assessment identified the following as strengths of the UK education product: culture, tradition, safety, and diversity. British education's weaknesses were its relatively higher cost and the unfriendliness of its people, who emerged as cold, eccentric, superior, and with a tendency to see foreigners as inferior (British Council, 1999b).

The reimagining and reimaging of Britain and British education meant discarding tired, traditional images linked with the old world order and replacing them with a set of forward-thinking and inspirational images. But it also meant retaining parts of the old formula that had worked. A highly selective image of "the British university" was drawn up to guide the new brand:[16]

> An icon of classic excellence in education, Oxford and Cambridge are names
> to conjure with . . . the British sense of fair play and moderation appeals to

---

[15]The government departments included several that lie outside the discursive domain of education: the Ministry of Defence, the Departments of Trade and Industry, and Education and Employment, the Scottish Executive and the Welsh Office and the Department of Education, Northern Ireland.

[16]The British education system was also associated with weaknesses including: cumbersome admissions procedures, limited scholarships, poor supervisory support for postgraduates, and inadequate provision of student support services, in particular, welfare and accommodation. The system's strengths were noted as: academic integrity and the international recognition of British degrees, which led to employability.

them. . . . They have been taught to admire the quality of British teachers and the very personal teaching style in the British educational system. (British Council, 1999b)

The UK education brand was premised on the following meanings: "a dynamic tradition, the new world class and being the best I can be" (British Council, 1999a, p. 12). It was also given a personality: "responsive, welcoming and alive with possibilities" (p. 12). Education UK's targeted constituency, self-funded students, were described as "tomorrow's citizens" and conferred with the following subjectivities:

Ambitious . . . [they] see themselves as the future elite. . . . The prize is to be movers and shakers when they return to their country. . . . They know that an education in an English-speaking country is a passport to intellectual citizenship of the world. (British Council, 1999b)

By using terms such as *elite, investment, ambition, ownership,* and *movers and shakers,* the marketing lexicon presupposes and perpetuates a particular vision of tomorrow's citizens—an elite class, highly individualized, and competitive. Indeed, some British Council advertisements aimed at recruiting English language teachers have assumed the marketing message of 'Teach Individualism'. Whether a UK education steers international students to internalize liberal, individualistic values, or whether a more complex and nuanced set of hybrid values are assumed by students, what is noteworthy is the use of individualism to promote a UK education (Pegrum, 2004, p. 7).

Given that the majority of international students originate from cultures that can loosely be described as collectivist, these promotional narratives raise the question of whether a better fit could be achieved between the values underpinning a UK education and the backgrounds and needs of these students. Finally, although it is certainly the case that demand for English language is growing, it is also the case that the legacies of colonization, Cold War imperialism, and neoliberal globalization have created the conditions for eroding the already fragile identities of other cultures (Kramer, 2003b). Perceptions are powerful, and increasingly those that associate English language competence with development, whether of individuals or their country, pose problems in the long term for linguistic and cultural diversity (Pegrum, 2004, p. 5).

IMAGINEERING THE CONTEMPORARY, CUTTING EDGE, AND COLONIAL

Using classic colors of black and white with an occasional inflection of red, Education UK promotional brochures reflect seriousness, diligence, and austerity. In a bid to soften what could be construed as hard-edge commer-

131

cialism, the first few pages of the brochures associate the United Kingdom, and British education, as the means toward the fulfillment of a childhood dream (wish fulfillment). A tastefully minimalist, translucent transparency makes up the first page of the prospectus: Education UK: The Best You Can Be. It features an unfussy typeface, suggestive of a child writer whose dreams it seeks to capture (see Fig. 5.1):

> when i was a child i wanted to be a spaceman and travel to the moon. peter mwandawiro is in the UK to study postgraduate astrophysics.

Peter has come to the United Kingdom to fulfill the quintessential boyhood dream—to travel to space. This dream becomes reality with the help of Education UK, which gives him the opportunity to "study postgraduate astrophysics." The visual statements are cleverly crafted to produce two sides of

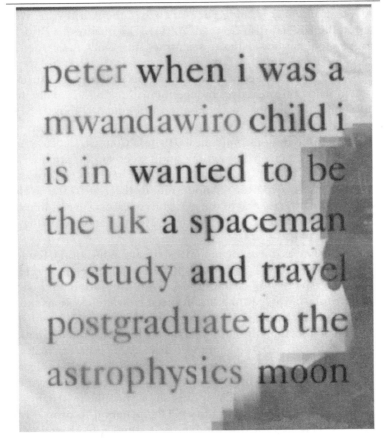

FIG. 5.1.   Education UK: The chance to be the best.

the one picture—Peter needs the UK to become a spaceman (see British Council, 2001a).

Peter's image in the advertisement is peripheralized to the extreme edge of the page. The text that captures his dream and the role of the United Kingdom is more important than he is and takes center stage. He is made visible as a young, smiling man, with eyes turned upward toward the celestial skies of his dreams. His otherness is effectively obscured. Juxtaposed with Peter's image is a set of molecules that works as an indexical sign to suggest an association between him and the serious endeavor of scientific inquiry. A UK education is the bridge that enables Peter and others like him to make that vitally important transition from childhood dream to the realization of adult ambitions.

A cluster of country-branding statements associate the United Kingdom with quality, dynamism, and innovation, legitimized by the generous use of facts and figures: "Those studying in arts . . . do so against a backdrop of an industry worth £12 billion" and "The principle of the World Wide Web was invented in the UK" (British Council, 2001a). The quality of a British education rests on its various claims to scientific fame: Dolly the cloned sheep and Stephen Hawking.

The benefits of a UK education are defined in largely instrumental terms—"emphasis on proactive, independent thinking . . . skills that are relevant"—and the means to economic enrichment—"look forward to better career prospects and higher potential earnings . . . students . . . are much sought after by top-companies" (British Council, 2002a). Associations among study, personal ambition, and career success are also prominent in Web sites. The modernization tropes are couched in terms of self-development: As an exporter of modernity to the rest to the world, the United Kingdom offers access to the new gods of career success in top companies, higher potential earnings, efficiency, science and technology (Pegrum, 2004, pp. 4–6).

At the same time as it sells the modernist dream, Education UK trades on tradition, using the cultural narrative of Britain as an imperial power and its historical role as educator of the other: "With a history dating back 800 years, the British way of learning has inspired education systems the world over." And, "where better to learn the international language of science business and politics than the country of its birth." The United Kingdom offers *the* authentic product, the genuine article. There is no discursive space here for acknowledging the cluster of hybrid Englishes that now exist such as Singaporean English or Indian English. Notably absent, too, is a critical engagement with the history of how English became the international language of science, business, and politics. The invitation to prospective students then is not to be reflexive but to come to the United Kingdom to "be fluent in a language that will boost career prospects the world over." English is held out as promising access to material benefits that presumably are not available to speakers of other languages. So, who is the subject that is being targeted and constituted by these narratives? Overwhelmingly, it is the self-developing individual who views education in instrumental terms and who will accept and perpetuate English's status as the world language.

In keeping with its ahistorical approach, a series of textual maneuvering in both the brochures and web pages challenge and dilute traditionally negative stereotypes of the United Kingdom as a society stratified by class and race: "[The UK's] much talked about class system is giving way to true multiculturalism as its diverse ethnic communities find their voice in British society." A history of class and race-based stratification is quietly obscured by ethnic communities finding their voice. A new United Kingdom, vibrant, vital, alive to new ideas and open to new influences is heralded as: "a country under change." Subsumed by this discourse of the new United Kingdom are the messy issues—how ethnic communities lost their voices in the first place (see Amin, 2002; Parekh, 2000).

The marketing message "Being the best I can be" and its variant forms ("A chance to be the best") is accompanied by a range of aspirational symbols (e.g., molecules, piano keyboards, skyscrapers, the hallowed Inns of Court, and fashion mannequins) along with images of individuals, all young and seemingly cosmopolitan (see Fig. 5.2). Youthful achievement presents as being within everyone's reach. Although some students are pictured smiling, the vast majority of the images in the Education UK brochure suggest serious and solitary subjects (see Fig. 5.3). Some are conventionally attractive and others have the look of bookish intellectuals ("nerd-like").

Student images also function as discursive markers of priority markets. Peter's image is one of the few of African heritage images, not surprising given that Africa is not a priority in the ECS' recruitment geography. In 2001, the brochures for postgraduate courses used images of Indian students, an ostensible discursive ploy aimed at wresting market share from the United States, which is the favored study destination for Indian postgraduate students (see Fig. 5.4). Chinese heritage students are useful discursive markers of any number of priority markets—Taiwan, Japan, Hong Kong, Singapore, China, Malaysia, and Indonesia.

To summarize, the Education UK promotional brochures seek to recraft the United Kingdom's identity as the place for intellectual elites and serious students. It is multicultural and (by extension) welcoming. A touch of altruism is injected into the promotional discourses—British education is the means to realize childhood dreams and opportunities. At the same time, a shadowy imperial text evident in the speech announcing the PMI and the Brand Report constructs a UK education as an instrument of for-

"I was a bit nervous to begin with, but I'm settling in now and making friends from so many different countries."

Yumiko Tmioko, Japan

Support when they first arrive

Student life in the UK is, by and large, a supportive and social one.

But even the most outgoing person can be forgiven for feeling a little apprehensive for their first few days in an unfamiliar country.

All educational institutions in the UK understand this and go out of their way to make their international students feel at home.

Many universities guarantee them accommodation in halls of residence for their first year close to all the campus facilities.

And most organise welcome meetings where students can familiarise themselves with their new surroundings.

In addition, counselling and special advice services are always available, while student unions and societies for foreign students also offer valuable support.

But the best cure for homesickness – and the one that always works – is simply for students to get out and get involved with UK life in all its unique character, colour and diversity.

Hisano Jahana, Japan

FIG. 5.2.   Seeking aspiration.

FIG. 5.3.　Solitary contemplation.

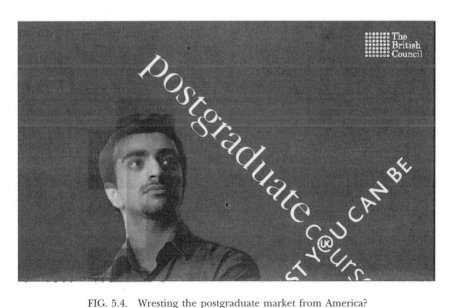

FIG. 5.4.　Wresting the postgraduate market from America?

eign policy. Educating the other is presented as a national investment to consolidate neocolonial power, with the state using the glamour of advertising and public relations spin to soften its hard-edged political and economic rationales. Along the way, the United Kingdom also deploys its foreign policy to promote the interests of its corporations. Britain's foreign aid contributions are increasingly tied to obtaining agreements from recipient countries to privatize their public assets.[17]

(Hyper)Real UK: Positioning for Global Success

Discursive events such as the Brand Report, *Positioning for Success,* and the host of branding the United Kingdom initiatives produce, perpetuate, and consolidate the symbiosis among government, markets, and the media, making it more and more difficult for consumers to distinguish hype and hyperbole from substance. The United Kingdom's image as a country is being actively resculptured to maintain competitive advantage in international education markets. The emergent "cool Britannia" is materially and discursively formalized by various other arms of government. The Foreign and Commonwealth Office (FCO)[18] is one such branch. It describes its role as improving perceptions of the United Kingdom overseas, which "may affect the attitudes of foreign governments, trade and investment decisions and personal choices such as where to study and what to buy" (FCO, 2002).

Strategic marketing approaches such as those recommended by the ECS-commissioned Gilligan Report[19] demand a keen awareness of what is happening at the coalface of individual markets. A well-dispersed network of agents, British Council staff, and consultants are engaged in gathering market intelligence. Local policy trends are carefully analyzed to ascertain whether these create opportunities for Education UK to increase its market

---

[17]Monbiot (2004, p. 24) notes that in Zambia the Department of International Development is spending £700,000 on improving sanitation, in contrast to its commitment of £56 million on privatizing copper mines. In Ghana, aid for improving water supplies was tied to obtaining agreement for partial privatization of Ghana's water boards.

[18]The FCO has embarked on a series of impression management strategies to modernize the United Kingdom's image. It commissioned a series of documentaries that were broadcast in more than 120 countries. These include *UK—Small Islands, Big Ideas; The Edge,* highlighting British achievements in science and technology, and *London Fashion Week . . . Style Tribes,* which showcased the creative and leisure industries. The FCO produced *Planet Britain 2000,* a CD-ROM directed at a target audience of 15 to 24-year-olds (FCO, 2002).

[19]The British Council–commissioned Gilligan Report in 1999 was intended to ascertain the standard of education marketing by UK education providers. It provided a long list of deficiencies in marketing and recruitment practices of British institutions, chief of which included the absence of a strategic marketing approach; a general attitude of complacency; and underestimation of competitor threat, failure to tailor promotional materials for individual markets, and the lack of a long-term vision (British Council, 2000, pp. 5–7).

share. This excerpt from the British Council's Australian Web site is instructive:

> The past four years of Australian Government has seen an acceleration of privatisation, including in education. . . . Even though Australia now has world class universities of its own, its geographic location has led to the feeling that some overseas exposure is essential for career development. (ECS, 2002)

This vignette is revealing of how other geographies and various others are constructed even in this era of globalization. Australia's geography sees its reconstruction as a remote colonial outpost. Going abroad and leaving the outpost for the colonial homeland and imperial metropolis is still regarded as essential for one's career development, if one desires to be part of the transnational elite.

Real UK, a recent Education UK marketing initiative campaign continues the emphasis on the United Kingdom's welcoming and accessible characteristics (British Council, 2002b). It takes market intelligence to another dimension by inviting young people between 16 and 18 to enter a competition to make a 3-minute video outlining their life goals, their perceptions of the benefits of a UK education, and their honest impressions of the United Kingdom[20] (British Council, 2003b). Competitions such as these provide valuable market knowledge that can be used to offset negative perceptions and to generate new technologies of spin for subsequent promotional campaigns.

Positioning for Success, the latest market report sponsored by the ECS calls for a new marketing strategy based on relationship management to develop long-term, sustainable relationships to nurture a market for lifelong learners (British Council, 2003a, p. 23).[21] It is replete with references to research, projected demand, demographic trends, competitor strategies, and geodemographic search instruments, all intended to make visible other territories and present and future temporalities (pp. 23–28). These informational devices and technologies map, analyze, record and construct market intelligence to pinpoint with increasing precision where and who the customer is in the present and the future. An all-pervasive sense of permanent

---

[20]The promotional Web site for Real UK invites candor from participants, stating, "[Tell us] what you honestly think of the UK . . . the more honest, the better." Entrants have the potential to win a 2-week "trip of a lifetime" to the UK to experience the "real" UK, to visit universities, businesses, and colleges, places of significance and to meet interesting and famous people.

[21]As part of its broader relationship marketing strategy, ECS has identified the need to offer international students an expanded range of services such as career guidance assistance, training, and personal development opportunities (British Council, 2003a, p. 25), the intention being to establish relationships before students return to their home countries.

competition with other countries is present in and perpetuated by *Positioning for Success*. A discourse of crisis and threat pervades its pages. All that is missing are the explicitly military metaphors that define open warfare: "We must ensure that we are not taken by surprise" (p. 31), "the threat is rising dramatically" (pp. 8–9), "we cannot afford to stand still" (p. 2). At the same time, there are hints that branding has its limitations as research indicates that the most influential information comes from "people that [prospective students] know and trust" (p. 7).

A powerful subjectivity is conferred onto the student who emerges as "media, advertising and brand literate" (British Council, 2003a, p. 7), "demanding in terms of customer care" (p. 7), "conversant with technology" (pp. 10, 30), and with high expectation of choice and flexibility (p. 9). The technically literate customer is used to argue for more sustained investment in IT infrastructure (pp. 10–11, 30). At the same time, references to students having to "continually upgrade their skills and knowledge to meet the needs of the high performance workplace" (p. 7) is suggestive of less autonomy, greater anxiety, and generally less secure lives than those lived by earlier generations of professionals: "On average each potential international student will follow six or seven different careers sequentially . . . life long learning will be a necessity" (p. 7).

Positioning for Success makes explicit references to the links between international education and globalization. The report's discussion of globalization, trade in education, and possible scenarios arising from General Agreement on Trade in Services (GATS) suggest that education is unambiguously regarded as a capitalist commodity and a service:

> The future of international education will be inextricably linked to the future of globalisation. Countries perceive that by internationalising their education they will be able to reap substantial benefits and improve their overall competitive position in the global economy . . . by internationalising . . . they are able to attract intellectual capital . . . internationalisation can also provide destination countries with a highly skilled labour force particularly where there are skill shortages. (British Council, 2003a, p. 60)

It is a resolutely 'First World' exposition on globalization with numerous references to the financial benefits stemming from international education for the 'First World'. What is missing? There is no mention of the need to develop more sophisticated expressions of international education that could author a more progressive politics of globalization. The old colonial narrative of consuming other geographies is telling. Where in the past other spaces were consumed for spices, gold, rubber, tin, and slaves, today these exotic geographies are regarded as markets for potential customers and as potential sources of highly skilled labor to be consumed to meet shortages in the 'First World' (Prasad, 2004).

Beyond the fairy tale of a new United Kingdom where ethnic groups have found their voice is a vision of international education that is vitiated to its core by national self-interest. It is a vision that regards plans to entice skilled people away from developing countries, which themselves face serious shortages of skilled labor, as entirely ethical (Batty, 2004). It is also a vision that exhibits unswerving fidelity to the sublime wisdom of the bottom line. Financial remuneration looms large in the order of things as the following narrative, which quotes a British Council staffer, reveals so tellingly: "Entrepreneurs from British business schools are rushing off to Moscow drawn by the strong economy. . . . Russia is getting near what financiers call 'investment' grade, thanks to the Iraq war which has pushed up the price of Russian oil. . . . Russians are riding high and can afford the cost of a British MBA" (Batty, 2004, p. 24).

The trend toward branding entrenches the importance of perception and impression management to the point where in the eyes of government and policymakers it has eclipsed the importance of the educational process itself. Education is reconstructed as a consumption good; its importance lies in its exchange values, in the pecuniary returns it offers the United Kingdom, and in the ambitious, self-improving international student.

How we think, write about and speak about international students and international education tells us something about how we govern others who are located in vastly different geographies. Despite attempts by various state and media instrumentalities to project a modern and multicultural image of Britain, a close reading reports and promotional materials reveals a national desire to perpetuate the imperial ideal in the new world order. Therefore, although short-term national economic goals are critical, international education is also viewed as "a long term investment in our future" (see British Council, 2003a, p. 29) as "people who are educated in Britain have a lasting tie to the country and can deliver tremendous political, trade and economic benefits" (p. 14). It is a view confirmed by those charged with the responsibility of marketing the authentic article of a British education:

> Also, the political benefits . . . it is very much why the government is supporting this initiative. . . . Tony Blair went to China, met the Mayor of Shanghai . . . talked to a lot of influential Chinese people who had studied in the UK. And that is really good for us. (interview with ECS manager, November 15, 2000)

QUALITY SLIPPAGES

In 1987, approximately 8 years after the introduction of full fees for international students, the United Kingdom's Council for Overseas Students (UKCOSA) introduced a code of practice, Responsible Recruitment. It was the precursor of several of the existing codes of practice[22] (Bruch & Barty, 1998, pp. 22–23). The number of quality assurance systems in place, however, are deceiving, as their generally non-prescriptive nature and the absence of serious regulatory frameworks impede their effectiveness (Hodson & Thomas, 2001). Offshore programs where courses are provided in partnership with private institutions in students' home countries are particularly susceptible to slippage in accountability and quality. Steering from a distance has its limitations as this comment from the QAA reveals:

> Whilst in no way implying that commercial partners are not as reliable as public institutions, the commercial aspirations of a partner can change the way a partnership is conducted. This can be to the detriment of the students in a way that is less likely with partners in the public sector. (QAA, 2001)

A 2002 QAA audit of franchise and articulation partnerships between UK universities and private higher education institutes in Singapore rated most partnerships as 'satisfactory', while highlighting concerns about the quality of student learning and the standards of awards.[23] One audit noted "a preponderance of Lower Second Class degrees," which it attributed to "a tendency for students to report on what they had learnt in texts rather than demonstrating skills of analysis and reflection" (QAA, 2002b, p. 8). A 1999 quality audit undertaken in Malaysia arrived at similar findings—teaching and assessment practices appeared not to facilitate the higher order critical thinking skills required of university-level study (QAA, 1999). Other issues

---

[22]These include: (a) the two codes of practice developed by the CVCP, presently known as Universities UK, *The Management of Higher Degrees Undertaken by Overseas Students* (CVCP, 1992), and *International Students in the UK: Code of Practice* (CVCP, 1995); (b) the HEQC's Code of Practice for Overseas Collaborative Provision in Higher Education, which covered franchises and articulation arrangements (HEQC, 1995); (c) the British Council's Code of Practice for Educational Institutions and Overseas Students (British Council, 1995), which governs the areas of marketing, information provision, admissions procedures, welfare support, and the management of complaints. The penalty for violating this code can result in the suspension of higher education institutions from the membership of the ECS. However, the monitoring of institutions' adherence to the code is ad hoc with institutional self-monitoring being the preferred modus operandi (Bruch & Barty, 1998, pp. 23–24); (d) the QAA's Code of Practice, which covers domestic and international student guidance and support (QAA, 1997).

[23]The requirement is that offshore programs should be equivalent in standards to the home programs. But it is difficult to monitor equivalence, especially given the practice by UK universities of devolving monitoring responsibilities about standards to their overseas partner. The QAA's (1999) audit in Malaysia reported several instances where the locus of responsibility for monitoring quality and standards had been relegated to the corporate arms of the universities, where they should have resided with academic staff. It argued that there was a potential for a conflict of interest given that the personnel from development offices had negotiated the establishment of the collaboration in the first instance. A separation of the roles was recommended.

of concern raised were poor student access to journals and hardware facilities in certain courses (QAA, 1999).

The high use of part-time and casual staff along with limited opportunities for UK universities to provide input into staff professional development was noted (QAA, 2002a, 2002b). Given that the standards of university awards are governed by loyalty to the standards of individual academic disciplines, the casualization of staff and their limited exposure to research and staff development programs cannot augur well for overall standards and quality. These findings also imply that consumers are not the arbiters of quality they are purported to be, as they lack the experience and knowledge to identify gaps in the programs of study they have purchased.

The very fact that overseas audits are conducted may be read as indicative that a trade-based orientation to international education does ensure some level of regulation. It was, after all, a concern with safeguarding the United Kingdom's reputation as a quality provider of education in a highly competitive market of international education that influenced the decision to place international franchises under the same level of scrutiny that British universities face at the hands of the QAA. Yet, there is a risk that quality audits will be reduced to performative charades, more concerned with image management than quality enhancement (Hodson & Thomas, 2001, pp. 104–106). This is particularly so in a marketized environment where the results of quality audits are increasingly used as marketing tools. The significant ambiguity surrounding the concept of quality across disciplines, institutional contexts, and social actors thus makes quality assurance an elusive goal, particularly for courses that are offered overseas (see also Ball, 2000).

To conclude, the development of the British international education export industry has been shaped by national policy vectors. Commencing initially as a cost-recovery undertaking aimed at reducing state expenditure by imposing fees on international students, the 1990s saw an intensification in recruitment activities including offshore collaborations. British rationales for internationalization are firmly anchored in the political and economic spheres, evident in the national desire to be internationally competitive and to develop and retain influence overseas. The international education sector is largely monitored by quality audits; however, these are entirely voluntary. The link between marketization and quality are, at best, tenuous.

Academic Discourse: Research Into International Education

Where the discursive field of academic research in international education was previously dominated by writings on development and educational aid, it has diversified significantly over the last decade to include different disciplinary perspectives. Academics writing on international education now come from a variety of disciplinary areas including business management, economics, sociology, development and comparative education, psychology and international relations. Equally diverse are the conceptual frameworks, methodologies and heuristic devices used in their analysis. These range from quantitative studies to qualitative studies; from policy analysis to ethnographic case studies and interviews. Within Education, the research on international education continues to focus on teaching, learning, supervision and support issues for international students. By contrast, in Business, the preoccupation has largely been with issues of marketing, branding strategies and predicting future demand.

How is the relationship between globalization imagined and understood by universities? An examination of public pronouncements by Universities UK (UUK),[24] the primary interest group that represents British universities, is instructive and illustrative. The following extracts refer to a speech delivered by the chief executive of UUK at a conference titled "Globalisation: The Challenges and Opportunities for UK Higher Education":

> Take a look at this ad in the Guardian [newspaper] just a couple of weeks ago. The University of Chicago is offering an MBA in Barcelona, and marketing it in London, Madrid, Brussels and Frankfurt. It's delivered in 14 weeks spread over 18 months, and access to the internet is implicit in the registering procedures. This is a typical example of what we mean when we talk about globalisation. (Warwick, 1999)

The technological and economic dimensions of globalization are privileged, and globalization is perceived and constructed as a borderless education space, a level playing field where anyone from anywhere can participate. Language, finances, and national affinities represent no barriers to the student who has the requisite cultural capital to flit from home base to Barcelona. The subject of this discourse is the elite Euro resident who lives in one of the global European cities (Frankfurt, Madrid, Brussels, London) and is wired up. In this brave new world, knowledge is a commodity and the international university is a trader. The professional subjectivities created by this discourse are proudly entrepreneurial:

> In the global economy, knowledge and information have become commodities—with a premium placed on their possession and exploitation. The flow of information and the acquisition of knowledge are commercial ventures in themselves. And, of course, universities throughout the developed and developing world have been taking advantage of the globalisation of knowledge too.
>
> Now, more than ever, higher education is subject to the market forces we traditionally associate with the world of business and commerce. Terminology

---

[24]UUK was formerly known as the CVCP.

that we associate with competition, clients, and markets is more commonplace in the academic vocabulary. (Warwick, 1999)

Having portrayed the future and the present in rosy terms, the past is
constructed as uniformly bad, a time when higher education was distant
and elite. It has taken this brave new, globalized, and virtualized world of
commodities, competition, clients, and markets to throw off the shackles:

> Higher education has thrown off the shackles of the "ivory tower"; the con-
> ceptual and physical borders that may once have restricted academia are dis-
> solving with the emergence of new technologies. (Warwick, 1999)

The seamless logic of this discourse constructs international education as
markets and income:

> In the global competition for students, UK universities have adapted admira-
> bly. They have adopted sophisticated marketing strategies to attract students
> from overseas and to take our teaching to overseas locations, and we've been
> remarkably successful.... The growth of overseas franchised courses, and
> soon campuses, validated by UK universities has also been phenomenal.... It
> is reckoned that this "business" is worth £250m a year. (Warwick, 1999)

Education, business, and commerce are constructed in discourse as well-
adjusted siblings in the one discursive family. A series of win–win outcomes
is constructed for both the developed and developing world. The speech
does not elaborate on the impact of marketization on the teaching and research missions of universities, nor on the types of student and professional
subjectivities emerging from this marketized terrain. Given that UUK is the
primary interest group charged with representing the concerns of universities, we can take these statements as the normative position of UK universities on globalization.

That the international education terrain is largely privatized is confirmed by Bennell and Pearce's (2003) empirical study of offshore courses
offered by British, Australian, and American universities in developing and
transitional economies. They found that 75% of overseas collaborations in
Asia, the Middle East, and Africa were with private higher education institutions. The figure was 50% for Europe (Bennell & Pearce, 2003, p. 224).
Public universities in transitional economies are beginning to join the
trend of seeking alliances with overseas universities, but these alliances are
concentrated in fee-paying professional development courses rather than
in student exchange programs where fee waivers prevail. Typically, the fee-
paying courses tend to span a narrow range of disciplines with demand
greatest in undergraduate Business, Computing, and Accounting courses.
The rising demand for offshore courses was attributed to the transna-

tionalization of economic activities and the hegemony of the English language.[25]

However, Bennell and Pearce (2003) also warned of "a wave of credentialism" within developing and transitional economies, sparked off by the easy availability of foreign qualifications (p. 230). Education credentials are increasingly viewed by both universities and their clients as tradable goods, just like any other commodity:

> Just as Coca-Cola and McDonalds corporations award franchises to companies and entrepreneurs in overseas countries to produce their products under tightly defined and rigorously enforced conditions, so too are a rapidly growing number of universities franchising other overseas institutions to offer their degrees and other qualifications. (Bennell & Pearce, 2003, p. 217)

The normalization of international education as a tradable commodity and service "just like Coca-Cola" is both revealing and unnerving given that the beverage is widely regarded as an icon of uber-capitalism, starkly evident in Coca-Cola's use as a metaphor for commercial colonization ("coca-colonization"). Where does such an analogy lead? Could there be other similarities between Coca-Cola and those that inform the brand of education sold on the global market, both offering a product that is cheap, convenient, universal, and ultimately not the best for one's health? The question of whether these discursive links between education, Coca-Cola, and McDonald's function as playful metaphors, or whether they are devices intended to establish the systems of thought that normalize knowledge capitalism is ultimately a politico-ethical question. Supporters of education markets might argue that universities could learn from the successful practices of the fast food and soft-drink multinationals. Critics, on the other hand, might equate the relentless drive for more markets and ever more profits with a myopia induced by 'coke-bottle lenses'.

There are obvious benefits stemming from the practice of conceptualizing education as a tradable service or good that can be provided from within the borders of nation-states. For transitional and developing economies the outflow of capital from the developing or transitional world to the North or West is reduced, local providers have access to the expertise of UK institutions, and students have access to an overseas credential at reduced cost (Bennell & Pearce, 2003, pp. 228–229). At another level, these international collaborations raise other pressing issues such as the normalization of privately funded education, and whether a sufficiently broad and rigorous education to meet the challenges of the 21st century can emerge from education markets.

---

[25]In 1996, 31% of all part-time courses undertaken in Singapore in private higher education institutions originated from the United Kingdom (Bennell & Pearce, 2003).

In contrast to Bennell and Pearce's (2003) largely positive depiction of how international education is responding to globalizing trends, a more sobering assessment of power–knowledge relations is provided by Tikly's (2001) situated study. His starting point is the relationships between globalization and national education systems in the African subcontinent. First, Tikly cautions against taking the developmental Asian state as the normative case study in any investigations into the relations between education and globalization. Second, he argues against premature celebrations of a polycentric world order. He observes that the colonial legacies of earlier forms of globalization have not yet been erased. Here, he cautions against using the presence of non-Western intellectuals and professionals in business, political, and education networks as the litmus test of reordered power relations.

Can universities become drivers of *postcolonial globalization*, and what does this term mean? Scott (1998) suggests that globalization offers universities the opportunity to go beyond the old neocolonialisms, nation-centered imperialisms, great power rivalries, and rhetorical, internationalisms that characterized the modern, nation-building university. Scott's hopeful vision is that the marketized international university with assistance from the postmodern nation-state will increase possibilities for greater intellectual pluralism and reflexivity and author a postcolonial globalization. So far, early indicators suggest that trade in education services is doing little to unsettle the nation-centered discourse structures of First World universities.

Media Discourses

Media constructions of international education offer a useful insight into the 'public common sense' about international education. The following news headlines highlight the competitive ethos that drives international education:

- "Scramble for Lucrative Foreign Students Is Corrupting Universities, Claims Leading Don" (Bright, 2004)
- "British Universities Ride in Pursuit of High Spending Russian Students" (Beckett, 2004)
- "Overseas Students Are Being Exploited" (Basnett, 2004)
- "Dons Bring in the Dough" (2003)
- "UK Must Keep Grip on Market" (Tysome, 2003)
- "Desperate Colleges May Turn to Foreign Students" (Miles, 2003)
- "Overseas Students 'Bankroll' Colleges" (Hodges, 1999a)

- "Dash for Cash or Trade Tactic?" (Hodges, 1999b)
- "Dons Blunt Global Push" (Major, 1999)
- "UK Universities Are 'Exploiting' Foreign Students" (Wallis, 1999)
- "New UK Brand Is Launched" (Kingston, 2000)
- "How to Woo Students From Overseas" (2001)
- "Pay Your Money, Take Pot Luck" (Court, 1999)
- "Colleges Rebranded for Overseas Appeal" (Carvel, 1999)
- "Slipping Abroad" (Major, 2000b)
- "Derby Dumbs Down to Gain Israeli Cash" (Baty, 1999)
- "How to Be Sensitive to Chinese Minds" (Leon, 2000)
- "Britain Must Fight to Keep Foreign Trade" (Tysome, 2000)
- "A Small Degree of Danger" (Major, 2000a)

Three broad themes are identifiable in the reporting: education exports and the issue of competition from other sources ("New UK Brand Is Launched," "Britain Must Fight to Keep Foreign Trade," "A Small Degree of Danger," "Dash for Cash or Trade Tactic?"), the financial problems of British universities ("Overseas Students 'Bankroll' Colleges"), and the issue of standards and quality ("Slipping Abroad," "Derby Dumbs Down to Gain Israeli Cash," "UK Universities Are 'Exploiting' Foreign Students," "Pay Your Money, Take Pot Luck"). The lexical items in these reports construct a sobering set of perceptions about the UK higher education sector—danger, desperation, gambling (*pot luck*), dumbing down for cash and branding for overseas appeal, exploiting foreign students, and bringing in dough.

Broadly, British media discourses constructs two types of subjectivities for international students: Students are either exploited consumers and recipients of "dumbed-down" degrees or discerning and ambitious cosmopolitan ambassadors who regard education as the means to competitive advantage. Compared with their Australian counterparts, British newspapers have been more critical of universities and the government and more thorough in pinpointing lapses in institutional processes and values. British universities emerge from much of the reporting as poor custodians of educational quality, interested mainly in offsetting their financial difficulties. Unlike Australian media discourses, the tenor of these reports places blame for declining standards not on international students but on a truncated leadership by "successive governments who have not funded universities adequately and ambitious Vice-Chancellors" (Wallis, 1999).

In both Australia and the United Kingdom, a preoccupation with issues of market accountability steers the discursive imagination toward privileging the economic domains, leaving little discursive space to explore the nontechnological and noneconomic dimensions of international education. These visions are premised on, and seek to produce, the self-sufficient, individualistic, autonomous, modern subject.

PROTECTING BORDERS: RETERRITORIALIZATION

The international airport in the First World is one space where the status of the nation-state is unambiguous. Here, a range of practices assert the state's sovereign rights to monitor its borders and the flows of people that try to cross them. The curiously paradoxical logic of globalization, which accepts capital's right to unfettered journeys across any number of borders but sees the free passage of people from one space to another as profoundly problematic, becomes evident at the airport. A type of reterritorialization takes place as people are screened to ascertain their suitability to enter and reenter the sacrosanct territorial space of the nation-state. Tomlinson (1999) reminds us that border crossings are hardly ever power neutral. The First World business traveler is likely to have a set of cultural experiences that are not too far removed from his or her home culture. The unskilled labor migrant or asylum seeker, on the other hand, will experience fewer familiarities (pp. 146–147).

This is my sixth visit to the UK and I have learned the protocols of entry that I need to follow. I know that I can expect a few more questions than the average Australian traveler and I prepare myself accordingly. It's nothing "personal." It's because people from the Indian subcontinent, people who look like me, are still considered high risk of illegal entry into the United Kingdom. So, even though it is approaching 100 years since my ancestors left Bharat, the Indian subcontinent, a resurrection of the material and historical links between appearance, place, and culture means that I am transported back in time and phenomenologically located in an Indian spatiality. I need to convince the immigration official in front of me that I represent the more desirable element within the highly differentiated ethnoscape that they see everyday. I rattle off answers to his questions, politely, calmly, and confidently: the names of friends I will be staying with, their addresses, the people I will be interviewing as part of my research, when I will see them, when I will leave the UK and how much money I have with me.

Because I have the ultimate signifier of respectability, a 'First World' passport, which declares that I have right of residence in a sun-drenched antipodean paradise (Australia), after 5 minutes or so of questions and a quick check of the list of people restricted entry to the United Kingdom, I am rubber stamped to legal visitor status. I am released from my embodied identity and allowed to reclaim my 'First World' identity without having to experience at first hand the punitive practices of reterritorialization that an asylum seeker or refugee might face. The term 'Third World' may have left the sociological annals but it continues to reside in the rationalities and practices of airport officialdom. International students are no less susceptible to being ordered by their embodied and spatial identities, and these are scripted by geoeconomic and

---

CHAPTER 5

geopolitical referents within the global polity. Being an international student from Japan means a much easier passage through Customs and Immigration checkpoints than being a Nigerian or Mainland Chinese.

A hundred or so years ago, the ethnoscapes would have flowed from this European Old World to the New World. By the start of the 20th century a quarter of Europe's population had left the Old World for the New World. From 1846 to 1930, approximately 52 million people left Europe to settle in the United States, Latin America, Australia, New Zealand, and Africa (Canclini, 2000, p. 44). Then, the push factors were overwhelmingly poverty and oppression. Whole continents such as the Americas and Australia were subsequently 'bleached white' by means fair and foul, as these Old World ethnoscapes tried to recreate their cultural homes. The whiteness of these spaces is so naturalized that today few can imagine that it was ever different. Nowadays, the flow of people is the other way around—from the continents of color to the old imperial centers and temperate colonial outposts. The push factors are largely the same: war, poverty, and oppression.

THE LONDON SCHOOL OF ECONOMICS (LSE)

The LSE was established in 1895 by a group of intellectuals aligned with the Fabian Society. Prominent among its founders were Sidney and Beatrice Webb and George Bernard Shaw. The Webbs were inspired to develop an institution along the lines of the Ecole Libre des Sciences Politiques in Paris, an institution that could be counted on to further knowledge and research in economics and social matters (Dahrendorf, 1995, pp. 4–5). The LSE was not born in a liberal age. Its very existence, which arose from the bold motivations of its founders, reflected the symbiosis of power and knowledge. It was positioned at the center of intellectual currents, some progressive, some radical, others conservative, and some retrograde.

Writing about the history of the LSE, Dahrendorf (1995) notes that the founders of the LSE were motivated by the 5 Es: Education, Economics, Efficiency, Equality, and Empire (p. 29). It was inevitable, then, that these strange bedfellows would give rise to a series of disjunctive relations across places over time. Thus, equality in the metropolis coexisted with empire in the colonies. Dahrendorf notes that at the start of the 20th century, when the LSE was consolidating its identity, British imperialism was closely associated with economics. British politics was an instrument for advancing economic interests whether by protectionism or free trade (pp. 44–46). For the Webbs, equality extended to welcoming students from Asia to study at the LSE but it did not mean relinquishing the empire. The cosmopolitan Webbs visited India in 1898 and then again in 1911–1912, when they also traveled to Japan, Korea, China, Malaya, and Burma. During their 1912 visit they secured a generous grant from Indian industrialist, Ratan Tata, to study social problems in the United Kingdom. Examples like this suggest that transnational ironies existed even then, where a rich benefactor from a poor country gave money to an intellectual center to undertake research into social problems in the imperial metropolis. The central mission of the LSE, education, would have a practical dimension, with a particular focus on economics so as to contribute to efficiency, then a pressing requirement of 19th-century British industry. Against this background, education was able to coexist quite cheerfully with the juggernaut of industrial capitalism.

These contradictory ideals led to the young LSE receiving support from sources as diverse as the business community; intellectuals, including Fabians like the Webbs; and politicians (Dahrendorf, pp. 29–31). Although it would be relatively easy to fix the LSE into the values of the world of its inception, Dahrendorf offers this cautious injunction, "One must resist the temptation of identifying an institution, a university at that, with particular ideas or intellectual currents. Good universities are never of one piece" (p. 47).

By the 1990s, the LSE (or the School, as it is referred to by its community) was facing financial pressures similar to that facing many other UK universities. It responded with a series of market-like behaviors and practices including forming alliances with other private and public sector institutions, providing consultancy services, increasing student numbers, and introducing higher fees for international students.[26] In 1990, the LSE won the Queen's Award for Export Achievement, acknowledgment from the government of the day for its financial contributions to the economy (Dahrendorf, 1995, p. 500). It is arguable whether it would have received an equivalent award for its contributions as an academic institution (see Dahrendorf, 1995, p. 507; Halliday, 1999, pp. 107–108).

As a member of the Russell Group of Universities,[27] the LSE is considered a high-status institution, noted for its intellectual seriousness and con-

---

[26]In 1999–2000, the LSE reported an annual income of £85 million. It had 6,490 full-time and 790 part-time students; 18% of the LSE's international students are from Europe and 42% are from "more than 130 countries," making its international student body 60% of the total student population. The LSE is a popular choice in Southeast and East Asia, where it is regarded as an elite institution. Revenue from international student fees constitutes 29.7% of the LSE's total income (approximately £25.25 million). The LSE has 1,400 staff, of which 40% come from countries other than the United Kingdom (LSE, 2000). In addition, 53.3% of its students are non-UK nationals (almost the 60% referred to in another LSE publication). The greatest proportion of students is from Europe (19.6%) and Asia (19.5%). Together, the United Kingdom, Europe, and North America constitute 75.8% of its student body. In 2000, an international student at the LSE could expect to pay fees of £9,500 a year, compared with the £1,000 paid by E.U. and British students.

[27]The Russell Group of universities takes its collective name from the practice of its Vice-Chancellors of meeting once a year at the Russell Hotel.

sistently ranked within the top 10 British universities. In introducing itself, the School makes the following claims on behalf of its staff and alumni: "Seven Nobel laureates . . . 28 past or present heads of state . . . 32 UK Members of Parliament and 31 members of the House of Lords have either studied or taught at the LSE" (LSE, 2000). The theme of intellectual substance, a dominant part of the LSE's identity, reappears in the School's promotional materials as "the leading social science institution in the world" and "a place of genuine intellectual excitement and cutting edge research."

BRANDING FOR TRADITION: "WE HAVE NO SET VIEWS HERE"

A compelling impression of the LSE's prospectus and Web sites is its liberal use of traditional icons to promote itself. Chief among these are those icons that symbolize Britain's imperial history: Westminster Abbey, Nelson's Column at Trafalgar Square, the perfect circular dome of St. Paul's, Tower Bridge, and Big Ben (Fig. 5.5). What do these imperial signifiers represent in the form that they appear in the promotional brochures? Whom would they appeal to? What is the effect of their juxtapositions against a series of statements celebrating the LSE's cosmopolitanism and its regionalization as part of Europe? What do these images tell us about the LSE as an international university?

These imperial visual statements have a dual function: First, they construct England and the LSE as places of intellectual eminence and sites of power. Second, by perpetuating the grandeur of an old imperial city, these images are reworked into a discourse of education tourism. These imperial icons also help to create a discursive continuity between present-day intellectualism and the tradition of the Western canon. Offering continuity, certainty, and reliability, the suggestion here is that the Western canon is the assured route to success. A series of visual statements identify the LSE as the disseminator of, and the conduit through which, the 'timeless' Western canon is accessible.

In all, the majority of the images in the prospectus reassert the power of imperial traditions and imperial discursive practices. They suggest the perpetuity of imperial knowledges and their capacity to function as valued cultural capital and the source of positional goods in this new, regionalized world. We may now live in a more interrelated, interdependent world, where maps have been redrawn, where passports are no longer required at European border crossings for the 'right people', where new alliances are being made with old enemies, but we can be confident that these old and established knowledges will continue to have gravitas in this new world. Given all this, it is hardly surprising to find this statement in its prospectus:

FIG. 5.5. Big Ben.

151

"LSE believes in a traditional approach to teaching methods, ensuring students have a solid understanding of their subjects" (LSE, 2001a, p. 13).

This representation of the traditional as solid understanding imparts an authority and respectability to traditional teaching. It implies a particular perspective of society, social relations, and scholarship as this next statement confirms: "The LSE seeks to promote the impartial pursuit of knowledge and understanding about how people organise themselves into, and interact within social groupings" (LSE, 2001a, p. 8). The inference here is that the construction of knowledges, and their subsequent transmission and validation, are neutral undertakings unencumbered by power relations.

This is an astonishing claim to emerge in an epoch in which intellectual disciplines such as feminism and the "posts"—postcolonialism, poststructuralism, and postmodernism—have challenged normative conceptions of knowledge and the impartiality of scholarship. Such claims to impartiality disguise the geopolitical asymmetries of knowledge production, transmission, and validation across the globe. It is not being suggested that the School's scholarship does not engage with critical knowledges and other forms of social organization. What is surprising is the discursive romance with imperial cultural forms in its marketing materials. By default, what is being inferred is a geopolitical and historical amnesia about scholarship's complicity in conquest, colonization, and domination (see Said, 1993; Tuhiwai-Smith, 1999).

BUILDING SELF-RELIANT AND INTELLECTUALLY SERIOUS SUBJECTS

A deep-seated discursive regularity that is at work in the LSE's promotional brochures is the implicit valorizing of individualism. "It's up to you" is the overriding message. Although the institution claims, "We have no set ideas," a closer reading of the statements in the prospectus reveals an espousal of ideas and practices that are embedded in the individual.

The School's prospectus pays special attention to the discursively powerful world of work and careers. References to the careers available to LSE graduates ("at banks, industrial companies, professional firms, insurance companies . . . as stock brokers, management trainees, personnel officers, researchers and analysts, publishers and booksellers, lawyers, charity and social workers and civil servants"; LSE, 2001b, p. 16) are sprinkled throughout the promotional brochures. Some employers such as the World Bank and the IMF are selected for special mention. Importantly, there is promise of access to particular forms of social capital: "We have alumni in many countries providing a very useful contact network" (LSE, 2001b, p. 16).

A large number of visual statements are used to signify student life at LSE. These are accompanied by captions that construct openness, energy, and dynamism: "no set ideas"; "tremendous opportunities to challenge and debate"; "opening up new avenues of thought"; "relevant, outward-looking, always looking to the future"; and "you can't get away with stating the obvious." However, a perusal of the prospectus suggests a disjuncture between the meanings embodied in the captions, and the images of student life.

Most of the student images convey an impression of a solitary and serious student life. Students are depicted staring at computers, reading, taking notes, listening in a lecture, and raising their hands, presumably to answer a question. It is all about hard work. Other images depict students striding purposefully forward. But most of the images depict a passive student body that is pictured listening intently to an authoritative figure, taking note of what is said. Nearly all images feature individuals, although there is the occasional picture of a group or pair of students. Many student images occupy whole pages, suggesting the attribution of some significance to their role. Complementing these images of student life are images of instructors, both male and female, in what appear to be powerfully didactic poses (LSE, 2001a, 2001b).

Read against an associated discursive field that features tradition and intellectual seriousness, these visual statements can be said to construct a preferred subjectivity of the solitary, responsible, self-sufficient individual. Elsewhere in the prospectus, a number of statements espouse the merits to individual achievement: "Self motivation is key to reaching your goal"; "There is complete openness and it is up to the individual to make the most of this opportunities" (LSE, 2001a). The message is explicit—there are no barriers at the LSE, only those that individual students may put up. These statements can be said to function as instruments of individualization and responsibilization: Students are constructed as free and autonomous beings who are located in an open environment. Each individual is a sovereign subject, with a unified and substantive sense of self, and master of his or her destiny. They simply have to be responsible to make the most of this opportunity.

Finally, despite the strength of its promotional message as a "a world centre of research and teaching" and "a global and cosmopolitan institution" (LSE, 2001b), a corpus of statements privilege a First World spatiality. The flow of knowledge from center to periphery is subsequently normalized: "The LSE has been a laboratory of the social sciences, a place where ideas are developed, analysed, evaluated and disseminated around the globe" (LSE, 2001a). There is something potentially problematic about conceptualizing an international university as a First World laboratory whose goal is to develop ideas that are "disseminated around the globe." It carries traces of an older cultural text of the colonial educator who generates ideas in the metropolitan center and thereafter transmits them as universal. It is entirely possible that the large percentage of the School's intellectuals, including the 40% of the staff who are international, may contribute to a deterritorialization of knowledge but we can't be sure, given the strong marketing emphasis on tradition and claims to the objectivity of knowledge.

"GLOBAL AND COSMOPOLITAN": SELF–OTHER RELATIONS

By boldly describing itself as global and cosmopolitan, the School constructs an image that has moved beyond the internationalist orientation of the nation-state to a globalist vision. How convincing is this? Certainly, a striking impression of the LSE's promotional materials is of very significant numbers of students of non-Western, non-White appearance. The School's commitment to recruiting a culturally diverse student body sees its multicultural student body featured on the front cover of its prospectus (see Fig. 5.6). Shot in sophisticated black-and-white photography, these images of others exude both seriousness and dynamism and are present in all of the School's promotional brochures and Web sites. The culturally diverse group of students include those of African, Caucasian, Chinese, and South Asian heritages. Both genders are equally represented. There are also several images of Muslim women with head coverings within the prospectus.

The international and intercultural composition of the student body is promoted as one of the strengths of studying at the LSE: "I'm in the company of so many different people from around the world," "You make friends from all over the world," and "You make connections all over the world." Captions such as "you make connections all over the world" can be read as a tentative recognition by the School of social relations that cut across cultural, linguistic, and national boundaries. But such references appear to privilege the instrumental ahead of other modes of relation, as exemplified by quotes such as this: "We have alumni in many countries providing a very useful contact network." A notable omission is the relative dearth of images of phenotypically different students interacting with each other. The majority are images of solitary students who appear to be working tenaciously toward their goal. Student life is presented as a serious endeavor. The largely monocultural images could also be read as implying conservatism, perhaps even a reticence, to embrace the possibilities of cross-cultural social relations.

The international student presence is normalized by front cover "pin-ups." A strong message emerges from the prospectus: This is no exotic side-

FIG. 5.6.   No exotic sideshow, diversity up front.

show; these people are a vital part of the LSE. We expect these subjects to
have particular attributes—they are intellectually elite and cosmopolitan.
However, when read against the discourse of tradition, the tacit assumption
is that their brand of cosmopolitanism must be inscribed within acceptable
parameters including acceptance of Britain's role as an imperial educator
and recognition of the superiority of the Western canon.

The global and cosmopolitan marketing message, then, works discursively to brand the LSE as international and global by way of the countries,
cultures, students, and alumni communities it embraces. The key question
is how substantive are the LSE's engagements with difference and multiple
globalizations? The LSE prides itself on its highly differentiated ethnoscape
(60% of students are non-British and 40% of staff are international). Are
these impressive statistics translating into productive transcultural and
transnational exchanges? The answer invariably depends on who answers
the question:

> Most of us, I don't know if it is our fault or not but we . . . hang out with
> Singaporeans more often . . . even in class, you seldom talk to your class-
> mates. . . . I think it is because we are a little bit afraid . . . in a way, to talk to
> new people. . . . You feel sometimes intimidated and like that there is nothing
> much to talk to them about because there is no common ground. . . . I mean
> they drink beer and the general feeling is they don't study as much as the
> Asians do.
>
> If I go by my experience . . . there are very few interpersonal relationships.
> In the class, it is not really like that [student refers to a picture of diverse
> group of students, pictured in the prospectus as engaged in animated conver-
> sation]. (Singaporean female student, undergraduate, 2nd year economics)

These feelings of anxiety and intimidation, of not having common
ground, act as barriers against the development of cosmopolitan sensibilities on both sides—international and home-country students. This is com-
pounded by the prevalence of ethnocultural stereotyping ("they don't
study as much as the Asians do"). At the same time, the desire to develop
and consolidate a sense of community and build affinities with similar people is strong.

Yet, the official view is that the institution is about providing international education, which is translated as: being educated in a global way, not
just looking at your particular backyard. This is perceived to be major factor
that distinguishes the LSE from other British universities:

> I think the mistake that many recruiting institutions make is only to look at in-
> ternational students as . . . money . . . or as a kind of opportunity to teach
> them about British culture. International [education] both in terms of . . . be-
> ing away from home but also international in terms of who they are studying

with. . . . In a small class of ten people here, you will find that most people come from different countries . . . 40% of our staff are international . . . we do have . . . both [a] universal and international curriculum here, I would say. . . . If you are in a tutorial group with six or seven people from six or seven different countries, no one country dominates. So they have to mix. . . . Except the Americans. There are 600 Americans here. (LSE staff, White, male)

The suggestion here is that the close confines of the campus, tutorial groups where no national group dominates, like the much vaunted Internet, are sufficient preconditions to rewrite the geographical imagination and the social imaginaire. Also, there is a disjuncture between the official view—that studying in a renowned international university such as the LSE means that you meet people from all over the world—and the lived realities of some student interviewees. Studying overseas offers an opportunity to engage in a kind of border crossing, an opportunity to encounter the other, to develop new sensibilities, and to refine old ones. Studying *with* international students offers home-country students the same opportunities to experiment, to challenge their values and affiliations, and to consolidate or transform them into new ideas and values. Yet the lived realities can be disappointing.

Globalization and the Social Imagination

What is thinkable and sayable about globalization at this global and cosmopolitan university? The following two narrative accounts are instructive of how the global is embodied and translated into practices:

Globalization is . . . the formation of transnational governance where sovereign power is less important and transnational power is much more important. So, it is the switching around of . . . huge amounts of capital . . . without any national barriers. And it is the group of organizations like the EU which break down national barriers and national identities. . . . The key factor of globalization is how quickly the communication revolution has hit us all and education is just one aspect of that. Anybody can sit at home, look at our website and decide that they want to come to LSE. Now, 15 years ago it was impossible. It would have been difficult to find out the information in the first place. You would have to track down . . . not necessarily even the British Council, you would have to track down a former student. (LSE staff, male)

Two clusters of statements are discernible from this vignette. First, capital is constructed as an object with the ability to glide effortlessly across time and space. Its hypermobility confers a transnational power that exceeds the disciplining efforts of the nation-state. Second, a form of governance is in place that is dismantling national identities. All-powerful instrumentalities such as the European Union are invested with considerable power to "break down . . . national barriers and national identities." There is an implicit disquiet here at the subsuming of nation-centered identities, despite the positive rhetoric in the recruitment literature linking the School to Europe. Globalization is also understood as a technological phenomenon, a communication revolution. Here, the inference is to a force that has rapidly, and with stealth, crept in ("hit us all"). Education's role in the globalization agenda is imagined in somewhat powerless terms, able only to react to the awesome forces of globalization: "Education is just one aspect of [the communication revolution]."

These statements construct globalization as a punitive phenomenon with considerable risks: It destroys national identities and it means unruly capital that cannot be disciplined by the state. The subjects produced by, and presumed in, these statements have limited agency. Economic globalization is placed at the top of the hierarchy of globalizations. Its awesome power suggests that we are being carried by its rapid torrents and flows. Citizen subjectivities are being broken down by supranational bodies such as the European Union. The corollary of the erosion of national identities is reduced possibilities for a national society to support funding of nation-centered universities. Under these conditions, the emergent subjectivity for the university is necessarily marketized, and the university becomes vulnerable to the machinations of economic and technological globalization.

The flows of information and people, and the reduction in communication barriers do not necessarily manifest in a reimaging of identity. This Singaporean student observes that the globe cannot be a referent for her identity; it is the nation-state that has a prior and enduring claim:

> Globalization? Movement of people and capital and information between countries. . . . It becomes easier to get information transmitted across countries and people can move more freely, yes . . . maybe less barriers. . . . If you are Singaporean you will always feel Singaporean at heart . . . no matter how you like to . . . emulate other nationalities. (Singaporean, undergraduate, female)

Here is an instrumental view of globalization that focuses on its possibilities and opportunities. At the same time, it is a response anchored in the continuing importance of the nation-state. Globalization cannot dilute or minimize a person's affinities and relationships to the nation-state: "You will always feel Singaporean at heart. No matter how you like to emulate other nationalities." She raises another point, namely that the compression of space associated with studying overseas can have a countereffect by intensifying affinities with the local-national and producing the loyal, national, ethnocultural subject:

After coming here . . . in a way . . . it makes you appreciate home more. . . . It makes you appreciate Singapore even more. . . . So, I would say that I am more of a Singaporean now than less. . . . If you are in your own country and you have everything . . . you take everything for granted. It is only when you leave your home that you start to miss things, just little things about your country. . . .

Most of us are still quite tuned towards Singapore. We keep up an active interest in what is happening. . . . It's not that after we come here, we forget everything about Singapore. We don't. We still mix with Singaporeans, we talk to each other about what is happening in Singapore and things like that. (Singaporean undergraduate, female)

What these statements reveal is the existence of a set of counterforces to the extraterritorial processes associated with globalization. These create and sustain heterotopias,[28] which have the potential to inscribe and reinforce particular subjectivities including nation-centered identities, religious subject positions, and ethnocultural affiliations. Against this backdrop of complex affiliations, even brand-name international universities such as the LSE find themselves hosts to myriad heterotopias that yield uncertain consequences. Former LSE student and terrorist, Omar Sheikh's conversion to Islamic militancy is noted to have occurred when he was recruited to the cause while a mathematics student at the LSE in 1992 (McCarthy, 2002).[29]

BRANDING THE INTELLECTUALLY SERIOUS UNIVERSITY

A few general comments about the type of marketing used by the LSE is instructive in understanding its engagement with the international education market. Although an intellectually elite institution in Britain, the LSE does not have access to the sorts of endowments available to the American Ivy League universities or those commanded by the Oxbridge universities. Its financial difficulties have been a major driving force for its increased recruitment of international students.

Nonetheless, despite being forced to engage in market-like behaviors, there are some differences in how it constructs its marketing message and the recruitment geography it targets. First, it seeks to convey an image of a serious university, as these staff comments suggest:

---

[28]Heterotopia is a concept that Foucault introduced to refer to "the ways in which different spaces can come into contact with other spaces that bear little relation to them" (Danaher, Schirato, & Webb, 2000, p. 113).

[29]Omar Sheikh, British born and a former LSE student, was convicted of terrorism activities including the murder of Daniel Pearl, an American journalist in 2002. He is thought to have been recruited while a member of the LSE Muslim Students Association.

> Serious, international, academically of the highest standards . . . Very diverse
> community. Very vibrant community. Pretty classic. That is why it [prospec-
> tus] is black and white and gold. Simple colours. (LSE staff, male, responsibil-
> ities for marketing)

In seeking to sustain its 'intellectually serious' image, the LSE distinguishes itself from 'other' institutions including those in Australia so as to
maintain its positional status:

> It [Australian approach] is too brash. I mean, it is very young. It is very dy-
> namic. But it reflects the types of students who go to Australia and the types of
> students who go to the UK. The education, to some extent, in some institu-
> tions is incidental. It is a lifestyle choice. . . . There are key institutions in Aus-
> tralia that will attract students that are very, very serious. But they really are
> the minority of institutions, I think compared to the UK . . . it is a much less
> serious student . . . a much less serious student. (LSE staff, male)

Country-name branding has emerged as an important discursive practice in
international education markets. The Education UK promotional campaign has been emulated by other countries such as Australia, New Zealand, and Singapore.

The LSE's intellectually serious branding means avoiding the mass-
marketing approach of education fairs and exhibitions:

> We have dropped out of all the education fairs elsewhere in the world. . . . For
> us they do not work. . . . For us as a brand, our participation in education fairs
> helps those around us rather than helping ourselves.

Building a serious brand name means promotional brochures that outline comprehensive information about the courses offered and lists of pre-
liminary readings (in the undergraduate prospectus). There are no student
testimonials, suggesting two things. First, the intellectual elite who attend
the university do not market anything. Second, there is no need for a customer to endorse the LSE brand as its credibility is universally accepted.

Its Web site reflects the LSE's understated approach to marketing (see
Fig. 5.7). It has a simple graphical layout, and it is uncluttered, unpreten-
tious, and easy to navigate. Visual stimuli are minimalist and orderly so as
not to intrude onto or subordinate the textual narratives. There is a pur-
poseful use of colors that delineate key areas of information rather than dis-
tracting the viewer. In this era of self-promotion the School is not entirely
averse to extracting currency from good news. In a bold public relations
spin, the News section announces, "Another Economics Nobel Laureate
With an LSE Link." However, there is nothing that suggests a hard sell here.

**London School of Economics
and Political Science**

■ **News**
Another Economics Nobel
laureate with an LSE link
■ **Events**
24th October 2001
Language & Citizenship
■ **New arrivals** - information for
new students
■ Job opportunities at the LSE
■ **School moves**
■ Language Centre

Directories

■ Telephone and E-Mail directory
■ Teaching timetables
■ Web access to E-mail service
■ Experts
■ Webguide
■ LSEjobs

About LSE
Departments and Institutes
Students
Services and administration

Studying
Undergraduate & Postgraduate,
General Course, Language Centre,
Summer School and more.......

Departments and Research
Current research, publications ,
academic staff, news and events,
Experts.

Library

LSE for YOU
Personalised access to School
databases for students and staff.

FIG. 5.7.   LSE Web site (LSE, 2002).

Although it strives hard to be intellectually serious in its marketing and promotion of international education, the School's image-management strategies have more than a passing reference to tourist discourses. By deploying national and local tourist icons, the LSE is constructed as a desirable institution in which to study. The School's location and character as a campus located in London are marketed as particularly strong distinguishing points. The LSE offers a study experience that embraces highly localized, place-based benefits: "[in] the heart of London [which is], one of the world's great capital cities and a focal point in the increasing integration of Europe." The LSE is "less than a mile from the legal, financial and business centres of Europe lending the School a dynamic and 'real world' feel, which is not found in the tranquillity of a rural campus or the traditions of dreaming spires" (LSE, 2002).

These examples confirm the importance of place construction and place branding in the marketing of international education. In celebrating its links with London, the LSE expresses a particular spatial identity: that of a key financial and political center. London is constructed as the nerve center where interconnections are made with capital, power, influence, and authority. It is these types of social relations that are highlighted in the prospectus rather than others, which may have less utilitarian value to an intellectually ambitious clientele of students. Not surprising, the deep-seated animosity to British integration with Europe, a salient "Little Island" discourse currently being transmitted and validated by significant proportions of the British establishment, has no place in this promotional message. Instead, the prospectus describes London as "a focal point in the increasing integration of Europe."

London's now-significant and visible cultural hybridity is repackaged and represented by the signifying term *cosmopolitan,* an altogether more acceptable term than *multicultural,* with its suggestions of migrant ghettos. *Cosmopolitan* suggests a desirable habitus; it brings to mind the finesse of cultural capital and is more likely to be associated with governing and globetrotting elites. *Cosmopolitan* is, in other words, less suggestive of the other and otherness.

What, then, can we conclude about the discursive constructions of international education in and through the LSE's promotional materials? How is this international university imagined? Who is the international student subject? Which notions of subjectivity are being normalized by the LSE's promotional discourses? Although the textual messages uphold the School's commitment to intellectual openness and debate, expressed in such declarations as, "we have no set ideas," the semiotic and textual representations provide both conjunctive and disjunctive messages. There is a suggestion of intellectual freedom, but the images of individual students pictured immersed in some aspect of solitary study suggest a pliability and intellectual subjectivity that celebrates the quiet absorption of received wisdom. The large numbers of culturally different people in brochures and Web sites normalize the cultural diversity on campus, but a closer reading reveals less emphasis on transcultural social capital networks.

Like any 21st-century university, the School's global and cosmopolitan mission will need to embrace the local, national, and international, and to mediate the creative tensions emerging from its multiple missions. It faces the challenges of training professionals toward sustainable and socially just visions that are both national and international, local and global. A starting point could be in recognizing the mutually reciprocal relationships between power and knowledge. Making claims in support of an apolitical, objective body of knowledge will do little to create possibilities for developing new knowledges and practices that can make some contributions to a polycentric world (Allen, 2000, pp. 18–19; Slater, 2003, pp. 324–327).

From an elite university, I now examine a mass university and former polytechnic—Oxford Brookes University—to contrast how a new university is responding to the opportunities and exigencies within the highly competitive international education market.

Having access to state-of-art First World communication technologies, I arrange interviews at Oxford Brookes using e-mail contact and telephone calls. Heeding warnings from friends to "avoid Paddington Station at all costs," which was reported to be undergoing essential engineering works and track replacements after the 1999 Paddington train disaster (an indictment of privatization?), I decide to travel by road to Oxford. My first time–space barrier is negotiated successfully at 5:30 a.m. The aging Northern Line, consistently voted as "the Tube line most likely to break down," delivers me to a connecting station with no problems. I arrive at Victoria coach station in good time to catch the Oxford Citylink bus. It is a wet and windy day, and the bus negotiates the already busy streets slowly. We drive past Marble Arch and Hyde Park, its leafless trees shrouded in soft mist. Then the traffic snarls to a halt on the M40. The bus waits motionless for 45 minutes. A truck has overturned on the M40, some inflammable chemicals have leaked onto the highway, and we are stuck, as police cars and fire engines with sirens blaring drive past.

My anxiety grows and I am now convinced that compressing space and time is a luxury open to a wealthy elite. The person next to me, who tells me that he is an Oxford don, becomes chattier and more cheerful. He is of that rare breed of persons that need a crisis to come out of their shell. "I have been traveling on this bus for 7 years and this has never happened," he announces, his face breaking out in a boyish grin. He offers me use of his mobile phone to contact my interviewees and then plunges into a discussion of his promising Ph.D. student who is having a crisis about an academic career, "Her thesis is easily the best I have supervised for 5 years, but there you are. Says she needs to find out what she really wants." At 11:45 a.m., I arrive for my 10:30 appointment. Stuttering my apologies, I am ushered through Headington Hill Hall, a magnificent stately home previously occupied by the failed media tycoon Robert Maxwell. It looks onto landscaped lawns, which are dotted with beautiful and rare trees.

OXFORD BROOKES UNIVERSITY

Founded in 1865 as Oxford Polytechnic, Oxford Brookes (hereafter referred to as Brookes) was conferred with university status in 1992. Brookes has a student profile[30] that is fairly typical of the newer British universities.

---

[30]The majority of its students are undergraduates (73.9%), with 21.2% undertaking postgraduate coursework and 2.9% of its students enrolled in research-based degrees. In 1999–2000, Brookes had 15,935 enrolled students; 13.5% of these were non-E.U. international students (approximately 1,800). Revenue from international student fees contributes approximately £8.5 million to the university.

For young universities like Brookes, which entered the international education market without a recognizable brand name and traditional reputation, their ability to reconfigure themselves according to market contingencies will determine their success or failure in the market. New universities tend to brand by emphasizing their contemporary relevance, their flexibility, and their ability to offer prospective students an experience akin to educational tourism. The discursive construction of their place of location as a desirable tourist commodity is another strategy to create interest and to boost their recruitment statistics. To this end, it is not unlikely for universities to steer themselves toward educational tourism to balance their budgets.

MEDIATING LOCAL–GLOBAL TENSIONS

Brookes' marketing materials make much of its location in Oxford. A senior staff member observes, "We are successful . . . partly because of the location, partly because Oxford is a name associated with education." Brookes introduces itself as thus: "Set in the majestic city of Oxford where a world-renowned tradition of academia is partnered by new technologies, Oxford Brookes is the ideal place to further your education" (Oxford Brookes University, 2001a, p. 1). Place, tradition, and dynamic new technologies are seamlessly linked here, bringing the past and present together. Oxford, historical place of learning, is a signifier of tradition, continuity, and academic quality. Brookes, on the other hand, is the bridge that connects a world-renowned academic institution with new technologies to "further your education." A successful place-branding strategy marries the nostalgia of tradition with educational utility to construct Brookes as a "great university" (see Fig. 5.8).

Like many new universities, flexibility is elevated to the status of the main selling idea. Educational flexibility is translated to mean the provision of accelerated programs in keeping with an ethos of just-in-time production. Multiple pathways are a central signifier of this flexibility, realized through advanced standing and credit transfer arrangements with other overseas public and private higher education providers. Flexibility, then, is about increasing opportunities to access a Brookes credential. It also means offering something of interest to everybody, "a programme, similar to the American system . . . vast choice of courses . . . subjects which interest you . . . while building a foundation for your career" (Oxford Brookes University, 2001a, p. 1). Here, highlighting the cultural capital of the American university credential serves as a strategic marketing ploy to make Brookes a more attractive destination not only for study abroad students from the United States but also those from East Asia, where a U.S. style higher education is

FIG. 5.8. Oxford: "Seat of centuries-old learning."

FIG. 5.9.   Winning medals.

now considered to have a higher status than other country brands. The marketing narratives also consolidate the education–work nexus: The international education experience is about building a foundation for your career and the Brookes' path to success is graduate employment.

> Oxford Brookes is one of the UK's most successful new universities. This continuing success is based on addressing the needs of our students as well the reputation of our graduates whose success places us in the top ten universities for employment prospects. (Oxford Brookes University, 2001c, p. 1)

What is sayable and thinkable about the quality of international education and the international university are shaped by markets through audits and league table rankings (see Fig. 5.9). Dispersed throughout the prospectus are images of medals, used to signify an award-winning university.[31] Given that medals and league tables are derived from, and base their appeal on competitive sport, the use of these metaphors normalizes competitiveness not only between and within universities, but also in the educational experiences of individual students. Sports analogies work to displace moral and ethical considerations from the university's mission. By normalizing competitiveness, these metaphors depoliticize the current global trade in education services. The myth of a global education market as a gigantic playing field where an honest and fair contest is played out, by willing parties, emerges from this discourse (see Agnew, 1998, pp. 46–47, 71–72, for a discussion of myths and metaphors).

---

[31]Examples of the awards won by Brookes are scattered throughout the international prospectus. These include: Guardian Newspaper University Guide: 1st in UK, Catering and Hospitality Management. Other "medals" to be found in the prospectus include: Guardian Newspaper University Guide '99: Built Environment, 2nd in the UK and Quality Assurance, Planning. Rated Excellent.

The global trade in education services is strongly influenced by ever-changing forces that affect national, economic, health and nation-state policies. The nuances of working with different markets demands attention to the project of impression management. Marketing geographies change, and having accurate ethnocultural student profiles in priority markets—countries where the marketing effort is concentrated—is vital. Incorporating the changing semiosis of ethnicities and cultures into promotional materials is particularly important. There are risks of disjunctures between promotional images and the nuances of particular markets that may well be multiracial and multicultural. Crude racialized categories, which are informed by a residual pseudoscientific 19th-century dividing technology, usually fail to capture these ethnocultural nuances. The Kenyan market for Brookes, for example, does not constitute Kenyans of an African heritage but those from a South Asian–Indian heritage (see Fig. 5.10). Here, the director of Brookes' International Office remarks on an image that is disjunc-

FIG. 5.10.   "Not the right Kenyan."

tive for one of its priority markets: "I was a little concerned about putting him there because our market is not . . . Black students. It is predominantly Asian. . . . Even in Kenya, it is mainly Asian students."

At the same time as recruiting full-fee-paying international students, British universities also compete with each other for domestic students to secure government funding. The images and narratives in generic publications must therefore reflect and resonate with the typical domestic customer base if it is to appeal to this group (Oxford Brookes University, 2001c). Here, as in the international prospectus, getting the right mix of genders, colors, and ethnicities is paramount. A semiotic translation of international thus involves balancing images of blonde students (discursive markers of the European or UK market for students) with Asian (Indian heritage market) images and Asian (overseas Chinese heritage markets) together with images of African heritage students, who may be local or overseas students.

> We are an international university and we [need to] have a good mix of students . . . it is trying to get a balance on these students. So we have . . . white students, blondes [and] Asians. (staff member, marketing responsibilities)

Constructing a favorable representation of university life is central. Impression management tactics are a vital complement to the university's ability to produce internationally recognized credentials. To this end, a type of censoring takes place so as not to draw attention to local libertarian attitudes to relationships and alcohol consumption. A staff member notes,

> There are certain images that we don't show. . . . A lot of our Malaysians students [are] . . . Muslims. We try to keep away from pictures of students drinking in the bars unless they are drinking orange juice. . . . One of the pictures in the front page of the Summer School brochure had a nice picture of an Asian with a big glass of orange juice. Which is a good image. . . . We try not to have students sitting in a bedroom of mixed sex, that would be appropriate for the European market but . . . you couldn't show that overseas.

In one image, two Chinese heritage students (see Fig. 5.11) in the section of the international prospectus titled 'Leisure Activities' appear to be window shopping, suggesting an altogether safer pastime and one suited for international students. What is the purpose of this censoring and what does it suggest? A close reading of these images and the interview data suggests that universities are increasingly sensitive about offending parental, cultural, and religious sensibilities. Studying overseas is in several respects a high-risk undertaking in the eyes of the families of students. Aside from the considerable financial costs, there are commonly held fears of losing one's cultural and religious identity. It is far easier to respond to this type of con-

FIG. 5.11.   Constructing the "right" image.

servatism with a series of window-dressing strategies than to undertake a critical engagement with what is being taught as international education or to reexamine how subjectification processes reproduce a passive and deficient international student.

Brookes' transformation within a decade, from a vocationally oriented polytechnic in the heart of Oxfordshire to a university that draws its students and financial revenue from international sources, has seen it become part of a geographically spatialized network. It deploys a range of procedures and strategies, including the use of agents, advertisements, interview sessions, and British Council–sponsored education exhibitions or fairs to reach its multiple constituencies. Practices are fine-tuned and emphases shifted while keeping an open mind to the types of offshore collaborations that will work in the university's interests.[32] Engaging with a geography of markets involves

---

[32]Brookes has two types of agents: List A agents and List B agents. List A agents are those who are "key agents" who "almost run the office for us." In addition to recruiting students, they supply the university with market information at local sites, information that could affect student

significant expenditures, and on occasions, uneasy alliances between not-for-profit educational organizations and agents whose interests are overtly commercial and centered around more immediate profits. Monitoring the efficacy of using private agents is an ongoing process:

> A huge amount of effort is involved in working with agents . . . huge amounts. And the market returns that we get . . . for example out of 295 postgraduate students, 26 came from agents. Which isn't many. (staff, International Office)

A host of factors, national and international, tend to influence recruitment targets, a reminder of how risky it is to peg the long-term financial viability of educational institutions on international education markets. Here, a staff member comments on the impact of national government policies in two sites, Malaysia and Singapore:

> There is encouragement from the Malaysian government for students to stay at home rather than to go overseas. . . . We now have a 3 + 0 with Nillai and we have a 2 + 1 with Sunway. And we are just starting one with KDU [Kolej Damansara Utama].[33]
> We are not on the major lists [of] the Singaporean government. So, for engineers and lawyers, we are not on the major lists. So they [students] are not recognised if they come to do Engineering or Law at Oxford Brookes. So, we are unlikely to get these students.

In response to the Asian financial crisis of 1997, the Malaysian government imposed controls on the outflows of foreign exchange and encouraged students to choose a local provider to complete their education. The economic downturn that accompanied the crisis also affected the numbers of middle-class families with sufficient resources to send their children overseas to study. In the case of Singapore, government-controlled professional association boards wield tremendous influence in deciding which

---

interest in Brookes' courses including labor market trends. They are also pivotal in establishing relationships with key organizations and authorities as a means of furthering Brookes' interests. List B agents are those that recruit students for Brookes and are paid a percentage of student fees as a commission. Typically, List B agents represent several universities. The effectiveness of agents in some markets is increasingly under question as the previous response suggests, although in other markets they remain the most effective means of recruiting international students (personal communication, director, International Office, November 10, 2000).

[33]A 3 + 0 arrangement means that the student completes all 3 years of study in the home country in a Brookes' approved and assessed course. A 2 + 1 arrangement is an advanced standing arrangement where 2 years are completed in the home country and 1 year at Brookes. Nillai, Sunway, and KDU are private colleges.

credentials are recognized by the state.[34] Marketization brings risks that can translate into an ongoing institutional anxiety. Universities such as Brookes, without the reputation of old brands, cannot afford to be heavily reliant on a narrow range of country-specific markets; they must always be vigilant of changes. A marketing strategy that spreads itself too thinly and attempts to attract students from too diverse a set of markets is risky.

Having the right touch of attentiveness without holding out glossy promises that cannot be met is also important:

> You need to have a rapid response with everything that they wish to know about the university. Rapid response. . . . In a professional way without being overtly commercial. . . . They can see through glossy promises . . . people are bombarded by glossy promises. . . . So you can't make it too commercial. It is a soft sell . . . it's nurturing, nurturing . . . converting applications . . . [to] students. (Staff, recruitment)

To what extent is education perceived as a commodity like any other, to be bought and sold in a global market? There is some disquiet about conceptualizing education in commodity terms, as these responses show:

> There is no advantage, no value to the student and no value to us to bring a student half-way around the world, spending an enormous amount of money and then failing. . . . I think that it is a big responsibility. Now, I am not sure that it is so in the car industry or any other industry. . . . My view about selling education is that it is an enormous responsibility. . . . What we would not do, and I drum this into everyone who goes overseas, we do not bring students over here unless we are 90%, maybe 100% or 90% certain that they are going to succeed! (senior staff, male, recruitment)

This view is a somewhat unusual one to emerge from education marketing circles where the view is to allow consumers to exercise choices as they see fit and to manage whatever risks that arise accordingly, including the likelihood of failing to graduate. Here is a position that rests on the producer (university) bearing responsibility to assess the student's potential for succeeding before entering into an arrangement to provide access to a range of education services such as lectures, tutorials, teaching materials, computer facilities, library resources, and so on. There is an implicit acknowledgment in this statement that education cannot be considered as a simple commodity or service. There is also recognition that these ideals can, and have been, subverted: "[Bringing someone who doesn't have a

---

[34]Graduates can still work in their designated fields if their qualifications are not recognized by these state boards but they are limited to private sector employment.

chance of passing] does happen, admittedly, it will happen" (senior staff, male, Recruitment Division).

The gatekeeping roles of faculty present problems to younger universities like Brookes which are not guaranteed high-caliber international students and face pressures of earning income:

> Just getting the academic schools to develop courses that are attractive to students is difficult. They will tend to develop courses that (a) they are interested in and . . . (b) they have the expertise to deliver. . . . When they find that their numbers [of international students] are not increasing in a way they would like them to increase, then it is time to start talking to them about developing different courses. . . . They don't listen to us instantly. (senior staff recruitment, female)

Faculty do eventually capitulate, iterating Slaughter and Leslie's (1997) finding that universities and individual academics will employ market-like behaviors to maintain revenue flows and to protect and maximize personal and institutional reputations.

Brookes' profile, then, is typical of many younger universities in the United Kingdom and Australia. Faced with the demands of national policy, it has successfully reconfigured itself into an international university. However, its engagement with the international has largely been in terms of recruiting international students. The university is faced with balancing the tension between constructing an image that appeals to its local constituents at the same time as sustaining a global appeal. Its ability to function as a facilitative node in a network of cultural processes is by its own admission limited. By default, then, its construction of international education continues to be shaped by an earlier neocolonial text, where the primary focus is to educate others while itself remaining aloof from deep and complex engagements with the global other.

"One-Way" Internationalization

The four dimensions that make up Brookes' internationalization policy—recruitment of international students, internationalization of the curriculum, collaborations to run academic programs offshore, and international links to undertake joint research—are not accorded equal status. The institutional priority has been recruitment of international students:

> In terms of having a concerted, concentrated effort on developing the internationalisation of the university . . . that hasn't really started yet.
>   They [students] tend to be taught a very British style . . . and they learn how to assimilate. . . . Then they get a credential and they go back again. I think that we have a long way to go. (recruitment staff, male)

There are many, many issues that we have to get to grips with. One would be to try to encourage our UK students to think about the benefits that international students bring to the curriculum or to the way of life here. We haven't really exploited that. Likewise, some of the staff may be . . . we need to get them to think more flexibly about international students. (recruitment staff, female)

Two key areas have been flagged for internationalization: internationalizing the student experience on campus and staff development. Putting this vision to work, though, has been less straightforward. Here, a senior manager in the university talks about the lived realities of providing international education at the ground level:

There is certainly evidence that students will work within their own groups because they feel comfortable within that group. . . . And whether it is right . . . whether we should integrate these groups and what is the best way to do so. The other strand is staff development . . . an understanding of the different processes that students go through when they are coming over. I mean UK students will question, they will ask you, "What are you doing that for . . ." whereas students from China will not. . . . I mean they will listen . . . they will soak . . . it takes a while to get into that. In terms of writing essays . . . whereas students from another part of the world will come at it in a different way . . . and . . . a member of staff could look at this one as waffling, because "OK, you are coming over to a UK university, you will get a UK experience and we expect you to be like a UK university student." (staff with responsibilities in international recruitment, male)

"Not questioning, different writing style, waffling" suggest that staff perceptions remain anchored in problematizing the international student rather than addressing the situational dimensions (e.g., learning in a second language, adjusting to a vastly different institutions, etc.). The deficient subjectivity imposed on the international student resonates with staff and domestic students:

In many cases, they are seen by the UK students as being possibly a hindrance to their work. Particularly where there is group work. Many of them don't want to work with international students. They don't understand them, they think their English is not good enough. And that is a problem. What some of the staff may see is . . . international students can be difficult. . . . One of the biggest problems we have is plagiarism. (recruitment responsibilities, female)

These candid accounts suggest that students' affective geographies, or social relations, continue to be ordered along territorial (place-based) lines. Notions of "them and us," "stranger and friend," "remoteness and closeness," remain with us. This is hardly surprising given that there has been little attempt by this new, and until recently, strongly local university to address issues of otherness. Indeed, one view expressed was that Brookes is caught between the tensions of projecting an image of itself as a predominantly British and European university, while at the same time trying to reflect its openness to students from its priority markets in Asia. Staff narratives paint a picture of an institution that is still grappling with the affective dimensions of internationalization; how to change attitudes, perceptions, and social relations:

> From our prospectus, you would have no indications that there were international students there. We need to present a much more international image in our prospectus. . . . Because students arrive . . . like at our Business School which is 50% international students and they [British students] are not going to know that! Until they have arrived and then it may be a shock! (director, International Office)

> One of the things about the UK students is that we don't tell the UK students that they are coming . . . to a university as diverse as this in terms of the numbers of students we have got. Should we? . . . Does that matter? (manager, International Recruitment)

A close reading of the information brochure for the master's in International Management illustrates the deep-seated ambivalence toward cultural diversity. The front cover of the brochure declares its mission as "developing tomorrow's global managers in a multicultural environment" (Oxford Brookes University, 2001b). Elsewhere, the prospectus declares that "the programme . . . has received students of 21 nationalities, providing a wonderful opportunity to experience the cultural diversity within which international business is conducted," and "the design of the learning experience is innovative and uses the rich cultural mix of the participants" (p. 1). There is a strongly instrumental value attached to the presence of international students, with their "rich cultural mix" creating a real-life laboratory that approximates the environment in which international business is conducted. We are not told how the university intends to enrich its teaching to include something that is more than a pedestrian appreciation of cultural diversity. Left unsaid is the issue of *relevance*—why it is important to have a curriculum that engages with different cultures, nationalities, and places, and that takes past, present, and future time horizons into account.

Pronouncements of an institutional commitment to cultural diversity are thus not very convincing:

> An important part of the mission of the university is to ensure that cultural diversity is fully appreciated in the teaching and learning environment. Students are encouraged to share their cultural heritage and learn about the

British way of life and business. British families can be introduced that welcome international students into their homes. (Oxford Brookes University,
2001b, p. 5)

It is by steering, prompting, and encouraging students toward particular
subject positions, that they become governable subjects. The statements
above are suggestive of a lingering assimilationist ethos which encourages
students to "learn about the British way of life and business," although it is
debatable how relevant British norms and practices will be in other contexts. The implication here is that the British way exceeds the ways of the
rest: It's hard to avoid arriving at a deficit subjectivity for the international
student—introverted and inward looking, the international student needs
explicit direction to share their cultural heritage, and assistance to meet
British families.

The inclusion of student testimonials in the brochures is now a standard
feature of most education marketing, designed to inspire trust in the university's brand. Here, Anita Yan from Beijing, China testifies to the suitability of the course, focusing on the course's vocationalist input.

[It] has opened my eyes to the dramatic changes taking place in international
business . . . provided me with strong foundations in the knowledge and skills
that I shall need in the future. . . . [It] has been good for me and my career.
(Oxford Brookes University, 2001b, p. 6)

An intellectually passive other who is striving for a singular future—a business future—emerges from this testimonial. The use of vocationalism as a
sales pitch and a passive student subjectivity foregrounds authority in the
master's of International Management credential.

REIMAGING THE UNITED KINGDOM?

Two points are worth repeating in concluding this chapter. The first is that
the promotional discourses of all three institutions, the LSE, Brookes, and
ECS depict a deep-seated ambivalence toward the other. Although at the official level, the merits of culturally diverse communities are acknowledged,
backed by the liberal use of semiotic vignettes in marketing materials, these
are effaced by various icons of Empire. Multiple references to tradition
work to reinforce the continuity and reliability of the Western canon in the
face of a changing and disjunctive present. Ambivalence also inflects the
subject positions created for the international student. The student is imagined and constructed as an elite economic subject for whom an international education means acquiring a credential that has currency in the
global economy. At the same time, an othering discourse is also at work, res-

urrecting an intellectually passive other who seeks tutelage from the West/ North.

There are subtle differences between the types of others constructed in the United Kingdom compared with the United States. British discourses are largely centered on an imagination of localized elites, reminiscent of the colonial era. In America, othering is allied with a discourse of American exceptionalism that is aimed at maintaining its hegemony. Notably, in both the United States and the United Kingdom, the economic and political rationales for international education have more than a passing resemblance to modernity's twin discourses of imperialism and capitalism. The presence of a strongly neocolonial discourse suggests that despite a great deal of talk about the global, the power relations in international education markets militate against plural and reciprocal engagements with the global.

The second point concerns the strongly instrumentalized educational imaginary that is present in all three institutions. When read against a neoliberal governmentality that has been in place in the UK for close to 2 decades, this thematic continuity between education and work is not surprising. Despite official declarations of a "new" and revitalized United Kingdom and a "Third Way" governance, there are strong indicators of a discursive continuity between the rationalities and practices of the Third Way and neocolonial and neoliberal persuasions. Where does this leave the "new" international university?

Despite institutional claims and commitments to "flexibility" and customer service, there is little evidence to suggest that lean, autonomous, fit, and disciplined university departments which are staffed by managerial and entrepreneurial faculty and administrators are offering the intellectual space to explore otherness (see Harley, 2002; Lemke, 2001; Miller & Rose, 1997). Indeed, as Foucault observes, the constructions of personhood selected by the individual are "not something that he/she invents. They are *patterns that he finds in his culture* and which are proposed, suggested and imposed on him by his culture, his society and his social group" (Foucault, 1991c, p. 11). A policy and institutional context that emphasizes competition and the use of market-friendly criteria to assess efficiency and performance makes it more difficult for the international university to honor its civic responsibilities and duties to both national and international constituencies.

Australia: "Diversity" ma non troppo

The focus of this chapter is Australia, a country which can be regarded as having played a vanguard role in the commercialization of international education. The chapter does two things. First, it explores the different meanings surrounding international education in the Australian context by analyzing three types of public discourses, policy, academic, and media texts. I examine the different interpretations of international education made by each of these texts—the public 'truths' they produce and circulate about international education and international students. Together, these public discourses (policy, academic, and media), their fields of emergence and the authoritative bodies that institutionalize them, establish the basis for identifying the power/knowledge constellations underpinning international education.

Second, this chapter examines the micropractices of marketing and promotion used by two Australian institutions: the Queensland University of Technology (QUT) and Monash University. It explores what is 'thinkable' and 'sayable' about international education and uncovers the regimes of truth that are generated by, and through, promotional practices about the international student, the international university, and international education. It is these regimes of truth, and their acquisition of authority, which provide understandings of how international education is assembled by the nation-state, universities, and markets under conditions of "globalization."

In a globalizing environment, national dimensions of higher education are frequently referenced against global trends, indicators, and benchmarks (Marginson & Mollis, 2000, p. 53). Governments and universities frequently invoke "globalization" and "international competition" as rationales for their selective borrowing of policy initiatives. Taking globalization as a governmentality requires us to contest its inevitability and challenge the benchmarks and standards termed 'global'. As part of the 'intellectual machinery', policies are a reflection of how local, national, and global forces pull and push against each other. Policies link the concerns of government and institutional practices with the individual behaviors of the worker-subject (see Marginson, 1997b, p. xiii; Rose, 1993, p. 289). As governmentality theorists have demonstrated, effective governance in globalized times requires mobilizing the productive imperatives of capillary power by encouraging individuals to employ particular technologies of self, so that they will self-steer toward particular subject positions. Similarly, in institutional settings, policy discourses are central to understanding the exercise of influence and power. They embody meaning by shaping what can and cannot be said and done; who can speak, with what authority and under what circumstances. Thus, "policies create circumstances in which the range of options available in deciding what to do, are narrowed or changed" (Ball, 1994, p. 12). Within the context of higher education, policies have a role not only in producing and sustaining institutional practices, but also in constituting the subjectivities of staff and students.

However, as this and earlier chapters argue, policy discourses are not the sole sources of meaning and knowledge about international education. Academic discourses—what is sayable in discussion papers, research papers, and conference proceedings—also shape knowledges about international education. Academic texts are powerful instruments in shaping academic 'realities' including academic subjectivities and 'academic commonsense' about international students and internationalization. They also have the potential to influence the experiences that international students have at universities. Finally, media discourses about international students and international education offer valuable insights into how power is embodied in, and through, people and institutions. Media texts are part of "networks of heterogeneous materialities," "things" which collectively define the complex social world surrounding the production and consumption of international education (see Law & Hetherington, 2000, pp. 35–36).

THE HIGHER EDUCATION POLICY TERRAIN

From the postwar period to the 1970s, a series of policy initiatives transformed Australia's universities from elite to mass institutions. These developments took place against a backdrop of postwar reconstruction, rising community aspirations, high economic growth, and Keynesian economic management. Education was defined as a public good with a vitally important role to play in Australia's modernization and nation-building projects (Marginson, 1997b, pp. 11–15). In a move designed to accelerate the momentum of massification, university fees were abolished in 1974 by the incoming Labor government led by Gough Whitlam. Some 10,000 government-funded places were provided for international students who, up to then, had paid fees to attend Australian universities (Jones, 1986; Throsby, 1985). To regulate and control regional flows of international students, the government introduced country quotas. This brief period of free education for private overseas students was abolished 5 years later with the introduction of the Overseas Student Charge (OSC).[1]

In the second half of the 1980s, a series of micro- and macro-economic reforms saw the introduction by the government of what were essentially private sector practices into the management and operations of the public sector in Australia. A steady stream of reports and commissions[2] supported arguments for the marketization of the public sector (see Marginson & Considine, 2000, p. 45). Beginning with the privatization of several government enterprises, the sites for marketization were rapidly broadened to incorporate health, education, and welfare services. A raft of technologies were used to reconceptualize and reconfigure public services to "a form of economic production" (Marginson, 1997a, p. 85; Pratt & Poole, 2000). The government's rationale for these sweeping changes was the urgent need to improve Australia's international competitiveness. Indeed, the imposition of full fees for international students in 1986 took place against a backdrop of a deteriorating trade deficit, when the government saw the export of education services as replacing the declining revenue from manufacturing exports. Universities were exhorted to do their bit to alleviate this national economic crisis by admitting fee-paying international students.

The 1988 White Paper on Higher Education, popularly referred to as the 'Dawkins reforms', established the basis for the introduction of market rationalities in the higher education sector by introducing changes to the financing, structures, operations, and governance of universities.[3] Governments of all political persuasions took the stance that the operational efficiency of the higher education sector required a performance culture and improved management (Kenway & Langmead, 1998). A series of accountability frameworks were subsequently introduced, ostensibly to moni-

---

[1]The OSC was set at one third of the average cost of a university education in 1979. It rose to 50% of the cost by 1988.

[2]They included the Industries Commission, the Productivity Commission (reforming the public service), and the Hoare Report (on governance within universities; see Marginson & Considine, 2000).

[3]These changes included: the abolition of the binary system of higher education that had been based on a two-tiered system of universities and the more vocationally oriented Institutes of Technology and Colleges of Advanced Education into a Unified National System (Marginson, 1997b, pp. 231–233). New systems of funding were introduced to allow institutions greater autonomy in managing their budgets and planning their operations, while placing greater emphasis on reporting and evaluation of institutional performance.

tor the progress of universities but also to discipline and steer universities toward market-like behaviors, often using a discourse of falling standards and transparency (Brett, 1997; Currie, 1998a, 1998b; Marginson, 2000b, 2004; Meadmore, 1998, pp. 28, 31–34; Meek & Wood, 1997, p. 262; Vidovich & Slee, 2001, p. 35).

The introduction of the Higher Education Contribution Scheme (HECS) in 1990 for all students reestablished the basis for a user-pays system of student funding, which predated the abolition of fees in 1972. To counter criticisms to this policy, the government argued that free university education had not improved socioeconomic representativeness of students in universities[4] (Chapman & Ryan, 2003, pp. iii, 10–14; Marginson, 1997b, pp. 2, 224–231; see also Marginson, 1997c). However, like any policy field, the higher education field features settlements and trade-offs, the result of the different agendas of multiple actors (see Ball, 1994, 1998; Taylor et al., 1997, pp. 22–35). Thus, in the midst of a broader push to propel universities toward market-like provisions and forms, an equity agenda, *A Fair Chance For All: Higher Education That's Within Everyone's Reach* (DEET, 1990) emerged, aimed at increasing the representativeness of university student population. As part of this policy, universities introduced a series of initiatives to address the needs of students from non-English-speaking backgrounds, including international students.[5] It is a fair comment that with few exceptions, these pedagogical initiatives have remained peripheral to mainstream teaching and administrative practices.

In the latter half of the 1990s, several proposals emerged aimed at steering higher education toward the market.[6] The *West Review* (1998), which was

---

[4]Set originally at a fixed fee (A$1,800) for full-time students and payable through the taxation system when students joined the workforce and acquired the capacity to pay, by 1997, HECS had escalated so that students were paying a yearly fee between $3,300 and $5,500, depending on their course of study. In other words, Australian students were contributing anywhere from 35% to 125% of the cost of the course (Marginson, 1997b, pp. 2, 228). In effect, changes to HECS in 1996 have resulted in an average 40% increase to students (Marginson, 1997b; see also Universities in Crisis, 2001, pp. 276–280).

[5]These equity frameworks steered higher education institutions toward formulating policies aimed at recruiting and retaining students from six identified equity groups through a series of funded initiatives. These groups were students from lower socioeconomic backgrounds, rural and isolated students, Aboriginal and Torres Straits Islanders, students with disabilities, women in nontraditional disciplines (technosciences), and students from non-English-speaking backgrounds. The criteria to consider an individual from a non-English cultural background was that they had to have English as a second language and to have lived in Australia for less than 10 years. A resident of Australia for more than 10 years cannot be considered in this category regardless of language abilities. A 1996 review subsequently found that students from non-English speaking backgrounds were no longer underrepresented (DEET, 1990).

[6]These included the *West Review* (1998), *Knowledge and Innovation* (DETYA, 1999) and its action plan *Backing Australia's Ability* (2000), *Higher Education at the Crossroads* (2002) and its manifesto *Backing Australia's Future* (DEST, 2003b). The spirit of reform proposed in these papers and reviews went on to inform the Higher Education Support Bill (2003).

dominated by submissions from the private sector, took the stance that education was a commodity to be globally traded and called for greater differentiation within Australian higher education to enable the higher education industry to be globally competitive. The Review argued for student-centered funding, which it declared would establish the basis for student choice to be incorporated into the funding equation. It highlighted the importance of lifelong learning and the educational possibilities offered by the digital revolution. Significantly, the *West Review* called for accreditation arrangements that would enable the inclusion of more private providers in the higher education sector. Although it framed its recommendations against a grid of world best practice in the global education marketplace, its recommendations were considered politically risky and were temporarily shelved only to be resurrected in 2003 by broad-sweeping policy reforms.

The 1999 ministerial white paper on research and research training, *Knowledge and Innovation* (DETYA, 1999) and its action plan, *Backing Australia's Ability* (2000) echoed the market focus that had featured in the *West Review*. Universities were regarded as having an important role to play in enhancing Australia's competitive position in the global economy. In contrast to the *West Review*, which excited much interest from corporate bodies, *Universities in Crisis* (2001), a parliamentary inquiry by the Senate Employment, Workplace Relations, Small Business and Education Committee received feedback from universities, individual academics, students, and professional associations. Collectively, the submissions expressed the concern that Australia's ability to participate in the global knowledge-based economy was hampered by insufficient public funding of its universities (see *Universities in Crisis*, 2001). University entrepreneurialism had not replaced lost public funding in real terms (p. 353) and public funding was noted to compare unfavorably with the OECD country average (pp. 5, 34–40),[7] contributing to greater institutional segmentation. Declining student–staff ratios (from 13.7 in 1989 to 18.8 in 2000; p. 166) were associated with a reduction in the quality of the education experience for both international and domestic students (pp. 356–357). This ratio was noted against a 300% increase in the numbers of pro- and deputy vice-chancellors from 1987 to 1998 (pp. 40, 126). Submissions by academics painted a picture of demoralization in a sector facing a fiscal crisis and strangled by bureaucratic practices (Anderson, 2004).

The inquiry noted the worsening financial problems of regional and newer universities. A number of regional universities had attempted to respatialize their identities to appear more attractive to international students and, in doing so, boost their income. They did so by opening branch

---

[7]The committee noted that government outlays accounted for 47% of university revenue compared with 57% in 1996 and 85% in 1987.

campuses, in reality, managed offices, in the central business districts of major Australian cities. The higher education success story of the decade, the international education export industry, was unsettled by several submissions that argued, first, that the export income earned has not replaced lost government funding, and second, that the international export industry had little impact on broadening Australia's engagement with the Asia-Pacific region and the broader international community (Lawnham, 2002; *Universities in Crisis*, 2001, p. 344).

Of particular concern was the concentration of international students and by extension, revenue, in a handful of disciplines (e.g., business and IT) and the small numbers of international students enrolled in research degrees, a trend that was anticipated to do little for Australian efforts in becoming a knowledge society (Marginson, 2004, p. 233). Furthermore, some submissions alleged subtle steering by universities toward soft marking to allow international students and other full-fee-paying students to pass their courses. Their heavy reliance on international student fee income was also noted as exposing some universities to high levels of financial risk (Moodie, 2002).[8]

Although many of the submissions to the hearing into *Universities in Crisis* used a discourse of national interest as the basis for arguing for greater public investment, other submissions, including some from leading education bureaucrats, called for the self-sufficient public entrepreneurial university (Gallagher, 2000, 2001). These arguments used the virtual, for-profit, corporate university as a benchmark for assessing performance and quality. Universities were accordingly exhorted to provide "customised convenience programmes, 24 hours a day, 7 days a week" (Gallagher, 2001, p. 7). The use of a shopping metaphor confirms the subtext: "It hardly matters what is being sold so long as the store remains open" (Zemsky, 1989, as cited in Dill, 1999, p. 60). A supermarket philosophy had permeated the imagination of senior education bureaucrats.[9]

Higher Education at the Crossroads (2002), the next significant proposal, presided over what was to become the largest restructuring of the university system since the Dawkins reforms of the 1980s. *Crossroads* was promoted as framed by four principles: sustainability, quality, equity, and diversity

---

[8]Institutions drawing more than 20% of their revenue from international students' fees were noted to fall in this category. The three universities whose operational budgets were noted to be excessively reliant on fee income of international students were: Royal Melbourne Institute of Technology, Central Queensland University, and Curtin University. The external risk factors identified were the changing government policies of sending countries, changes in currency exchange rates, and the changing economic circumstances of students and their families (Moodie, 2002).

[9]Gallagher was the head of DEST, which is the nation's most important education bureaucracy.

(DEST, 2003c). Paradoxically, under the existing funding regime, these principles are in tension with each other, and how these tensions will be worked out in the daily grind of institutional practices remains to be seen. What appears clear this far is that universities have expanded opportunities to raise revenue from students (Duckett, 2004; Marginson, 2004). One issue that received significant public coverage in the debates surrounding *Crossroads* was whether government support should be directed to supporting one or two world-class universities. The tenor of this discussion was focused on league tables as a grid with which to determine "world class" and "excellence" (Duckett, 2004). The U.S.–centric indicators that underpin these grids means that they are not entirely appropriate for other national systems of higher education (Marginson, 2003b). This is not being acknowledged in official commentary, which also fails to recognize the redundancy of using such calculative technologies as determinants of academic quality.

One of the most contested issues surrounding *Crossroads* and its accompanying manifesto, *Backing Australia's Future* (DEST, 2003b), was the linking of government funding to industrial relations conditions. Ostensibly promoted as "a workplace productivity programme," the government proposals required universities to enter into individualized contracts, Australian Workplace Agreements (AWA), with all of their staff. This demand was criticized for impeding academic freedom and reducing institutional autonomy. The ensuing Higher Education Support Bill (2003) was eventually diluted to remove its more intrusive proposals following consultations and negotiations by bodies such as the AVCC and the National Tertiary Education Union (NTEU), and from concessions extracted by Independent political representatives in the Upper House. It is anticipated that the Bill will change internal governance protocols to those that favor central control mechanisms (Duckett, 2004, pp. 231–233).

The major purpose of the Higher Education Support Bill—to introduce new funding arrangements for the higher education sector—steers universities further toward the market. It has increased fees for students (up by 25%) and permitted universities to increase the full fee-paying percentage of the total-course cohort (up to 35%). To offset electoral backlash, other initiatives such as loan packages to help students pay their course fees are being introduced (Marginson, 2004, p. 238).

INTERNATIONAL EDUCATION: A BRIEF HISTORY

Although the earliest records of overseas students in Australia point to their presence in Australian universities in 1904, Australia's engagement with international students really commenced with the introduction of the Colombo Plan in 1950 (see Tootell, 1999). The plan's rationales reflected a mixture of political self-interest and humanitarian concerns. The withdrawal of colonial rule and the success of communist rule in mainland China had created Australian anxiety about the north. The plan was to be a 'gift' to establish affiliations and affinities between Australia and the local elites and middle classes in the newly independent states (Alexander & Rizvi, 1993, pp. 17–18; Auletta, 2000, pp. 47–51; Rizvi, 1997, pp. 6–17).

In the latter half of the 1980s, major shifts in higher education policy designed to reduce reliance on government funding led to the introduction of full fees for international students. The shift from an aid to trade policy can be traced to two significant government reviews in the 1980s. The Jackson Review (1984), which was appointed to evaluate the Australian overseas aid program, recommended the introduction of a policy to impose full fees on international students.[10] The Jackson Review argued that such a policy shift would provide a source of export income for Australia, using the United States as a benchmark:

> The demand for education services throughout the Asian region is likely to be quite large in the next 20 years or so. The expansion of Australian education to meet this demand would encourage cultural exchanges and tourism. It would provide jobs for Australians directly, and there would be multiplier effects through the provision of food, shelter, clothing and entertainment for students. In American university towns, one "town" job is generally added for every additional "gown" enrolled. (p. 93)

The Goldring Review (1984), by contrast, recommended the continuation of the 1980s program based on offering a subsidized number of places for international students to study in Australian universities.[11] Both reviews had arrived at opposing recommendations, yet the recommendations of one, the Jackson Review, were translated into subsequent government policy, leading to one of the most significant transformations in Australian higher education. The will to marketize had engulfed the entire public sector, producing the conditions for the development of an international education export industry in Australia. Not all the Jackson Review's recommendations were accepted. A recommendation to substantially increase the number of aid scholarships to 10,000 by the mid-1990s was not taken up.

With the endorsements of the Jackson Review, the government began to establish the foundations for the export industry in Australia. To stimulate interest by universities, the government provided grants of up to A$200,000 to enable them to develop promotional and marketing plans for overseas recruitment (Back, Davis, & Olsen, 1996, pp. 6–7; Marginson, 1997a, p. 233;

---

[10]See Australian Parliament Joint Committee on Foreign Affairs and Defence (1984).
[11]See *Mutual Advantage Report* (Goldring, 1984).

Marginson & McBurnie, 2004, p. 169; Meek & Wood, 1997, p. 259). Institutions were allowed to retain a large proportion of the international student fee income. Where quotas had once been in place to assuage domestic disquiet at the potential displacement of Australian students by large numbers of wealthy overseas students, these were now removed.[12]

In place of the earlier aid discourse aimed at regional stability, which was linked to Australia's national and geopolitical concerns, the official discourse mutated toward highlighting the private benefits enjoyed by international students. A clever misuse of egalitarian discourse saw their construction into an elite group whose eligibility to receive education subsidies from Australia was now called into question: "In many cases subsidised students had been relatively well off or from relatively wealthy countries" (Back et al., 1996, p. 7; Jones, 1986, p. 105). A new discourse of trade thus emerged, leading to a meteoric rise in international student numbers.[13] It came as no surprise when the government policy of offering subsidized places to private students was discontinued in 1990.

From a marketing and promotional perspective, Australia's incursion into the international export market depicted a peculiarly "back-to-front" quality, which contradicts international business axioms. The usual sequence of events that accompanies the sale of a product in an international market is such that a product is usually first marketed domestically. Through this experience the product is improved continuously and thereafter launched into an international context with appropriate refinements and accommodations for what is recognized as a different customer base. In Australia, a market-driven industry had been grafted onto a publicly funded, regulated system—all within a space of 5 years.

Market "Fallout"

The deregulated, trade-dominated focus of international education ran into problems quickly with the collapse of several English language schools, concerns about a 'corporate cowboy' approach to recruitment, and accusations of immigration fraud. By 1991, the shortcomings of the deregulation policy were starkly evident, and in a bid to reign in the excessively entrepreneurial practices of some Australian educational institutions, the government introduced the Education Services for Overseas Students (ESOS; Registration of Providers and Financial Regulation) Act. ESOS, the Beazley

---

[12]The regulations specified fee levels and international student quotas in universities (Smart & Ang, 1993).

[13]Limitations on fees and student numbers were removed; a new market was established (Marginson & McBurnie, 2004).

Ministerial Statement,[14] and the AVCC's Code of Ethical Practice for the Provision of Education to International Students were all part of a broader discursive ensemble aimed at curbing the fallout from the free-market era of international education.

The Beazley Statement, for example, tried to introduce a more inclusive internationalism in place of a more inward-looking nationalism. By its references to cultural understandings, it highlighted the importance of inter-subjective cultural literacies for Australian students as prospective members of the workforce and, on a broader scale, for Australia's international relations (Rizvi, 1997). It also attempted to link the internationalization of education with the emerging processes of globalization, although it clearly privileged the economic dimensions of globalization, in this respect reinforcing the tenor of the government-initiated Productive Diversity platform.[15] An amalgam that sutured together market, social equity, and cultural diversity principles, Productive Diversity sought to put cultural diversity to work for capitalism. It positioned a multicultural Australia as an active player, mediator, and facilitator of Euro-American business incursions into an economically dynamic Asia. It was also concerned with capitalizing on the skills, knowledge, and networks of Australians who were born and educated overseas (see Karpin, 1995). Concerns that its social justice impulses were subordinated by its commercial imperatives have dogged the Productive Diversity platform since its inception.

The discourse of Productive Diversity has recently reemerged in *Engaging the World Through Education* (DEST, 2003d), a 2003 policy statement on international education. Australia is constructed as a bridge between Asia, Europe, and the Americas: "a Western Country located in the Asia-Pacific region with close ties and affinities with North America and Europe" (DEST, 2003d, p. 3). I return to the East–West theme later in this chapter given its dominance in the branding of international education.

Also intended to temper rabid entrepreneurialism in the international education industry was the AVCC's Code of Ethical Practice for the Provi-

---

[14]The 1992 Beazley Ministerial Statement articulated a wider interpretation of international education. It claimed the following as its guiding principles: educational values and quality, a policy and regulatory framework, quality infrastructure to enable the provision of broader expressions of internationalization (staff exchanges, joint research, study abroad opportunities, etc.), an Asia-Pacific focus (which included America), and partnerships between government and education providers aimed in part at introducing flexible and streamlined processes.

[15]The concept of Productive Diversity was part of a state-led initiative intended to encourage Australian enterprises to prepare Australia's managers to meet the challenges of the Asia-Pacific century. Firms were encouraged to develop greater cultural and gender diversity in their management and to expand their vision to trade in the Asia-Pacific.

sion of Education to International Students. The code covers the promotion, recruitment, admission, education, and welfare dimensions of international education. Recent revisions have extended its reach to include offshore education provisions involving Australian universities and their partners. Importantly, the code specified the types of customers to be targeted by universities: "only those international students who have reasonable chances of success." It also acknowledged the economic, psychological, and intellectual challenges that accompanied study overseas:

> By accepting a place international students have taken a major step in their lives; they may leave their home countries for long periods, travel considerable distances and undertake considerable expense. The Code has been formulated with this in mind. (AVCC, 1998)

The AVCC's guidelines for the promotion and marketing of international education also made several references to the need to uphold national interest by protecting the reputation of Australian education.

In 2000, a new version of the ESOS Act was introduced, ostensibly to protect Australia's reputation as a exporter of quality education. ESOS (2000) embodies the complex, contradictory, and incoherent side to policy responses. In some respects, it privileges border protection ahead of national economic concerns, a concern that has been raised by the AVCC.[16] Students' spatial or geographical identities have assumed greater significance in determining whether they will occupy the positions of valued customer, illegal immigrant, or potential terrorist, suggesting that we are a long way from a borderless world. ESOS places a renewed emphasis on English language competence as a screening device, along with more stringent admissions requirements. It also vests greater monitoring and enforcement powers in the education and immigration arms of government.

Australian policy responses have been aimed at maintaining a competitive edge in the global trade in education services (Marginson & McBurnie, 2004). This rationale has the greater political currency, a fact recognized by the preeminent higher education lobby group, the AVCC. Its *Discussion Paper on International Education* (AVCC, 2001), for example, proposes the fol-

---

[16]Prospective students from regions considered to be at high risk for illegal immigration must now sit an examination to ascertain their English language proficiency, even if a significant proportion of their education has been in English. The introduction of English language examinations for applicants from the Indian subcontinent was singled out for criticism by the AVCC, which argued that "key markets stand to be wiped out" (AVCC, 2001). Here, the concern was about the effects on the Indian postgraduate market, which is dominated by the United States and which was being nurtured by Australian marketers to bring promising returns in the way of increased enrollments.

lowing measures to strengthen international education: more marketing, easier and cheaper visas, and financial initiatives to encourage Australians to study at universities in the Asia-Pacific. The AVCC did not offer a more complex vision for international education, preferring instead of stay with the trade agenda. The marketization agenda is also present in *Positioning Australia's Universities for 2020*, an AVCC vision statement that calls for "greater participation in the international education market" (AVCC, 2002, p. 6). The AVCC notes that "Australian educational exports will give Australia a pre-eminent place in the global education revolution" (p. 2) and calls again for more streamlined visa processes and assistance from government instrumentalities in supporting education exports (p. 6).

A New Trade Agenda

Engaging the World Through Education (DEST, 2003d), the first major policy statement on internationalization after the Beazley Statement continues to highlight the economic importance of international education to Australia. Its launch was followed up by the signing of education agreements with both China and India for the mutual agreement of qualifications, a move anticipated to increase demand from both markets. Although trade considerations have been dominant in shaping the international education agenda for most of the 1990s, *Engaging the World Through Education* goes a step further. It reflects the arrival of a different set of relationships between the nation-state and Australian higher education, and between Australian universities and the world.

Engaging the World Through Education normalizes education as a tradable service commodity and maps a more ambitious vision of marketization, not seen in its predecessor, the Beazely Statement. The expansion and subsequent success of international education is clearly not happenstance but the outcome of active steering by the nation-state. Where education was once shaped and framed almost entirely by national economic and cultural forces, this new policy statement brings the global into the equation.

Amid government pronouncements of increased funding, what is left out in the statement is the fact that the A$113 million committed by the government toward implementing *Engaging the World Through Education* is to be raised by additional taxes and levies on international students and education providers such as universities (AVCC, 2003). The lion's share of the A$113 million—A$41.7 million—goes toward promotion and marketing activities (DEST, 2003c). The rationale for a global trade in education borrows heavily from the knowledge economy–'New Economy' discourse. *Engaging the World Through Education* makes explicit references to Australia's commitment to liberalization in the trade of education services and GATS as a means to "reduce trade barriers" (DEST, 2003d, p. 22). As an exporter of a value-added commodity (education), Australia faces stiff competition from established exporters such as the United Kingdom and the United States as well as from newer nations such as Singapore and Malaysia (pp. 11–12).

The trade discourse so firmly entrenched in *Engaging the World* is made visible in a style of language more familiar to the world of agriculture and mineral export commodities than learning and higher education. Statements such as this one declare a commitment "to engineer" and maintain "a high quality, high yield, sustainable export sector delivering services in Australia and in other countries" (DEST, 2003d, p. 16). Couched in win–win terms, there appears to be something for every stakeholder in this statement. International education offers national, economic, trade, and diplomatic benefits to Australia *and* to developing countries; it generates individual, institutional, and community benefits: "Trade in education also contributes to . . . strengthening institutional viability . . . education institutions are strengthened through the pressure of student consumers on service responsiveness and value for money" (p. 5); "There are benefits for Australian firms . . . they recruit employees and form business partnerships with Australian educated graduates from different countries" (p. 4); "It is easier for Australian executives and diplomats to do business with people familiar with Australia." An adroit use of language sees the representation of trade as eclipsing aid in importance:

> Trade in education services enables Australia to contribute more broadly to provide individuals with training and education where their own countries have insufficient capacity to meet demand. . . . Trade increases numbers of students, the range of countries of origin and courses that can be offered far beyond the gains delivered through aid alone. (DEST, 2003d, p. 5)

Engaging the World Through Education identifies three main risks to quality: inadequate inputs, inappropriate processes, and insufficient outcomes (DEST, 2003d, p. 15). Interestingly, inputs are conceptualized in terms of student selectivity: "quality students," the "top end of student abilities rather than the bottom end." The introduction of an expanded (albeit modest) program of scholarships and fellowships is one of the measures designed to attract quality students.[17] What is left unsaid is the extent to which teaching and research quality is governed by state provision of adequate funds. Indeed, the AVCC has criticized *Engaging the World Through Education* for "the seeming lack of importance given to the significance of working partnerships between the Government and the higher education sector within the policy statement" (AVCC, 2003).

---

[17]The government has committed A$7.9 million over 4 years to the Endeavour Programme (DEST, 2003c).

Engaging the World Through Education does not provide a definition of international education and carries no references to globalization. Although it supports "market access for trade and investment in education" (DEST, 2003d, p. 22) and by implication the removal of barriers that impede the movement of services, people, information, and capital for this purpose, the policy statement also makes several references to "the integrity of Australia's immigration programme" (pp. 30–31). So, geography still matters, and the statement's nuanced language suggests that some are more welcome to Australia than others. Student visa applications are assessed for risk on a country basis (p. 31), suggesting a more than fleeting resonance with the discourse of border control.

The place of border protection in the official and popular imagination in Australia has historical roots. Both xenophobia and its sibling, racism, have been long-standing fixtures in the Australian nation-building project (see Castles & Miller, 1998; Fiske et al., 1987; Hodge & Mishra, 1991; Turner, 1994), most evident in the discursive logic of the 'yellow peril' and a White Australia policy.[18] Given the historical links between national interest, national security, and educating the other (see Alexander & Rizvi, 1993), this continuing preoccupation with territorial identities is not entirely surprising. Recent developments have seen a broadening of the thesis of nation-state vulnerability to international terrorism.

"Study in Australia": Buying a Kangaroo?

Approximately 2 years after the United Kingdom launched its Education UK brand, the Australian government agency, Australian Education International, commissioned work[19] to identify a distinctive Australian education brand that would differentiate it from its major competitors, the United States and United Kingdom. A strongly positivist discourse, linked to an empiricist methodology, was used to create the impression of objectivity. The market research used the needscope technique to identify six principal needs that students seek to fulfill in an international education: freedom,

---

[18]The White Australia policy came into being with the new Immigration Restriction Act in 1901, which placed restrictions on the immigration of people of color along with several other categories of persons such as prostitutes, those deemed insane, and criminals. The Act stated the migrant had to "write out dictation and sign in the presence of an officer, a passage of 50 words in a European language directed by the officer." Non-White refugees who were permitted entry into Australia during World War II faced deportation at the end of the war. In 1966, the Australian government declared that people of different races would no longer be prohibited from applying to immigrate. Migrants were to be selected on their ability to integrate readily and their possession of qualifications positively useful to Australia (Department of Immigration and Multicultural and Indigenous Affairs [DIMIA], 2004).

[19]The market research was carried out by public relations firms Keystone Corporate Positioning and Taylor Nelson Sofres.

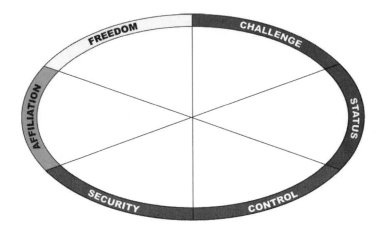

FIG. 6.1.   The Australian brand.

challenge, status, control, security, and affiliation (see Fig. 6.1). Options
were subsequently identified for 'testing':

> Four options, Affiliation, Freedom, Freedom/Challenge/Status and Chal-
> lenge/Status were *tested* [italics added] in focus groups with students using po-
> sitioning statements and collages of images expressing the emotion or mood
> associated with each positioning. (AEI, 2002)

Education marketing is constructed as a set of neutral activities, informed entirely by an instrumental rationality (Odih & Knight, 2000). The
quasi-scientific discourse has the overall effect of rendering invisible the
complex and polymorphous, such as the politics and ethics underpinning
education's transformation into a commodity, and the privilege extended
to Western epistemologies in a historical era described as polycentric by the
more optimistic globalists.

The ensuing Australian education brand would embody the traits of
freedom, challenge, and status, with fine-grained variations by country and
sector. Freedom would be the selling idea behind education promotion in
First World markets such as North America and Europe, whereas status and
challenge would assume more importance in the Asian markets.

A brand without a logo has limited scope and reach in commodity capitalism; therefore, further research was conducted to "identify the types of
images and colours that best express the positioning [of Australian educa-
tion]." The logo subsequently developed to give the Australian brand of education a distinctive identity was a red kangaroo, a native animal that also
serves as the logo for Australia's national airline, Qantas (see Fig. 6.2). The
logo signifies the institutionalization of a new discursive formation, educa-

FIG. 6.2.   Study in Australia logo.

tional tourism. It confirms what is becoming a self-fulfilling prophecy: Australian education is not intellectually serious. Indeed, close analyses of government-sponsored marketing campaigns suggest that the selling ideas that underpin Australian education are its 'adequate quality', cheaper price compared with the United States and the United Kingdom, and its closer location to countries in Asia-Pacific (Marginson, 2003a).

The concept of selling a multicultural imaginary remains an important part of Australian education marketing. However, the imaginary functions largely as a governmental project to promote success in the highly competitive global education market (Sidhu, 2004). It does not, for instance, offer inspiration or ideas about possible ways in which Australian models of plurality can be incorporated into a uniquely Australian brand of international education.

> Multicultural Australia is a safe, friendly, sophisticated and harmonious society in which students can learn and travel in an English-speaking country. . . . Crime and political unrest are limited in Australia . . . your study plans and progress are not likely to be upset by political turmoil.
>
> The multicultural nature of Australian society means international students are readily accepted by other students and teachers. . . .
>
> Australians value the wealth of cultural diversity and social sophistication that international students bring to our campuses and our communities. We take great care in looking after international students and helping them to adjust to the Australian way of life. (*Study in Australia*, 2004)

This message is clearly directed at multiple audiences. First, it addresses the Middle Eastern market of students, which previously selected the United States as their study destination but which has redirected its choices following the fallout from the political turmoil of 9-11. Second, it is directed at the Asian market, which remains wary of Australia's history of race-based immigration and ongoing populist suspicion of the Asian other, and in this context requires reassurances that they will be readily accepted. There is also a message for the Euro-American market, invited to contribute its social sophistication to a distant outpost and its inhabitants. A mildly paternalistic and assimilatory tenor, barely discernible but present, suggests that these rational customers have to be "helped to adjust to the Australian way of life" (*Study in Australia*, 2004).

The escalating demand by international students and the positive outcomes it delivers to individual students makes it difficult, on the surface, to fault the brand of international education offered by Australian universities. Individual international students attain an internationally recognized credential that is well regarded in their home countries while providing Australian universities with much-needed fee income (Brown, 1997; Cohen, 2003; DEST, 2003d). For ethnic minorities such as the Chinese heritage communities of Indonesia and Malaysia whose participation in local universities has long been impeded by discriminatory state policies, the marketization of Australia higher education has been perceived positively, although escalating tuition costs remain of concern to students and their families. Some students have used their Australian credentials to relocate to countries that offer them better opportunities. Finally, through the proliferation of franchises and articulation arrangements, the flow of capital and investment from West to East is partially reversed.

These outcomes, all positive for the short term, distract from issues that have long-term consequences, including whether the 21st-century Australian university should continue to enact the 19th-century eschatological master plan. Instead of merely training up model minorities for a global economy, the responsibilities of universities should extend to educating for global citizenship, global community, and sustainability (Kramer, 2003a, 2003b). Policy initiatives such as the Beazley Statement and the more recent *Engaging the World Through Education* (DEST, 2003d) simply have not addressed the issue of how Australian universities can provide a quality education to culturally and linguistically diverse students from postcolonial nation-states. Instruments such as the AVCC's Code of Ethical Practice function more as a set of guidelines than as a set of prescriptive norms or set policy, leaving institutions to self-monitor their adherence.[20]

Critics of international education point to a prevailing short termism on the parts of many Australian universities, coupled with declining government support, that has hindered the sector from developing into a unique and viable, globally oriented higher education system. What is produced is a poor imitation of an American brand of higher education (see Clyne et al., 2001; Marginson, 2002, pp. 420–423; Marginson & Considine, 2000, pp. 182–183). Also of concern are the low levels of intercultural mixing on university campuses, which suggest that spatially and culturally based conceptions of self and other remain in place even in universities that pronounce themselves to be cosmopolitan and international (Chen, 1999; Smart, Volet, & Ang, 2000; Volet & Ang, 1998).

---

[20]The *Universities in Crisis* (2001) inquiry, for example, revealed concerns about entry and assessment standards (see also Burgess, 2003), a concern that resurfaces in *Engaging the World Through Education* (DEST, 2003d). However, there is no evidence of any action being taken against any institution for breaches of the code (Senate Employment, Workplace Relations, Small Business and Education Committee, 2001, p. 350).

More recently there have been concerns that trade-dominated expressions of international education are contributing to uneven economic and educational development in client countries. Reliance on foreign knowledge-building capabilities, the concentration of demand in market-friendly disciplines (Business), and the continuing flow of capital to overseas-based institutions are all factors identified as undermining and weakening universities in the developing world. Marketization also affects 'First World' universities by drawing funds and scholarly efforts away from knowledge areas deemed to lack market relevance (Marginson, 2003a; Turpin, Iredale, & Crinnion, 2002).

Although many Australian universities have expressed their commitment to policies of internationalization, these rest on limited understandings of the power–knowledge relations underpinning notions of diversity. A liberal concept of cultural diversity, for example, fails to recognize the links between the politics of difference and the power–knowledge relations that constitute educational discourse. Issues of academic content and pedagogy have been subordinated, and student diversity—the recruitment of students from different countries—has become the litmus for internationalization (Rizvi & Walsh, 1998). After an initial flurry of activities in individual universities, little progress has been made in systemic internationalization of the curricula of Australian universities.

Internationalization requires the discourse structures of the nation-centered university to be unsettled to enable the unhinging and unlearning of values that support civilizational plurality (Sadiki, 2001). It should seek to create opportunities for both students and staff to acquire a global imagination and qualities of openness and self-reflexivity (Rizvi, 2000). An international university, narrowly preoccupied with national economic interests, cannot subvert the power relations that continue to produce and perpetuate monoculturalism and neocolonialism (Alexander & Rizvi, 1993; Morris & Hudson, 1995; M. Singh, 1998).

Academic Discourse: Research Into International Education

Academic research and commentary about international education falls into two broad camps. One strand has taken the position that a governmentality committed to fiscal savings, earning institutional income, and upholding financial independence has done little to institute wide, deep, and complex expressions of international education. The argument is that governments of all political persuasions have connected the state, the market, universities, and individual employees, using a "there is no alternative" reasoning about the need for international competitiveness. The disciplinary power of the market is noted to have done little to institute deep-seated curricular changes that respond to the cultural dimensions of globalization

(Marginson, 1999, 2002, 2003a; Rizvi, 1997, 1998). The general finding of this body of research is that power–knowledge relations within the Australian international university continue to privilege cultural singularity at the expense of cultural plurality. Market-attractive disciplines and knowledges have not made changes to the hegemony of a Euro-American inspired monoculturalism (Marginson & McBurnie, 2004).

A second strand of academic commentary has normalized notions of education as a tradable commodity and international education as an export industry. Within this discourse, universities are regarded as service industry providers whose primary responsibility is to meet the needs and expectations of their customers by providing a low-cost, high-quality product. Globalization is regarded as having created an irreversible momentum and escalating demand for higher education that cannot be met by public sector universities. There is no alternative but to open the field for private, for-profit institutions.

In this hyperglobalist context, there is no need for a singular institution called *university*. Rather, the different functions of the university—from preparation of curriculum materials to teaching and assessment—are best separated and outsourced. Different producers develop "packages of learning resources," to be delivered to customer-students "anywhere, any place" by other links in the production chain (Chipman, 1998, 2000). Students and employers are assumed to be rational utility maximizers who will seek value for money in the form of quality credentials that provide access to employment. Within this discourse, understandings of quality are couched in commonsense understandings of meeting customer needs and cost effectiveness, or value for money (see Gilbert, 2000; Norton, 2002). Academic entrepreneurialism is lauded not only for the benefits it delivers to talented hard-working academics but also to their institutions, to individual students, and ultimately to the nation-state.

Regarding education as just another commodity creates serious concerns not only about entry standards but also about issues of institutional transparency and accountability. Here, a marketing manager describes how the deployment of a value-for-money discourse has manifested into a discount war:

> There are a great number of local agents working in Sydney. . . . Many are discounting tuition fees to international students. And they do that often through giving the students a share of the commission they earn from the institution. They are [also] giving students cash and laptops . . . and trips to the Gold Coast. (manager, IDP, October 22, 2000)

How, then, do policy discourses assemble the international university in Australia, and how do these assemblages enact the global? The international university in Australia is clearly an agent of globalization through its perpetuation of a monolingual, largely Westernized, monocultural brand of international education. The international education field is also premised on and normalizes education as a tradable commodity, and to this end, international education is an expression of Anglo-American neoliberal orthodoxies. However, the push toward the market has delivered productive possibilities, hence the vested interests among education bureaucrats, faculty, administrators, and students not to withdraw but to engage with, adapt, and become more compatible with the new global terrain: the market in education services.

"There's Gold in Those Hills": Media Appraisals

Media texts construct commonsense understandings about international education and international students. They shape institutional and individual realities, which ultimately influence the subjectivities of both academic staff and international students. In analyzing Australian media discourses about international education, two themes are discernible. First and most prevalent is an economic theme that celebrates the success story of the international education export industry. Second is a set of discursive practices that reinforce the position of international students as the other by textually linking students with illegal immigration, crime, and declining academic standards.

Exemplifying the economic theme is a collage of dynamic phrases ("boom in exports") and a vocabulary of 'competition'. Much is made of a 'world market' for education. In the face of stiff international competition, Australia is portrayed as 'winning markets'. The headlines of news reports are fairly typical:

- "Foreign Uni Students Lack English Skills" (2002)
- "Nations Plot to Grab Share" (Lawnham, 2001d, p. 36)
- "Asian Demand to Endure" (Illing, 1999a, p. 40)
- "British Push for Bigger Share" (Illing, 1999b, p. 36)
- "Education Gold in Japan" (*Courier-Mail*, 1999)
- "There's Profit in Ideas" (Lyon, 2001, p. 43)
- "Joint Degree Opens Door to China Market" (Lawnham, 2000)
- "Oz Shopfront in the UK" (Lawnham, 2001a)
- "Uni Push to Export Courses" (Illing, 1998)
- "Chinese Market Ready for Boom" (Illing, 1999c)
- "A New Boom Sweeps Clean" (1999)
- "Conference Showcases Education as Business" (Lyon, 2000)

FIG. 6.3.   Frequent Flyer?

- "There's Gold in Them Commercial Arms" (2000)
- "Ideas Flow in a Sellers' Marketplace" (Leon, 2002)
- "Australia's Universities Must Raise Their Standards Before They Raise Students' Fees" (Dunstan, 2003)
- "Overseas Uni Students Lured Here With False Promise" (Reddy, 2004)

The melding together of the discourses of trade and markets with education assumes particular prominence in advertisements such as Frequent Flyer?, which appeared in the higher education section of the sole national newspaper (see Fig. 6.3).[21] "International education, Cash in your network, and $115k ++ neg package" suggests a particular institutional subjectivity—

---

[21]Frequent Flyer? appeared as an advertisement in the Higher Education section of *The Australian* newspaper on 11 July 2001.

that of an education entrepreneur. International education emerges as just another commodity, and the selling of education is no different from selling other goods or services. A few articles such as "Dark Side to Export Boom" (Illing, 2001b), "Overseas Students Lured With False Promise" (Reddy, 2004), and "Australia's Universities Must Raise Their Standards Before They Raise Students' Fees" (Dunstan, 2003) report on the problems which have arisen from an export approach to international education such as poor quality teaching and support in universities, overzealous marketing by institutions, and the high levels of emotional and financial stress faced by many international students. On the whole, these cautious tales have a subordinated status compared with the boom stories of commercial success.

In the Australian media, reporting on international students largely takes three forms: their "insatiable" demand for an Australian education; immigration fraud ("No Entry Under False Pretences"; Boucher, 2001); the issue of soft marking ("Marking Row Leads to QUT Inquiry"; Illing, 2001a; "Marking Inquiry Exposes Glitches"; Lawnham, 2001b) and declining academic standards ("Marks and Sparks"; Lawnham, 2001c). A series of rhetorical strategies are also used in news reports to position Asian students as powerful entities who deploy their power as consumers of Australian education to discipline the democratic impulses of the broader Australian community, such as the right to elect populist politicians. Articles such as "Unis Fear Asian Student Backlash" (see Cole, 2001) impose a powerful subjectivity onto the Asian student who is able to discipline fearful universities.

To what extent are academics, who face large teaching and administrative workloads, vulnerable to the othering practices depicted in some parts of the media discourses? Judging by the following statements, some academics equate the presence of international students in Australian universities with declining academic standards and the loss of their professional integrity:

> In the eyes of many academics a good service for the fee paying clients is the same thing as prostituting your academic standards for the sake of a dollar. . . .
>
> It is a common claim among academics that overseas students are accepted under spurious entrance criteria ahead of qualified students then herded through courses despite inadequate performance so that they can make way for the next lot of milch cows. Another common grumble is that paying for their degrees gives them unrealistic expectations of passing. (Armitage, 1996, p. R01)

Here again, international students are conferred with a powerful subjectivity—their power resides in their capacity to buy degrees and their associations with powerful advocates within their institutions:

> In the campus international offices that recruit them, international students
> have powerful advocates which local students lack. These offices have power
> because they bring in money: between $200 and 300 million a year in to-
> tal. . . . It is perfectly normal for the international office to intervene when in-
> ternational students are failing. (Armitage, 1996, p. R01)

By contrast, the National Liaison Committee (NLC), which is the peak international student lobby group in Australia, observes that as a group, international students tend to be highly motivated and regard their education
very seriously. Many students experience high stress levels in making the academic, linguistic, and cultural adjustments required of overseas study
(Dunstan, 2002; Reddy, 2004). Many are supported by families who make
significant financial sacrifices to educate their children. All of these accounts challenge the powerful customer identity who merely purchases a
credential as is implied by media discourses on international education.
The NLC has been critical of tendencies by universities and the government to treat international students as "cash cows" (Maiden, 2004).

To summarize, the 'policyscapes' that have shaped international education have been intersected by national interest considerations. Where con-
taining communism and winning allies was a key national desire in the educational aid phase, by the end of the 1980s, national interest was framed by
the demands of the national economy. International education was thus
propelled into the role of earning export revenue. Allied to considerations
of national interest was a neoliberal discourse that argued for corporatization and deregulation of the Australian public sector. State instrumentalities subsequently deployed a series of governmental technologies such
as national quality policies to produce and sustain market-friendly relations
of power and knowledge.

That the market dominates is reinforced by analyses of media discourses
on international education. International education is discursively constructed as a tradable export commodity that has yielded gold for Australia.
International education markets are the new frontier to be conquered. Together, policy, academic, and media discourses construct the international
student as a favored customer who seeks privileges, an uneducated other
who has an insatiable demand for things Western, and a duplicitous character who is involved in immigration fraud and soft-marking scandals.

If power does have a capillary quality, power relations at the micro levels
are vital for developing and sustaining alternative discourses, institutional
visions, and practices for the international university. How do Australian
universities imagine international education? What types of subjectivities
are created by institutional discursive practices for the international student? How do these discursive practices resist the twin hegemonies of market and cultural singularity? I explore these questions through the promo-

tional narratives of three Australian institutions, beginning with the promotional materials of one Australian university whose slogan is "The University for the Real World."

My 'entry' as a researcher into this setting is not without problems. After two rescheduled appointments and one no-show appointment, I finally obtain an appointment with a senior executive manager with responsibilities for international marketing. The interview proceeds with considerable caution in a chilly atmosphere. My interviewee expresses concern that as I am a student in a rival institution, commercial-in-confidence considerations will prevent him from providing information about his university's marketing strategies. I run through my institution's ethical requirements of its researchers in a bid to ease his discomfort but to little avail. At the end of the interview I am exhausted and have not taken sufficient notes, having concentrated so hard on trying to develop rapport and trust. It is the ultimate fieldwork nightmare. Fortunately, other sources lower down the hierarchical ladder are more forthcoming.

A UNIVERSITY FOR THE REAL WORLD

As part of the broad reforms that engulfed Australian higher education at the end of the 1980s, the Queensland Institute of Technology amalgamated with the Kelvin Grove College of Advanced Education to form a new institution, QUT, in 1988. Following its elevation to university status, and unencumbered by the artifices of tradition, QUT aggressively marketed itself both locally and overseas and in doing so crafted an image of itself based on its previous incarnation as a practical institution. Its promotional slogan, "A University for the Real World," seeks to maximize leverage from its vocationalist orientation.

Like most Australian universities, the institution's marketing activities range from soft marketing, involving its alumni who facilitate word-of-mouth endorsements, to the use of education exhibitions and recruitment visits to schools and other educational institutions. From its early days, QUT has used a variety of market behaviors to build its profile in Southeast Asian student markets; for example, it was one of the first Australian universities to use agents to recruit students. Today, the nurturing and careful management of its agents remains central to achieving its recruitment targets.[22]

The dispersion of promotional messages through the university's Web site and its alumni magazine, *Links*, indicates the use of a set of generic mar-

---

[22]Agents' commissions are a closely guarded secret, known usually only to the executive director of International Marketing. On the average, an agent will receive 10% of the students' first-year fees; however, this figure varies depending on productivity factors such as the recruitment targets achieved by agents. Depending on the market in question, individual agents may represent several Australian universities, many of whom are in competition with each other.

keting messages by the university that are directed at both local and international audiences. The institution's marketing slogan, "A University for the Real World," was initially developed to appeal to a domestic audience, but it is also pitched to international audiences. *Real Global Giant* and *Buffy* are two such examples. Both advertisements reveal the attributes of the educated subject that this real-world university prides itself on producing. It is through an analysis of the educated subject that we are able to identify this institution's values, establish the criteria it uses to define professional success, and identify its vision.

Real Global Giant features an image of a young man positioned in the center of the page, in sporting attire, pictured running (see Fig. 6.4). In the background are two Australian icons drenched in the departing, golden light of day: the Sydney Harbour Bridge and the Opera House. The subject in this image is introduced to us as Michael Baxter. The accompanying promotional narrative describes him with three captions: "QUT business graduate," "real global giant," and "runner." He does not look at us, the viewers, but gazes intently ahead, presumably focused on his goal, completing the "circuit across the Harbour Bridge and around the Opera House." Against Michael's chest is emblazoned the slogan of the corporation that employs him—Accenture. In one sense, his body is portrayed as corporate property—he is an object of business at the same time as he is its agent: "to keep his mind and body ready for business, Michael runs a circuit across the Harbour Bridge and around the Opera House nearly every day." He is pictured as a giant who dominates the landscape—a modern-day Colossus of Rhodes, a young, fit, White, male sprinting toward his goal. The image and accompanying text in the advertisement valorizes the education–economy nexus by constructing Michael's mind and body as serving business.

What can we infer about these ascribed identities—QUT business graduate, Real global giant, and Runner? A literal reading would produce the following meaning: QUT business graduates can aspire to be real global giants and have a career that is "up and running." However, a critical reading of *Real Global Giant* also identifies statements about the meaning of education, what success as a professional means in a real world, and the normative role for the university in society. Professional success in the real world is constructed as being a real global giant, that is, being employed by one of the world's leading management and technology consulting companies. The QUT credential is portrayed as a vital ingredient for achieving success. It enabled Michael to acquire a job with amazing haste, "before he even had the chance to frame . . . his Bachelor of Business degree." The narrative ends with flourish, investing QUT with the agency and kudos associated with creating employment opportunities: "QUT puts more degree graduates into full-time employment than any other university in Australia." Quantity matters in this Fordist world. The imperative to the reader to "call . . . or visit qut.com to

QUT business graduate

Real global giant

Runner

ven had a chance to frame his Bachelor of Business degree in Management and International Business, Michael Baxter
a job with Accenture, one of the world's leading management and technology consulting companies. He moved to Sydney
ffices in 46 countries) and his feet have hardly touched the ground since. To keep his mind and body ready for business
s a circuit across the Harbour Bridge and around the Opera House nearly every day. QUT puts more degree graduates
employment than any other university in Australia. Call (07) 3864 2000 or visit **qut.com** to get your career up and running

a university for the **real** world

Queensland University of Technology, Brisbane

FIG. 6.4. Real global giant.

get your career up and running" confirms the institution's belief in its job-creating prowess. The bold typeface for "qut.com" portrays the institution's unabashed commercial focus. It is a training ground, a factory for developing productive bodies for the fields of commerce and technology. The subject positions that are normalized by this advertisement are competitive, on-the-move individuals who keep their minds and bodies fit for business and who grasp opportunity wherever they may be.

The QUT business degree is represented as the bridge to a spatialized world of opportunity, evident in the references to Accenture with its offices in 46 countries. The QUT graduate is constructed as geographically portable, and the QUT credential is *the* immutable credential that transcends national, linguistic, and cultural boundaries to exploit the spatialization of opportunity in the brave new world of global markets. *Real Global Giant* demonstrates that the instrumentalist orientation of university education and the subjectification of graduates as human capital for the corporate world have become stable, rhetorical forms. Using Foucault's (1972) conceptual language, these discourses have crossed the 'threshold of epistemologization'.

How has this state of affairs emerged? This response from a staff member locates the cause firmly with national-level forces:

> There is no turning back now. . . . [It has been] a deliberate strategy by the Commonwealth to make universities less reliant on government revenue. (marketing personnel, male)

Another discursive reinforcement between the worlds of work and education is *Buffy*, another high-profile QUT advertisement that has appeared in TV advertisements in Brisbane, and on QUT's Web site and alumni magazine, *Links* (QUT, 2001b).

"QUT graduate," "Real Buffy fan," and "Slaying them at Microsoft" are the captions used to showcase the achievements of Ilana Smith (see Fig. 6.5), whose success as a professional is based on working at Microsoft's head office in Seattle, Washington. She describes Microsoft as "the best company in the world" and Seattle as "the place all the best and most exciting things call home." Ilana's aspirational goal, working for Microsoft, have been inspired by Microsoft's position in "*Fortune* magazine's . . . list of the top companies to work for." She observes, "What appeals to me about IT . . . [is] . . . the industry changes all the time and coming to work is exciting and interesting because there's always some new technology development." A particular image of progress is being constructed—it is technologically driven, fast, furious, and heart-thumpingly exciting.

Ilana 's "fiercest passions" are noted—"rally cars [and] . . . hobbies which involve anything that requires excitement and adrenaline." We are offered a glimpse of a key signifier of her success, the personalized registration plate of her car "LIKEDIS" (see Fig. 6.6). She is pictured against the Seattle skyline in a caricatured posture in celebration mood (see Fig. 6.5). We are also informed that Ilana is an avid fan of the TV show, *Buffy the Vampire Slayer*, hence, the caption, "Slaying them at Microsoft." In some respects, it is a promotional message anchored in a discourse of conflict and competition.

Here, QUT's use of a theme from a popular TV show is intended to appeal to the younger cohort of prospective students, in particular, young women. In one sense, this advertisement can be read as a positive move to unsettle the normative associations between males and IT by positioning a young woman as the subject of an IT success story. Less inspiring is its reliance on masculinist norms to define what it means to be a successful professional and its role in reinforcing a technologically deterministic view of success.

FIG. 6.5.   Buffy: Slaying them at Microsoft.

FIG. 6.6.   Buffy's car plates.

The issue of gender has considerable visibility in the academy, its cause ministered by departments with comforting names, such as 'The Office of Gender Equity', which help produce institutional policies, operational plans, and mission statements and helpful tracts on how to avoid sexist language. These documentary monuments are designed to make visible and address issues of gender discrimination in the academy. Yet, as this promotional narrative indicates, copious visibilities and transparencies about gender can still end up invisible and marginal if female characters like Buffy alias Ilana are used to promote resolutely masculinist norms (see Strathern, 2000; Tsoukas, 1997).

There is little that is distinctly local about the images of success portrayed in *Buffy* and nothing to suggest that local cultural norms or attributes have a part to play in producing professional success. Instead, what emerges is an unabashed celebration of mainstream North American norms of success and an associated celebration of the types of subjectivities required to succeed in this cultural environment. The discursive subject positions that are legitimized are those of technologically driven high achievers who can identify with, and replicate, the normative American dream of success. The cultural and symbolic capital required to win is resolutely American in flavor. The overriding message to QUT students is that the formula to success is to replicate an American script.

What is missing is an alternative vision of success aside from the limited ones of technology and consumption. Ilana's success is based on her acculturation to the 'center'—the United States and Microsoft—where professional success and material rewards beckon. QUT is portrayed as a vitally important conduit, a springboard to the supremely successful center of technological enterprise and cultural hegemony, the United States.

Positioning the Other in a Real World

Like many Australian universities, QUT declares its commitment to a global and multicultural vision: "Our campuses are cosmopolitan . . . a significant proportion of our students speak at least one other language than English. As a result, QUT is a vibrant place to study and work" (QUT, 2001a). Here, the mere presence of international students is equated with an intellectual engagement with cultural diversity. The official imagination assumes that a cultural osmosis will happen naturally (Kelly, 2000). There are no statements about the need for reciprocal learning and symbiotic exchanges among the university's cosmopolitan student body. Coexisting with this vision is a set of counternarratives reminiscent of an older colonial past, which reinforce images of a passive, inert other that requires help from the West.

These othering counternarratives appear in various guises in QUT's official material. Three examples—"QUT Staff Reach Out to Preschools in India" (QUT, 2000), "Students Aid Struggling Fijians" (QUT, 2004), and "Making a Difference in Mozambique" (QUT, 2001b)—are now explored. "QUT Staff Reach Out to Preschools" appeared as an article in *Inside QUT* (International), a campus newspaper that is distributed at international education exhibitions to overseas agents and prospective students. "Making a Difference in Mozambique" appeared in the *Weekend Australian Magazine*, the country's only national newspaper; a local Brisbane news magazine, *Brisbane News*, which is distributed free to Brisbane residents; and as a story in *Links*, the magazine that is forwarded to domestic and international alumni. It also appeared in advertisement in public spaces, such as bus shelters.

"QUT Staff Reach Out to Preschools in India" (QUT, 2000) describes the institution's commitment to be a responsible global citizen (see Fig. 6.7). The article notes, "Staff from QUT's schools of Early Childhood and Human Services are planning to work with a group that runs community

QUT staff reach out to preschools in India

By Andrew Hammond

Staff from QUT's schools of Early Childhood and Human Services are planning to work with a group that runs community preschools in Indian slums.

Academics will investigate the best ways to train more than 3,000 teachers working for the Pratham-Mumbai Education Initiative, as well as help with the development of teaching resources.

Professor Heather Mohay said the Pratham group was keen to begin involving parents in their programs so that they were better able to support their children's learning and development.

She has just returned from a trip to India where she visited the preschools as well as a number of Indian universities which have early childhood programs.

"Pratham is a charitable trust which as a societal mission to make early childhood education available to all children," Professor Mohay said.

"Without preschool, Indian children are ill-prepared for school and frequently drop out in the first few years and remain illiterate."

Professor Mohay said that Pratham was using a community mobilisation model to set up early childhood programs in the Mumbai slums, where approximately 60 per cent of the city children lived.

"They go into the slums and talk to the parents – if they want a balwadi (preschool) for their children, they must identify a suitable 'teacher' from their midst

Indian children take a break from lessons in their balwadi (community kindergarten).

who has at least a grade-eight education," she said.

"Pratham then provides a few days' training and some basic materials and pays the teacher a minimal wage that is the equivalent of about $8 (Australian) a month.

"Parents have to pay a small fee and the community must find a space for the balwadi.

"This means that many balwadis are held in people's homes or in community offices or temples or even out-of-doors. The spaces are usually very cramped and there are, typically, 20 children and a teacher working in intense heat with very little ventilation. But they all seem to enjoy themselves."

Professor Mohay said Pratham, which was formed in 1995, had grown to operating more than 3,000 balwadis catering for 55,000 children in the Mumbai slums, and was extending its program into other cities.

"The challenge now is to ensure that the balwadi program is of good quality and really gets the children ready for school," she said.

"This is problematic as the balwadi teachers have had limited education themselves and there is a turn over of about one third of the teachers each year."

Professor Mohay said the Pratham program also facilitated the advancement of women and the whole community.

She has applied for funding from a number of sources to enable the development of collaborative programs between QUT, Pratham and a number of Indian universities.

"The community mobilisation model which has been used so successfully has clear implications for community programs in Australia and we are keen to learn more about how it works," Professor Mohay said.

FIG. 6.7. Third World children in India.

preschools (balwadis) in Indian slums. [They] "will investigate the best way to train more than 3000 teachers working for the Pratham-Mumbai Education Initiative" (QUT, 2000, p. 2). A QUT staff member is quoted as saying: "Without preschool, Indian children are ill-prepared for school and frequently drop out in the first few years and remain illiterate" (QUT, 2000, p. 2).

A cursory reading of this article conveys the impression of a responsible global citizen who is using knowledge in the field of early childhood to alleviate an entrenched problem that disadvantages Indian children. However, a closer reading reveals the prevalence of significant material poverty:

> Many *balwadi's* (pre-school establishments) are held in people's homes or temples or even outdoors . . . [in] cramped spaces, [with] teachers and children working in intense heat. . . . Teachers [have] limited education and [there is] a high turnover of staff . . . they are paid A $8 a month. (QUT, 2000, p. 2)

In the face of such material poverty, the solution of sending First World academics to educate the Third World begins to appear ineffectual. The article is sparse in its descriptions of the commitment of the Pratham-Mumbai Initiative or the work undertaken by Indian staff and patrons at the front line. The overriding impression is of First World agents of knowledge and compassion saving the Third World. It is a familiar replay of the White Man's Burden, a theme that dominated colonial education technologies. Then, as now, the colonial authorities from the center emerge as moral, compassionate, and wise, and the other appears with cultural and educational deficits (see Ashcroft, Griffiths, & Tiffin, 1995, pp. 425–427; Loombia, 1998, chap. 2). Positioned in the center of the article and confirming this impression is an image of bedraggled Indian children with their teacher staring passively at the camera.

"Students Aid Struggling Fijians" (QUT, 2004) generates a similar discourse:

> Five Business and Law students gave up their holidays to teach locals in the island nation elements of human resources, marketing, strategic management operations, accounting and law. Team member Giuletta Brown said, "we found it a fantastic challenge putting into practice what we have learned from our studies and life experience to help others that may need that help, and hopefully helping alleviate some of the more poverty stricken areas in remote Fiji." (p. 8)

Poverty in Fiji is constructed as a lack of core knowledge in "human resource management, marketing, accounting and law." A kind master positioning is evident here, with the QUT students represented as a benevolent, selfless group who have given up their holidays to educate the Fijians out of poverty (QUT, 2004).

These manufactured images of the institution as a compassionate global citizen and the voiceless, agentless other also appears in "Making a Difference in Mozambique" (QUT, 2001b). The advertisement invests a QUT graduate with the agency to save "tragic," "war-scarred" Mozambique (QUT, 2001b, p. 15). With no images or statements from Mozambicans, the implicit suggestion is that they are excluded from the job of making a difference. The article refers to the lack of preparation by the government of Mozambique for the 2000 flooding disaster and the "help of international governments and 200 international organisations" (p. 15). It is hard to get away from an impression of incompetent Mozambicans and a dynamic, compassionate West that is called on, once again, to assist the natives. The language is nuanced, but the thematic continuity with an older colonial text where enlightened Westerners brings civilization and learning to the backward other remains securely in place.

The artifices of QUT's marketing message are not able to capture other vitally important complexities in this scenario—that Mozambique pays US$1 million per week in debt service as a result of Structural Adjustment programs that continue to be broadly endorsed by First World governments and intellectuals, or that two thirds of its population live in poverty (Inter-church Coalition for Africa [ICCAF], 2000). In the face of such grinding poverty, forward planning for natural disasters is an understandably low priority.

If we take internationalization as the strategic response of higher education institutions toward globalization, what conclusions can we reach from this analysis of promotional narratives? QUT's promotional archive reveals the existence of two coexisting discourses: first, an instrumentalist discourse premised on a technological and commercial normativity, and second, a residual colonial discourse that generates and maintains ciphers of otherness, premised on passivity, poverty, inertness, and ineptitude, while depicting the West as agents of knowledge and compassion. The habitus of the educated subject is steered toward dispositions, desires, and aspirations to enable them to succeed in, and contribute toward, a largely technological and commercial world. The lauded qualities associated with the educated subject as depicted in *Real Global Giant* and *Buffy* are competitive individualism, a reverence of the norms of success that are premised on Western or American values, and a colonial attitude toward the other. There is little attention given to developing alternative subjectivities or in steering students and staff toward alternative images of success, progress, or alternative futures. The international relevance of the QUT credential is anchored in space-bound, Western, and ethnocentric notions of progress and professional success.

In the highly competitive field that constitutes the global trade in education services, the Australian government's desire is to establish a credible brand position that secures its place as an education destination. Australia's largest markets for international education are located in the geographic space termed Asia. Constructing an image of friendliness and respect for the Asian other is especially important, given Australia's past history of race-based immigration and ambivalent engagement with the region. Therefore, the marketing message necessarily deploys a discourse of cultural hybridity to promote Australia as a study destination in Asia. But it is an impoverished interpretation of diversity, anchored largely in the availability of home-country cuisine and the presence of an immigrant diaspora. Marketing narratives project an image of friendly, multicultural campuses and cities, free from racist violence and law-and-order problems. Place and lifestyle are also used to sell Australian education to First World clients. The outcome is a tourist discourse, featuring elaborate place-branding strategies that seek to construct and sell an imagined place to live for the duration of one's study sojourn.

Educational Tourism

Place branding is now an important component within the political economy of international education. The tourist-traveler discourse emerged in the trade era of internationalization, commencing around 1988 and gradually assuming greater importance. Today, the tourist landscape is a permanent landscape in the marketing of international education. The types of images that are used are continuously changed, updated, and linked to themes and premier events. For example, in 1999 and 2000, many universities used the upcoming Olympic Games to promote their educational wares. Today, standard university promotional brochures highlight the modernity of Australian cities, their safety, and their proximity to key tourist attractions such as wildlife attractions (see Fig. 6.8) and pristine beaches.

QUT's promotional materials are no exception. They make much of the attractions of Brisbane—"modern, vibrant, blessed with subtropical climate. Clean, safe, easy to travel around ... beaches, abseiling" (QUT, 2001c)—these adjectives are intended to appeal to a particular customer market, the parents of prospective students and women students. References to abseiling also suggest that a particular type of clientele is being feted by the institutions, wealthy and well acquainted with expensive rugged, outdoor activities. The profusion of tourist images is particularly strong in the study abroad prospectus and web pages—a program dominated by First World clients.

FIG. 6.8.   Rugged tourism.

As Australia's foreign policies have reorientated toward the country's historical links with the Euro-American world ahead of its geographical proximities to the Asia-Pacific region, education marketing narratives have subtly tempered the unspoken concerns that prospective students from the Asia may have about their acceptance by Australians. Populist backlash against immigrants, refugees, and asylum seekers, along with moves to counter the emergence of a revisionist history of Australia's conquest, and government support for the Coalition of the Willing in world affairs, have led to concerns about the resurgence of a fortress Australia mentality. The subjugated discourse of multiculturalism that has been lying dormant in recent years has been resurrected to counter concerns among a largely Asia-Pacific client group about the possible reemergence of a governmentality based on racial and cultural ethnocentrism. Pronouncements such as this one, which appeared in the government-sponsored *Study Queensland*

(Queensland Government, 2001) brochure, are used to confer particular psychological meanings onto places aimed at normalizing difference and diversity in the spatial landscapes at the same time as entrenching the right to practice difference in law and authority:

> Queenslanders are a friendly people who will make you feel at home, while you are studying away from home. . . . The relaxed atmosphere, beautiful environment and perfect weather allow for an unparalleled lifestyle while you study. . . .
>
> One of the great aspects of life in Queensland is the high level of personal freedom that comes with a truly multicultural society. People in Queensland have a wide variety of beliefs, philosophies and practices and live harmoniously with personal freedoms and rights protected by laws. (Queensland Government, 2001)

This discourse of personal freedoms hints of a state-sanctioned belief in a liberal discourse of cultural diversity intended to assure people that they are entitled to engage in religious and cultural practices in their private lives. Images such as Fig. 6.9 featuring the Australian Halal Butcher and goods priced in Chinese text embed difference and multiculturalism into the social and semiotic landscape. At the same time, such images are also comforting to traditionally conservative families who may perceive studying overseas as a high-risk venture with the potential to unsettle their essentialist identities and expose their children to liberal excesses.

In short, the politics of marketing and representing international education have significant material and political consequences (see also Harvey, 1993, pp. 17–18). Attracting overseas students means a boost to local economies and governments are increasingly lending rhetorical and material support to the international education sector. Part of this support includes the reconstruction of places to re-make them as being safe; of tourist interest; and most important, as being multicultural, nonracist, and free of violence. Safe cities are a key marketing signifier used to promote Australia as a preferable study destination to the United States, whose cities are perceived as dangerous.

As a cultural artifact, promotional materials tell us something about how the international university and international education are construed and constructed. So, what conclusions can we reach from the analysis of QUT? The university's promotional slogan, a "University for *the* real world," suggests a collapsing of all narratives and all realities into the one spatiality and the one teleology: There is only one real world and one teleology, a commercial and technological one. Here is an assumption of a linear view of time that is less inclusive of diversity than we are led to believe by the plethora of official declarations supporting multiculturalism. Allied to its real-world message is the assumption that the use and exchange values of a

Food

Due to Queensland's multicultural population, there are many supermarkets and speciality shops which cater for all tastes. You will be able to buy almost every product you have at home including Halal meats, Chinese vegetables, American style burgers, pasta, pizzas, European breads and pastries and all kinds of

Accommodation

FIG. 6.9. Australian multiculturalism.

QUT education can seamlessly be transferred to different national and cultural contexts, and that the educated subjects who are QUT's graduates will live and work within an identical episteme to that of the real world of QUT, regardless of their geographical, cultural, and economic positioning.

Such marketing messages are premised on and reinforce the grand narrative of modernity. The habitus of the educated subject is steered toward dispositions, desires, and aspirations to enable them to succeed in, and contribute to, a largely technological and commercial world. The lauded qualities associated with the educated subject as depicted in *Real Global Giant* and *Buffy* are competitive individualism, a colonial attitude toward the other, and a reverence of norms of success premised on Western or American values. There is little attention given to developing alternative subjectivities, or in steering students and staff toward different images of success, progress, and alternative futures. The international relevance of the QUT credential is anchored in space-bound, Western, and ethnocentric notions of progress and professional success. Such an education, which is largely conceptualized in instrumental and universal terms, is limited in its capacity to unhinge knowledges and institutions that are informed by notions of a civilizational polarity.

From a 'university for the real world', the focus now shifts to Monash University, a university that is working to reinvent itself from a popular, city-based institution to that of Global University.

MONASH UNIVERSITY: GLOBAL AND "SELF-RELIANT"

In 1998, Monash University, a prolific actor in the Australian international education scene, replaced its Italian motto *Ancora Imparo* (I am still learning) with "Australia's International University" (Marginson & Considine, 2000, p. 40). Its recent promotional slogan, "The Global University," suggests a further spatialization of its vision. The university's strategic plan, *Leading the Way, Monash 2020* (Monash University, 2000a), uses the term *Greater Monash* as a self-descriptor of its ensemble of bricks and mortar campuses in Australia, South Africa, and Malaysia; its International Centers in London (UK) and Prato, Italy; and numerous educational partnerships with institutions throughout Europe and Asia.

Monash's declared goal in *Leading the Way* is to establish "an educational network that spans the globe." Through a range of positive national stereotypes, the university's strategic plan links its national and global aspirations. A narrative of the nation sees Australia constructed as an enthusiastic, adventurous, and pragmatic country, "willing to take on a challenge, pursue opportunities." There is an explicit reference to globalization, the opportunities it offers, and how these opportunities resonate with national aspirations and national values:

> Monash is at once international and Australian. Like the Australian nation, it is comparatively young, but built upon ancient traditions. Like Australia it is a tolerant, multi-cultural community spanning both urban and regional areas, but sharing common values and aspirations. Like the Australian people, Monash is characterised by its willingness to take on a challenge and to pursue new opportunities. And like modern Australia, Monash has embraced the challenges and opportunities of globalisation. (Monash University, 2000a)

The logic of marketing and public relations that thrives on uncomplicated and unambiguous images also requires a selective imagination. Accordingly, this discursive logic has established a set of rules about what can be said about Australia. The grids of specification of conquest, disenfranchisement, and assimilation are necessarily airbrushed, whereas the tolerant and social democratic face of Australia is highlighted. At the same time, national and global, as well as urban and rural, relations are seamlessly sutured together without a hint of any contradictions.

Leading the Way also declares a three-fold commitment to internationalization: the internationalization of curriculum, the pursuit of internationally relevant teaching and research, and "developing Monash in a way which broadens the international opportunities [and] strengthens its capacity to perform its national and international roles" (Monash University, 2000a). It is unclear just what these roles are. Essentially, these statements have an impression-management function to depict a dynamic, forward-thinking institution, keen to broaden its international role while seeking inspiration in a national imaginary. Given that the concept of international relevance is produced in and through the configurations of power–knowledge, it is not a sufficient guiding principle with which to capture the rich mosaic of ideas and epistemologies from different regions and cultures. Power–knowledge configurations are well noted for selecting out, ordering, and prioritizing what is important enough to appear in curricula and research agendas.

Monash declares its vision to be "self-reliant . . . a learning organisation, conducting innovative teaching and research of international quality and relevance . . . with . . . industries and professions which it serves" (Monash University, 2000a). The institution's aspirations are to seek deliverance from its reliance on state hand-outs and to diversify its revenue streams to include the "industries and professions which it serves." The university's director of marketing confirms this institutional desire and links it to a shifting national policy as well as to broader macro-level trends:

> We could have chosen to resist Dawkins' reforms and we could have remained . . . a Redbrick institution. . . . But with the demographics of Australia, and given the way education services are evolving around the world, there would have been problems of critical mass in adequately servicing [our] multi-

campus operations. . . . So to be a university of excellence, we needed to get bigger in order to get better and we needed to be much more outward looking. So, this pattern of global interaction started to emerge, partly by happenstance. (director of marketing, male)[23]

The forces driving Monash's strategic push to build overseas campuses and establish international centers, then, were distinctly local and included its competition with a local competitor, Melbourne University, as this response by a senior staff member based at Monash's London Center suggests:

Monash's campus is located 20 km out of the city centre [of Melbourne]. It is not well serviced by public transport. . . . Melbourne University is 100 years old and located in the city centre. What is a university like Monash going to do? Sit there like some surburban university and fade away quietly?

That was not our idea at all. . . . If the university is to have influence in the scholarly world, it better get out into the world. . . . So we have campuses in other countries and they are in strategically placed sites. There is no point trying to put a campus in a first world country . . . [although] we want to have links. So we have campuses in places like South Africa and also Malaysia. . . . In Europe we have an office which is just like an embassy. . . . Possibly some day we will get around to having one in North America and East Asia too. (senior executive dean, male)

These accounts point to the intricate workings of local- and national-level processes, suggesting that processes with a global reach often have their origins in the local and that the local, national, and global should not be regarded as ontologically separate categories. In Monash's case, its decision to reinvent itself was motivated by a series of national government policies aimed at increasing competition between universities. The rivalry between Monash and Melbourne University created the conditions for its ambitious offshore expansion project, which included locating itself in strategically placed sites, namely, developing countries, to attract a critical mass of consumers. The emergence of Greater Monash, then, cannot be attributed to an external power and exogenous force (globalization).

Monash University's international arm, Monash International Pty. Ltd., has primary responsibility for the recruitment and support of international students and all general administrative practices to do with international students. Monash International's logo does not carry any sign of its status as an education institution (see Fig. 6.10), presumably a strategic move aimed at increasing the university's flexibility, maneuverability, and leverage in a com-

---

[23]*Redbrick university* is a generic term that is used to refer to the postwar British and Australian universities.

FIG. 6.10. Monash International Pty Ltd.

mercial world. The logo positions *Monash* above the world, which is signified by an arc, and crowned by a shining star to signify its enduring quality (star status). It suggests an institutional aspiration to be instantly recognized. The seven-pointed star, also present on the Australian flag, is an embodiment of Australianess (the nation-state is made up of a total of seven states and territories). The star indicates Monash's strong ties with the nation.

Monash's diverse markets are captured semiotically in a range of student images (see Fig. 6.11). Earlier prospectuses used the Chinese heritage student to symbolize the international student; however, later publications use images suggesting a greater ethnocultural diversity. As a consequence of changes in educational markets in the period following the Asian Financial Crisis, Monash, like many Australian universities, had to diversify its customer base. Although there are some images of mixed-gender and culturally diverse groups, the more common image is that of single-gender pairs of students and solitary individuals looking studious, reassuring for the conservative parent who might have a limited appreciation of difference and diversity. In a bid to secure customer loyalty, the university offers a 10% discount to siblings of existing Monash students, suggesting a growing isomorphism with the selling strategies of commercial, for-profit companies who have long realized that relationship marketing is the most cost-effective and efficient way of ensuring financial return.

In keeping with its goal to construct an educational network that spans the globe (Monash University, 2000a), Monash's strategic objective has been to deterritorialize its production and provision of education services. Thus, Monash University Malaysia is promoted in the international prospectus, the institution's Web site, and regional education exhibitions as a lower cost option to studying at Monash's Australian campuses: "[It] offers students a very affordable opportunity to gain a Monash qualification" (Monash University, 2002). Monash Malaysia was developed in partnership with the Sunway Group, a Malaysian construction company with interests in real estate; tourism; and now, education.

Monash has constructed for itself the role of a multinational enterprise and is in partnership not only with a Malaysian private corporation but also

FIG. 6.11. Monash students.

with the South African nation-state. The opening of its South African
branch campus was hailed as proof of:

> a long term commitment to South Africa's future. . . . The campus will be part
> of the new South Africa's continued integration into the global economy, and
> will play a major role in educating the country's workforce for tomorrow's
> challenges. . . . If we can follow the example of our campus in Malaysia, a full
> 25 per cent of the student population will come from outside South Africa,
> thereby bringing enormous economic benefits to the country. (Monash Uni-
> versity, 2000b)

Through a declared mission of training human capital, the university aspires to facilitate flows of 'finanscapes' and 'ethnoscapes' to reinvigorate

the South African nation-state's moribund economy. Monash South Africa is expected to "produce global citizens who will be able to contribute a great deal to their own countries" (Monash University, 2000b). The Monash graduate, described in the institution's Web sites, is expected to have the following attributes: "self-reliant, open, egalitarian, contemporary, and international" (Monash University, 2000a). The presumption here is that these qualities will enable Monash graduates, wherever they might live and work, to function as global citizens and to mediate successfully any conflicting responsibilities that may arise between the global and local–national. Yet, the smooth, seamless unicity featuring productive flows used to explain its incursions overseas is only part of the Monash story.

For an institution such as Monash with an espoused commitment to the broader social good within Australia, its physical incursions into non-Western geographies change its identity. In crossing territorial boundaries, Monash becomes a private institution and, by default, displaces the publicly funded nation-building university in the developing world. Its 'First World' budget permits Monash to operate at a loss in South Africa for a nominated time frame of 5 years while building itself a brand name. South African universities, by contrast, lack the largesse to operate in deficit for any length of time while facing very significant challenges in building a postapartheid nation-state and society.

Monash's incursions into the imperial center, the United Kingdom, by way of its association with King's College, have less serious ramifications. King's College, described by the Monash promotional narrative as "a founding College of the 170 year-old University of London and a member of the Russell Group of leading United Kingdom universities" (Monash University, 1999) is an established, high-status university whose association with Monash is collaborative and not competitive.

The university's Web site notes that:

> King's College London will join the Monash Malaysia campus as a major destination for Australian-based Monash students completing part of their course overseas. Conversely, King's College London plans to arrange that its students will have ready access to Monash courses in Australia and Malaysia. Monash and King's will plan joint courses and cooperate in the recruitment of students in Australia, Britain and elsewhere around the world. (Monash University, 1999)

The London Center is intended to smooth the way for negotiations between King's and Monash to enable the streamlining of courses. The partnership between the two institutions is also mooted as creating productive possibilities for collaborative tenders for Australian, European Union, and internationally funded projects, and credit transfer arrangements for each institution's students. Negotiations were being finalized to institutionalize a convergence to "get the undergraduate courses as parallel as possible so that it is very easy for someone to move back and forth . . . as seamless webs, so to speak" (personal communication, executive dean, 2000). On one level, this streamlining of courses can be read as a trend toward homogenization, a key position taken by some globalization theorists. However, interactions with different national systems of higher education, involving different institutional and departmental cultures, do not weave themselves into seamless webs. Local inflections—departmental cultures, institutional norms, and faculty autonomy—are all factors that impinge on Monash's progress toward global university status:

> Things proceed very slowly in this country. I don't find it a particularly efficient country. . . . London is so expensive that a lot of the academics only come up when they have a class. That slows everything down. It takes weeks to set up meetings. The Computer Science course has taken ages to move but is moving now. King's department felt they were overworked and were not keen to take anything extra . . . It was only when they were convinced that collaboration would not mean extra work but would mean extra money that they started to become positive about it. (senior executive)

Significantly, what is left unsaid in the university's promotional mantra to be self-reliant are the risks involved in shifting to market-based incomes. Market-like practices create other complexities that are different from but perhaps commensurate with the pressures associated with a reliance on state funding. For example, markets favor some disciplines ahead of others, resulting in a narrowing of educational options and the scope for institutional diversity (Marginson, 2003a; Marginson & Considine, 2000, pp. 214–215). Neither are universities any less subject to censure by private sector charities than governments. The University of Oregon's failure to secure the continuing financial support of corporate giant Nike is a case in point. By supporting the Worker Rights Consortium, a labor rights organization that had criticized Nike's practices in the developing world, the university raised the ire of the corporate giant, which discontinued its endowments (Drier & Fox-Piven, 2000; Jacobsen, 2000; "On Your Bike," 2000).

Notable and paradoxical is the fact that Monash's own engagement with the international domain arose from its concerns to protect its identity as an institution committed to educational diversity and the public good. Its slow reconfiguration into a private, educational multinational offshore institution is a sobering illustration of how universities are imbricated in the geometries of power. Monash's desire to deterritorialize and to expand its reach to strategically significant sites as a strategy to self-reliance is likely to have long-term consequences for developing countries. The following view offers a grim and sobering prognosis for that national university's public good functions:

> Without private participation the educational expectations of most countries will never be met. There is no capacity in many countries to make the investment from the public purse because the tax base is insufficient to fund it. . . . Groups like the World Bank are now moving away from lending for education to governments and lending to corporations as they feel a business model will make a difference. (director of marketing)

"The Edge": Selling Positional Goods With Global Appeal

In the highly competitive international education market, Australian universities such as Monash have resorted to branding as a way of establishing a distinctive identity and an edge. Monash has assumed a multipronged approach aimed at being all things to all people:

> Everyone is looking for an edge and we focus on things like diversity and the ability to find a pathway into Monash for different people. . . . And we are increasingly, emphasising the global nature of university, its engagement with other countries. So "this can provide you with networks, a high reputation quotient." . . . If you have a Monash degree you won't have to explain what a Monash degree is. (director of marketing)

A recurring instrumental theme is one of education as a source of positional goods for the ambitious, self-improving individual: "Advanced study at Monash can open many doors."[24] A series of branding statements aimed at setting Monash apart 'from the rest of the pack' permeate the text: "The Monash approach is leading the way in higher education not only because of our absolute commitment to teaching excellence, but also because we offer a truly global education" (Monash, 2002). These lexical items—"absolute commitment" and "truly global vision"—suggest an almost evangelical belief in its position as a unique university. Monash's educational vision for the 21st century, however, seems largely pedestrian, tempered by the goal of preparing its students "for the increasingly competitive job market" via flexible pathways:

> As a large and diverse university of the 21st century, Monash offers a wide range of postgraduate courses that give our students access to flexible learning options and innovative research opportunities. We are *dedicated to prepar-*

---

[24]See Welcome Address, International Prospectus 2002.

ing . . . students for the increasingly competitive job market [italics added], as a result, Monash graduates are highly sought after by employers internationally. (Monash University, 2002)

So, Monash sees its primary mission as producing human capital for the "competitive job market."[25] That it takes its instrumental role very seriously is clear in the proportion of the prospectus devoted to career opportunities, a comprehensive spread presented in a tabular form and cramped with details of career pathways, against which are listed corresponding Monash courses. The foregrounding of the job market in the production, transmission, and validation of knowledge is implicit, and the privileged student subjectivity is the ambitious individual who equates education with career success.

The Welcome address in the International Prospectus from the Vice-Chancellor and President hints at the university's preoccupations with its market position. Including the title 'President' with 'Vice-Chancellor' reflects a deference to the U.S. model as the norm. The term *president* is largely associated with the North American higher education sector and is the preferred term in countries such as China, Japan, Taiwan, and Korea. Vice-Chancellor, on the other hand, has currency in the Commonwealth countries only (see also Marginson & Considine, 2000, p. 68).

The notion that a Monash education has universal utility emerges as an enduring theme throughout its international prospectus: "A Monash education qualifies you for success in the global community" (Monash University, 2002). The assumption being that Monash's graduates will operate within a singular episteme, unencumbered by cultural or national specificities. Likewise, the global community is imagined and constructed as a homogeneous entity.

As is the case with the university's other international education programs, the marketing message used to promote the study abroad program also extends to the instrumental, although with a touch of adventure and spice thrown in. The study abroad Web site (Monash University, 2000c) features numerous images of young people pictured on mountain tops, against waterfalls, and in forest settings. A form of educational tourism is being manufactured for the young, fit, and possibly elite student-tourist: "We are committed to making your stay as easy and pleasurable as possible." It reads as an official endorsement of the 'dumbing down' of education.

---

[25]The instrumental orientation of the university is detectable in p. 4 of the International Prospectus under the caption, "Study at a Global University for a Global Career." Again, we are told that Monash offers: "a university qualification that is recognised around the world and opens up exciting international career opportunities"; "Our graduates are widely sought after by employers internationally for their academic abilities and their reputations as independent learners, innovators and leaders."

Monash University's Study Abroad Program is for the serious student traveller who wants an advantage. The competition for good jobs is more intense than ever before. With the greater integration and internationalisation of the world economy, companies are looking for employees who can take a world view. Studying in another culture will give you an advantage. Australia is the perfect place to strengthen your career prospects. . . .

To study and travel is to get the best of both worlds. The travel spices up the study by setting it in a context of adventure. It gives you a chance to test your resolve, your boldness and your ability to deal with the new and the un-expected. . . . Together, study and travel bring about real change in a person. And of course, employers and graduate school selection boards like to see that you have done something that *sets you apart from the pack.* . . . [italics added]

Students who choose to come to Australia will find: a bridge to a diverse range of cultures, a great and stable democracy, a skilled society, a sporting society, an achieving society, an open society, people from the world's most ancient civilization, the sophistication of Europe, state-of-the-art communication systems. . . . We are committed to making your stay as easy and pleasurable as possible. (Monash University, 2000c)

At work here are two discursive clusters: First is an instrumental discourse that seeks to position the study abroad experience as offering cultural capital in the form of competitive advantage: "something that sets you apart from the pack"; "will give you an advantage." The Darwinist ethos is evocatively captured in the use of "the pack" as a metaphor and its accompanying image of wolves. Second are traces of a explorer-adventurer discourse, which is reminiscent of the colonial travel narrative: "a context of adventure"; "a chance to test your resolve, your boldness, your ability to deal with the new and the unexpected." The openly ethnocentric othering narratives present in QUT's materials that construct the foreigner as passive, helpless, and hopeless are thankfully absent. But an intertextual reading of the Web site's references to Australia's Indigenous population— "people from the world's most ancient civilization"—is suggestive of a museumized people, making it difficult to escape the colonial narrative with its fetishization of difference.

Imagined Places

Like QUT's prospectus, a tourist discourse permeates Monash's print and web-based promotional materials. The international prospectus carries the following captions: "Australia—The Young Country," "Melbourne—Study in Style," and "Explore Victoria" (see Fig. 6.12). The textual prominence of the headlines anchors a set of meanings about Australia, Melbourne, and

FIG. 6.12.   Explore Victoria.

224

Victoria as spaces to visit and live in: beautiful scenery, sophistication, and access to a leisurely lifestyle. Accompanying the headlines are tourist images such as the beach at dusk, a scene at a coffee shop, glimpses of the Yarra river framed by autumnal foliage, and a rainforest retreat (see Fig. 6.12).

A series of country branding strategies are at work here to attract overseas students:

Australia is . . . known for its . . . unspoiled beaches, natural rainforests, dramatic deserts, vibrant cities, open spaces. . . . Australian is chosen by over 150,000 students each year seeking an international perspective on their university education. (Monash University, 2002)

Each visitor's experience is unique, but all international students discover:

- a friendly and tolerant people
- a cultural bridge between East and West
- an academic tradition of intellectual inquiry
- a healthy outdoor lifestyle
- a great and stable democratic tradition
- the sophistication of Europe and the excitement of America without the price tag. (Monash University, 2002)

References to the Australian Tourist Commission's Web site (www.australia.com) confirm the strong links between international education and tourism. A vivid and polychromatic collage that features icons such as the Sydney Opera House, white sandy beaches, the rich red profile of Uluru, uniform blue skies, and of course, the 'star', a koala (see Fig. 6.13; see Australian Tourist Commission, 2001). The Web site images have a discursive continuity with the top-down ascriptions of national identity that were premised on crudely stereotypical 'Say G'Day' and Crocodile Dundee campaigns of an earlier era where Australia was epitomized as a place with simple and friendly people like the Crocodile Man and a wilderness paradise with a cluster of big cities. Clearly, these images of Australia operate on broad and essentialized national stereotypes, constructing a hyperreal world that would not stand the scrutiny of sociohistorical analysis. But they are considered sufficient for marketing Australia as an attractive study destination.

A marginally more refined form of place branding is evident in Monash's international prospectus. Here, attempts are made to construct as 'a cultural bridge between East and West'. A more sophisticated image of Australia is implied, one that breaks from the simple, unidimensional and stereotypical projections of the Crocodile Man, koalas, and kangaroos. The East–West

³³ See Australian Tourist Commission (2001).

FIG. 6.13. Australia.com.

theme alludes to Australia's unique history and geography: Although peopled by a predominantly Western population, its geographical positioning places it firmly in the Asia-Pacific region. And despite a historical ambivalence to its cultural hybridity, this East–West celebration of hybridity has been marketed as desirable, particularly in promoting Australia as a study destination to Asian markets: "With its unique blend of Asian and European lifestyles . . . Melbourne has something for everyone" (Monash University, 2002). Figure 6.14 captures the contrasting bricolage of images used to both portray and define Australia as a hybrid of East and West, both modern and a naturalist paradise. These images include a group of sophisticated cafe society members, an "Asian"-looking couple on what seems like a Venetian gondola, and a beachside promenade that portrays a relaxed lifestyle, birds in flight, palm trees—a veritable outdoor bliss featuring people in groups walking alongside the beach, cycling, roller blading and relaxing in the company of others. Finally, the marketing of Australia as a low-cost option that "has the sophistication of Europe and the excitement of America" is instructive of an underlying insecurity in the Australian identity—Australia needs the referents of Europe and the United States to make its mark.

FIG. 6.14. The young country.

The tourist discourse is widely dispersed, and present in promoting Monash's branch campuses. Monash's Malaysian campus is constructed as an attractive option for study-abroad-type programs and other educational tourism encounters. We are told that Malaysia is famous for the "variety and excellence of its food, the abundance of beautiful beaches . . . and outdoor activities such as skin diving and jungle trekking." It is "friendly and safe," "modern," and noted for "its shopping" (Monash University, 2002). South Africa, on the other hand, "abounds with natural beauty including deserts, forests, wide unspoiled beaches, coastal wetlands and amazing wildlife." Johannesburg, where Monash's campus is located, is "the gateway to Africa," "headquarters of numerous international corporations" (Monash University, 2002).

What can we make of this strong reliance on a discourse of educational tourism as a recruitment technology by Australian universities? And is this an adequate discourse to prepare the educated subject of the 21st century? What is missing? Could Oceania have been used as a referent to inform the Australian brand of international education instead of a Euro-American spatiality? Schapper and Mayson (2004) argue that universities should use different sets of ontological and epistemological referents to guide their teaching and research. The vision below is a stark contrast to the marketized expressions of international education:

> If universities were to contribute positively to sustainable futures . . . it means lending support to reclaiming local and indigenous knowledges and philosophies that are culturally inclusive and sustainable. . . . It means incorporating local and indigenous knowledges in the university research and teaching agenda. . . . Every civilization used to view the Earth as alive, an organism with a set of living relationships that work together. . . . Too many of us are becoming detached from the Earth and people. Indigenous wisdom is about the connectedness and interrelatedness of all things and all people. (Thaman, 2002)

CONCLUDING COMMENTS

This chapter described and analyzed both the macrocontext and micropractices that constitute the field of international education. It began with a selective analysis of key national policies that have shaped the discursive field that is international education in Australia. It discussed defining themes, issues, and rationales, that is, the visible objects of discourse and their fields of emergence. It also identified the key authorities responsible for legitimizing particular interpretations and expressions of internationalization.

A discourse of national interest has been influential in shaping power–knowledge relations within international education. Various institutional reforms have been undertaken in the interest of national competitiveness to develop an education export industry. At the same time, an older colonial text, premised on Australia as an educator of Asia and Asians, remains in place, along with a national fear of being swamped by the other.

The promotional and marketing narratives offer glimpses of the values of universities, how they imagine and enact the global, and the types of knowledges they consider worthy of creating and transmitting. Despite elaborate claims by university executives, what is offered as international education remains monocultural and instrumentalist. So-called hybrid knowledge constellations are skewed toward economic, scientific, and technological rationalism. The result has been the development of a model of international education that has continued to endorse cultural singularities in knowledge production. An institutional preoccupation with recruiting international students is associated with "a will to commodify." The comments below are from a university administrator:

> It [international education] should be about more than just selling things. . . . It's not fashionable to talk about these things. There's all this money, all these students. . . . A lot of people talk about internationalisation of the curriculum but I see little evidence of it. . . . I think that there is a lot of lip service given. . . . But I think the education system in universities would be richer if there was an opportunity for people to study these other things. . . . I think we will make some token gesture, sooner or later. . . . The argument that is given is "you want an Australian qualification, that means Australian content." . . . I think that is a despicable cop-out . . . especially if you are a distance education postgraduate student staying in your own country . . . it is preposterous. (staff, Australian University, male)

Cultural hybridity is increasingly deployed as a governmental project to increase Australia's market share in the highly competitive education market. This requires the representation of Australian universities as open, cosmopolitan, and safe. Visibilities of cultural hybridity are manifold and include cultural diversity policies, international days, cultural diversity awards, and antiracism pronouncements by senior university staff. These are comforting signs that the 'bad old days' of exploitation are over and that things are improving. Universities are not monolithic institutions, and some faculty are clearly striving to undertake creative and transformative work aimed at challenging the twin hegemonies of the market and monoculturalism. However, such work is often relegated to the status of subjugated knowledge. In a competitive work environment that privileges market fundamentalism and monoculturalism, it is easier for university staff to go with the flow than to work against the prevailing orthodoxies.

Singapore: East Meets West

The next two chapters focus on two countries that are described in marketing jargon as priority markets for international education: Singapore and Brazil. Both have very different histories and both are facing different challenges from the globalized economy. Understanding the 'take-up' or demand for international education in both contexts requires a macro-contextual and micro-level analyses. The macro-contextual approach involves mapping the historical, economic, cultural, and social contingencies that shape the desire for international education. The micro-level analysis concentrates on ordinary and inconsequential texts such as university marketing materials, and the multiple mundane texts which capture the life-worlds and lived realities of individual students (e.g., chatroom discussions and interviews).

This chapter begins with a historical snapshot of Singapore to understand its political economy. It explores the largely instrumentalist model of education that has so far prevailed, recent moves by the government to re-invent Singapore as a global schoolhouse, and the Singaporean desire for brand-name international education. It argues that as a group, Singaporean consumers of international education are not likely to demand or choose a brand of international education that is transformatory unless it fits within the instrumentalist parameters defined by the state. *Exposure*—the Singaporean term used to describe the international education experience—refers to sets of benefits that variously involve the acquisition of an internationally recognized credential and access to instrumentally appropriate Westernized sensibilities. The desire for exposure is partly related to a pervasive national trait to stay ahead of the competition. Governmental practices, on the other hand, seek to produce spatially fixed identities that are premised on ethnocultural nationalisms and essentialized notions of race and nation.

GLOBAL DREAMS

In Singapore, global city of the 21st century, old ways and old disjunctures jostle with 'New Economy' miracles and high-tech icons: 'postcolonial' Singapore; where East meets West; home of the famed Singapore girl in her Pierre Balmain-designed *sarong kebaya* (see Heng, 1997); tiger economy; a spectacular success, corruption free, a glowing free-market node, proof that the other has what it takes to succeed in the aggressive world of capitalism.

The aesthetic world of Orchard Road, one of the city-state's major shopping precincts is a good place to absorb and analyze Singapore's contradictions. December in Orchard Road marks the start of the Christmas season. The extravagant and ostentatious Christmas lights on Orchard Road equal, if not surpass, those in London's West End. Every one of the street's air-conditioned shopping centers has a collection of Christmas trees, huge edifices that are visible from every tier of the giant escalators. Festooned with gold and silver bows, and sprayed with powder-fine 'snow', these arctic heterotopias are a defiant symbol and reminder of the continuing importance of the Northern Hemisphere to this part of the world. What would it be like to celebrate Christmas using a geographically suitable theme, I wonder? A monsoon Christmas perhaps? A tropical Nativity scene perhaps, depicting a burnished brown Baby Jesus under a coconut palm? Would this match the splendor of a Christmas trading on colonial memory and images?

Orchard Road is more than a site in which to observe boundary crossings. It also represents the aspirational desires of Singaporeans: the "5 Cs"—cash, credit cards, condominiums, country clubs, and cars (Wei, 2000).[1] Shopping is a national pastime, not surprising given that consumerism is perhaps the main arena of freedom in Singapore. Orchard Road is a magnet that draws everyone from the average Singaporean to bored and overpaid 'expats' (expatriates) and the lower end of imported human capital, the unskilled guest worker. At street level, the symbols and signs are asymmetrically inclined in favor of First World multinationals, largely Euro-American with the occasional Japanese name: Louis Vuitton, Armani, Prada, Chanel, Hilton, Taco Bell, McDonald's, Marks and Spencer, Starbucks, Isetan, and Takashimaya.

---

[1]Cars are a rather precious commodity in the city-state where the government requires prospective car owners to obtain a Certificate of Entitlement. These COEs sell at prices upwards of S$80,000.

Understanding globalization's effects by studying it through peripheral places and marginal others is illustrative and instructive. You cannot strive for the 5 Cs without the army of domestic helpers who make up the lower end of the ethnoscape of guest workers: Filipinas, Indonesians, Indians, Sri Lankans, and Bangladeshis. They, too, claim a provisional space at Orchard Road. Sunday is the day off for a large number of Filipinas who come to shop at Orchard Road's Lucky Plaza, and more important, to meet with each other and to speak their own language. Their energy, humor, and collegiality are palpable to any bystander. Local Singaporeans, however, keep their distance, including the shopkeepers in Lucky Plaza. We are all Asians but some of us are more superior Asians. In Singapore, Filipinas are considered to be among the lower tier of Asians and are best managed in this way. The Filipinas might buy, but they are hardly deserving of a customer service approach, evident in shopkeepers' offhand, brusque answers to the women. Singapore has a population of 4 million people and in 2002 employed approximately 140,000 foreign domestic workers, making it the second biggest employer of migrant domestic workers after Luxembourg (Seneviratne, 2002).

At the Singapore Cricket Club (SCC), the scene is different. A favorite haunt of Nick Leeson, the rogue trader reputed to have single-handedly brought down Barings Bank, there is a different kind of guest worker here. They represent the top end of human capital, largely Western, predominantly male expatriates, recruited to work in an island working feverishly to reinvent itself as a high-tech node and financial services center. The SCC is another heterotopia, a place where modernity's icons of money and masculinity coalesce to re-create a peculiarly 19th-century type of social relations between men and women and between the haves and have-nots. Not only do they represent the city-state's nostalgia for its colonial past, but country clubs such as the SCC, Tanglin, Seletar, and Keppel have been reworked into the Intelligent Island's indexes of success and social standing.

Singapore has been a node in the 'survival circuits' for much of its history (see Sassen, 2002). People have been coming here for all kinds of reasons. For some, it is and was "pull" factors—a sense of adventure and curiosity to explore the Far East and the chance to get rich quickly. Today, it is a stopping point for foreign talent—the knowledge merchants who can assist Singaporeans to become more innovative, more productive, to help it value-add to the new knowledge-based economy. For other sojourners, it's the old "push" factors such as grinding poverty and unemployment in their home countries that bring them to this global city. The maids who work for my family today, like the Filipinas at Lucky Plaza, fall in this category.

Lydia, 49 has worked for a branch of our family for almost 20 years. Having raised one generation of our family, she is on the way to raising a second. She has also paid for the education of an entire generation of children in her family and provided

for the old. Mariam, with two children, aged 3 and 5 years, is from Indonesia and de-
cided to try her hand at getting a job in Singapore after the children's father left her.
She has been engaged to care for the newest baby in our family, my nephew, Jai.
Mariam's children may get to see her biannually, if they are lucky. Shahu from India,
cares for my intellectually disabled masi (maternal aunt), Hardial. The mother of
adult children, she too talks of the day when she can go home, although she is con-
cerned that her sons may have been a bit cavalier with the remittances she has sent
home. It is these sobering ironies, these disjunctures that continue even in this spectac-
ularly successful high-tech bubble. Local and global forces pull and push against each
other in ways that are strangely unpredictable and barely discernible to most of us,
and particularly to 5- or 3-year-olds like Mariam's children.

In every story of disjunctures, displacements, and desperate human emotions there are also win–win tales. The women's lives away from their families represent a productive absence. Their earning power as guest workers
enables them to renegotiate their places in paternalistic family hierarchies.
Of course, if one probes too deeply into the private spheres of their lives,
other stories may emerge about a crisis of care—of children whose mothers
or fathers have spent most of their childhood overseas earning to educate
them, and resentful, feckless spouses who fritter away the nest egg. But on
the balance, there must be more gains because there is no shortage of guest
workers.

The big picture surrounding guest workers makes exporting nation-
states anxious to maintain the win–win argument. Remittances from guest
workers provide vitally important income for many poorer countries. The
Philippines earns almost US\$7 billion a year from remittances (Philippines
Bureau of Statistics, 2004). It is estimated that some 34% to 54% of its population are dependent on remittances (Parrenas, 2003, p. 39). In 1993, remittances equaled 44% of Bangladesh's merchandise exports, 13% of India's export earnings, and 24% of Pakistan's foreign earnings (see Puri &
Ritzema, 1999). Host countries such as Singapore also benefit from taxes
such as the 'maid levy'. The levy is estimated as contributing S\$400 million
to the government (Baker, 2002; see also Heng, 1997, p. 32). Employers pay
a monthly sum of S\$345 to the government for the maid levy and often use
this as a rationale for paying maids lower wages.

It's 5:00 a.m. and the working day of many maids has already begun. I pass sev-
eral women nervously washing their employers' cars, their eyes open for any sign of
danger in the street as they ferry buckets of water from monster homes—awkwardly
large, double-story homes squeezed into plots that were originally meant for modest
single-story dwellings.

The local newspaper carries the occasional horror story of maids who endure assault, starvation, and isolation. Some maids have fallen off high-rise
apartment blocks because their employers insist on their cleaning the outside surfaces of apartment windows ("Singapore Curbs," 2003). No days off,

a 16-hour working day, no telephone calls, and no relationships—these practices are not uncommon (Baker, 2002; see also Henson, 2002). Maids can be dismissed without notice or right of appeal and sent home immediately if an employer lodges a complaint to the government. Maids who are found to be pregnant in regular medical screening processes are deported (Baker, 2002). A recent survey of 284 foreign maids by the city-state's flagship newspaper, *The Straits Times*, provided more heartening news and noted that physical abuse of maids was rare, that "more than three quarters of the sample were rewarded for good work with extra money and presents" and "95% eat the same food as their employers." That only 50% of its sample reported days off, and then once a month only (Arshad, 2003), was not considered an abusive labor practice by the newspaper that used the headline: "Maid Abuse Not Rampant Here" (Arshad, 2003). Unlike Hong Kong, where the law requires employers to pay maids a minimum wage and provide them with at least 1 day off from work each week, the Singapore government does not specify or require minimum welfare guidelines to be included in contracts between Singaporean employers and their maids (Agence France Presse, 2003; Baker, 2002).

As I am making my way home, I observe several maids running to open the gates as "sir"—the industrious Asian manager/professional—drives off to work. It is 6:00 a.m. It is these comforting sights that must have convinced the apostles of the 'New Economy' in the Northern Hemisphere, the transnational capitalist class, that the 21st century would be the Asian century.

THE POLITICS OF COMPETING EMPIRES

Singapore's acquisition and settlement by the East India Company (EIC) is a story of competing empires. The island was purchased by Stamford Raffles of the East India Company for 1,000 Spanish pounds in 1819 after he had installed a preferred and illegal heir as ruler of the Johor sultanate (Heidhues, 1974, pp. 18–19). Within a few years of colonial settlement, Singapore had subverted Batavia's (Jakarta) position as a premier trading center, and in doing so, the British wrested the highly lucrative Far East trade monopoly from the Dutch (see Boulger, 1897).[2] Its strategic importance to the British colonial government as a naval base and entrepôt saw Singapore separated from the two other Straits Settlement colonies, Malacca and Penang, both of which were reunited with the newly independent Malaya in 1957. Singapore achieved a limited autonomy from the British colonial government in 1959 and in 1963 joined the federation of Malaysia before se-

---

[2]Boulger's (1897) biography on Stamford Raffles offers a colonial history of Singapore's beginnings.

ceding in 1965 (Chua, 1998, pp. 28–29; Han, Fernandez, & Tan, 1998, pp. 65–83).

The starting point for understanding Singapore's political economy is the colonial legacy of its administration which influenced the development of a unique form of postcolonial governance. As a newly independent nation in Southeast Asia, Singapore sought to maintain close cultural and economic links with the former colonial powers. The political leadership of the largely English-educated and multiethnic People's Action Party (PAP) that led Singapore to political independence took a decidedly unsentimental view of retaining the colonial legacy, as its first prime minister, Lee Kuan Yew, observed:

> We were not ideologues. . . . We had no raw materials for them to exploit. All we had was the labour. So why not if they [foreign companies] want to exploit our labour? . . . And we found that whether or not they exploited us, we were learning how to do a job from them, which we would never have learnt. We were in no position to be fussy about high-minded principles. We had to make a living. (Lee, as quoted in Han et al., 1998, p. 109)

In analyzing Singapore's postindependence development and systems of governance, what is immediately obvious is the significance of a rubric of local factors specific to its geography, population, demography, and internal politics. These factors interacted with a series of macro-level forces including those arising from the superpower rivalries at that time. First, Singapore's status as a city-state with minimal natural resources made redundant any notion of constructing a sheltered socialist economy, choices that were open to other postcolonial nations such as India (see Chua, 1998, p. 29). Out of deficit and crisis also came opportunity. Singapore had, in the words of Lee (2002), "the whole export oriented freeway open to us. . . . China was isolated, out of the world's markets. Most developing countries rejected the MNCs [multinational corporations] . . . they believed that MNCs would exploit their labour and natural resources."

Second, Singapore's adoption of English as the official language was designed to build the required pool of human resources to engage with international trade markets. This choice also enabled the English-educated Chinese political leadership to assert their dominance over the more left-leaning, Chinese-educated community, many of whom held positive sentiments toward communist China (Han et al., 1998, pp. 43–61; Rodan, 2001, pp. 143–144; Sai & Huang, 1999, pp. 132–143).

Singapore's success as an economic powerhouse has been touted as a paean to the seductive power of capitalism. However, according to a Foucauldian theoretical schema, the Singaporean success story in leapfrogging from the Third World to the First World must be taken as one particular historical-geographical incarnation of postcoloniality. Singapore achieved political independence at a particular historical moment—during an era of Cold War rivalries—and it used superpower rivalries to strategically position itself as a willing and able free-market node. In a postcolonial Southeast Asia, fiercely resistant to the possibilities of continuing exploitation by capitalism by the region's former colonial masters, Singapore's political alignments with these powers and its strategic geography combined to provide it with a competitive advantage. Singapore was a willing and able postmodern colony long before it became the norm for nation-states to travel to various international fora to court the business and political elites. Indeed, the following vignette could just as well have been written with Singapore in mind, given the city-state's modus operandi of securing investment:

> The sellers [politicians and government ministers] hustled investment opportunities, and all their numbers were as bright and shiny as the exhibits at a trade show—low inflation, high growth, willing workers, beautiful girls, democratic institutions springing up like mushrooms, responsible fiscal policies, broad vistas, a compliant press, courageous police. Their will to please spoke to the terms and conditions of post-modern imperialism—the lesser nations of the earth become colonies not of governments but of corporations, the law of nations construed as the rule of money, and the world's parliaments intimidated by the force of capital. (Lapham, 1998, pp. 16–17)

At the same time, the threat of communism meant that Singapore's governing elites had to give the *Ah Bengs*, the 'heartlanders', enough or face growing popular support for communism.

A MODERN COLONY: SINGAPORE INC.

Much of the analysis of politics and governance in Singapore has drawn on crude top-down models of power deployed by an authoritarian government to exercise power and to suppress their citizens. Certainly, authoritarian instruments of state do exist, although it is convenient for Western journalists to forget that Singapore's most repressive laws are remnants of the biopolitical arsenal used by the British colonial authorities to discipline dissent in the local population in their colonies.[3] The newly independent govern-

---

[3]Some examples of the disciplining technologies that were used to suppress anticolonial dissidence included: the Internal Security Act, which enabled detention without trial; a statutory requirement for everyone above the age of 12 years to carry an identity card at all times; and the requirement of all aspiring university students to undergo a security clearance at the hands of the intelligence police, the Special Branch.

ment found it convenient to retain these instruments of state to crush communalism, industrial militancy, and communism.

A more sophisticated analysis of governance in Singapore is possible by focusing on *disciplinary modernization*—the deployment of disciplinary strategies, technologies, and instruments to govern (George, 2000, pp. 39–40, 65–69; Kwok, 1999, p. 54; Lam, 1999, pp. 11–12). Thus, the potentially explosive communal and cultural politics that were to be the nemesis of so many postcolonial states were neutralized and displaced by instituting English as the official language, introducing constitutional protection for religious freedom and steering the multiethnic population to identify with the nation rather than with their ethnocultural communities[4] (Barr, 2000, pp. 18, 29–30, 144–145; Chua, 1998, pp. 34–36; Purushotam, 1998, pp. 51–55).

Another important aspect of governing is the state's capacity to influence the popular imagination through discursive means. As Coe and Kelly (2002, p. 342) note, citizens are also political actors with the potential to resist or reject change. Steering citizens' capacities to act and harnessing their desires and aspirations toward ends and objectives that are convenient for the state is the cornerstone of successful governance. Top-down models of power, by contrast, fail to take into consideration the use of pastoral power or 'governance by care' to win popular support.[5] Singaporeans achieved First World living standards with a capable and financially astute, technocratic government at the helm within 30 years of independence. They remain cautious in expressing electoral dissent against the PAP.

Perhaps most prominent among the discursive tropes deployed by the PAP to govern, is the crisis and survival discourse aimed at rallying Singaporeans to pull together to survive (see Barr, 2000, pp. 226–234; Birch, 1993, pp. 72–75; Chan, 1976; Emmerson, 1995, pp. 95–96; George, 2000, pp. 52–56; Rodan, 1993, pp. 58–59). As a discursive strategy, narratives of crisis have been immensely powerful in both shaping and instituting acceptance of the government's policy platform of market pragmatism and its concomitants: individualism and meritocracy. Premised on Singapore's vulnerability as a small nation with no natural resources and echoing the catchcry, 'we have no choice', the government has consistently deployed narratives of impending crisis and the need to survive to both win popular support for its policies and to strategically circumvent ethical dilemmas such as trading with the apartheid government of South Africa or with the military regime of Burma.

---

[4]These included constitutional recognition of cultural and religious diversity including religious freedom, public holidays on cultural and religious festivals, and guaranteed political representation for the indigenous Malay population.

[5]Singapore's policy of subsidized public housing is one example of the exercise of pastoral power. Access to high-status educational goods via Public Services Commission Scholarships is another.

George (2000) uses the metaphor of "air-conditioned nation" and an attendant politics of "comfort and control" to describe and analyze the workings of the Singaporean government. After years of being disciplined by "OB Markers" (out-of-bounds markers), Singaporeans are largely depoliticized. Political autonomy remains elusive while the freedoms of consumption are pervasive (pp. 39–56). The relatively high living standards enjoyed by the populace have assuaged community concerns about the limited discursive space for a civil society (see also Birch, 1993; Chua, 1999; Rodan, 1993, 1996).

MANAGING GLOBALIZATION

Singapore offers a unique site from which to understand how the contemporary nation-state is simultaneously both agent and object of globalization. The official line on globalization is that Singapore does not have the choice open to other nations with natural resources, "for us globalisation is a necessity" (Goh, 1999). Many of its policies, including its education policies, discussed later in this chapter, can be read as responses to the new iterations of global capitalism that have emerged in the 1990s. A strongly developmentalist state, Singapore has largely eschewed the minimalist state approach ("roll-back liberalism") that informed the neoliberal state in the West over the last two decades. The direct involvement of government in various nation-building projects has tempered the dictates of the market (Rodan, 2001, pp. 143–152). The Singaporean government also engaged in various projects of culture building to define the nation in particularistic or culturally unique terms even though, more than any other Southeast Asian country, the city-state personifies cultural pastiche and melange (see Kahn, 1998, p. 5). These culture-building rationales have been deployed to manage the risks represented by globalization.

In the period immediately following political independence, the state accommodated cultural, linguistic, and religious diversity, as long as this diversity sat within state-prescribed parameters of economic modernization, individualism, and meritocracy. Politics was reduced to economics and a relatively deculturalized approach to nation building was deployed (Chua, 1998, pp. 30–31). By the 1980s, there was a discernible shift toward a culturalization of the political terrain. This shift was justified as necessary to counteract the 'dangers' of Westernization: individualism and deculturalism. Individualism was acceptable only insofar as it promoted economic achievement and self-sufficiency (Rodan, 2001, pp. 160–161). Its other dimensions were less welcome. Singaporeans, according to the government, required a 'moral ballast' to anchor them to their collective responsibilities to the state and the family unit.

Crafting Confucians

The Confucian values discourse that emerged as a result of this cultural turn was part of a broader discursive ensemble, premised on an East-versus-West discourse that effectively positioned a homogeneous, decadent, and individualistic West against a hardworking, thrifty, and community-minded East. Ironically, the Confucian hypothesis that discursively linked Confucian values with economic performance and modernization emerged from the West.[6] In some quarters, there were concerns that the culturalization of Singapore politics was not only subverting its multiethnic, cosmopolitan beginnings but also discursively privileging the Chinese-Singaporean contribution to Singapore's nation-building project (Rajaratnam, as cited in Hong, 1999, pp. 104–105). Nonetheless, it was enthusiastically embraced by the government before its metamorphosis into the more culturally inclusive Asian values discourse (see Chua, 1999; Kwok, 1999, pp. 53–66). The Asian values discourse can be read as an attempt to distract the population from the growing wealth disparities within Singapore in the same way that the Asian way or Asian-style government has been invoked by various authoritarian governments to variously justify their oppressive tendencies (see Barr, 2000, pp. 33–34; George, 2000, pp. 49–56; Mitton, 2000; Rodan, 2001, pp. 161–164).

Culture building presided over the resurrection of the racialized identity where previously the emphasis had been on neutralizing race and culture. Several reasons have been proposed for the cultural turn in Singapore's political terrain. Barr's (1999, 2000, pp. 120–126) thesis attributes the official state engagement with Confucianism with Lee Kuan Yew's "sinicization," which included his espousal of biological and cultural eugenics, although it can be reasonably argued that this shift toward the sinicization of the Singaporean identity was a strategic preparation for the Singapore's engagement with the sleeping giant, China.

For Chua (1999), the official engagement with Confucianism was aimed at artificially grafting an elite Mandarin culture onto an ethnically and linguistically heterogeneous Singaporean-Chinese community (see also Kong, 1999). That the raft of policies aimed at an ethnocultural fixing of the Singaporean identity were unsuccessful (see Chua, 1998) is also borne out by the findings of a 1999 survey of young Singaporeans which revealed that a large number expressed a desire to be either Caucasian or Japanese, cultures that they associated with the leading economic and cultural powers—

---

[6]Perhaps the scholar most associated with the Confucian values discourse is Tu Wei Ming, originally from Taiwan but who has spent the greater part of his university education and working life in America. He has been employed as a professor of Chinese history and philosophy at Harvard University from 1981.

the United States, Europe, and Japan (Chin, 2000). The hyphenated Singaporean, whether Singaporean-Chinese, Malay, Indian or other, is characterized by 'productive absence', a hollow quality that allows the Singaporean government to change what being Singaporean means to fit in with the situational demands of the moment (Chua, 1998). Culturalization also fulfills a pragmatic role—it helps create various community self-help agencies that are organized along ethnocultural lines. These bodies instill an ethos of looking to the community, and not the government, for assistance (Tan, 2003, p. 43).

By the end of the 1990s, in response to a global rise of religious and ethnic fundamentalisms, the Singaporean government's interest in policing[7] race relations and religious activities had increased. In a telling nod to power's enigmatic qualities and its finely dispersed, nearly invisible textures at the capillaries, activists from the Singapore-based group Jemaah Islamiah were able to establish working partnerships with the al-Qaida terrorist network. They were able to foil one of the most networked, technologically superior nation-states in the world and a government that had perfected surveillance to an art form (de Beer, 2004).

Membership in the advanced capitalist world does not guarantee a stable prosperity; countries have to keep competing fiercely with each other to establish themselves as financial, consumption, and entertainment centers (Amin & Thrift, 2002; Harvey, 1989; Olds & Yeung, 2004). Courting investors and meeting the needs of a mobile, libidinal capitalism means marketing and "talking up" the virtues of a city by selling a dream image, vision, and spatial myth (Sparke & Lawson, 2003). It is with this goal that the Singaporean government has embarked on rebranding the island as a Renaissance City.

The Renaissance City

Over the past decade, the situational demands of a globalizing economy have prompted the government to reorient the island-state's economic base toward value-added business- and research-intensive high-technology industries (Coe & Kelly, 2002, p. 343). There has been an increased importance attached to recruiting foreign talent by the Singaporean government along with concerted moves to reduce the emigration of highly qualified Singaporeans. To redirect some of the foreign investment away from low-cost sites such as China, the Singaporean government has worked hard at

---

[7]It is government policy not to allow Muslim girls to wear head coverings to school. In 2002, four Muslim girls were suspended from their primary school for wearing a *tudung* (hijab). The policy was defended by the Singaporean government on the grounds that maintaining secularism in state schools was critical to maintaining racial harmony.

transforming the city-state's image away from that of an authoritarian, 'nanny state' with repressive media laws. It has done so by rebranding Singapore as an international cultural center, by emphasizing a cosmopolitan, renaissance image to make it attractive to the supermobile, transient largely Euro-American elite of knowledge workers (see Olds & Thrift, 2004). Slogans such as this, "I saw a city with its head in the future and its soul in the past," capture and transmit a manufactured East–West cosmopolitanism (see Fig. 7.1). Urban sociability, the 'soft' factors such as leisure, entertainment, and quality of life for families are noted as significant in the business services and knowledge industries where the core assets are the capabilities of knowledge workers (Amin & Thrift, 2002, pp. 74–75). Global cities are meant to be "places of orientation and vitality for the *deracine* knowledge entrepreneur/worker" (p. 59).

New place-branding expressions have emerged to give Singapore an identity that exceeds its earlier incarnation as a safe, modern, business friendly city (Singapore Inc.). The 'Lion City' is reconfigured as vibrant and livable with a thriving arts culture, a 'Renaissance City' and a global

FIG. 7.1. City with soul.

hub for the arts (Wee, 2001). The vision for a Renaissance City is anchored in earlier nation-building narratives providing a cultural ballast for Singaporeans. As a Renaissance City cannot be occupied by a parochial citizenry, the state has embarked on remolding the Singaporean citizen. A new subjectivity, the Renaissance Singaporean, emerges, described as "well rounded, [with] an inquiring and creative mind, a passion for life, . . . a civic-minded active citizen. He [*sic*] appreciates and cherishes his heritage. His graciousness is underpinned by a fine sense of aesthetics" (Lee, 2000). The earlier 'survivalist' Singaporean is chastised:

> Let us get rid of our self-centred, selfish and overly materialistic streaks. Let us be more cultivated and refined, with a keener sense of the beauty in human relationships, music and our cultural heritage. (PM Goh Chok Tong, speaking at NTU in December 1996)

The singular cultural heritage endorsed by the collective 'us' hints of a state-defined vision of a [singular] cultural heritage. The Renaissance Singaporean draws discursive inspiration from the nation-building Shared Values[8] and Singapore 21 visionary platforms (see Chua, 1998, pp. 38–40). Both construct a qualitatively different ballast from the ethnocultural identity fixing of the 1980s and are premised on Singapore as home, a place where you can establish emotional ties while at the same time making the most of economic opportunities. Singapore 21's stated objectives are to produce a more "gentle, caring and gracious" society, a nation with "a heartbeat" where every Singaporean matters (Singapore 21 Committee, 2002). What remains to be seen is how the gracious and civic-minded Singaporean can coexist with the hypercompetitive economic subject that predominated in Singapore's history. In small and large ways, then, the government embarked on a discursive reconstruction of the nation-state. The rhetorical purchase on graciousness, refinement, and aesthetics does not detract from hard-edged pragmatism aimed at producing a 'cultural renaissance economy'.

Encouraging highly skilled returnees is also an important dimension of producing a Renaissance culture. Where in the past, emigrants earned the ire of the government, the official stance now is to keep the door open to encourage returnees. The Singapore International Foundation (SIF), a key instrumentality with a declared mission to create "belongingness and rootedness" for Singaporeans, thus works to encourage "talented" Singa-

---

[8]Singapore's Shared Values are: nation before community, society above self, family as the basic unit of society, regard and community support for the individual, consensus instead of contention, and racial and religious harmony.

poreans to return home. The foundation's mission statement captures the practices used by the Singaporean government to manage globalization: "To enable Singaporeans everywhere to think globally, feel Singaporean, be responsible world citizens and foster friendships for Singapore" (SIF, 2002b). Using magazines,[9] newsletters, fellowship programs,[10] and conferences,[11] the SIF participates in the construction of the Renaissance Singaporean who is a global citizen but whose roots and identities are firmly anchored in Singapore.

The survival of 21st-century capitalism demands the marketing of a more intelligent brand of capitalism, one that is more open to its audiences and speaks the language of partnerships, diversity, and transparency (Thrift, 1998). Peddling this kind of soft capitalism is about "eating the bread of globalism and drinking the milk of dialogue" (Lapham, 1998, p. 41).

THE INTELLIGENT ISLAND: ALWAYS AHEAD

Seeking to appropriate Western knowledges and practices has never been a problem for Singapore as long as it contributes to the national project of attaining economic success as a capitalist, free-market powerhouse (see Chua, 1998, pp. 32–34; Coe & Kelly, 2002; George, 2000, pp. 171–172; Olds & Thrift, 2004; Olds & Yeung, 2004). From its founding principles—striving for economic survival and the material improvement of its citizenry—Singapore has constructed a particularly strong nation-building role for its education

---

[9]A typical SIF magazine would carry a mix of stories aimed at conveying these two images of Singapore. Accordingly, the magazines feature hard newsworthy items that focus on government and private sector opportunities and development stories (e.g., the opening of a new museum, hospital, etc.) and profiles of successful Singaporeans. A series of soft stories that trade on memory and nostalgia are positioned at the tail end of the magazine, for example, "Homecooking" (which features a favorite childhood recipe), and inevitably a story of the peripatetic Singaporean who is nearly always quoted as saying that their roots are firmly in Singapore.

[10]Programs such as Singapore Internationale are intended to "promote the Singaporean image and identity overseas." Similarly, the Singapore-Australia Young Business Ambassadors Programme "offers young professionals from Singapore and Australia a unique opportunity to network while living and working in each other's country as part of their career exposure and professional growth" (SIF, 2002b). The SIF also coordinates the Humanitarian Relief Programme, sending the message to Singaporeans both at home and overseas that the country does not adhere to the materialist, hyper-competitive stereotypes.

[11]For example, SIF sponsored a conference titled "New Asia and Emerging China: Challenges and Opportunities," which was held in Shanghai in February 2004. In 2002 a conference titled "A World in Transformation: Impact and Implications for the Asia Pacific Region" was conducted at the nominal cost of A$50, which was refundable for all students attending, suggesting that this was a targeted group.

system, which features strongly instrumental and symbolic dimensions. In the first instance, it is concerned with cementing a sense of national identity among its multiethnic citizenry and loyalty to the nation. Second, education produces a pool of human resources that will enable the economic survival and success of the nation (Ashton & Sung, 1997, pp. 209–214; Gopinathan, 1997; Spring, 1998, pp. 75–79). The Minister of Education captures the evangelical hopes held of the education system in this speech:

> How each generation turns out depends critically on education. Whether our young have the skills, drive and entrepreneurship to make a living, whether they uphold the principle of meritocracy, whether they love Singapore and are prepared to give their lives in her defence are shaped by the education they receive during their formative years. (Teo, 2002)

Presently, Singapore's educational vision is focused on maintaining a competitive edge for the nation-state. It is a vision that sees the best way forward as developing a technically competent and highly educated labor force for the next lap of Singapore's development, to join the First World club of knowledge economies. In the words of officialdom, the next challenge is "to establish Singapore as a vibrant and robust global hub of knowledge-based industries" (Tan, 2001, 2003; Teo, 1999).

Both schools and universities have been charged with the responsibility of securing Singapore's place in the knowledge-based economy. Schools are now required to develop critical thinking and creativity in their student-subjects. Thinking Schools Learning Nation, the IT Masterplan, and Technopreneurship 21[12] are just three expressions of a broader policy platform intended to steer the educated subject toward innovation, creativity, and self-improvement (Chang, 2000; Goh, 1997; Spring, 1998, pp. 79–83; Tan, 2003; Wee, 1998). Schooling is also a site where strategies are put into place to develop affiliations or affective connectivities with Singapore, the nation. National Education, a form of citizenship education, is one such attempt to anchor the Singaporean identity and to inspire loyalty to the country (see Spring, 1998, pp. 83–88). Together with platforms such as Shared Values[13] and Singapore 21, National Education represents an attempt to offset brain drain by encouraging talented, innovative Singaporeans to remain in the country instead of leaving for the Western First World.

---

[12]Technopreneurship 21 is a government-led initiative aimed at establishing the infrastructure and culture for technological entrepreneurship in Singapore.

[13]The Singapore 21 vision is based on the following ideas: every Singaporean matters, opportunities for all, the Singapore heartbeat, strong families, and active citizens (see Singapore 21 Committee, 2002). National Education is a form of citizenship education aimed at developing national cohesion (Ministry of Education, 2002).

THE GLOBAL SCHOOLHOUSE

On the economic front, we have had a bumpy ride since the Asian financial crisis in 1997. . . . In football parlance, Singaporeans are beginning to play in the first division. . . . It is not easy to stay at the top of the league all the time. It is a struggle for a small country but we cannot opt out of this race *or we do not deserve to survive* [italics added]. (Wong, 2003)

The global demand for international higher education will exceed 7 million students by 2025. Asia will dominate, accounting for 70% of this future demand. . . . A large part of this demand will be met in Asia itself in advanced cities like Singapore. Our objective is to make Singapore a *"Global Schoolhouse."* (Yeo, 2003)

The key idea is the creation of a virtuous circle: draw in the "best universities" with global talent, this talent then creates knowledge and knowledgeable subjects, through their actions and networks, then create the professional jobs that drive a vibrant KBE [knowledge based economy]. (Olds & Thrift, 2004)

As part of its Industry 21 platform, the Singaporean government embarked on a plan to establish Singapore as "a Global Schoolhouse" (Yeo, 2003), "a world class education hub, a centre internationally renowned for its intellectual capital and creative energy" (Singapore Economic Development Board [SEDB], 1998). The Global Schoolhouse rests on three broad strategies: The first is to attract brand-name, world class universities to establish a base in Singapore. These institutions are expected to attract students from Asia, "raise the intellectual and education standards of Singapore," and establish industry–university links to increase the potential for commercialization of new technologies and new industries (SEDB, 1998). The second strategy is to steer local universities toward an entrepreneurial 'American mindset' while strengthening the local, private higher education for-profit sector. The Singapore Quality Class for Private Education Organisation Scheme is a quality framework sponsored by the Singaporean government intended to help Singaporean private institutions achieve business excellence (Yeo, 2003). The third strategy involves concerted campaigns by the Singaporean government to recruit large numbers of international student to "double or triple" the current numbers of 50,000 (Yeo, 2003; see also Olds & Thrift, 2004).

The world-class universities have differed in their modes of entry into Singapore, and these differences stem from the level of financial and product risk they were prepared to enter into (Olds & Thrift, 2004). INSEAD, a leading French Business School, established a 'greenfields' campus, INSEAD Asia, sprawled over 2.86 hectares and estimated to have cost US$40 million (so far). It is regarded as a branch of the home base in

Fontainebleau but with its own research priorities and latitude to develop different management education products. Its entry into Singapore was the most high risk in financial and product terms. At the other spectrum of risk, Olds and Thrift (2004) place the entry of Wharton. Although official declarations referred to the Singapore Management University as a 'beachhead' of the University of Pennsylvania's Wharton Business School, it is not a branch campus of Wharton, as such. Rather, the government has entered into a 5-year contract with Wharton Business School to establish the Singapore Management University (SMU), which is being described as Singapore's first business university and poised to "take on the American mindset for management education" (Cohen, 1997, p. A71; see also Davie, 2002; Olds & Thrift, 2004). The risk of this venture has been largely devolved to the state and Wharton's responsibilities are to provide intellectual leadership (Olds & Thrift, 2002).

The term *beachhead* is an interesting choice to use in official pronouncements. It is defined in the *Collins Dictionary* (1991) as "an area on a beach that has been captured from the enemy and on which troops and equipment are landed" (p. 81). What types of subject-positions are perpetuated and assumed by the use of a discourse of war? Who is the enemy here? What are the textual links between a war metaphor and that of Global Schoolhouse? What do the discursive links between war, education, and market suggest about the 21st-century university?

The GSB, another prominent world class university, is located in a 120-year-old heritage building, the House of Tan Yoek Nee, at the edge of the shopping precinct of Orchard Road. Its architecture and aesthetic features, complete with glassed-off security doors and guards, suggest a hybrid institution halfway between a miniaturized imperial Chinese palace and a fortified corporate headquarters. The Singaporean branch of the Chicago GSB offers executive master of business administration (MBA) degrees that are delivered by faculty from its Chicago campus. Its brand name derives its appeal from its home base, which looms large in its promotional narratives: "the home to Nobel laureates, leading economists, market theorists and business experts." A raft of promotional statements reassures prospective applicants and presumably GSB alumni that "the professors who will teach in Singapore are the same ones who teach on our main campus" and "students who complete our new program in Singapore will receive the same MBA degree as students in our six other MBA programmes" (Friedman, 1999). The high-cost strategy of flying in faculty to deliver courses does present greater financial risks to the GSB. However, its presence in Singapore is premised on a need to have a global presence (Olds & Thrift, 2004). The GSB's targeted customer base—leading companies throughout the Asia-Pacific region and Singaporeans who undertake MBA programs in overseas high-prestige universities—suggest that the GSB is assured of dividends on its investment.

In terms of risk taking, the strategy undertaken by the University of Chicago's GSB in establishing its Singaporean branch campus, fell between INSEAD Asia and Wharton (Olds & Thrift, 2004). In the sanitized language of the market, the GSB's intention was simply to export a 'fixed product', a strategy designed to reduce product risk (Olds & Thrift, 2004). However, the process of reducing risk has created the conditions for the export of a curriculum product from a metropolitan center to a (post)colonial periphery, or 'beachhead'. Now, this is not about a top-down subordination as anyone who has taught an international classroom, particularly at postgraduate level, would be aware. Students do debate and challenge theoretical paradigms from the reference points of their personal and professional life experiences. Similarly, professors who teach postgraduate courses are usually well versed with adult learning principles, and many would profess to being reflective practitioners. So what is wrong with such a strategic approach of regarding university courses as 'immutable mobiles' that keep their overall forms as they move across geographical and cultural spaces if the classroom dynamics and professor–student interactions will dilute some of its American centeredness?

Yet the vastly unequal cultural exchanges between the Euro-American 'First World' and 'the rest' must surely impose barriers to the insertion and operation of reflexivity into the social. Questioning existing power–knowledge constellations and building new knowledge requires academic rigor and sustained effort on the parts of educators and students. It is not sufficient for "reflexivity to [operate] only in relation to the individual as an autonomous subject and not in the individual's relationship to the social" (Olds & Thrift, 2004). Flying in for a week or so to deliver an executive MBA course or attending evening and weekend classes as an add-on to a busy professional life may steer teachers and students away from introducing reflexivity into their specialist knowledge and practice. The rationale of choice is conveniently used to explain away the need for a strong and fearless intellectual leadership[14] to build new knowledge paradigms.

The government's plan to reconfigure Singapore from manufacturing center to a center for global knowledge production reflects a continuation of its developmentalist role. A technocratic, pragmatic bent has long characterized Singaporean governance. In refashioning its economy, it is continuing its historically pro-business and foreign investment role. However, from a geopolitical perspective, the world is a vastly different place today from what it was in 1965 when Singapore achieved independence. Where Singapore once drew 'free world' interest and investment from its position as a willing and able 'free market' node in a strategic geography, it now has to compete with other willing and able nodes to secure foreign investment.

---

[14]In the course of this study I came across marketing personnel and in some cases faculty in universities who confided that Asians want the stock-same educational product that is that offered in the metropolis. The standard position was "we are simply giving them what they want."

248

CHAPTER 7

TABLE 7.1
World Class Presence in Singapore

	Initiative
INSEAD	Greenfields campus. Offers INSEAD degrees.
Chicago Graduate School of Business	Urban branch campus. Offers University of Chicago MBA degrees.
Massachusetts Institute of Technology	Partner in Singapore–MIT alliance (SMA). Teaches postgraduate engineering and computing programs with National University of Singapore (NUS) and Nanyang Technological University (NTU) Graduates credentialed by either NTU or NUS.
Georgia Tech	Collaborates with NUS to provide programs in global logistics, information, and decision technologies at The Logistics Institute Asia Pacific (TLI–AP).
Wharton (University of Pennsylvania)	Contracted by the Singapore government to assist in the planning and intellectual leadership of the Singapore Management University (SMU).
Technische Universiteit Eindhoven	Jointly runs the Design Technology Institution with NUS offering engineering education.
Technische Universitat Munchen	Offers a master of industrial chemistry program in collaboration with NUS.
Johns Hopkins University	Runs Johns Hopkins Singapore Biomedical Center and numerous programs with NUS.

Note. Adapted from Olds and Thrift (2004).

The significant presence of other world class universities is realized through their collaborations with local institutions (see Table 7.1). The Singapore–MIT Alliance (SMA) established in 1998 to promote global engineering research, is a postgraduate program. Alliances and partnerships have also emerged between these elite Euro-American universities positioned in Singapore. INSEAD and Wharton have cemented an alliance intended to conduct joint teaching and research on global management. Although many of these partnerships are discursively constructed as alliances and although the official aspiration is for Singapore to be a node in the network of world class universities, some partner universities appear to have inserted the necessary clauses to protect their brand names. The graduates from the SMA, for example, will be credentialed by the two local Singapore universities—National University of Singapore (NUS) and Nanyang Technological University (NTU)—not by MIT.

Australia is the favored destination for a large number of Singaporeans; however, Australian universities were not considered first choice to participate in the Singapore government's world class education hub plans. An Australian university, the University of New South Wales, was eventually invited to come aboard in 2004 (O'Keefe, 2004). Surveys of Singaporean impressions of Australian universities have repeatedly ranked Australia at number 4 in terms of quality after the United States, the United Kingdom, and Singapore (Milton-Smith, 2001). Partnerships between Australian universities and local private higher education providers are also considered detrimental to the Australian reputation, as these private institutions tend to cater for students perceived to be academically weaker. In a country where positional status is key, the hard sell of Australian degrees that are a daily feature in the city-state's main newspaper is perceived to further dilute reputation and quality (see Fig. 7.2).

FIG. 7.2.   The hard sell.

The Global Schoolhouse project is revealing of state–market relations at this historical moment. The global spread and embrace of neoliberalism, and the emergence of a postmodern capitalism, mean greater tolerance by governments of all political persuasions toward unemployment and poverty among their citizens. The issue of global economic justice has disappeared from the horizon in light of intensified competition between governments to attract capital. 'Roll-out neoliberalism', whereby considerable sums of government money are used to fund numerous initiatives to attract and retain capital, has taken a hold in many First World and transitional economies. It is these capital-friendly policies and practices by nation-states that have enabled "the stretching of the institutional architecture of elite Western universities across global space" (Olds & Thrift, 2004). The rationales for roll-out neoliberalism are framed in the soft language of market, technocracy, individual responsibility, and choice (see Peck & Tickell, 2002). In Singapore's case, what helps give roll-out neoliberalism its gravitas, momentum, and ultimately electoral support are two factors: the internalization of the discourses of crisis and pragmatism as discourses that govern the imagination, and the government's firm embrace of the "cultural circuit of capital" which has convinced Singapore's citizens that they are "factors of production . . . like a mineral resource with attitude" (Olds & Thrift, 2004).

The Singaporean government has provided financial incentives for the foreign universities in the form of soft loans, research funding, and reduced land values (the INSEAD site was purchased for one third of its commercial value, reported in Olds & Thrift, 2004). The government contributed to the renovations of the House of Tan Yoek Nee, a 120-year-old heritage building and site of the University of Chicago's GSB. The SMU also received government support in all aspects of its planning, development, and financing. The Ministry of Education subsidizes the tuition fees of all SMU students including international students, who are required to work in Singapore for 3 years after graduation. SMU has been described as "a publicly funded private university" which will have free rein to adopt the best practices of world class universities (Tan, 2002).

The Singapore Education Brand: "Springboard to a Better Future"

The global trade in education services which Altbach (1998) describes as the multinationalization of education requires all the artifacts and symbols one would associate with selling fully capitalist commodities. The Singapore Tourism Board has been charged with the responsibility of building a Singapore Education brand. The brand's selling ideas are centered on the country's educational excellence, its quality infrastructure, and its cosmopolitanism, all of which are promoted to serve as a "springboard to a better future" to the aspiring professional:

> By being in Singapore, you will get a chance to be plugged into an educational system that promotes excellence and be part of a progressive cosmopolitan community. (Singapore Education, 2003)

Selling the country is as important as selling the strengths of its education system. Much is made of Singapore's "GDP of S$160 billion," "the world's busiest port," "the best business environment in Asia," "the most competitive economy," "quality of life that surpasses London and New York," "young, fast growing" (Singapore Education, 2003).

The Singapore Education brand logo is a butterfly—a curiously feminine symbol—its meaning is explained in the descriptive text below:

> Like the butterfly which exists in a proliferation of different species, shapes and colours, Singapore's offering of education services is equally diverse. The wings which flutter as the open pages of a book remind us of the foundations on which we build our aspirations. . . . Just as the pages of the book converge at the spine, Singapore too acts as the hub for international networking opportunities in the region. The vibrant red and green of the butterfly tells of Singapore, a young fast growing country . . . lush and green . . . warm tropical weather . . . easily accessible. (Singapore Education, 2003)

Superimposed within the butterfly is an image of an open book. The flowing cursive typeface that denotes "Singapore" suggests an exoticism and feminism whereas the stolid typeface of "EDUCATION" is suggestive of the serious, uniform, and modern (see Fig. 7.3). The symbol personifies the complementary and opposite forces of yin, depicting the feminine East, and yang, suggesting the masculine and West. It is premised on classic orientalist codes of a feminine East and a modern, masculine West. Also

FIG. 7.3. Singapore education.

featured on the Singapore Education Web site is a stack of three books, secured firmly with a clasp, suggesting the control (clasp) of knowledge (books). It is a symbol that more closely approximates a 19th-century American education imagery than a 21st-century education in a country claiming an East–West heritage. Sitting on the top of the books is an apple—a fruit not traditional to Southeast Asia—that symbolizes a reward. It is a stunning pictorial depiction of how human capital theory manifests in modern "postcolonial" Asia.

Descriptive texts like the one above are also highly visual in effect. Using tropical imagery to market Singapore, the text calls on a historical repository of Western images about the tropics. "Lush," "green," "young" Singapore has an imaginative resonance with "positive" colonial stereotypes about the tropics as an "earthly paradise, with landscapes of extraordinary natural abundance and fertility" (see Ryan, 2004, p. 18). Visual strategies are now recognized as having a vital role in the knowledge-making enterprise. Given this, what provisional conclusions can we make about the Singaporean brand of international education? First, the types of hybrid formations likely to arise from a Singapore education reflect the government's embrace of a Western/North American model of modernity. Knowledge must have market value and education an instrumentalist and functionalist orientation. Second, the East is conceived of and constructed through an orientalist discourse. By implication, we can expect an orientalist appraisal of non-Western epistemologies as second rate and as having little contemporary relevance aside from selling tropical fantasies of paradise.

The promotional narratives in the Singapore Education Web site also hint at the growing profile of the consuming Singaporean subject, who manages the vicissitudes of life by shopping and eating out: "Dining and shopping are two of the top-rated activities of locals" (Singapore Education, 2003). Like the Education UK and Study Australia promotional campaigns, Singapore is also marketing its multiculturalism:

> Singapore is a great place to live in . . . what really appeals to many about Singapore is the multi-racial and multi-cultural environment. Broaden your horizon in this vibrant nation with a melting pot of Chinese, Malay, Indian and Eurasian cultures. (Singapore Education, 2003)

Yet, there are parameters governing permissible expressions of cultural diversity. Singapore's success as the locational choice for INSEAD Asia ahead of Hong Kong was shaped in part by perceptions by INSEAD staff that "Singapore is more international than Hong Kong. Hong Kong is a Chinese city" (Olds & Thrift, 2004). The commodification of its ethnicity has long been a feature of Singapore's tourism marketing, but its appearance in the marketing of education suggests two things: first, the emergence of a new discursive formation, educational tourism, and second, the growing importance of place branding as a strategy to market education.

WHAT KINDS OF SUBJECTS?

In the Singaporean context, steering the soul toward productive ends involves the deployment of a range of discourses including the crisis and survival discourse and the notion of individual merit that decrees that "no one owes another a living" (Chua, 1998, p. 33). An East versus West discourse is also deployed to craft the Singaporean as a unique subject—hard working, communitarian, and respectful of authority (George, 2000, pp. 49–56; Oehlers, 1998, pp. 7–8). In the face of the pressures never to be complacent, one subject position that has emerged is that of the driven, hypercompetitive, and individualistic Singaporean.

Having been subject to intense competition for all of life's amenities—education, jobs, status, physical space—some Singaporeans have reacted to the state's ambitions to always be ahead, never be complacent by developing a *kiasu* subjectivity. *Kiasu* is a Hokkien term that when literally translated means "fear of missing out" or competitive anxiety (Humphreys, 2001, pp. 99–102; Oehlers, 1998, p. 7). *Kiasu-ism* is generally associated with hyperindividualism and hypercompetition despite official pronouncements on the virtues of communitarianism.[15] It is increasingly the object of soul searching from younger Singaporeans:

> The Singapore dream has always been about the 5 C's. You are only somebody if you have the latest and best products. . . . This pursuit of material wealth combined with the constant need to be No. 1 has created the Singaporean we hear so much about—the *kiasu* Singaporean. Everything that revolves around the Singaporean ego is measured in terms of costs and benefits. The "what-will-I-gain-by-doing-this" mentality is foremost in the *kiasu* psyche. And because this psyche is part of the Singaporean identity, rude traits surface. (Ho, 2002)

These comments from Australian alumni confirm the extent to which *kiasu-ism* governs the Singaporean soul:

> Singaporeans are very kiasu, always wanting to be number one and all that. . . . Australians . . . they learn things for knowledge rather than to be

---

[15]The traits associated with being kiasu are myriad and are described popularly as: "Grab first talk later, Help yourself to everything, I first, I want, I everything, Vow to be number one, Winner takes it all! all! all!, Don't trust anyone" (Ho, 2002).

number one. (Chinese-Singaporean, Australian educated IT professional, female)

As a steering technology, *kiasu-ism* expresses itself at work, in schools, and even when Singaporeans are studying overseas:

Singaporean students, they end up like, hog the reference books. . . . So when everyone else was trying to get it they just keep it to themselves. . . .

It has become so competitive over here. . . . Even like at work. You get people who tell you, "I don't have this, I don't have that, I don't know this, I don't know that." And then you realise they are keeping everything from you. (Arab-Singaporean, IT professional, male)

Of course, like all 'isms', *kiasu-ism* produces unintended consequences. Singapore's plummeting birthrate, particularly among the highly educated, has been a source of concern to the state for some time. Work-related stresses are now being associated a condition termed *lifestyle impotency* (Aglionby, 2003).

Countries such as Australia indirectly benefit from this national trait as *kiasu-ism* propels many Singaporeans toward upgrading their qualifications. The following comments from Australian-educated Singaporeans are fairly typical in describing the instrumental approach to education: "Singapore is a very paper-based society"; "Singaporeans learn things to be number one." Regionally, there have also been rumblings that *kiasu-ism* has established itself in the mentalities of rule adopted by the government and is (particularly) evident in the Singaporean government's foreign policy.[16]

Popular Singaporean aspirations are widely thought to include the 5 Cs; however, these should not be seen as reflecting the definitive Singapore desire or dream. In keeping with a poststructuralist position, the Singaporean subjectivity should not be considered essential and fixed, even if the official position has been to engage in identity fixing. The reception of public discourses, whether capitalism, ethnocultural nationalism, or *kiasu-ism*, is never simple and passive but mediated by individual histories, subjectivities, and positionings of class, gender, and ethnicity. Recent debates about what it means to be Singaporean in the 21st century suggest that young Singaporeans are just as likely to ponder their identities as their counterparts in other countries (Teo, 2001).

Although a *kiasu* subjectivity with its corresponding emphasis on hyper-competitivity is recognized as dysfunctional to cooperation, it also has a productive dimension. Singapore's spectacular economic progress, its ability to exploit the opportunities presented by economic globalization, and

---

[16]Criticisms of a "kiasu mentality" in foreign policy have been directed against Singapore by members of Malaysia's Keadilan Party.

its ability to reinvent itself can be attributed at least in part to a *kiasu* mentality. What is less clear is how functional this hypercompetitiveness will be for the future, although the indications from the architects of Singapore's future suggest that a refashioned *kiasu-ism* has a role to play.

In the next lap of its development, Singapore intends to establish itself as a center for knowledge production. Where education was once intended to produce docile bodies, the knowledge-based economy now demands a particular type of critical thinking, preferably one that lends itself to entrepreneurialism.

> There is a dearth of entrepreneurial talent. . . . We have to start experimenting . . . the easy things—just getting a blank mind to take in knowledge and become trainable—we have done. Now comes the difficult part. To get literate and numerate minds to be more innovative, to be more productive, that's not easy. It requires a mind-set change, a different set of values. (SM Lee, as quoted by Hamlin, 2002)

The discursive construction of the citizen is as an utterly malleable object of experimentation. A new breed of Singaporean is being crafted for the 21st century: a risk-taking, innovative being who is both willing and able to assist the nation-state in its endeavors to become a hub for knowledge-based industries.

> We are seeking to inject entrepreneurship and innovation into the Singaporean DNA. It is not a project we can complete quickly. But we have to find every way to encourage enterprise and create a culture supportive of risk—a culture that cheers on those who fail and try again. . . . It is also a culture that sees heroes in those who break with convention and forge their own path. That's how we will get the diversity that we need to continue to be a successful economy. (Acting Education Minister, Shanmugaratnam)

The Singaporean government has tackled the task of changing its citizens' mindsets with its trademark tenacity, by committing itself to "inject entrepreneurship and innovation into the Singapore DNA." In discourse, the state presents itself as a facilitator which unlocks the workings of a genetic template. The ideal citizen-subject of the knowledge-based economy is a passionate and courageous risk taker whose patriotism drives him/her to contribute toward the national project of remaking Singapore as a hub for knowledge-based industries. The government's call for a culture change which recognizes those who break with convention as 'heroes' suggests a radical rupture from a rule-governed society long known for demanding conformity of its citizens.

That the Singaporean education establishment is also looking to America to be a role model is clear from the following pronouncements by key authorities in Singapore. The president of the NTU notes: "We are con-

scious that a lot of our investments come from the United States . . . thus
the university will be modelled on the American way" (Cohen, 1997). Another key university official observed, "The very future of our economy is
based on this realisation" (Cohen, 1997). The national desire for American-
style education has been translated into academic programs aimed at producing an "entrepreneurial drive and zeal"[17] (see Davie, 2002; see also Olds
& Thrift, 2004; Prystay, 2004). The subjectivity being fashioned by the
Singaporean government through its higher education system takes the
American entrepreneur as a grid of specification.

The Global Schoolhouse initiative is also premised on a particular Asian
subjectivity: "hard working . . . prepared to work for low wages" and holding
educational aspirations for their children so that their lives will be improved:

> With the end of the Cold War and the re-entry of China, Vietnam and India
> into the global market place, the Asian landscape is changing dramatically.
> Over 2 billion people want a better life for themselves and their children.
> They are prepared to work very hard and for very low wages. . . . They in turn
> want their children to be better educated so that their lives will be im-
> proved. . . . The hunger for education is creating a huge flow of knowledge
> from the developed countries to the developing Asian countries. . . . By tradi-
> tion Asians know that a good education can alter decisively the life chances of
> a child. Many are therefore prepared to pay large amounts to secure the best
> education for their children. . . . Singapore will increasingly become a global
> player in this education market. (Yeo, 2003)

Education is perceived as the means to greater security and socioeconomic mobility for the poor, the only catch being that it is a private good,
not a public good. This is a neoliberal discourse that vests the responsibility
for education on private citizens—in this case, parents—whose unrequited
aspirations are transferred to their children. It also imposes an all-powerful
subjectivity on the consumer who is described as having a hunger for education and thus driving demand. There is no mention of the role of the nation-state in creating this demand or the state's responsibility to alleviate
the conditions that create this hunger. In fact, the linking of education with
Asian tradition normalizes its value as a private good. A frontier or pioneer

---

[17]Also part of an ongoing commitment to foster creative talent among the best and the
brightest, the NUS and the NTU have intensified their focus on programs on entrepreneurship and "technopreneurship" courses with American institutions: Stanford University will be
the partner institute for NUS and Washington University's Center for Entrepreneurship and
Technology will be the American partner of NTU. Both schemes are backed by generous
scholarship schemes from the Singapore Economic Development Board and endowments
from the private sector. The NUS internship is the more comprehensive and better resourced
of the two initiatives.

subjectivity premised around the adventurous, self-improving, self-sacri-
ficing, risk-taking individual is faintly discernible: Asians are on the move
and they are prepared to do what it takes to have a better life.

What of the subjectivities perceived and constructed by the world class
universities? In declaring that "INSEAD's expansion in Asia illustrates our
commitment to globalism and multiculturalism" (INSEAD, 2002), the
founding dean of INSEAD Asia also revealed that the university intended to
use Singapore as a springboard to access the lucrative Chinese market for
management education:

> China is a special case. It is potentially the biggest market in the world. A Gal-
> lup survey indicates that one in ten Beijing-based companies wants MBA train-
> ing for their executives. The same survey also found that 4,000 companies in
> Beijing alone are willing to spend up to US$30,000 per executive for suitable
> MBA programmes. (INSEAD, 2002)

Here, China is perceived as a vast market that has the potential to offer
huge profits ("4000 companies in Beijing alone"). The statements imply
and perpetuate a subjectivity of insatiable consumer of Western educational goods for the Chinese. It also perpetuates an unflattering institutional subjectivity for this world class university—one that regards the Far
East as a giant market and source of profits.

Having mapped the key initiatives that are being introduced by the
Singaporean government in its bid to leapfrog into the value-added world
of international education markets, this is an apt moment to pause and ask
what these discussions into the minutiae of micropractices underpinning
the Global Schoolhouse and education hub reveal about the nation-state's
role in a global economy. I attempt to make a provisional summary of the
meaning of these discursive practices.

First, the broad raft of policies under Industry 21 and the Global Schoolhouse blueprint for world class universities has seen the government use its
powers and resources to develop a private university system that features
links with brand-name, predominantly American, providers of higher education. Steering toward a U.S.-modeled education hub reflects an open acknowledgment by the government of the reciprocal relationships between
power and knowledge. Singapore's national desire for an American-style
higher education with its strongly instrumental and entrepreneurial focus
indicates a changing global economic order evidenced by the eclipse of its
former colonial master, Britain as a geopolitical and economic power and
the consolidation of America's dominance into the 21st century (see Hamlin, 2002; Olds & Thrift, 2004).

Second, the Singapore government's commitment to bankroll these initiatives by offering large number of subsidies grants or scholarships sug-

gests a continuity with its developmentalist role. It also exemplifies how the government deploys pastoral power by facilitating access to the provision of high-status educational goods for its citizens to seal its legitimacy to govern. In a society where education is held in reverence, the ruling PAP is able to continue to win popular support from the broader community.

At the same time, the government is renewing its commitment to the two public sector universities, arguing that

> left to the market, there will likely to be underinvestment in basic research and in capital-intensive scientific disciplines . . . the public sector must step in to correct market deficincies in disciplines critical to our continued growth and to safeguard objectives that would otherwise not be served. (Tan, 2002)

Singapore's economic success was attained by instilling a particular set of attitudes and values in the citizenry, with education being one of the key sites where the state inscribed the development of 'appropriate' desires and subjectivities among its citizens, desires that effectively concurred with its national interest and goal of economic prosperity. The state controls the curriculum to promote a human resource model of education, which along with national education and compulsory military service for men (National Service), aims to promote loyalty and obedience to authority (Spring, 1998, pp. 75–81). The highly competitive nature of the education system is also noted for cultivating and perpetuating conservative values in students (Oehlers, 1998).

What vision is being constructed for Singapore by its leadership? What deductions can we make about the types of nation-building strategies that are at work in an era of postmodern capitalism from this example of Singapore? What types of subject positions will be privileged in the future? In a speech titled "An Entrepreneurial Culture for Singapore," Senior Minister Lee Kuan Yew provided hints of the preferred future:

> For over 30 years we have aimed for an egalitarian society. If we want to have successful entrepreneurs, Singaporeans have to accept a greater income disparity between the successful and the not-so-successful. . . . We are in a new era of the global economy. China will be a vacuum cleaner for Foreign Direct Investments (FDIs) and its production capacity is enormous. We must get part of the FDIs in higher value added and higher technology sectors. . . .
>
> Some of our energetic, resourceful and able people must go into business, and not just take salaried jobs. This is a change of culture, of values and mindset. . . . The world has changed and so must we. (Lee, 2002)

Lee (2002) declared, "The Cold War is over," and argued that the strategies that were used in 1960s to win the hearts and minds of people were no

longer appropriate. Where Singapore had once introduced state-sponsored initiatives to reduce the considerable poverty gap at the end of colonialism, such as universal schooling and public housing, Lee's vision for the
future requires "Singaporeans hav[ing] to accept a greater income disparity between the successful and the not so successful."

To conclude, educational attainment in the Singaporean context is regarded not only as an important individual goal but also as a collective aspiration that is linked to national success, given that "people are Singapore's
only natural resource" (SIF, 2002a, 2002b). A unique implementation of
human capital theory has been put to work, through the state's deployment
of various steering technologies to ensure that a skilled labor force is at
hand to enable Singapore to leapfrog into the next phase of development,
the knowledge-based economy (Coe & Kelly, 2002; Olds & Thrift, 2004).
The knowledge-based economy is understood as an inevitability in light of
globalization.

Globalization is viewed by the Singaporean government in terms of necessity not choice, and the state has moved swiftly to diversify its economic
profile to one based on a knowledge-based system of production. Higher
education is a critical nodal point in such a system of production. The ruling PAP has adopted the position that Singapore needs to produce a strong
entrepreneurial culture. This requires Singaporeans to engage in more risk
taking instead of choosing stable and well-paid positions in the government
and local and foreign multinational companies (Cohen, 1997; Hamlin,
2002; Lee, 2002; Olds & Thrift, 2004; Schein, 1996; Tan, 2001, 2002; Wong,
2003). There now appears to be a view that the future demands an "entrepreneurial soul" and the normalization of a neo-Darwinian ethic, "but we
cannot opt out of this race, *or we do not deserve to survive* [italics added]"
(Wong, 2003).

The constant crafting and recrafting to build the intelligent subject has
also had the effect of creating elitist mentalities in younger Singaporeans. A
web debate in 2004 that commented on a relationship between two young
Singaporeans—a high-achieving female student from an elite school, Raffles Girls School—and a young man from a 'neighborhood' school—
brought forth a series of worryingly explicit neo-Darwinian responses:

> The one weaker in academics will not be able to provide nourishment for the
> mind . . . and the more intelligent one will have to lower his/her standards
> and will eventually degenerate to the same level. . . . We are afraid of genetic
> dilution [person a].

> There will be a great communication problem. I mean what has a graduate
> from Cornell in common with Ah Beng in the streets? [person b]. (adapted
> from Seah, 2004)

STUDYING OVERSEAS: DESIRE AND AMBIVALENCE

The basis of mapping the policy terrain in Singapore is to acknowledge that
the experience of studying overseas, the subject positions that it forms, cannot be analyzed in isolation from local discourses. How students experience
and make sense of overseas study in Australia, the United Kingdom, or
America is necessarily intersected by the public common sense surrounding overseas study. A complex assemblage of competing and complementary public discourses shape the educated Singaporean subject. These include: nationalism, ethnocultural identity fixing, *kiasu-ism*, individualism,
and capitalism. Although recognizing that ultimately it is the individual
subject who makes sense of, and acts on, the public discourses, the function
of these discourses merits closer examination.

Given Singapore's hypercompetitive professional and business environments, many Singaporeans have been steered toward viewing education in
largely instrumental terms. It is a national and individual desire to stay competitive and to always be ahead that propels many Singaporeans to seek
multiple educational credentials in overseas universities, a process described by Chua (1998) as an endless 'paper chase'. A term widely used in
Singapore to capture the cultural capital that accompanies overseas education is *exposure*. The most coveted exposure is obtained by studying in a
prestigious, high-status university in a discipline attractive to the market.
Australia is a popular choice in terms of its cost effectiveness and proximity.
However, the most desired credentials are from the Ivy League and
Oxbridge institutions in America and the United Kingdom, respectively.

The large numbers of self-funding undergraduate students, who desire a
degree but have been streamed into the lower status polytechnics by Singapore's elitist system, tend to come to Australia to upgrade from diploma to
degree. Postgraduate students who wish to acquire competitive advantage
in the workplace will also seek exposure by undertaking further study, preferably in an institution identified by league tables as prestigious. The British Council's *Grow with UK* marketing campaign cashes in on this desire.
Singapore differs from other countries that have placed restrictions on students seeking to study overseas.[18]

However, exposure has to be kept within acceptable parameters. A series
of power–knowledge mechanisms are at work in mediating the raft of processes broadly termed *cultural globalization* by globalization theorists. As
noted earlier, the state uses a complex range of steering technologies to position a morally decadent and highly individualistic West against Singapore's Asian-style democracy where Asian values such as respect for author-

---

[18]The sole exception is males who are of the age to serve the compulsory military service,
or National Service.

ity prevail (see Chua, 1998; Lam & Tan, 1999). In doing so, the state steers the populace toward acceptable forms of transcultural and transnational exchanges. Unacceptable forms of hybridity, whether locally inspired or exported from overseas, are roundly criticized by the government. Thus, technological know-how, critical thinking, innovation, and creativity constitute a valued habitus. Less desirable is "the atomistic approach to life," loosely translated to mean "Western individualism" (Lee, as cited in Han et al., 1998, pp. 190–191; see also Barr, 2000, pp. 150–154). Developing entrepreneurial and competitive subjectivities is acceptable. Acquiring overseas education credentials is permissible, as is the consumption of some Western cultural products.

Frowned on are Western borrowings, such as liberal democracy, which is officially regarded as having high social costs. Unabashed self-interest is also poorly received, as evidenced in the government-sponsored cartoon series *Mr. Kiasu.* In recent times there has been a rise in the numbers of Singaporeans who, having been the recipients of state largesse in the form of overseas scholarships, have put self-interest ahead of their commitments to honor their responsibilities to serve the state on graduation. Such acts of self-interest have been pilloried and bond breakers publicly named in the city-state's newspapers in a bid to discipline those who put self-interest before the nation ("EDB Names," 1999).

Locally inspired hybridities can also be problematic. The government's Speak Good English Movement, for example, has sought to discourage the use of Singlish, a hybridized patois, on the grounds that it will reduce Singaporeans' employability in a global economy where English has hegemonic status. In doing so, the state is selectively privileging one aspect of globalization—economic globalization against cultural globalization, which is expressed through the emergence of a hybrid language form. The national desire to erase Singlish was rapidly seized on by the British Council, which is offering Singaporeans Speak Good English courses for a fee. These are aimed at teaching adults how to "understand common differences between Singlish and good English, avoid common Singlish mistakes and learn how to use good English in your personal and working life" (British Council Singapore, 2001).

Injunctions against hybridities are not restricted to official institutions. Several local discourses, too, are often called on to discipline the Singaporean who steps too far toward a hybrid identity. The Sarong party girl is a caricature of the Singaporean woman who dates or weds White men (*ang moh*) and is the object of derision. A cursory reading of the discursive construction of the Sarong party girl is revealing in its gender and racial stereotyping. There is, for example, no equivalent term for Singaporean men who date or marry White women. The famous Singapore Girl marketing campaign which promotes the city-state's national airline embodies the

conflation of a number of discourses of dominance. A gendered neocolonial, Oriental discourse is harnessed by postcolonial corporatism to normalize patriarchal social relations (see Heng, 1997).

There has been a long history of individual and collective resistance to
surveillance and typecasting among Singaporeans. It is no less evident today. Notions of the passive, uncritical, and instrumental Asian subjectivity
would be rapidly dismissed by perusing local popular culture. Mandarin
language films such as *Twelve Storeys* (1997) by Eric Khoo, *Street Angels*
(1999) by David Lam, and *Money No Enough* (1997) and *I Not Stupid* (2002)
by Jack Neo, deal with key issues such as poverty and alienation faced by Singapore's 'heartlanders'.[19] Similarly transgressive is the local TV comedy,
Phua Chu Kang, featuring a money-minded Singlish-speaking building con-
tractor (Humphreys, 2001, pp. 173–175). At another level are organizations
such as AWARE (Association for Women in Research and Education) and
the Singapore Internet Community which have been significant in creating
a space for civil society in the imagination. However, the use of the 5 Cs as a
grid for evaluating success, the demands involved in living and working in a
hypercompetitive environment, and an illiberal political culture make it
difficult to galvanize robust support for a civil society (George, 2000, pp.
40–48, 133–143).

In the next section I examine the micropractices and mundane discourses surrounding studying overseas. I use transcripts from chat room
discussions, newspaper reports, and interviews from Singaporeans who
have studied overseas to explore the types of subjectivities associated with
overseas exposure.

MANAGING 'EXPOSURE'

The relative strength of their currency, the high-tech wired nature of their
Intelligent Island, their familiarity with technology in education, and their
English language competency set the Singaporeans apart from the other
Southeast Asian and Pacific Islander student communities. In Australian
universities, Singaporeans are generally regarded as having First World status. As a group, they can also be described as focused and highly competitive. They have long been acculturated to regard academic achievement as
a status marker and the means to upward mobility.

How do students describe their experiences at British, Australian, and
American universities? Student narratives from three sources—chat rooms,[20]

---

[19]*Heartlanders* is the descriptive term given to the battlers of Singapore, who are largely the
poorer members of the Chinese-Singaporean community.

[20]All chat room discussions which are referred to in this chapter are accessible through
Straits Times Interactive, which hosts these discussions.

interviews, and student magazines—were analyzed. Their voices suggest that acquiring a global imagination and an accompanying supraterritorial subjectivity is complicated. A range of disciplining strategies are in place in both private and public spheres to remind students of their ethnocultural and national identities. These strategies, along with a dominant and instrumental discourse, steer students away from the reflexivity required of the educated subject in the 21st century.

Three desires underpin exposure. First is the desire for self goods such as personal growth, independence, empowerment, the opportunity to acquire independent living skills, and the ability to develop a different identity from a family-centered one. Second is the desire for positional goods: career success and monetary rewards, or in Singapore-speak, the 5 Cs. Third is the desire for a cosmopolitan habitus that comes from living and studying in a different cultural and national milieu. This response is fairly typical:

> I'll lend my voice to the support of overseas studies. The culture, independence, lifestyle. . . . Living abroad also makes me grow up. No longer sheltered by my family . . . learn to do things myself . . . learn from my mistakes. (mav)

Living and studying overseas also invites comparisons with Singaporean society:

> I used to think that Singapore was the best and I wanted all foreigners to believe that too. My dream was to become a highflyer with a swanky job in Raffles Place and achieve the "5Cs." . . . England gave me a great sense of freedom . . . to interact with people from diverse backgrounds, to be free to think independently and speak freely on socio-economic-political issues. (rlw)

> Mind opening . . . an eye opener to the reasons why other societies are more successful or ranked more favourably in terms of education, social grace and creative thinking. . . . Most people here usually want one of their sons or daughters becoming doctors or lawyers, making good money. . . . OK but a tad bit too restrictive and mundane. (mav)

> I like the idea of owning a car and a house/apartment at AFFORDABLE prices, without having to be in debt up to my ears. . . . There is no perfect country in the world. . . . If you obtain an education abroad you will realise the change and impact an overseas experience has when you return to Singapore . . . you'll have a broader acceptance of things. (ladyi)

It is interesting that the overseas sojourn also appears to intensify identification with Singapore and a renewed commitment to their responsibilities as citizens:

Makes you more appreciative of Singapore yet more critical as well (a good thing). Without critical thinking there will be complacency and the society suffers. (starcancer 1377)

The postings also reveal some awareness of the state-sponsored disciplining strategies that draw on East–West binaries:

I know that there is a stereotype in Singapore that those who return are often arrogant trendy, foreign attitudes and American accents etc. That much hasn't changed since the last century when Dr. Sun Yat Sen tried to promote western values into China. . . . I would like to say that not all graduates from American or Australian universities are like that. Many are the children of neighbours, hawkers, taxi drivers. (manhatten)

This response is an attempt to normalize overseas study—it is not just an elite undertaking but is an aspiration of ordinary people such as hawkers, taxi drivers, and so on. However, the overseas experience is also perceived as high risk and potentially disappointing. This can take the form of a poor experience of teaching and poor university facilities: "Not all Aussie unis are good. . . . For the past two years . . . my exams are all multiple choice questions." Some postings raise the issue of racism, although on the whole, student narratives such as this one suggest that actual incidents overseas are rare:

Racism exists not only in Australia but Singapore too. I have Singaporean friends who are not comfortable shopping in Lucky Plaza or Serangoon Road on Sundays. . . . Racism happens everywhere not just in Australia. Anyway, if you have the opportunity to study overseas consider it, racism in Australia isn't that bad. (weiho)

Perhaps the least contested interpretation of exposure is the access it offers to positional goods. There are numerous references to "prestigious institutions," and indeed, countries too are ranked accordingly ("u should try to go to great world class research universities . . . aren't any in australia . . . about 50 in the US and 50 in europe"). At the top of the list of positional goods are those offered by American Ivy League institutions, followed by Britain's Oxbridge institutions. Australia's research-focused Group of Eight Universities has some fans but overall narratives from Australian graduates and students focus more on the overall experience of being overseas: "more for the exposure than . . . the academic aspect."

The chasm between institutional reputations and students' expectations can create some disappointments as this account suggests:

I transferred to the University of Texas because it was more prestigious. . . .
My main concern is that Singaporeans (and many other nationalities) are
caught up in name recognition (and rightfully so in answering to friends and
relatives). I transferred to a school that was more reputable but I hated it. It
was too big and the education substandard. Sure the name sounds decent but
I'll be very candid and say I do not appreciate my so-called alma mater. My advice is that if you are happy in a university that is "not as famous" but offers education, that's all that matters! (etsb23)[21]

A few postings such as this one also point to some concerns about the
quality of Australian education:

Do not expect Aussie uni to be like what you see at NTU or SMU. Buildings in
some or most Aussie uni are terribly old . . . be aware and assess critically the
brochures you are given by agencies like the Australian Education Centre.
(interstudent)

Because university credentials are a form of investment, criticisms such
as interstudent's tend to be rapidly met with refutations:

Maybe you are in a mediocre Australian universities or perhaps you can't get
into the G8 Australian university. This guy is all out to damage the reputation
of Aussie universities. . . . If you see the Asiaweek rankings of the universities
you will see the truth. Don't listen to what interstudent posted, its naive and
immature thinking (no wonder he is in some "ulu" Australian university, envi-
ous of those students who made it to top Aussie unis. (victoria 73)[22]

Just don't spoil the reputation of all Australian universities just becos your
university is not up to standard. (sinful)

I suggest that you stop scaring people, just based on your experience.
(avaleon)

The postings rarely make references to lasting friendships made overseas, suggesting perhaps that social capital across national boundaries is not
a notably common or valued aspect of exposure. Some postings do refer to
the instrumental benefits of understanding difference and diversity in the
new global economy:

---

[21]As with the posting that criticized Australian universities, this message from etsb also received responses from two "longhorns" from the University of Texas, Austin, which refuted his
or her claims.

[22]Ulu is a Malay language term that means backward. It is usually associated with a rural
backwardness.

Its all too easy to seek the familiar faces of Singaporeans and Asians when you are in a new land. If all the people you are going to interact with are fellow Asians . . . then you have lost out in your most valuable asset of having an overseas education. This is the chance to understand a set of people who have grown up completely differently with different values and attitudes. This will be an advantage in the new global economy where the barriers will not be national boundaries but cultures and language. (manhattan)

This response warns of the discipline meted out to those who seek to move out of culturally homogenous comfort zones:

Many of the Singaporeans viewed me as a "traitor" because I was surrounded by Europeans. . . . I had very few Singaporean friends not because I did not like them but because they tend to stick to themselves and to do the same things they would do in Singapore . . . with little interest in interacting with other international students or experiencing the British way of life. (rlw)

However, a warning to students thinking of using overseas study as a springboard to leave for greener pastures. This impassioned posting is one of several boundary-maintaining narratives, framed in a discourse of cultural authenticity and national loyalty:

This is Where I Know I'm Home!
My fellow Singaporeans, being able to study abroad has really broadened my social skills. . . . Ironically, I actually feel more in touch with my Singaporean identity. . . . COME BACK MY FELLOW COUNTRYMEN. So that we can contribute together in our unique way to achieve a better future for all Singaporeans. EVEN A HAWKER KNOWS HOW TO IRON THE FLAG NEATLY BEFORE HANGING IT OUT WHILE SOME EDUCATED ONES DAMNED IT. . . . an Englishman's home is his castle and so is mine. (BG YANG IN PARLIAMENT 1997: A TURTLE MAY SWIM IN THE OCEAN BUT IT NEVER FORGETS THAT TINY STRETCH OF BEACHES FROM WHICH IT SWUM OUT). (gabrielkoo)

Here, loyalty to the nation is constructed as natural, cutting across all class boundaries. By creating a binary between self-interested elite ("educated ones") and the quintessential battler ("the hawker"), the message is never to forget home and never forget one's origins.

A satirical piece titled "When East Meets West" (see Fig. 7.4) captures the psychological boundaries to border crossings. "When East Meets West" traces the journey of Tao Hu Hua, a Hokkien-speaking student who comes to Australia to study. His journey is marked by numerous attempts to "assimilate," which includes adopting a "westerner friendly name" and "[a] fascination with Caucasian girls." It ends with his unfortunate metamorphosis into "a banana." The statements within the story problematize the notion of

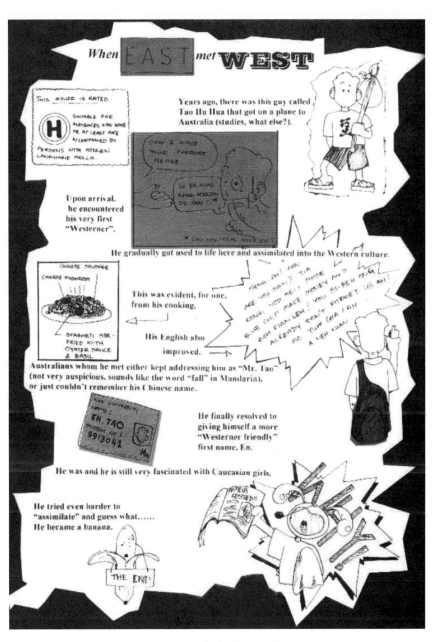

FIG. 7.4. East meets West.

split and agonistic subjectivities. You are either Hokkien Chinese or a banana (yellow on the outside, white inside). Exposure is constructed as a high-risk venture involving the possible loss of one's roots as an Asian. The safest option is a fixed subjectivity. "When East Meets West" offers a powerful message with a colonial resonance. It is a reminder that colonial governance was effected by the co-option of local leaders. Hu Hua is portrayed as the agent of his assimilative downfall. He actively chooses to alter his name, to speak English, albeit the patois form, Singlish. "When East Meets West" is a parody of the experience of being the other and a thinly veiled attack on cultural exchanges and hybridization.

CONCLUDING COMMENTS

Singapore offers an appealing case from which to explore the links between discourses of globalization and the policy responses adopted by the nation-state, which drive both the production and consumption of international education. Rather than treating globalization as imbued with agency to dominate the local, and an evolutionary force ("the next phase of societal development"), the chapter highlighted how globalization functions as a governmentality. Globalization is used as a legitimating metaphor to justify particular policies and practices by the Singaporean nation-state. A hegemonic understanding of globalization as exogenous forcing is reworked into a long-standing cultural discourse of crisis and survivalism to reconstruct higher education and build new capacity through the Global Schoolhouse Project. Long regarded as a source of international students ("priority market") by Australian and British universities, the city-state is now building itself to become an exporter of international education through the Global Schoolhouse Project.

Several conclusions can be drawn about the relations between the nation-state and education under contemporary conditions of globalization. First, the Global Schoolhouse Project highlights the importance of moving beyond zero-sum thinking about the effect of globalization on the nation-state. The Project illustrates the creative and imaginative ways in which the Singaporean nation-state is remodeling itself in response to the new iterations of global capitalism. As a strongly developmentalist state, Singapore has largely eschewed the minimalist state approach. Instead the dictates of the market have been mediated by the direct involvement of government in nation-building projects like the Global Schoolhouse and Renaissance City, which are concerned with reengineering the city-state's economic base.

The case of Singapore also suggests the existence of hybrid variants of neoliberalism. Neoliberalism is articulated with the political project of economic survival in the city-state, but in more ways than one, the state remains an important actor in economic production. While the scope of this chapter does not extend to an analysis of Singaporean articulations of neoliberalism, the city-state is a potentially useful focal point for investigating the variants of neoliberalism arising outside its heartlands in the United States and the United Kingdom. Second, the case of Singapore prompts reflection on what the unrelenting quest for global competitiveness means for the citizen-subject. More specifically, whether the fast, globalizing processes that manufacture 'spaces of intensity', as embodied in global cities like Singapore, increase the likelihood of producing 'fragile subjects' (see Thrift, 2000).

Third, Singapore offers an instructive case study on hybridity under conditions of globalization. The Global Schoolhouse reveals the value and worth attributed by the government to the American mindset of entrepreneurialism. Hybrid formations whether as business practices, educational developments or ethnocultural identities are monitored to ensure that they do not interfere with the nation-building project to develop an internationally competitive, entrepreneurial culture that will allow Singapore to prosper into the 21st century. Such state-sanctioned hybridities can embody hierarchies and create the conditions and possibilities for differential rewards and greater disparities in status and income. Culture-building technologies continue to be used to govern although more recently, less fixed and less essentialized discourses of culture, home and belonging are being employed to anchor Singaporeans spatially and emotionally to the city-state. Furthermore, in its aims to encourage entrepreneurialism, innovation and creativity in its citizens, the government is encouraging Singaporeans to break with convention. That stated, the East versus West discourse remains in place, reappearing periodically to discipline the local population. The kind of exposure sought by Singaporeans studying overseas reflects the instrumentalized and racialized parameters that delimit acceptable hybridities. Although globalization is represented in some quarters as replacing boundaries through the enlistment of places, regions, and countries into large-scale networks, the overseas study sojourn is suggestive of the emergence of new boundaries within these 'new' networks. Singaporeans encounter and engage in various boundary-maintaining practices that ultimately influence their social subjectification as citizens of a 'global city at the crossroads of Asia'.

Chapter 8

Brazil: "Priority Market"

Ravinder Sidhu
Cecilia Torres

Brazil offers a good case study of top-down globalization. It has been subject to, and governed by global military, economic, cultural, and political processes, starting with colonization and continuing with its inclusion into an integrated global market. As this chapter shows, Brazil continued to experience globalization from above, as defined by corporations, major multilateral agencies, transnational policy communities, and powerful national governments. These forces have done little to alleviate the inequalities in Brazilian society. How can a democratic globalization-from-below be effected, what role can intellectuals and professionals play, and is there a place for international education in bringing about change?

In marketing parlance, Brazil is considered by the international education export industry to be a priority market. Both the United Kingdom and Australia have intensified their recruitment activities in this country, albeit in different ways, to wrest market share from the United States. America's long involvement in Latin America has fostered political, economic, and cultural links between its governing elites and Brazilians who choose to study overseas are most likely to select the United States.

The chapter begins with a historical overview of Brazil, an exposition of its political economy, and the challenges facing its higher education system. It explores how the broader context shapes the ways Brazilian students who study overseas choose or arrive at particular subjectivities. It concludes with a discussion of the global imaginaries presumed and perpetuated by international education in Brazil, and what prospects are created for globalization from below.

270

TRADE WARS?

The early 1400s brought about great advances in European exploration. *In or-der to make trade more efficient,* Portugal attempted to find a direct water route to the India and China. By using a direct water route, Arab merchants, who owned land trade routes, were not able to make a profit off the European trade merchants. (Koeller, 1998)

This vignette reads as part of a broader historical tale of the efficient and dynamic European explorer-trader. Here, he is driven by an entirely rea-sonable motivation—to put an end to Arab profiteering; elsewhere, though, he is conferred with a vastly different motivation. Nearly every schoolchild in Southeast Asia learns about Vasco da Gama, the Portuguese navigator, who in 1498 found the sea route to India through the Cape of Good Hope. His voyage inaugurated European imperialism in Asia. The Portuguese were driven by an anti-Islamic ideology—a desire to find Chris-tian nations with which to build anti-Islamic alliances—and solid commer-cial concerns—a desire to wrest control of the spice trade from Arab traders who monopolized the land routes (Keen, 1992, pp. 52–54; Levine, 2003, pp. 33–34).[1]

As a small kingdom with a population of about 1.5 million and a rela-tively small navy, the Portuguese were aware of their vulnerability in the East. They had 'restless natives' to contend with, having taken Goa (in In-dia) and Malacca (in the Malay peninsula) by force. They faced competi-tion from other ambitious European kingdoms who nursed aggressive am-bitions to establish trading monopolies. These imperatives drove Portugal to establish a presence westward, in the Americas. The Portuguese explorer Pedro Cabral claimed the territory of Brazil for his country in 1500, a claim given legitimacy by the Treaty of Tordesillas of 1494, which saw Spain and Portugal renegotiating the original papal dictum by Alexander VI.[2]

---

[1]Koeller's (1998) rationale of European expansionism as driven by the desire to "make trade more efficient" is mired in controversy. In India the quincentenary of da Gama's arrival was greeted with criticisms. Although some historians attribute the military attack and coloni-zation of Goa in 1510 to da Gama's rival Alphonso de Albuquerque and not da Gama, there was enough disquiet about celebrating da Gama's arrival for proposed celebrations to be re-duced in scale and significance. Portugal's expansionism saw the colonization of Malacca (in Malaysia), Ceuta (in Morocco), Portuguese Guinea (west Africa), and the islands of Azores and Cape Verde. Goa remained a Portuguese colony until it was reclaimed by the Indian gov-ernment in 1961.

[2]In 1493 the Spanish Pope Alexander VI issued a decree establishing Spanish and Portu-guese sovereignty by an imaginary line running north and south through the mid-Atlantic, 100 leagues (480 km) from the Cape Verde islands. Spain would have possession of territories to the west and Portugal to the east of the line. The Portuguese renegotiated these territorial claims in the Treaty of Tordesillas in 1494 (Levine, 2003, pp. 38–39).

The conquest and settlement of Brazil proceeded at a relatively slow pace compared with the rest of the Americas,[3] and in 1535 the Portuguese Crown established a system of hereditary captaincies to accelerate the process of populating, exploring, and exploiting the resources of its new colony. The captaincies were a fusion of feudal and capitalist imperatives, and they set the precedent for a form of regional governance that remains a feature of Brazilian politics today (Crow, 1992, pp. 141–142; Keen, 1992, p. 146; Levine, 2003, pp. 42–43).

The European conquest and settlement of Latin America was driven by 'God, gold, and glory', although Portuguese incursions into Brazil are noted for their relatively sober ambitions compared to the Spanish. 'Old school' historians of Latin America, such as John Crow, write of the demise of first nation people with a resigned inevitability. Crow (1992) observes that no European nation, no race or creed was exempt from cruelty to the indigenous peoples, "Then as now, too much idealism in government did not seem to work out," adding that attempts at a just leadership of the colonies ended up as "complete fiasco" (p. 144). A ringing endorsement of the "superiority" of a Western civilization is discernible in Crow's references to indigenous cannibalism, internal warfare, and an implied promiscuity by their women who "consorted" with the Europeans to produce "half-breeds" or *mamelucos* (p. 140). Forced abduction and the slavery of indigenous "Indians" accompanied colonization efforts to open up the country, and these efforts assumed greater momentum with the introduction of cash crops such as sugar (Levine, 2003, pp. 19, 34–36). Indigenous people resisted enslavement[4] and received limited protection from the Portuguese crown through the advocacy of the Jesuits. Influenced by a discourse of benevolence, the Jesuits led a secular and theological struggle for greater rights for the Indians by contradicting the popular Christian belief that, like animals, the native population had no souls and could therefore be dealt with accordingly. Although the Jesuits and other missionaries are thought to have protected indigenous peoples from settlers and landowners, their legacy is now contested by historians and anthropologists.[5]

---

[3]Brazil was first sparsely settled by a trickle of sailors, castaways, temporary settlers, and criminals (Keen, 1992, p. 55). Commodities such as brazilwood did not create the same fervor as gold, which drove the conquest and settlement of Mexico, Peru, and Colombia (Crow, 1992, p. 143; Keen, 1992, pp. 145–146).

[4]They did so through means as varied as absconding and committing suicide instead of serving in slave labor gangs. They also engaged in guerilla warfare in isolated parts of the country against settlers (Levine, 2003, pp. 34–37).

[5]Well regarded by numerous Portuguese kings, the Jesuits enjoyed power and authority in Brazil, which they exercised through the *Mesa da Consciência*, a royal council appointed to run religious affairs in the colony. One of the most prominent Jesuits in Brazil was Antonio Vieira. The role of Jesuits in protecting the indigenous peoples is ambiguous. Jesuit-run missions, *aldieas*, where indigenous people lived and worked, were also sites for assimilating tribes into

Power and Politics in the Modern State

By the mid-16th century, sugar's status as a mass commodity in Europe and the lure of large profits led to the introduction of slavery to obtain labor for sugar plantations (Levine, 2003, pp. 18–28, 45–47).[6] Commercial and religious discourses were galvanized to justify the need for slavery, with the settlers arguing that there were no moral dilemmas to enslavement as Africans were the unrepentant sons of Ham (Keen, 1992, p. 85). The governance of indigenous peoples had been similarly inflected by the racial principle. Declared uncivilized, and associated with cannibalism, the impetus to offer them protection and education disappeared. They were considered as deserving enslavement. Allied to these other practices was a racial taxonomy centered on the purity of blood deployed as a dividing practice. Blood impurity was said to be visibly manifested in skin color and even after they had seen the light and converted to Christianity, these new Christians, which included Africans slaves, indigenous people, and the various mixed races, were declared to be impure. From this racial principle, it was impossible for those with impure blood to occupy positions of power, receive noble titles, or belong to prestigious collectives such as fraternal societies (Fausto, 2002, p. 31). Although a law was passed in 1773 abolishing the distinction between old Christians and new Christians, practices of discrimination continued (p. 31). An ethic of general obedience to authority was further instilled by the Catholic church's exercise of pastoral power. Obedience to the state was an extension of this governance of care and control (p. 29).

The sugar economy consolidated the power of large plantation owners and established Brazil's land-holding system—*latifundio monoculture* (great estate monoculture). A system of rural oligarchs emerged who consolidated their power over small land holders by imposing steep charges for their use of expensive sugar refining mills (*engenhos*). Slavery and debt pe-

---

alien cultural practices. Many Indians died after being released to work for settlers. The missionary zeal of the Jesuits spurred their exploration into the interiors of Brazil, inadvertently causing the deaths of many indigenous people through diseases to which they had no immunity. The predictable animosity between the clergy and the plantation owners and settlers eventually resulted in their expulsion from Brazil in 1756 (Levine, 2003, p. 36).

[6]The northeast provinces of Bahia and Pernambuco became major centers for the importation of African slaves. The fortunes of the planter aristocracy in the northern provinces declined with falling sugar commodity prices and the restrictions on the slave trade stemming from intervention from the British. The British navy intercepted and destroyed slave-carrying frigates. These actions were motivated largely by commercial sentiments as British plantations were unable to compete with slave-produced commodities. The writings of the British consul general in Brazil, Sir Francis Burton, of slave life in Brazil between 1865 and 1867 suggest that the humanitarian persuasions of the British may have been overstated (see Burton, as cited in Levine & Crocitti, 1999, pp. 131–136; Levine, 2003, pp. 66–67).

onage continued till the end of the 19th century. These historical relations of power have remained in force. Present estimations suggest that 1% of landowners control 50% of arable land in Brazil (Alai-Amlatina, 2003). Brazil retained the colonial institutions of slavery and imperial governance at independence from Portugal, the result being a ruling class largely united in its interests (Levine, 2003, pp. 66–71; Levine & Crocitti, 1999, p. 60). Governance in contemporary Brazil is characterized by the power of an educated elite, the presence of strongly racializing logics, the political influence of the military (p. 206), and an extreme form of federalism ("politics of the governors") whereby the provinces or states continue to exercise significant autonomy (see Keen, 1992, pp. 235–239, 342–347).

Like other Latin American economies, its export-driven economic foundation would link Brazil to Britain, and later the United States, into a series of broadly neocolonial relations. Brazil's integration into an international economic system began during the Industrial Revolution, but did little to arrest its diminution into a neocolonial economy. Its transition from an export-based monoculture to a predominantly industrialized, manufacturing-based economy dependent on one or two commodities made it highly vulnerable to changing demands. Booms were punctuated by slumps and in some cases, total collapses. By the 19th century, foreign control of Brazilian natural resources and infrastructure had increased significantly. Britain was the leading foreign investor until World War I, when it was replaced by the United States. With foreign investment came political intervention—'dollar diplomacy'—and where necessary, 'strategic' military intervention by various American governments. However, any analysis of governance must engage with the precariousness of insider–outsider distinctions. Labor leaders and intellectuals may well be justified in attacking foreign interests but the role of the entrenched Brazilian elite in contributing to the country's economic problems and extreme income disparity should not be understated (Levine, 2003, pp. 22, 90–92).

GOVERNING TECHNOLOGIES

Engaging with contemporary political culture of Brazil is a first step toward understanding its higher education context, which this next section attempts to do. It examines key governing discourses and links these to the emergence of particular self-steering technologies and subject positions. The historical presence of an oligarchic dimension in Brazilian politics produced possibilities for various models of authoritarian governance. These were based on coalitions between the military and various right-, centrist-, and left-wing political parties. The Liberal Alliance party headed by the populist politician Vargas, for example, used military support to install the

Estado Novo (New State)[7] from 1937 to 1945. The New State's developmentalist policy platform was premised on modernization and industrialization. It exercised strict control over the press and civil rights movements, but also introduced limited social welfare programs for the middle classes and sections of the working classes (see Levine, 2003, pp. 111–119; Tota, 1999; Vargas, 1999, pp. 186–189; Vianna, 1999, pp. 184–185). After a brief period in the 1950s when a democratically elected government was in office, the military returned to power in 1964 having ousted the left-wing Goulart government (Levine, 2003, pp. 124–127). Cold War politics underpinned American support for the military government, which was largely dominated by graduates of the *Escola Superior de Guerra* (School of Higher Military Studies), an institution known for its hard-line approach to communism (*linha dura*), acceptance of U.S. leadership in foreign affairs, and support for foreign investment (Keen, 1992, p. 339). The military government was also backed by Brazilian property owners, industrialists, multinationals, the urban middle classes, and several provincial governors (Keen, 1992, pp. 359–362; Levine & Crocitti, 1999, pp. 225–229).[8] In 1967, under the auspices of national security, the military regime introduced a new Constitution, which led to a series of repressive laws (Levine, 2003, pp. 128–133; Levine & Crocitti, 1999, pp. 238–240).

The military government's economic policies were intended to stimulate the entry of foreign capital and denationalize key sectors in the Brazilian industry.[9] By 1968, the motor vehicle industry was entirely in foreign hands, and 90% of the pharmaceutical industry was controlled by foreign multinationals. The United States was the largest investor, controlling more than half of total foreign investment, followed by Germany, Britain, France, and Switzerland (Keen, 1992, pp. 359–360). Wages were frozen and strikes banned to ensure a cheap, abundant, and pliable labor force. An earlier nationalist model of economic development was abolished. At the same time, the regime deployed nationalism to galvanize loyalty and support from its citizens, with such measures as the mandatory teaching of *civismo* (citizenship education) in schools, and TV, radio, and billboard campaigns that exhorted citizens to display patriotism (Levine, 2003, pp. 129–130).

---

[7]The outcomes of the *Estado Novo* were mixed. Educational reforms remained largely insignificant. The plight of the poorest people in the community, Afro-Brazilians, peasants, and urban poor in favelas (slums) remained largely unchanged (Levine, 2003, chap. 5).

[8]Runaway inflation prompted the urban middle classes to support the military regime. The support of the U.S. government was driven by its concerns about the prospect of communism taking hold in Brazil.

[9]These measures included reduced taxes for foreign firms and the lifting of capital controls to enable the free export of profits. In accordance with the IMF's prescriptions to curb inflation, access to internal credit was restricted, resulting in an increase in bankruptcies among Brazilian-owned businesses.

The years from 1969 to 1974 were regarded as particularly repressive.[10] The state coordinated a campaign of violence against members of the political opposition, clergy, students, intellectuals, journalists, and labor leaders, who were subjected to arbitrary detention, torture, and institutionalized censorship (Ginway, 1999, p. 248; Keen, 1992, pp. 360–362; Levine, 2003, pp. 130–132; Tavora, 1999, pp. 231–234; Tota, 1999, pp. 235–237). Resistance to the state's repression was conducted through a variety of means—popular support for liberation theology, organized protests by labor, and the creation of art and literature.[11] In the latter part of the 1960s, musical movements such as *Jovem Guardo* and *Tropicalismo* provided forums for criticism and dissent toward the state through popular music. Groups and artists such as *Chico Buarque, Caetano Velloso, Gilberto Gil, Geraldo Vandre, Edu Lobo,* to name a few, used their music to envision and call for social and political change. Today, music and poetry remain powerful mediums to express solidarity with the disenfranchised, with groups such as *Barao Vermelho* and *Legiao Urbana* noted for giving voice to the hopes, dreams, and dilemmas of those at the margins of Brazilian society (Torres, 2003).

Spurred by their technocratic visions, Brazil's military rulers pushed for the development of technologically advanced industrial plant and an agribusiness sector. Despite rises in the export of primary and manufacturing commodities, the promised economic miracle did not eventuate. Brazil's export income did not improve balance of trade payments, in part because of the rising costs of servicing its foreign debt and in part because of the oil recession. IMF bailouts merely imposed greater austerity measures on the population. In 1978, it was estimated that 70% of the population was living below survival level (Keen, 1992, pp. 360–362; Levine, 2003, pp. 137–138). Land grabbing in the Amazon by large landowners displaced the rural poor, who drifted into cities looking for work. In the face of growing opposition by Brazil's peasantry and working class, and with support from the middle classes and sections of the capitalist class, a policy of *abertura* (opening toward democracy) was entered into, limited political freedoms were introduced, and by 1983 the transition to democracy had begun. Brazil's economic problems, however, continued to escalate with brief periods of remission from inflation and unemployment.

---

[10]By December 1968, after protracted public protests and following the defeat of reformist elements in the military by the "hard-liners," President Costa e Silva dissolved Congress, suspended the Constitution, and granted the office of the president dictatorial powers (Keen, 1992, p. 361).

[11]The rise of literary forms such as the political novel, documentary fiction, and testimonial fiction explored the human costs of the military's modernization and interrogated claims of the economic miracle, criticized state-sponsored brutality, and pondered ethical alternatives.

One of the biggest problems that has faced Brazil is the reach of institutionalized corruption.[12] Brazilian anthropologist Roberto Da Matta (1999) attributes the tenacity of corruption to "norms which protect the ethic of privilege" and "a state that indulges its elite and fends off its citizens" (p. 296). The elite expectation of deference is expressed in the ritual intimidation of everyday talk, exemplified most commonly in the phrase, "*voce sabe com quem esta falando?*" ("do you know whom you are talking to?"). Along with norms such as *jeito* (the way), there is widespread acceptance of the need to deploy extralegal behaviors to obtain services, extract favors, and purchase protection (Da Matta, 1999; Levine, 1999, pp. 402–407). Jeito does manifest in outright corruption although more often than not, it is simply a way of negotiating a bureaucratic labyrinth and getting things done.

Marginality and Civic Invisibility

The official view is that Brazil is a *racial democracy*. The origins of this thesis can be traced to the work of Gilberto Freire[13] and enjoys widespread support by intellectuals and policymakers. Freire argues that a less pernicious model of racial discrimination has always prevailed in Brazil. Compared with the United States, racial segregation was not enshrined in legal doctrine (Levine, 2003, pp. 12–14). Thus, the reasoning goes, intermingling between the races led to 'brazilianization' or a blurring of the racial boundaries between the groups. On the basis of this reasoning, the clustering of Afro-Brazilians at the bottom of the social and economic hierarchy can be attributed to class and limited access to education rather than to race-based discrimination (Levine & Crocitti, 1999, pp. 351–353). In contrast, the Afro-Brazilian perspective is sharply critical of any suggestion of Brazil as a racial nirvana and argues that the intersection of race and class are responsible for the large numbers of impoverished darker skinned Brazilians (Huggins & Mesquita, 2000; Klees, Rizzini, & Dewees, 2000). The official ideology of brazilianization is informed by a strongly assimilationist stance, anchored in a premise of 'whitening' the nation[14] rather than ac-

---

[12]The 1992 impeachment of Brazil's first democratically elected president in 30 years, President Fernando Collor de Mello, highlighted the extent of high-level corruption.

[13]Freire argues in his book *Masters and Slaves* that Brazilian slavery was more humane than American slavery (Levine, 2003, pp. 11–14).

[14]Critics of the racial democracy thesis also point to the divisions between the *pardos* (lighter skinned, mixed-race Brazilians) with *pretos* (dark-skinned Afro-Brazilians) as evidence that the issue of race and color remain salient in the politics of citizenship and identity (see Rout, 1999).

cepting and celebrating its racial and cultural diversity (see Caldwell, 2001; de Jesus, 1999; Nascimento, 1999; Rout, 1999).

According to the United Nations Development Program, Brazil is not a poor country—it is a middle income country with 53 million people living below the poverty line. Brazil is one of the most unequal societies in the world. The wealthiest 1% of Brazilians hold resources that exceed those held by 50% of the poorest (Andrews, 2004, p. 477). The issue of Brazilian poverty assumes a particularly visceral expression in the large numbers of Brazilian children who live and work in the street (Huggins & Mesquita, 2000, p. 83; Rosemberg, 2000, p. 130). Brazil's class polarization is vividly exemplified in the segregation of spaces, from the *favelas* to the gated communities with their elaborate home security devices intended to protect the haves from the have-nots. Destitute children and adolescents who resort to criminal activities to survive receive little understanding from middle- and upper-class urban residents (Milito & Silva, 1999). The complexities surrounding children's survival in the urban jungle of the streets have been vividly captured in internationally acclaimed films such as *Pixote, Cidade the Deus* (*City of God*) and *Central do Brasil.* Unflinching in their neorealism, these films capture the failure of the state and Brazil's elites to create the conditions necessary for families to live decent lives and provide for their children's intellectual, psychological, and social development and well-being. Children who work and live on the street, particularly those of Afro-Brazilian background, remain high at risk of being killed by state authorities such as the police (Brandao, 1999; Levine, 1999, pp. 423–429; Moulin & Pereira, 2000).

> Youth murders are part of the rational organisation of Brazilian society. The Brazilian image of the poor urban youth as dangerous street children individualises youth murder and mutes social consciousness about the relationship of these murders to such structurally rooted social problems such as . . . unemployment, debt, hunger and brutal wealth inqualities. (Huggins & Mesquita, 2000, p. 266)

Antipoverty policies have been on the agendas of numerous Brazilian governments since the 1930s. Their success has been limited by problems of coordination, excessive bureaucracies, and corruption. Following the election of the Partido dos Trabalhores (PT) there have been renewed attempts to refocus these policies to combat both the causes and the consequences of poverty (Andrews, 2004).

The normalization of practices that intimidate those considered social inferiors, huge inequality, and the vicissitudes of a neoliberal capitalism that demand fiscal responsibility are all factors that reduce the possibilities for social change (Andrews, 2004; Chagas, 2004; Munk, 2003). Brazil has an activist government that is trying to address the nation's inequality (Fisher & Ponniah, 2003, pp. 4–5). However, institutions such as representative government, civil liberties, and market freedoms are not in themselves sufficient for social and economic equity. As Tully (2004) argues so convincingly, in place of civil freedoms, what is required are civic freedoms. Such freedoms rest on the *agreement of the governed and their ability to participate in creating and sustaining new and better institutions that meet the needs of people previously excluded.* In short, meaningful change requires mobilization of those at the grassroots.

How to address the acute problems of social well-being that affect such a large proportion of Brazilian society? And what responsibilities does this place on Brazilian universities and on the educated Brazilian subject? These are complex questions to which there are no easy answers. A vital first step is to generate hope in the next generation of educated professionals that it is indeed possible to change structures and practices. And this requires the capacity to imagine and put into practice an emancipatory politics of globalization.

"THE EMPIRE OF THE MARKET"

The neoliberal orthodoxy is to attribute Brazil's macroeconomic problems to the profligacy of past governments and the existence of a predatory federalism, which, it is argued, give provincial (subnational) governments an excessive amount of power and make it difficult for central governments to curb their spending (Samuels, 2003). It is instructive to trace the reception and mixed outcomes of the *Plano Real,* a macroeconomic blueprint aimed at political and fiscal recentralization by the Cardoso[15] government, which led the country from 1995 to 2002. The *Plano Real,* originally praised for its fiscal responsibility, was invested with gargantuan expectations. It was expected to rein in inflation, reduce government expenditure, impose fiscal discipline onto subnational (state) governments,[16] attract foreign investor confidence, and reduce Brazil's debt level. Its effects included an intensification of income inequality and increased poverty (Amann & Baer, 2002; Levine, 2003, pp. 141–145) and capital flight, resulting in the free fall of Brazil's exchange rate and further increases in its debt.

---

[15]Cardoso was a former academic and proponent of dependency theory.

[16]In 2000, the central government introduced the *Lei de Responsabilidade Fiscal* (Fiscal Responsibility Law), which set limits for subnational debt and prohibited central government from refinancing future subnational debt. The law also placed restrictions on state banks, which up to then had been under the influence of state governors (Samuels, 2003, pp. 553–557).

The *Plano Real* could not subvert the economic crisis, leading First World theorists to observe, "Brazil needs to overcome the perception that its institutions encourage economic inefficiency" (Samuels, 2003, p. 564). Yet, perception, confidence, and credibility in the financial markets do not depend on rational grounds or, indeed, empirical evidence (Flynn, 1999). The Asian financial crisis is a case in point. 'First World' Brazil watchers trotted out the usual culprits, attributing the lack of confidence by money markets to Brazil's "political weakness" and "the lack of party discipline" to rein in the governors and fractious domestic politics (see Levine, 2003, pp. 158–159). Although acknowledging the existence of these problems, financier George Soros and former World Bank economist and Nobel laureate Joseph Stiglitz both argue that the basis of many of Brazil's problems lie in market fundamentalism—the belief that markets work perfectly and do not require regulation or any kind of state intervention. Financial market liberalization, for example, enabled raids by speculative capital on a Brazil's currency, increasing its vulnerability (Stiglitz, 2002a, 2002b). In the 3 months leading up to the 2002 Brazilian election, nervous international capital markets worried about the prospect of a victory by a political party led by a former trade union official caused capital flight estimated at US$6 billion. The currency lost up to 41% of its value (Branford, 2003).

What is clear is that the 'First World' markets' discourse has generated an excessive pessimism toward Brazil, leading economists to call for more balanced appraisals that recognize Brazil's strengths and potentials:

> Brazil may be called an emerging market but it has first rate financial, educational and research institutions. In Sao Paulo, discussions about economics are as sophisticated as in New York. University seminars are as lively as those in Cambridge, Mass or Cambridge, England. Brazil produces one of the finest air planes in the world, so good that competitors in more industrial countries have tried to raise trade barriers against it. (Stiglitz, 2002a)

The 2002 election victory of the *Partido dos Trabalhadores* (PT)[17] signified a symbolic break from the stranglehold of the political elite who have dominated for much of Brazil's history. The PT faces tremendous challenges at both the domestic and international fronts. Its supporters are pushing for an activist state that will introduce the necessary reforms to alleviate the twin problems of poverty and disenfranchisement. An estimated 55 million

---

[17]Brazil's current president and leader of the ruling party, the PT, Luiz Inacio ("Lula") da Silva, is a former metalworker, trade unionist, and the child of sharecroppers. In the lead-up to the 2002 election, the prospect of a PT victory led financier Soros to observe that da Silva's victory would be read by speculative capital as an opportunity to raid the Brazilian currency, the Real. Soros observed, "In modern global capitalism, only Americans get to vote, Brazilians don't" (Soros, as quoted in Beck, 2002).

Brazilians live below the poverty line and it is estimated that some 15 to 20 million Brazilians do not get enough to eat. Zero Hunger, one of da Silva's programs, is intended to tackle poverty of this magnitude (Chagas, 2004). Another area which demands urgent intervention is agrarian reform to benefit landless peasants (da Silva, 2003; Munk, 2003; Stiglitz, 2003b).

Brazil's large foreign debt, estimated in 2002 to be US$250 billion and an IMF-imposed regime of austerity, present huge difficulties for the PT to meet the expectations of an electorate who are anxious for social change (Chagas, 2004; Steele, 2002).The challenge facing Brazil is that facing many heavily indebted, socially stratified countries—how to introduce the far-reaching reforms urgently required if it is held to ransom by 'big capital' (see Branford, 2003; da Silva, 2003; Steele, 2002; Wilkin, 2003) and how to surmount the unequal terms for trade liberalization ('free trade') offered by the United States and the European Union (see Stiglitz, 2003a, 2003b).

Brazil's case supports the growing body of empirical evidence suggesting that a globalization agenda driven by neoliberal economics creates the conditions for greater wealth polarization in-country and between nations. There is evidence that the United States and European Union have benefited more than developing countries from the trade liberalization agendas and that the social costs of liberalization have been borne by the poorest—both in the developed and the developing world (Stiglitz, 2002b, p. 6). The key pillars of the Washington Consensus—capital and trade liberalization—have not insulated obedient countries such as Brazil from economic meltdown. The corollary effects of greed and adventurism in global financial markets have been severe unemployment, high interest rates, inflation, and "large-scale distributions of fear and misery" (Lapham, 1998, p. 37). It is not the responsibility of investment bankers, hedge fund principals, and multinational executives to concern themselves with the "crying in a foreign wilderness" (p. 37). But it is the responsibility of democratically elected governments.

Brazil unsettles the thesis that capitalism is a bridge to democracy. As Wilkin (2003) observes so astutely, capitalism has derived its strength from the denial of democracy in the peripheries. The Brazilian colonial economy is an illustration of how capitalism coexisted with feudalism and labor systems such as slavery and debt peonage.

MAPPING THE EDUCATION TERRAIN

Discussions about educational provision, its financing, and accountability invariably impinge on theories of the state. Brazil's educational system has long been criticized for supporting the privilege of the country's economic and political elite at the expense of low-income, working-class, and middle-class families. Graduate university education, for example, receives more resources than elementary and secondary schooling; the large cities and the southeastern parts of the country have tended to receive the lion's share of funding[18] (Wong & Balestino, 2001, pp. 597–598).

The first Brazilian universities, which emerged in the 1930s, had a mandate to introduce a limited modernization agenda. Brazilian universities were subject to legal control by the central government and a system of lifetime chairs ensured that they remained in control of the country's elites (Figueirido-Cowen, 2002; Kempner, 1994). The rectors of the country's federal universities were selected by the president of the country, cementing further the close links between the university and politics of government. This mode of top-down governance, reproduced within the universities, saw them likened to "personal fiefdoms, guild-like authority and control by a rigid State bureaucracy" (Figueirido-Cowen, 2002, p. 473). Legal fiat also prescribed 'minimum curricula'—what had to be taught for particular degrees.

During periods of economic growth, the Brazilian state, like other states that operated on a Keynesian model, invested in education, although the highly stratified quality of Brazilian society meant that benefits stemming from educational expansion and diversification were not equally shared. Various authoritarian governments also used education systems to advance their agendas (see also Torres, 2002). Thus, the 1960s and 1970s witnessed an increase in regional and public universities together. A further expansion of higher education took place in the 1980s.

The first half of 1960s is noted as a period of radical change and innovation in Brazilian higher education. A series of radical projects such as Freire's literacy program advocated new expressions of mass education, Cardoso's work on dependency theory, and the initiatives introduced by Darcy Ribeiro in the federal University of Brasilia accompanied a wider push to consider how higher education might facilitate social change. Freire's educational philosophy, anchored in *conscientizacao*—the awareness of sociocultural realities and translation by cultural action for freedom (Torres, 2002)—challenged the bureaucratic authoritarianism of Brazilian

---

[18]Brazilian law requires the federal government to invest at least 18% of annual tax revenues on schools, and city councils and state governments are required to spend 25% or more on schools. Article 227 of the Brazilian Constitution outlines the "duty of society and the state to assure the child and adolescent as an absolute priority, the right to life, health, nutrition, education, leisure time, vocational training, culture, dignity, respect, liberty, and the fellowship of the community" (Moulin & Peirera, 2000, p. 50). However, legislative fiat has done little to contribute to a high-quality public education system, which is plagued by poor financial management, insufficient schools, and poorly paid teaching staff (Moulin & Peirera, 2000, p. 47; Wong & Balestino, 2001, p. 598).

society. Freire was expelled from Brazil for 20 years (Kempner, 1994), along with other reformers following the military coup in 1964. The military government introduced a series of laws aimed at increasing the state's administrative and political control over higher education (p. 477). Students and staff could be dismissed or expelled if they were thought to be involved in activities declared to be subversive (Decree Law 477 of 1969). At the same time, the technocratically inclined military government embarked on a process of modernizing universities, expanding their numbers, and increasing student places to enact various nation-building initiatives, a move that won them support with the new middle classes and the elite.[19] The 1960s also heralded closer links between Brazilian and American universities through a series of educational aid programs sponsored by the American aid agency, USAID.

Like its systems of schooling, the challenges facing Brazil's higher education system today are centered around equity (*equidad*), quality, and efficiency. There are three types of public universities in Brazil: federal, state, and municipal. Public universities do not charge fees to students and enjoy a good reputation. Entry into the federal universities is particularly fierce and is based on the results of an exam, the *Vestibular.* Those most likely to succeed in the *Vestibular* are students from elite private schools, many of whom attend cram schools designed to prepare them for this exam. The *Vestibulars* are only held in metropolitan areas, creating another barrier of access for the rural poor. The exam-based entry system has been criticized for barring the entry of entrants from lower socioeconomic groups (Almeida, 2001). Recent government policy has revoked the *Vestibular*'s mandatory status as a screening device for university entry, and the elite National University of Brasilia has introduced a policy of reserving 25% of places for candidates who will be assessed on the basis of other criteria.

There are also a large number of private universities; in 1998, there were 83 private universities (Schwartzman, 2002, p. 7). They range from high-quality institutions that are focused on both teaching and research to teaching-only, single-facility institutions, many of which offer night courses only. Single-facility institutions are largely staffed by part-time faculty, although changes are in train following the 1996 introduction of the National Education Law (*Lei de Diretrizes e Bases da Educacao Law 9, 394*). This law requires at least one third of faculty to be employed on a full-time basis and to hold advanced degrees (master's or Ph.D.), for an institution to use the title of university (pp. 8–9).

The institutionalization of the neoliberal state in Brazil, together with pressure from supranational organizations such as the IMF and World

---

[19]Between 1968 and 1974, at the height of repression by the military dictatorship, the number of students increased from 158,100 to 392,600.

Bank, is now steering the higher education sector toward reforms aimed at increasing quality and efficiency, which can be broadly interpreted as reducing the dependence of public universities on state funding (Torres, 2002). The issue of maintaining universities' efficiency and quality mirrors some of the debates taking place in countries such as ·Australia and the United Kingdom. The solutions that are being proposed to tackle these problems—greater decentralization, the articulation of standards, mechanisms of evaluation, and improvements in teaching (see Beech, 2002)—have been criticized for failing to adequately consider the specificities of Brazilian contexts and for their neoliberal ideology. Torres (2002) observes that "historically the World Bank has reflected the threat perceived by the US and the wishes of the American business community" (p. 376). An entire dispositif or assemblage featuring education institutions, policies, programs, reviews and reports, managers, consultants, benchmarks, and measurement grids promulgate market-friendly solutions. Under the aegis of a neutral instrumentality, the power–knowledge dimensions in these assemblages are obscured (Samoff, 1999; Torres, 2002). In terms of quality, though, it is notable that staff–student ratios were lower in Brazil (13.3) in 1999 than in Australia (18.8). Brazilian educators face the challenges of extending the discursive space of possibilities for radical reform (Beech, 2002). It is worth considering what kinds of subjects the reform platform should aspire to develop—for citizens and for entities such as the state, business, and industry.

Brazil has been described as a dual society, or 'two nations', and this is echoed geographically in the distribution of higher education institutions (see Kempner, 1994). Seventy-eight percent of Brazil's higher education institutions are located in the south and southeast regions of the country. The issue of equity also extends to race and socioeconomic status. Higher education participation remains the preserve of the elite and upper middle class. Sixty-six percent of university students are from the top income quintile (Schwartzman, 2002, p. 10) compared with a country like Spain, for example, where only one third are from the highest income families. Students from public schools have a lower success rate in obtaining university places, and Afro-Brazilian students are less likely to attend university compared with other groups. Equity quotas have recently been introduced by some universities, although these remain controversial[20] (Davies, 2003).

Brazil's civil society has pushed for the establishment of a number of progressive education initiatives. Various grassroots movements are attempting to introduce a new form of thinking about education and society. The Citi-

---

[20]The University of Brasilia has reserved 20% of its places for Black students, and the University of Rio de Janeiro has reserved 40% of its places. Both institutions have declared that 50% of their places will go to students from public schools.

zens' Schools in Sao Paulo and Porto Alegre provide impressive examples of the collaborative synergies from top down and bottom up, which have led to the development of a new model of education for citizenship. The divisions between "those who know and will educate, and those who don't know and need to be educated" is thus being broken down (Gandin & Apple, 2002, pp. 8–9). In these schools, local knowledge is no longer considered marginal and extraneous, but deployed to find alternatives to social problems. The broader goal of these programs is to produce deep and enduring forms of democracy that inverts both elitist and neoliberal logics that have dominated Brazilian education (Gandin & Apple, 2002). In this respect, these programs are informed by Freirean critical literacy—a literate citizen is understood as willing to participate in building and rebuilding society (Roberts, 1998). In terms of epistemologies, these programs seek to unsettle what counts as core and peripheral knowledges. They seek to form links between people's lived realities and knowledge practices that are capable of translating utopian visions into actions. They place "those who live the problems in a privileged position to construct alternatives" (Roberts, 1998).

BRAZILIAN INTERNATIONALIZATION AND "ANGLO-GLOBALIZATION"

For the Brazilian elite, access to an international education may start in one of the many international schools located in major cities such as the British International School or the American School. These fee-paying schools are out of the reach of ordinary Brazilians, Their non-Brazilian dimensions are promoted and used as marketing tools. For example, several schools promote their North American staff ("70% Norte Americanos"). For the greater part, internationalization in the Brazilian context is driven by individuals traveling overseas to study either by private means or through scholarships funded by the Brazilian state or aid programs funded jointly by the Brazilian and various donor governments and international agencies. State-funded scholarship schemes are intended to contribute to national development by increasing Brazilian expertise in areas of strategic importance. In the past, these included areas such as biotechnology, chemistry, and computer science.[21]

Like other countries deemed to be outside of the key Euro-American knowledge nodes, the Brazilian academy faces the dual challenge of doing research deemed credible by international networks and retaining a focus on local problems. Greater academic reward for internationally oriented

---

[21]Brazil's economic problems and high unemployment rate contributed to a brain drain, deterring some recipients from returning home.

research; the hegemony of Western, scientific culture; a residual colonialism; and the elite nature of their society mean that researchers have largely been discouraged from exploring how local cultural knowledges can contribute to transformative and emancipatory epistemologies (Kempner, 1994). This is not a problem unique to Brazil, and some in the Brazilian academy have been more successful in attaining this balance than others.

The United States is the most favored destination for Brazilians choosing to study overseas. In 2003–2004, there were 7,799 Brazilians studying in the United States. The majority (54.4%) were studying at undergraduate level (IIE, 2004). The United Kingdom and Canada are also favored study destinations, and a growing number are now choosing New Zealand. As a lower cost destination than either the United Kingdom or the United States, Australia's share of the Brazilian market tends to increase slightly during times of economic difficulty, as it did in 2002–2003 (Education Travel, 2003). Most of the Brazilians studying in Australia are undertaking English language courses. They numbered 1,067 in 2002–2003. The number of students undertaking full degree programs remains small (less than 100 in 2002–2003). A small number are also enrolled in high schools (approximately 300). Brazil is regarded as a market that holds promise, hence, its status as a 'priority market'.

To be profitable, international education markets must create and maintain connections between the 'First Worlds' of the planet. It is advice that is heeded by university marketing personnel as these comments suggest:

> We deal with the private universities because they have the money to travel . . . in Latin America, the opinion is that public universities don't have the money. . . . What they are interested in is 1:1 swops [but] . . . our students wouldn't want to go. . . . It's [because] [Latin American public universities] are [not] well resourced and also whether they teach in English. (marketing officer, male, major Australian university)

Marketing discourse glides smoothly over facts that might suggest the eliteness of international education and its hegemonizing impulses to present a pragmatic approach. Thus, after making the bland observation that "Brazil is a continental country, and one of many contrasts" (Austrade, 2000), the following advice is dispensed by the Australian government to institutions seeking to recruit Brazilian students:

> The cities of the south and the south-eastern states have more people who are likely to study abroad. . . . Three per cent to five per cent of Brazilians have the financial resources, the tradition and the desire to study abroad, which means that there is a potential market of over five million people. (Austrade, 2004)

Australian education is marketed in Brazil by IDP in conjunction with a string of private agents. The primary marketing message that underpins IDP's selling strategy is to represent Australia as a cheaper destination than both the United States and the United Kingdom, but one that also offers access to quality by way of an internationally recognized qualification (IDP Brazil, 2004). The tourism discourse is present but does not dominate the marketing message. The presence of the quintessential Australian icon, the Sydney Opera House, on IDP Brazil's home page sets the scene for vivid descriptions of the climate, breathtaking scenery, and recreation and entertainment facilities (Fig. 8.1). But a concerted discursive effort is invested in trying to reposition Australia as an intellectually serious study destination, perhaps in response to criticisms that Australian higher education has been represented and constituted as "a global polytechnic" (Marginson, 2004, pp. 232–234).

The drive to represent Australian scholarship in more serious terms sees a substantial part of the marketing message being directed toward Brazilian graduate students. A detailed exposition on Australia's world class research facilities and the numerous opportunities available for high-tech, knowledge-economy-type research, follows:

> Imagine yourself doing research in information techonology, biotechnology, robotics and sustainability. . . . Australia has facilities such as the Centre of Excellence in Information and Communication Technology, and a recently opened Australian Technology Park, backed by Commonwealth government investment of AU$129.5 million for five years. (IDP Brazil, 2004)

The marketing narratives offer the promise of a series of 'First World' to 'First World' interactions. The subject of discourse is the ambitious Brazilian professional, and Australian business education is depicted as offering the linguistic and cultural capital to mold Brazilians to work in an English-speaking global economy. The dominant global imaginary is of an integrated economy that is led by English-speaking professionals. An Australian education is a passport to a global career:

> Doing a management course in another country will equip you with the international experience necessary for a good position in medium and large size businesses. . . . In order to operate in the international market . . . business will require professionals with international expertise. . . . An understanding of foreign business and skills to negotiate with other cultures is very important. We have courses to help you to improve your understanding of business in emerging markets. (IDP Brazil, 2004)

The aspiring Brazilian business professional is lured by the promise of studying in a country that is a dynamic node in a globally dispersed business

FIG. 8.1. IDP Brazil.

network that spans the United States, Asia, and the Pacific region. Its unique geography positions Australia as a gateway, a springboard to emerging markets, and its "strong historical ties with Western culture" offer a comforting familiarity. Accompanying pronouncements about Australia's commitment to free trade suggest that the intended recipient of the marketing message is an individual whose aspirations are unconstrained by geography but who, nonetheless, seeks the comfort of a shared history and connectedness with a Western culture.

The strongly instrumental promotional narrative is reinforced by the paucity of images of people on the Web site, suggesting that people are incidental and subject to a world of emerging markets, multinational businesses, technology parks, corporate structures, and e-commerce courses. The strongly First World flavor of the marketing message is reinforced by the notable absence of persons of an Afro-Brazilian appearance on IDP's Web site. Cultural diversity is relevant only insofar as it contributes to successful business practices, as captured by this testimonial from a Brazilian graduate of an Australian university:

> My experience in Australia as an Accounting student made me capable of relating with other cultures to broaden my view of international business practices. . . . I believe this experience will position me favourably for a career in a global enterprise. (IDP Brazil)

The British Council has also flagged Brazil to be a priority market for its recruitment activities. It deploys a language of 'partnership' to soften both its commercial aspirations and the national desire to spread the use of the "imperial" language—English (see Fig. 8.2). There is a tactful use of phenotypically diverse persons, some fair and others of notable African appearance, in its Web sites and promotional materials. A considerable part of its marketing effort is concentrated on promoting myriad possibilities for educational, scientific, and cultural debates between the United Kingdom and Brazil. Thus,

> the British Council works in partnership with the Brazilian government and civil society to promote debate, and stimulate the development of knowledge in such areas as: human rights, justice, social inclusion and gender issues. (British Council Brazil, 2004)

The UK emerges as a good global citizen, concerned with offering its expertise to promote social reform. However, the messy complexities and ambiguities surrounding the lived power relations on the ground render these efforts cosmetic, and tantamount to tinkering at the edges while maintaining an economically and ecologically flawed status quo. For example, the deforestation of the Amazon for cattle grazing has escalated in response to

FIG. 8.2. Bringing English to Brazil.

demand for Brazilian beef from the United Kingdom and Europe in light of the mad cow disease (Vidal, 2004).

The British Council's brief in Brazil is also to "creat[e] opportunities for future generations of Brazilians to contribute to an international community." Strengthening English-language teaching is a means to this end. Encapsulated under this project is a variety of such activities aimed at developing English teaching material for Brazilian educators and initiatives intended to promote the teaching of science in English. All of these materials are designed to nest with the objectives of Brazilian national curriculum initiatives. By implication, English holds out the promise of engagement with the international scientific community, progress, and modernity.

What is clear from both the Australian and British marketing materials is the increasing role played by international education in consolidating the hegemony of English. From the perspective of the individual, learning English offers the opportunity for professional, cultural, and economic advantages. English-language 'technologies of the self' take on a different guise once they are delinked from the level of individual aspiration and considered at the macro level. In a globalizing world that purports to offer a stunning profusion of possibilities, how can it be that one language is gaining dominance? If learning English is pivotal to contributing to an international community, what does this tell us about its use as a technology of government? Should governing structures and governors be English speaking? Edge (2004) presses us to consider creative ways to dissociate English teaching and learning from the 21st-century neoimperial project given the strong links between English and empire building.[22] Edge acknowledges the power structures in place that reward the learning and teaching of English, but poses a challenge to educators to teach against this dominance, by paying careful attention to methods used in classroom and to the worldviews that are constructed by teaching materials. English, he argues, can thus be transformed from inducing compliance to 'the way things are' to being used as a language of protest.

FIRST WORLD CONVERSATIONS

How do Brazilians perceive the experience of studying overseas? The following personal narratives are instructive of what drives the desire to have an English-language university education. For some, it is the desire for a 'superior' credential that has currency in the global labor market, whereas for

---

[22]Here, Edge (2004) makes reference to the British Council's role in supporting the teaching of "peacekeeping English" to enable the "interoperability" among military and security forces in Eastern Europe.

others a curiosity and accompanying desire to explore a "fascinating" culture work as motivating factors.

> I decided to study overseas in order to get exposed to the American education system, methodology, and content, which is considered to be superior to the one offered in my country. . . . I got a Masters in Business Administration (MBA) degree from Boston College (1997) and I am currently in the process of getting a Doctorate in Business Administration (DBA) degree from Boston University. The decision to join these universities is primarily related to the high-qualification of their professors in the field of interest—Organizational Economics and Strategy. (male, completed MBA)

> US has always been a country that fascinates me. Maybe it is because the American way of life is advertised all around the world, including Brazil. (male, on a school exchange program)

The issue of how individuals' identities might change through the experience of studying overseas does not suggest a passive absorption of attributes and beliefs from the host culture, but for some, it offers an opportunity to reexamine previous identifications:

> I cannot say I feel less Brazilian now that I spent a year living in Australia, three months living in Italy or two years living in the USA. I can say, though, that my way of looking at things has changed a lot. . . . I feel I have a mind that is much more open than it was when I went to Australia and I think that happens because I have seen things from another angle. (male, studied and worked in Australia)

> No, it [identity] did not [change]. No, not a bit. Because, I have learned that each country has its own problems. We have ours and they have theirs. Even though US is the richest country in the world, there are still many problems, for example, quality of life. (male, went on exchange to United States)

> Unfortunately, I guess I am feeling less Brazilian, with less identification with local habits and feelings. But at the same time, I have come to the conclusion that to be Brazilian is a social construction, in the sense that there is not just one way to be Brazilian. In my opinion, to be Brazilian is to be loyal to the sovereignty of the Brazilian nation and people, regardless of the current culture. What it is considered to be Brazilian today will certainly be different 10–20 years from now. (male, MBA graduate from U.S. university)

So, in these quite different responses, the experience of studying overseas is commonly perceived to unsettle assumptions and to open up new ways of thinking. But elsewhere there are suggestions that for this group of individuals, who are positioned in the upper echelons of social class in

Brazil, globalization is about unconstrained mobility, connections, and synergies, 'where everyone has something to offer'; it is about 'a single integrated market' and the opportunities it offers a transnational class of professionals:

> Globalisation is the process of inter-connection among different entities (governments, countries, economies, etc) around the world. In short, it is the feeling that the world is becoming smaller. (male, former exchange student in the United States)

> Globalization could be understood as the breaking of a country's borders, the mixing up of different cultures and experiences in a world where everyone has something to offer and many things to learn. (male, with Australian experience)

> It is the creation and development of supra-national institutions and regulations to coordinate/regulate the allocation of resources (material, financial, and human) across national borders, as if the world was just one integrated market. (male, MBA graduate)

In their commonsense understanding of globalization, the interviewees' accounts seem to suggest that asymmetries, boundaries, and hierarchies are a thing of the past. Opportunities are deterritorialized and individual success is just as possible in another geographical and cultural space. What is striking about this globalized world featuring an integrated market and interconnections among governments, countries, and economies is the invisibility of power relations. The discursive invisibility of power relations also emerges in the interviewees' perceptions of what constitutes an international education and an international university. Understandings of what makes an international university and international education are largely framed by a liberal concept of multiculturalism, although there are hints about the need for reciprocal exchanges of ideas:

> In my point of view, international education is the kind of education that makes possible for a student to know life and culture overseas, in a country where another language is spoken and where it is possible to have an exchange of ideas and experiences. (male, with experience living in Australia)

> Boston University can be considered an International University because 40% of its students and faculty are originally from places outside the US. . . . An [international] education . . . takes into consideration the natural differences between cultures and regions, the different needs of individuals with diverse background, contributing to students' and professors' capacity to think and work on a global and intercultural basis. (MBA graduate)

THE PROSPECTS FOR A GLOBALIZATION-
FROM-BELOW

That international education is initiating dialogue among the First Worlds
is clear from the discussion so far. For the three Anglo-American producers, Australia, the UK, and the U.S., recruiting students from a very specific
social stratum in Brazil fits with their political and economic interests. The
analysis of education marketing narratives indicates that the 'selling idea'
that underpins the Anglo-American educational product is the offer of linguistic and cultural capital to enable Brazilians to work in an English-
speaking global economy. How appropriate and adequate is such a vision
given the significant challenges facing Brazil?

To contribute to an emancipatory politics of globalization, international
education must create the discursive space and foundation for an alternative pedagogy, and one that liberates the imagination so that upcoming
generations of professionals and bureaucrats will find hope, heart, commitment, and habitus to engage with the disjunctures of living that cause acute
problems of social well-being. Writing about the role of the imagination in
social life, Appadurai (2001) observes:

> The imagination is no longer a matter of individual genius, escapism from or-
> dinary life, or just a dimension of aesthetics. It is a faculty that informs the
> daily lives of ordinary people in myriad ways. It allows people . . . to resist state
> violence, consider social redress, and design new forms of civic association
> and collaboration across national boundaries. (p. 6)

The liberal logic that has so dominated political and intellectual thinking for the past two decades rested on the argument that a 'Democratic
Revolution' delivered freedom, prosperity, and peace. The claims are that
the best idea, market liberalism, won out in the end. The history of Brazil
suggests otherwise. Neoliberal policies have not reduced poverty in Brazil
(Amman & Baer, 2002). Market liberalism's construction as rational choice
obscures its neocolonial underpinnings (see Samoff, 1999; Torres, 2002).
At this historical moment, when a democratically elected government is
hoping to develop a new role for the state—tackling poverty and social inequality—it is unable to do so to the best of its abilities because of the threat
of 'discipline' at the hands of the fundamentalist market.

Brazil's future rests on galvanizing the forces and processes that define
globalization from below, that is, a grassroots globalization that engages
with visions, strategies, and practices for those at the bottom of the social
and economic hierarchy. In more respects than one, globalization from below involves putting the Freirean notion of critical literacy to work. Unlike
neoliberal globalization with its individualizing ethos, grassroots globaliza-

tion holds out the promise of improving social and gender equity, and protecting cultural and ecological diversity. For deeply stratified countries, such as Brazil, globalization from below provides the basis for the disenfranchised to bypass traditional institutions that have historically been skewed toward protecting the interests of the elite.

International education can create the discursive space for such engagements by enabling a social imagination for a different, more equitable world and by sponsoring dialogue across borders, for example, by facilitating transnational advocacy networks instead of transnational commercial networks. Crucially, this demands an alternative global imaginary from that of the integrated single global market.

Chapter 9

"To Market, to Market"

OVERVIEW OF FINDINGS

This book puts forward an alternative perspective of international education. Rather than viewing international education as a global trade in education, characterized by unproblematic flows of people, ideas, capital, and technology, and governed by simple supply-and-demand dynamics, this study seeks to map how international education is assembled and ordered by states, markets, institutions, and people under conditions of globalization. The study explores the types of subjectivities arising from, and informing, international education; the types of truths generated about international students and international education; the power–knowledge relations that inform these truths; and the practices that inform the governing of education markets—nationally and globally.

Each chapter identifies and examines various influential idioms that have shaped power relations in the field of international education: the residual and resurgent powers of colonial, neocolonial, and neoimperial persuasions; the power relations that surround the postcolonial desire for an English-speaking education; and the discursive power wielded by globalization. As cultural studies theorists observe, texts such as policies, academic research papers, media items, political speeches, and promotional narratives constitute a rich archive; they are not merely freestanding objects but components of larger cultural formations. They shape and inform commonsense understandings of, and about, international students and international education. All of these discursive frameworks—policy, media reports, academic writings, and marketing narratives—are connected with governance; they have power effects and are linked to aspirations to shape the conduct of others.

A Foucauldian sensibility is necessarily cautious about totalizing pronouncements. The emphasis of this study is to capture and link up micro-level practices with the broader context at the same time as describing continuities, discontinuities, and contingencies. That stated, a number of themes have emerged, suggesting the importance of geopolitical and geoeconomic rationalities in shaping how international education is imagined, understood, and enacted in policies and practices. Both of these rationalities are framed by a discourse of competitive advantage in the global economy. The desirability to be a participant in the global economy is not restricted to nation-states; it also encompasses the student-graduate who must compete for work in a globalized labor market.

In Australia and the United Kingdom, competitive advantage takes the form of earning export income through international education; the student is regarded as an object of trade. This emphasis is less pronounced in the United States where the international student is perceived as valued human capital with the potential to contribute to the American enterprise in the 'global talent race' and as an ally who will uphold America's interests overseas. The primary political rationality informing international education in America is the national desire to maintain its role as a world leader, politically and economically. This rationality is based on the foundational premise of Manifest Destiny, the United States' drive to bring the world the 'American way'—capitalism and democracy, liberty, the pursuit of happiness, and an American version of peace and prosperity. Complementing manifest destiny is the American economic frontier thesis, which is premised on the global imaginary as an integrated market under the management and influence of U.S.-driven rules and norms (Klein, 2003). The territorial imperialism that marked European colonization efforts has been muted in the case of the United States.[1] A more nuanced governmentality is at work that aims to harness the desires and aspirations of individuals to better themselves, to recraft their identities to be competitive, productive, and efficient individuals. Some analysts have dubbed this *soft power*, creating desires and aspirations through the use of cultural symbols and institutions that complement American interests.[2] Hardt and Negri (2002), on the other hand, have appropriated the term *empire* to describe a deterritorialized and decentered apparatus of rule that encompasses culture, economics, civil society, politics, and subjectivity.

---

[1] It could be argued that the war against terror has seen a new governmentality at work where "reason of state" rationalities are used to justify oppressive measures. Although it is accurate to state that some international students in the United States have been exposed to excessive state-sponsored surveillance, as a general rule, the form of governance has been more subtle and involved steering the soul toward the American dream.

[2] Soft power has been attributed to the work of Joseph Nye.

Whatever term is used, whatever concepts are in vogue, it is apparent that old geometries of power have not been redrawn. American expressions of international education suggest the resilience of an earlier Cold War discourse intended to win minds. The role of American universities in supporting the national agenda, whether in minor ways, through the development of Area Studies programs, or through more ambitious programs such as establishing a global standard for university–industry collaborations through the institutionalization of MBA programs, has been largely understated and underexamined. The American Constitution might prohibit the state from direct involvement in higher education, but state intervention is well established. The most exaggerated expressions of the national agenda take the form of American exceptionalism and triumphalism. These are so thoroughly embedded in state and nonstate institutions, and embodied in technologies of the self as not to require overt state intervention (Klein, 2003).

Postcolonial theorists argue that international education continues to be part of an elaborate intellectual machinery to justify and support the neoliberal, neocolonial, and imperializing expressions of globalization. In analyzing how the 21st-century international university understands self–other relations, a host of broad similarities is discernible across all universities. As a general rule, promotional narratives tend to highlight the 'First World' university's history of educating the other. These narratives do not foster a vision for reciprocity in learning across cultures, and by default then, they continue to reinforce insider–outsider subject positions. With one or two exceptions, where traces of crudely ethnocentric and neocolonial discourses are present, promotional discourses are largely expressed in a subtly imperializing tenor. The basis of resisting imperializing self–other relations requires identifying the governing discourses that are put to use by the various social authorities, the types of subjectivities they normalize, and the steering technologies they inspire in individuals.

The use of cultural hybridity as a governing discourse and marketing tool assures prospective students and their parents that the university, city, or country being marketed is safe, free of racism, open, and accepting of their difference. This safe multicultural imaginary is anchored in banal expressions of hybridity such as descriptions of an international student body, an immigrant diaspora, and the easy availability of ethnic cuisine and access to places of worship. I return to a fuller discussion of hybridity as a governing discourse later in this chapter.

Neocolonial impulses clearly predate the marketized era of international education, although their continued presence must cast doubts on notions of market accountability as an enforcer of quality. Neocolonial idioms are not restricted to the countries of the West and North, as the case of Singapore shows. The city-state's desire to acquire the 'American mindset' and the disciplinary regime it imposes on its unskilled guest workers suggest a reinsertion of the neocolonial imaginary into this postcolonial nation-state. In Brazil, the traditional discourse of a racial democracy serves to airbrush the combined effects of race and class on social disadvantage. Self–other relations on a geopolitical scale have historically positioned Brazil's political economy as other to various colonial and neocolonial economic powers. The explosion of interest by ambitious Brazilians for an English-speaking university education must be read with this in mind.

It seems that territorially based conceptions of self and other remain firmly in place despite the compression of space made possible by high technology and the talk of extraterritoriality in globalization narratives. The reasons for this are complex and require further study. However, I offer a provisional observation. First, the reterritorialization trends within nation-states and the persistence of nationalist discourses such as American exceptionalism must be considered. In this context, globalization's use as a governing discourse confers a sense of urgency about enhancing national competitiveness. Globalization discourse is framed in a language of competitive combat, where the adversary is positioned as the dangerously hypercompetitive foreign other.

Second, both international and domestic students deploy othering practices to build social cohesion among in-group members. Certainly, for some international students, the experience of being positioned as the marginal other has the potential to reignite an identification with the nation and ethnocultural nationalism, suggesting that international student subjectivities may be reterritorialized as a result of studying overseas. I argue that this is more likely if students are from a dominant or majority ethnocultural group in their home country than if they are from a minority group. Acton's observation that "exile is the nursery of nationality" may still have a resonance even if the form of exile afforded by studying overseas is voluntary, temporary, and increasingly punctuated by visits to one's home country (Acton, as quoted by Scholte, 1996, p. 42).

Along with similarities, there are national and institutional differences in the ways in which international education is marketed. The Australian and British approach to marketing international education is characterized by deliberate state steering. The state plays a significant role in formulating and promoting country-specific brands through instrumentalities like the ECS, and its parent institution, the British Council and Australian Education International, a division of the Department of Education, Science, and Training. A less overt role is played by the U.S. government, but this is not to suggest that American higher education does not promote the national agenda. Rather, an elaborate network of legislation and policy and the dispersion of market actors and American-centric knowledges have intensified the capacity of American universities to engage in academic capitalism at a global level.

In-country differences in promotional strategies exist largely between the older and more elite institutions and the younger and nonelite universities. Some newer institutions report using educational exhibitions and private agents to recruit students, whereas a rich and elite institution such as Stanford University prefers using its corporate and alumni network to recruit a highly selective clientele. The intellectually elite but cash-strapped LSE distances itself from the spectacle of education exhibitions but undertakes recruitment drives, or 'roadshows'. Promotional brochures from the newer universities are more colorful, suggesting a hard-sell approach, whereas the older, more elite institutions prefer an understated look.

Small differences are also evident in what institutions chose to showcase as their strengths. The promotional materials used in international recruitment drives in all three producer countries incorporate roughly similar themes. These include publicizing their faculty who are leading authorities in their fields and winners of prestigious awards and prizes, promising access to cutting-edge technology, celebrating histories as established intellectual centers, and highlighting graduate employability, alumni links, and so forth.

Nation-states are implicated in the cultural, political, and symbolic economies of education markets. Again, this is not to suggest an all-encompassing state apparatus, manufacturing a homogenous brand of international education. As the study shows, tensions and contradictions surround the discursive constructions of international education in all producer countries. The operations of power and knowledge employ and generate different sets of symbols in the United Kingdom, the United States, and Australia. A uniform understanding of the market is clearly not possible given the different sociopolitical and cultural situations, relations, and forces in each of the countries examined. However, it can be said that the nation-state plays a part in facilitating its universities' engagement with the business dimensions of education in all three sites—the United Kingdom, the United States, and Australia.

QUESTIONS OF AGENCY

A Foucauldian analytic rests on the active subject, namely, the notion that individuals are not ideologically interpellated but retain the capacity to resist, recode, transgress, or use the available discursive resources toward more productive ends. This raises the issue of agency in regard to how marketized and othering discourses are internalized by university staff and students. The argument can be made that universities and individual scholars retain the means to engage in reflexive practices, which challenge the neoliberal and neocolonial impulses within international education. To this end, this study can be faulted for failing to convey in more detail the productive possibilities that surround the active transgressive subject.

The study's primary concern, though, is to examine the dominant ways of assembling international education, the types of social relations and subjectivities that inform these assemblages, and the types of subject positions that are privileged. It maps the territory of international education consumption in Brazil and Singapore to introduce greater complexity to the largely ahistorical, disembodied, supply-and-demand dynamic. It does not seek to map out the incidence of resistance and reflexivity on the parts of the various social actors in the field of international education.

Further empirical research, perhaps using an ethnographic approach that follows the various actors and maps their day-to-day practices, is potentially helpful to investigate the subtle resistances, reflexivities, appropriations, and subversions of various social actors. For now, I return to the point made in chapter 2 about Foucault's work on the government of men and women through truth. An entire arsenal of truths has been generated by the machinery of public relations, marketing, and government that endorses the naturalness of education markets, the inevitability of globalization, and the 'rightness' of Western epistemologies. The steering mechanisms and technologies of the self that produce rewarded acculturation, by crafting market-attractive subjectivities, shapes the 'conduct of conduct' and limit the exercises of sovereignty by individuals. Furthermore, the absence of free-discourse communities and limited civic freedoms in sites such as Singapore and Brazil are additional factors that must be considered in any discussions of agency by individual social actors.

TO MARKET, TO MARKET . . .

Contrary to the liberal ideal, markets are not discrete entities separate from the workings of states. States are heavily implicated in markets through practices including "subsidised tuition, state-protected monopolies, state guarantees against bankruptcies and so on" (Marginson, 2003a, p. 3). Geopolitical factors also shape the operations of the global education market. Thus, American universities rate highly in the league tables, in part because they are located in a nation that is a military and economic global power (Marginson, 2003a). In the same vein, the English-speaking American Ivy League and, to a lesser extent, the Oxbridge universities, are better positioned to compete in the global sphere than Todai (Tokyo University) and QUT. Universities' individual histories also shape their engagements with, and treatment by, the market. Institutions such as Stanford and MIT have long histories of engagement with American industry and commerce and are far better positioned to engage with the national and global education market than universities in the Rocky Mountain states.

Having acknowledged the cultural and national particularities of education markets, some generalizations, nevertheless, can be made. The international education market cannot be divorced from the nation-states' desires for competitive advantage in the global economy. It is these power relations as they are worked out on the scales of nation-states and universities that privilege particular expressions of the international education and particular subjectivities for faculty:

> Markets do not directly reduce professional autonomy, in the manner that, say aristocracy or dictatorship eliminates the possibility of professionalism. Rather, the problem is that in markets, educational professionalism is redundant. The more important goals are profitability, economic efficiency and market share. (Marginson, 2003a, pp. 3–4)

Conceived in this way, there is a tendency to see faculty and university staff in general as being at the receiving end of broader structures and strictures, as victims of the vicissitudes of the narrow, marketized logics. Indeed, the intellectual work in many universities today is increasingly framed by a market logic evident in practices such as competition, ceaseless innovation, and accumulating surplus (Marginson, 2003a; see also Massey, 2002). Nesting within this logic, are just-in-time, flexible practices that are curiously resonant with the practices of fast capitalism. As Thrift (1999) notes so evocatively in his discussions of the complicity between the business world and intellectual communities, "there is no theory that cannot be made complicit" (p. 60).

The faculty subjectivities normalized by the market—as entrepreneur and education service provider—"imply loyalty not to institution, [nor to discipline], not to innovation but to marketable product" (Marginson, 2003a, p. 4). Much has been written about how education markets steer academics toward business technologies of the self, a topic that I discuss shortly. Clearly, the social structures and academic practices within universities contribute to, and reflect, the wider relations of power nationally and globally. That stated, faculty also contribute to the conditions of fragmentation and short-term-ism that surrounds their intellectual work (see Roberts, 2000).

The academic mission is now imbricated by the dual tyrannies of immediacy and newness (Massey, 2002; Roberts, 2000). What counts as success is performance, efficiency, speed, and quantity, disguised as quality. Few researchers manage to avoid the anxiety imposed by the imperatives of time and speed. This means hurrying to finish—a project, an academic paper, a thesis, or a book—*before* the caravan of ideas moves on to the next new, exciting topic. Although it is a good thing for knowledge to be challenged, renewed, and transformed, as a reflecting of and driving toward societal changes, the obsession to locate something new for the sake of newness does little for the academic mission. In British and Australian universities, annual accounting exercises such as the RAE do not only quantify the outputs of individuals and departments, they also calibrate professional worth. Most important, they shape the way research is planned and conducted with consequences for the types of knowledges that are being produced. Faculty are exhorted to be flexible, and many respond accordingly, by embodying particular expressions of flexibility within their teaching and research. Ultimately, the result of flexibilization is an academic mission that is fixed into a temporal horizon that is short term (see Fraser, 2003, p. 169, for a critique of flexibilization). *Short term* means a stress on outputs ahead of processes. It privileges instrumentality and in its worst manifestations creates a value-for-money approach instead of deep, reflexive engagement with the academic mission for the 21st century (Massey, 2002). In this context, it is easier to lapse into thinking of responsibility to rules, rule makers, and rule guardians ahead of responsibility for the well-being and dignity of the other (Bauman, as cited in Tester, 2001, p. 58). The world of ideas thrives on originality and freshness and ceaseless innovation. But without moral responsibility, there is an acute danger that new knowledges and new technologies will be used to get rid of, reform, or destroy particular values, particularly by those others who don't fit into the schema of the global market.

When I commenced the research that forms the basis of this book, globalization was all the rage in my school. The 'globalization story' was based on a declared wisdom that globalization was successfully rewriting social, geoeconomic, and geopolitical relations. Not quite the 'end of geography', but we were fast approaching this state of affairs. Globalization was hailed as a new paradigm, a new theory that made redundant totalizing 'old' ways of thinking. It brought a randomness, unpredictability, and contingency to social processes. The 'old hands' in the school who insisted on talking the 'old talk' of global poverty, class, dependency, and underdevelopment in the non-Western world were brushed off as outdated.

My school proudly declared itself international. We were, after all, part of a university whose marketing message declared us as 'international' and 'world class'. Officially, there were references to the multinationality of the student body, the school's ability to 'win' consultancy grants from international bodies, and its commitment to diversity. But at the same time, geographies of difference asserted themselves on a daily basis. Although the greater proportion of the international student body in the school were from regions of Asia and the Pacific, we established student exchange arrangements with First World, English-speaking universities. We tailored special courses for American study abroad students as a means to raise revenue.

The other international students were greeted with a flourishing rhetoric on arriving in the school but then relegated to the bowels of the school's buildings, where they struggled with the demands of producing a thesis in their second, third, or even fourth language. With a few exceptions among the more committed cosmopolitans among the school's teaching staff, the teaching and personal support that international students required was not forthcoming. Among graduate (postgraduate) students, research collaborations with international students were the exception rather than the rule. There was certainly no malice extended to them, just our own busy schedules and among the more ethnocentric, a benign lack of interest in plodding through their fractured verbal and written prose.

The pressing and deeply political complexities and ambiguities surrounding the practices of international education unfolded before our eyes. The long-term cultural and social consequences of unidirectional flows of non-Western students to Western universities, the equity of foreign students having to pay inflated fees compared with the rest of us, the selling of watered-down masters courses (in reality, undergraduate courses that were simply renumbered and given Masters level codes), the struggles that individual students faced when confronted by vastly different linguistic and intellectual traditions—all of these issues rose in our minds, occasionally causing a nagging discomfort. For most of the time, though, we pushed them further into the unexamined recesses of our thoughts. Our international peers did not offer personal stories and we did not ask. We continued working on various dimensions of globalization research, treating it as an exogenous event, something 'out there' that was to be abstracted and dissected theoretically. We did not see ourselves as active agents in the globalization of education.

BUSINESS TECHNOLOGIES OF THE SELF

One of the significant contributions made by scholars and theorists working from a poststructuralist position is to alert us to the productive and contingent dimensions that accompany all relations of power. Their work reminds us that we have at our disposal the ability to engage in 'practices of freedom'. We can acquire different subjectivities from those implied by the neocolonial and neoliberal persuasions of the global education market.

The market offers productive possibilities to meet individual ambitions and aspirations, but it remains an uneven terrain, underpinned by material and discursive relations that embrace gender, class, nationality, geography and disciplinary field, and geography evident in one's nationality, country of location, and training. Trophy professors and 'chainsaw' Vice-Chancellors and Presidents, for example are well served by the market. They may have once strutted the national stage but are now actors in a multinational academic enterprise. The aphrodisiac brew of prestige, high-status jobs, and money that arises from commanding large research grants and authoring multiple publications spurs faculty and executive managers to assume particular technologies of self that are inevitably centered around self-interest and competitive individualism. Such technologies are identifiable as 'business technologies of the self' (Thrift, 1998).

For faculty, the term *business technologies of the self* translates as modeling and crafting oneself to be competitive and networked, both nationally and internationally. It means adopting a postbureaucratic persona, a preparedness to jettison processes and procedures even if these compromise transparency and accountability, so long as market-relevant outputs can be furthered. It means being energetically confident and single-minded but giving the appearance of being consultative and democratic. It means taking on the role of a cultural diplomat, talking about 'special relationships' and 'partnerships' while carefully sorting and weaving the 'right' mix of cultural difference to give the appearance of openness to all cultures and classes, men and women.

In this context, the academic mission to educate is occluded by an evangelical push by university managers to find and develop new products: fast-track degree programs, new masters courses diluted for market value, and online flexible learning courses marketed as allowing the student freedom to work, study, and spend time with family. Taken collectively, these practices implicitly further neoliberal notions of personhood:

> For all the commitment to an open-ended view of subjecthood, in practice, the conception of the person (and the model of action) that is presumed *is more often than not, a narrow one that involves the superexploitation* [italics added] both of managers (who are expected to commit their whole being to the organisation) and workers (who are now expected to commit their embodied knowledge to the organisation's epistemological resources). In other words, the net effect may be to reduce the different conceptions and comportments of the person . . . and to transfer these reduced conceptions and comportments to other spheres of life. (Thrift, 1998, p. 60)

INVESTING LEVIATHAN WITH A MULTICULTURAL FACE

The use of globalization as a legitimating metaphor to justify policies and practices of nation-states and educational institutions despite being poorly theorized and analyzed is now well noted.[3] Chapter 2 discusses an alternative approach to globalization—taking it as a governmentality and a way of knowing—to disrupt its naturalness, its inevitability, and unsettle assumptions of its position as the next phase of human development.

A significant regime of truth to emerge from within the voluminous writings on globalization, and one that has been heavily used in mapping the

---

[3]See Marginson and Rhoades (2002) and Deem (2001) for a critique of how globalization processes have been studied in higher education; Dicken (2004) and Hay and Smith (2005) on the use of globalization discourse to govern political and economic spheres.

benefits of international education markets, is the notion of hybridity and hybridization. Along with the theoretical prominence given to 'flows' (another discursive trope of significant popularity), writings on hybridity have been reworked to create notions of reciprocity and equality across territorial and cultural spaces. The language of barriers and boundaries is replaced by a feeling of a new universe that features multiplicity, open doors, choices, opportunities, manifold pathways, and multiple identities. In this discursive logic, all geographical and cultural spaces are imagined to be in the same latitude. We can all be emotionally connected to this universe, unencumbered by class, gender, history, or geography. If our engagements with the global are destined always to produce hybrid outcomes, then there is something of ourselves in each of these formations and we should not worry. The mantra of 'choice' and 'free will' dictates that everyone has unlimited possibilities, that it is just a matter of selecting the right alternative.

The global subject who emerges from this imaginary is fluid, multiple, eclectic, mobile—unconstrained by boundaries, hierarchies, histories, and geographies. Allied to this discourse of hybridity is the prominence given to intercultural brokers and bicultural cosmopolitan scholars, often held up as litmus tests that the market values diversity. Yet, as this study shows, territorially based self–other relations remain firmly in place. The challenges of negotiating interculturality are profoundly individualized and are not assisted by curricular and pedagogical initiatives by the international university. Aside from a nodding acknowledgment, governments, too, have done little. In Australia and the United Kingdom, state-sponsored initiatives such as productive diversity, multiculturalism, racial equality, and antiracism have been countered by reterritorialization strategies that politicians have been eager to exploit.

For people who feel powerless to challenge elusive and mysterious forces such as globalization, it is easier to direct their energies toward objects closer to home. A range of responses that include suspicion and hatred of the stranger; fear about personal security; the desire to live intensely private lives, cocooned in gated communities work against a sense of responsibility and mutuality[4] toward the multiple others who are denied justice, dignity, and human security (Bauman, as cited in Tester, 2001, pp. 91–92).

The imposition of market fundamentalist regimes has contributed to growing income disparity within many 'First World' nations. These disparities are magnified manifold outside the 'First World'. Yet, inequality is increasingly understood as an individualized phenomenon; it is associated with deficits of the individual who subsequently experiences intense self-doubt, stigma, and shame. These feelings find relief in attacking the integ-

---

[4]I use Sennett's (2003) understanding of mutuality: "to act well towards others" through cooperation.

rity of those others, authoring a paranoid nationalism (Hage, 2003; see also Manne, 2004) or other virulent expressions of localisms. As Sennett (2003, pp. 46–47) observes, one's sense of self is recoverable by diminishing the integrity of others.

Thus, although sophisticated information, communication, and transportation technologies may facilitate space–time compression, these artifacts stop short of widening the "compass of moral indignation and sensitivity" (Bauman, as cited in Tester, 2001, p. 67). This is most evident in attitudes to national and global poverty that are broadly regarded as self-inflicted or as "facts of nature" that people have no choice but to accept. Global campaigns such as the Jubilee Campaign, aimed at debt cancellation of heavily indebted poor countries, generated soundbites of handwringing sympathy from 'First World' politicians and bureaucrats, but rhetorical commitment is a poor alternative to actual practices of canceling debt (Hertz, 2004). Noting that "the perpetuation of poverty no longer offends the sentiments of justice" (Bauman, as cited in Tester, 2001, p. 66), Bauman criticizes theorists for this state of affairs, observing that social theories and social thought have shifted from class to culture ("identity politics") and in doing so redirected the moral alertness of intellectuals and citizens away from the "class divisions, humiliations and indignities caused by the market-and-property game endemic to capitalist culture" (p. 66).

Some of this logic can be applied to the discursive celebration of hybridity in accounts of international education. While a genealogy of the concept of hybridity is clearly outside of the scope of this book, my provisional position is to argue that hybridity has displaced considerations of social equity and cultural mutuality. Hybridity's discursive prominence was achieved thorough the work of postcolonial writers who sought to destabilize notions of racial and cultural essentialisms and purities and to acknowledge the historical interdependencies between cultures. In other words, hybridity was a discursive attempt to first, interrogate the imperialist logic of difference which informed cultural racisms and underpinned assumptions of civilizational polarities (C. Klein, 2003, pp. 15–16) and second, to normalize intercultural mixing and synergies (Pieterse, 2004, chap. 4).

However, its use as a legitimating technique to deflect criticisms about the vastly skewed cultural and economic exchanges that constitute globalization and international education must now be questioned. N. Singh (1998) poses a number of pertinent questions about multiculturalism that can be usefully extended to the discursive positioning of hybridity: "Is it a corporate 'plot' to work through and profit from diversity? Is it a hopeful, global vision of cultural justice?" Both are possibilities for international education, along with other alternatives. So far, the indicators suggest that hybridity functions to reassure the corporatized First World universities by diluting their responsibilities for linguistic hegemony and neoliberal globalization. Hybridity makes it possible to dismiss criticisms about the failure of 'First World' multinational education corporations to internationalize their curricula, to support initiatives to reverse the largely East-to-West directional flows of students, and to tackle the issue of the growing linguistic hegemony of English in the academy. In the language of multiple and heteroglossic identities, the issue of linguistic diversity as a 'global public good'—something that benefits citizens of many countries[5]—is easily diminished.

In this context, cultural hybridity is a convenient governing discourse. It is part of the language of placelessness; it rests on an inclusive spatial logic that implies giving the peripheries a chance. It subtends the 'safe multicultural imaginary' that is discursively, territorially, and socially embedded within the political economies of economically dynamic places, featuring competitive governments, enterprising cities, entrepreneurial local governments, enterprising universities, and entrepreneurial subjects. The multicultural imaginary is used as a marketing signifier by governments and universities to create perceptions that their cities and campuses are signifiers of a new era marked by equality and reciprocity, while continuing to maintain strongly assimilationist curricula and perpetuating linguistic hegemony.

> Though the government website providing information about international education in Australia markets the national product in 11 different Asian languages, the actual programs of study are provided only in English, apart from a few bilingual programs in China. The cultural diversity of students is respected up to, and including, the point at which they hand over their money. After that, they have to take what they are given. (Marginson, 2003a, p. 31)

The global education market draws on, and simultaneously authors, the fantasies, dreams, and desires of its customers. The lifestyle-inclined, educational tourism programs such as Study Abroad, which constitute the main conduit for Americans to undertake overseas education, draw on two trends that have been the leitmotif of 'New Economy' marketing: aestheticization and fetishization. Education is promoted as an 'experience' and an opportunity for fun. Educational tourism presumes and generates an aura of youthfulness, adventure, and zestfulness. Establishing oneself as interesting and different marks out the tourist-student as an object worthy of recruitment and further investment.

Impression management techniques are deployed to package and commodify countries such as Australia as a rugged, pristine frontier for adventure and an East–West bridge. Universities in global cities, such as London and New York, promote the place of their location, and by extension, them-

---

[5]"Global public good" is defined by Marginson (2003a), who was informed by Kaul's (1999) notion of global common goods.

selves, as sites of dynamism, intellect, and opportunity—ideal places for ambitious, aspiring professionals. Oxford Brookes, on the other hand, tries to capitalize on its links to a place that resides in most of our imaginations as a historical seat of learning. The overlapping discursive fields of education and tourism are most unabashed in their proximity in Singapore, where marketing the Singapore Education brand and promoting the Global Schoolhouse is deemed the responsibility of the state instrumentality, the Singapore Tourism Board. International education networks today feature a range of actors, managers, media consultants, advertising agencies, and tourist consultants who act as place marketeers, brand architects, and web designers, along with the distinctly less sexy faculty whose job it is to educate.

In some respects, the international education market embodies the millennium grand fantasy of *the* postFordist 'New Economy', and its subsets, the network society and the knowledge-based economy. It deploys the imagination as a force of production and rides on the aesthetics and practices of design and style captured in the spectacle of public display and performance through education exhibitions, promotional brochures, Web sites and videos. It is premised on speed, newness, and novelty, offering accelerated degrees, "any time, any place" education in the form of online education (e-education and flexi-learning) and lifelong learning. International education is not immune to the "thermodynamics of being hot and staying cool" (Lofgren, 2003, p. 250), creating the risk that the education on offer is incidental. High-status, financially secure universities largely avoid the fads and gimmicks, the whistles and bells of the 'New Economy'. Although some did embark on online courses, these were discontinued when costs escalated and venture capital dried up.

The euphoric narratives of the new economy, which were heralded as the next phase of development, are now in abeyance. However, further research into the ironies that underpinned the phenomenon is potentially useful to chart a future path for international education. Of particular interest is the types of subjectivities that were or are privileged by this world, described variously as post-Fordist and featuring the culturalization of production. We need to ask how the university's engagements in the hyper-competitive, fast, new economy contribute to its role as a site where people learn not only to be critical, literate citizens of a democratic society at the national level but as ethical and informed global citizens.

The free-moving, eclectic, hybrid subject, which has been so dominant in the new economy discourse, continues to be actively deployed by nation-states toward convenient ends. The governmental logic that underpins the ideal citizen-subject encourages self-sufficiency, self-reliance, and flexibility. Rather than demanding a citizen's rights to economic and political security, the ideal citizen-subject is encouraged to deploy deterritorialized and hybrid sensibilities to remake themselves to meet changing economic and political needs. In universities, the visible and heavy hand of the state uses the invisible hand of the market as its governmental logic to impose a discourse of short-term pragmatism and flexibility on how individuals discharge their teaching, research, and administrative responsibilities.

In the developing world, the systematic failure of governments to tackle cumulative disadvantage, whether through poor governance; economic exclusion; and ethnoracial, linguistic, and religious discriminations, create the push factors for mobility (Papademetriou, 2003, p. 40). In many ways the mobile guest worker is the ideal 21st-century 'citizen'. Rather than agitating for citizenship rights, these individuals relocate themselves by legal and illegal means and, in doing so, contribute much-needed foreign exchange through their remittances. Given that guest worker remittances have now outstripped the aid contributions to the developing world by 'First World' governments, it is unlikely that governments from poor countries will interfere with these networks. Their economies may have once relied on exporting primary produce and natural resources, but now the emphasis is on exporting their people's labor to the economically dynamic centers. Indeed, countries such as the Philippines now actively promote labor migration of their nationals as a development strategy to gain access to foreign exchange (O'Tuathail, Herod, & Roberts, 1998, p. 18). The Philippines' role as provider of English-speaking professional labor for the First World is generally accepted as unproblematic by many of its citizens, who point to the scarcity of individual opportunities in their country.

Nation-states such as Singapore and Brazil, which embody hybridity, also provide us with useful focal points to understand the workings and expressions of hybridization at this historical moment, marked by globalization. Singapore, a 'significant other' that receives considerable attention from Western social theorists, is often held up as an example of an East–West hybrid. From the perspective of neoliberalism, Singapore functions as a signifier that the leviathan of capitalism offers every nation and every race the opportunity to leapfrog from 'Third World' poverty to 'First World' prosperity within a single generation. What types of hybridities are valued in the city-state? How are these reflected in subject positions open to Singaporeans? For individual students, Singapore's hypercompetitive working environment means a constant tension between *kiasu* technologies of self and more gentle alternatives based on cultural synergies. A subjectivity of productive absence allows the Singaporean government to steer citizens toward various incarnations of the Singaporean: the Renaissance Singaporean, the Confucian Singaporean, the secular citizen, and so forth. In its newly acquired role as the 'global schoolhouse', Singapore offers an educational vision for the 21st century that is focused on building entrepreneurial subjects.

Brazil is a hybrid nation by all measures, but it is also a highly stratified nation. Under such circumstances, the conditions for the reciprocal exchanges of cultural knowledges are skewed. Although the creation, use, and dissemination of hybrid music, performing arts, and food are widespread and well regarded, as a rule the most valued configurations of hybridity are those inclined toward the Euro-American world. Less valued are the hybrid constellations derived from the synergies or fusions between Western and indigenous ontologies, for example.

The liberal argument that is vested in the primacy of sovereign power is anchored in the belief that individuals cannot be duped, that they are able to see through such governmental technologies. There is certainly some credence to this argument. However, as Pierre Bourdieu points out, discipline in postmodernity has shifted from "normative regulation to seduction; from policing to public relations" (Bourdieu, as cited in Tester, 2001, p. 90; see also Bourdieu, 2003, pp. 76–77). Today, we are exposed to multiple and sophisticated 'technologies of spin' that give the impression of being anchored in facts and sincerity. The unpalatable reality is that partisan spinning and the selective release of information by the media and our political masters, combined with nationalist narratives, reduce the possibilities for a free-discourse community and civic freedoms. The opportunities to become a critical subject are thus significantly reduced.

BROADENING THE UNIVERSITY'S IMAGINATION

> What is wrong with the society we live in . . . is that it has stopped questioning itself. This is a kind of *society which no longer recognises an alternative to itself* and thereby feels absolved from the duty to examine, demonstrate, justify (let alone prove) the validity of its outspoken and tacit assumptions. This society did not suppress critical thought as such, neither did it make its members afraid of voicing it. . . . We are critically predisposed, but our critique is so to speak, "toothless," unable to affect the agenda for our "life-political choices." The unprecedented freedom which our society offers its members has arrived . . . together with unprecedented impotence. (Bauman, 2001, p. 99)

The modern university has habitually reformed itself to fit in with the project of the nation-state, not surprising given that it is a progeny of the modern nation-state. Nineteenth-century British and American universities were heavily implicated in the modernizing and imperializing missions of their nation-states (Scott, 1998). Early Australian universities were modeled on a British template and were cloisters for would-be gentry in exile, although later they would produce the agents of incipient nationhood (Marginson, 2002). Today, the notions of nation and national competitiveness continue to shape higher education systems in First World countries such as Singapore, Australia, the United Kingdom, and the United States. The same political rationalities, now couched in the language of competitive advantage in the global economy, are used to legitimate new forms of governance in universities.

The need to decolonize, to engage in self-reflexive scholarship as a means to internationalizing the university, is not restricted to the Western, First World university. With few exceptions, their roles as nation-building instruments have led these 'postcolonial' universities to defer to their political masters. They have not been particularly effective in civilizing the state or in creating the conditions for a civil society (see Rahman, 2000). As Nandy (2000) so eloquently argues, the non-Western university whether in Asia, Africa, or Latin America has not been an effective custodian of local and subjugated knowledges, preferring instead to defer to their colonial heritage and to model themselves on universities in the center.

Imperialism's sweeping impact on the material, technological, economic, and sociocultural conditions did not end with constitutional independence of the colonies. Postindependent civic societies, if they were allowed by the nation-state to emerge and flourish, steered themselves toward a Westernized template of civicness and Western-oriented epistemologies (Nandy, 2000; Venn, 2002). The pedagogical goals of the university in the former colonies sought sameness with the West rather than striving to author diversity. Today, Singapore's Global Schoolhouse project exemplifies this pedagogical impulse in its regard for and desire to emulate the American mindset. Brazil's universities were also strongly influenced by the drive to modernize. They were modeled on universities in the metropolitan center. Given the influence of elites and authoritarian governments, it is not surprising that the exploration and institutionalization of alternative epistemologies has been stunted.

We cannot escape the fact that we are now in 'a dark age for human kindness' (see Bauman, 2001). We need from our universities intellectual leadership for a more progressive politics of globalization that contributes to enhanced social equity, global human rights, and human security. Reworking the academic mission of the university means providing the space to investigate an alternative social order—whether of human nature, knowledge, governance, community, or systems of production. One of the most urgent tasks at hand is to find ways to build more sustainable and equitable systems of production, and to arrest the existing North–South inequities. This cannot be achieved solely through the market or by relying entirely on the nation-state, where the power politics of national interests and commercial imperialism will continue to get in the way of positive changes. Universities have long been implicated in supporting the hegemonic ambitions of nation-states—they do not sit outside these power relations. Of significant concern today is the extent to which governments are manipulating understandings of community and nation to reassert ethnocultural subjectivities.

These reterritorialization drives have the inevitable effect of splintering the lived experiences of citizenship.

A reinvigorated academic mission rejects the current definition of international education as the recruitment of fee-paying international students and the credentialing of domestic graduates with the instrumental skills to work in an economy without borders. It rejects the notion of the university as a service industry, and 'knowledge factory', staffed by entrepreneurs and service providers. Presently, there is limited discursive space within international universities for transformative scholarship or for building nonterritorial solidarities that liberate humane and democratic expressions of cosmopolitanism and foster authentic international collaborations.

In the case of international students, the pressure to finish their (often expensive) courses rapidly and to return home to secure employment encourages a largely instrumental view of education. In many public universities, including those studied in this research, the demands of bread-and-butter issues dominate, whether earning institutional income or juggling heavy teaching and administrative loads. The public sector university, deemed problematic by successive neoliberal governments, had to be reformed to save public money, to earn export income, and to position the nation-state favorably in the global economy. What is clear is that these factors are barriers to the intellectual engagements demanded of universities if they are to help author more humane and democratic global futures.

What role will the university take in developing a postrationalist social order? So far, legitimacy has been largely accorded to rationalist knowledges, and minimal discursive space has been given to examine its ontological assumptions. The primary aim of a university education is now to transmit skills and competencies, and to this end its privileged epistemologies all seek to inculcate reason (Marginson & Mollis, 2001; Scholte, 2000, pp. 315–317; Tikly, 2001). Yet, as the lessons of history have demonstrated time and again, relations of domination and oppression are usually rationally defensible (see Foucault, 2000; Parekh, 1995).[6]

An unreflective, instrumentally dominated education brings many, many risks as Bauman (2001) carefully and evocatively reminds us. It reduces our capacities for engagement with conscience and morality and for self-knowledge. It increases the possibilities for our subjection. It reduces our capacities to identify and challenge the special relationship between rationalization and the excesses of political power and it distances us from the other.

The world as seen by reason is a collection of useful objects. Reason has tried hard to annex value and dump anything that resists annexation; to make value into

---

[6]Parekh's (1995) study of liberalism and its complicity with the disenfranchisement of indigenous peoples and colonialism is a case in point.

the handmaiden or a spin-off of use . . . to enlist value in the service of use;
but value is the quality of a thing, while usefulness is an attribute of the thing's
user. . . . The world as seen by [regard, caring] is a collection of values.
(Bauman, 2001, pp. 164–165)

What can be done by individuals in their day-to-day activities? A starting
point is for faculty to direct their energies toward displacing the dominance
of the instrumental ideal in knowledge production. By themselves, instrumental educational visions do not offer the space to build social relations
informed by reciprocity, equality, and mutuality. Instrumentalism cannot
and has not provided the intellectual resources to tackle social equity or to
contribute to global common goods. The commitment to instrumentality
draws a special strength from the education market, where increasingly exchange has emerged as the definitive logic for producing, organizing, and
disseminating knowledge. A great deal of knowledge and research is now
tied to its capacity to earn income and profits. I will not elaborate on this
view, which has been amply corroborated by numerous studies into the political economy of knowledge.

What is urgently required is serious, reflective engagement with the issue
of how knowledge might be used to promote the proper use and distribution of resources for ecological sustainability, social justice, and social equity. This requires faculty to address the disjunctures between reason and
regard for the other in their disciplines and in their day-to-day practices.
Reworking the academic mission and broadening the academic imagination also requires universities to make a commitment to cosmopolitan
scholarship and to contribute to cosmopolitan democracy both within and
outside their political communities. As Archibugi (2003) observes,

Democratic states are not always inspired by the principles of their own consti-
tutions. . . . To be democratic with your own people does not necessarily en-
tail being democratic with others as well. (pp. 6–7)

As I try to show in earlier chapters, universities are implicated in the
power relations to which Archibugi (2003) refers. If universities are to develop a rigorous, plural, interactive, multiperspectival, and dynamic curriculum that breaks out of an implicitly nation-centered architecture (Appadurai, 2004), they must foster a commitment to cosmopolitan democracy to
counter the security rationale of knowing about other people, other cultures, and other spaces for the primary purpose of governing them. What
might such a cosmopolitan scholarship look like? It would commit itself to
an "ethics of care" that endures over the long term (Bauman, as cited in
Tester, 2001). Certainly, it would challenge the parochialism and orientalisms of the disciplines and it would seek a more active engagement with the
public sphere. It would also use and further epistemological pluralism by

engaging with non-Western epistemologies (see Sadiki, 2000) and knowledges outside the rationalist paradigm.

As part of this pluralism, universities would enable their graduates and faculty to solve problems in different environments using multidisciplinary professional knowledge bases that promote ecological sustainability and social and gender equity (see Kelly, 2000; Patrick, 1997). In their research and teaching, universities and their faculty would also be inspired by, and support, transnational imaginaries (Gough, 1999), premised on understanding the interconnections and interdependencies among individuals, communities, and nations (see also Francis, 1993; Sadiki, 2001; Whalley, 1997).

"FEARLESS SPEECH" OR "ENDURING THE UNWISDOMS OF ONE'S MASTERS"?

> My intention was not to deal with the problem of truth, but with the problem of the truth-teller, or of truth telling as an activity . . . who is able to tell the truth about what, with what consequences, and with what relations to power. [With] the question of the importance of telling the truth, knowing who is able to tell the truth, and knowing why we should tell the truth, we have the roots of what we could call the critical tradition in the West. (Foucault, 2001, p.)

> My role—and that is too emphatic a word—is to show *people that they are much freer than they feel* [italics added], that people accept as truths, as evidence, some themes which have been built up *at a certain moment in history* [italics added], and that this so called evidence can be criticised and destroyed. (Foucault, 1988a)

Foucault's 'technologies of the self' provide the basis for some practical strategies that can be used to arrest the ways international education has been assembled, including the social relations that underpin international education as we know it—a juggernaut hurtling toward the market, and at the same time trading and reproducing colonial nostalgia. An additional and critical dimension of Foucault's work that offers the means to acquiring ethical technologies of the self is exemplified in the notion of *parrhesia*. Literally translated, *parrhesia* means 'fearless speech', and Foucault understands it as knowing the truth and conveying this truth to others. Parrhesia, then, is a set of practices of 'civic freedoms' (Tully, 2003). Those who engage in fearless speech are termed *parrhesiastes* (truth tellers).

Foucault makes a clear distinction between the fearless speech of parrhesia and the speech act of rhetoric, by drawing on parrhesia's moral quality and its function as critique. It takes courage to speak the truth[7] in the face of risks and danger: "The commitment involved in *parrhesia* is linked to a certain social situation, to a difference of status between the speaker and his audience . . . the *parrhesiastes* says something which is dangerous to [herself] and thus involves risk" (p. 13). In other words, parrhesia "comes from below and is directed towards above" (p. 18). However, parrhesia should not be confused with permissiveness—the capacity to say whatever one wishes with no regard to the consequences for others. Rather,

> it is a civic responsibility or duty for both rulers and ruled. If citizens do not engage with governors by speaking frankly to them—by criticizing them— then citizens have to bear "unwise" governors. (Tully, 2003, p. 3)

Significantly, to develop a set of ethical practices, truth tellers have to take up a *specific relationship with themselves* and at the same time engage in the timeless dialogue between same and the other. Here, Foucault returns to his earlier preoccupation on how classical reason offers a spiritual basis to transform subjectivity. Where Cartesian rationalism considers truth as accessible through the exercise of reason and by the mere accumulation of knowledge, Foucault argues that the ethics within classical reason demanded that the subject "become other in order to find the truth" (O'Farrell, 1989, p. 73). An immoral subject cannot know the truth, no matter how much knowledge he accumulates (O'Farrell, 1989). As Bauman observes, "morality is about commitment to the Other over time . . . it is not about temporary whims" (Bauman, as cited in Tester, 2001, p. 12). He goes on to observe that moral acts often require people to challenge social norms and "majority opinions" (p. 53).

As with so much of his work, Foucault provides the opportunity to turn ideals into everyday practices. He poses several questions, critical to any reworking of the academic mission of the 21st century: 'What is the training of a good parrhesiastes? About what topics is it important to tell the truth? What is the importance of having *parrhesiastes* for a nation, society, community or university?'

FOR A FEARLESS SCHOLARSHIP WITH COMMITMENT

> I think it is us who make the future. The future is the way we react to what is happening, it is the way we transform a movement, a doubt into truth. If we want to be masters of our future, we must fundamentally pose the question of what today is. (Foucault)[8]

---

[7]Foucault does not regard truth as an eternal object but recognizes its historical specificity.

[8]Foucault (1994) Le monde est un grand asile, Dits et Ecrits, Vol. 11, p. 434 quoted by O'Farrell.

The hallmark of a 21st-century university education should be to educate professionals to be parrhesiates, individuals who have the ethical capacity to become of the other and to exhibit empathy to the other; professionals who push against market reductionism and national insularity. Instead of genuflecting to the rule guardians of quality assurance, parrhesiastes are willing to be fearless in their exposure of institutional rhetoric about quality. Rather than perpetuating an empty, short-term educational instrumentalism, parrhesiastes would have the capacity to distinguish knowledge from information and challenge the hyperbole of the knowledge-based, globalized society and 'New Economy'.

Parrhesiastes would not participate in practices that are unethical to communities and individuals in the non-West—whether in the form of crass educational entrepreneurialism or biopiracy. They would refuse the subjectivities that lend themselves to practices that amount to 'cash for expert comment'. They would fight hard against rendering theory complicit to abuses of power. This would require that parrhesiastes are not complicit in unethical power–knowledge relations that might cause environmental destruction, linguistic hegemony, and cultural imperialism. They would foster a commitment to an ethics of care that endures over the long term. Rather than promoting international education as a passport to a global career, parrhesiastes would engage in professional practices that contribute to the global public good—to democratic, humane, and sustainable global futures for this and succeeding generations.

References

Africa News Service. (2003, November 12). The rarely exposed side of global trade rules.

Agence France Presse. (2003, July 23). Singapore curbs maid abuse but "indignities" persist. Retrieved January 27, 2003, from http://www.singapore-window.org/sw03/030727af.htm

Aglionby, J. (2003, April 17–23). Singapore aims for a better sex life. *Guardian Weekly*, p. 22.

Agnew, J. (1998). *Geopolitics: Revisioning world politics.* New York: Routledge.

Ahier, J., & Beck, J. (2003). Education and the politics of envy. *British Journal of Educational Studies, 51,* 320–343.

Ahmad, A. (1995). The politics of literary postcoloniality. *Race and Class, 36,* 1–20.

Aid goes to cyberspace [Editorial]. (2001, August 3). *Australian.*

Alai-Amlatina, A. (2003). *The crime of the Latifundio.* Retrieved April 1, 2004, from http://www.landaction.org

Alexander, D., & Rizvi, F. (1993). Education, markets and the contradiction of Asia–Australia relations. *Australian Universities Review, 33*(1), 8–13.

Alexander, F. K. (2000). The changing face of accountability. *Journal of Higher Education, 71,* 411–431.

Allen, J. (1999). The new geopolitics of power. In D. Massey, J. Allen, & P. Sarre (Eds.), *Human geography today* (pp. 194–218). Cambridge, England: Polity Press.

Allen, J. (2000). Power/economic knowledge: Symbolic and spatial formations. In J. Bryson, P. Daniels, N. Henry, & J. Pollard (Eds.), *Knowledge, space, economy* (pp. 15–33). London and New York: Routledge.

Almeida, A. (2001). The formation of the elites in Sao Paulo. *Social Science Information, 40,* 585–606.

Altbach, P. (1998). *Knowledge, the university and development.* Hong Kong: Comparative Education Research Centre, University of Hong Kong.

Altbach, P. (1999a). Harsh realities: The professoriate faces a new century. In R. Berdahl, P. Altbach, & P. Gumport (Eds.), *American higher education in the twenty-first century: Social, political, economic challenges* (pp. 271–297). Baltimore: Johns Hopkins University Press.

Altbach, P. (1999b). The perils of internationalising higher education: An Asian perspective. *International Higher Education.* Retrieved March 15, 2002, from http://www.bc.edu/bc_org/avp/soe/cihe/newsletter/subject_index.htm#inteduc

Altbach, P. (2001). Academic freedom: International realities and challenges. *Higher Education, 41*, 205–219.

Altbach, P., & MacGill Peterson, P. (1998). Internationalize American higher education: Not exactly. *International Higher Education.*

Altenberg, L. (1990). *Beyond capitalism: Leland Stanford's forgotten vision.* Retrieved March 18, 2002, from http://dynamics.org/~altenber/PAPERS/BCLSFV/index.html

Amann, E., & Baer, W. (2002). Neoliberalism and its consequences. *Journal of Latin American Studies, 34*, 945–959.

American Association of University Professors. (1999). *Letter from Dr. Perley to North Central Association of Colleges and Schools.* Retrieved January 19, 2000, from www.aaup.org/3191let.html

American Association of University Professors. (2003, December 15). *HR 3077, The International Studies in Higher Education Act, Government Relations, Washington Update.* Retrieved January 18, 2004, from http://www.aaup.org/govrel/hea/2003/HR3077.htm

American Council on Education. (2001). *A brief guide to US higher education.* Washington, DC: Author.

American Council on Education. (2002). *Talking points refuting Stanley Kurtz's attack on HEA-Title VI area centers.* Retrieved January 19, 2004, from http://www.acenet.edu/washington/letters/2002/07july/titlevi.talking.points.cfm

American Council on Education. (2003). *Promising practices: Internationalization strategies.* Retrieved February 15, 2004, from http://www.acenet.edu/programs/international/promising-practices/

Amin, A. (2002). Ethnicity and the multicultural city: Living with diversity. *Environment and Planning, A34*, 959–980.

Amin, A., & Thrift, N. (2002). *Cities: Re-imagining the urban.* Cambridge: Polity.

Anderson, G. (2004). Voices from the chalk-face. *Studies in Higher Education, 29*(2), 185–200.

Andrews, C. (2004). Antipoverty policies in Brazil: Reviewing the past 10 years. *International Review of Administrative Sciences, 70*(3), 477–488.

Angelova, M., & Riazantseva, A. (1999). If you don't tell me, how can I know? A case study of four international students learning to write the US way. *Written Communication, 16*, 491–525.

Anthias, F. (2001). New hybridities, old concepts: The limits of culture. *Ethnic and Racial Studies, 24*, 619–641.

Appadurai, A. (1996). Disjuncture and difference in the global cultural economy. In *Modernity at large: Cultural dimensions of globalization* (pp. 27–47). Minneapolis: University of Minnesota Press.

Appadurai, A. (2001). *Globalization.* Durham, NC: Duke University Press.

Appadurai, A. (2004). Interview. *Items and Issues Quarterly, 4.* Retrieved April 28, 2004, from http://www.ssrc.org/programs/publications_editors/publications/items/online4-4/appadurai-interview.pdf

Apple, M. (1998). Education and new hegemonic blocs: Doing policy the "right" way. *International Studies in Sociology of Education, 8*, 181–202.

Apple, M., & Oliver, A. (1998). Becoming right: Education and the formation of conservative movements. In C. Torres & T. Mitchell (Eds.), *Sociology of education* (pp. 91–119). Albany: State University of New York Press.

Archibugi, D. (2003). Compolitical democracy. In D. Archibugi (Ed.), *Debating cosmopolitics* (pp. 1–15). London: Verso.

Ardolino, K. (2002, September 24). One student's choice of a lifetime. *Guardian Education*, p. 15.

Armitage, C. (1996, August 31). Degrees of doubt. *Weekend Australian*, pp. 1–2.

Arshad, A. (2003, December 28). Singapore: Maid abuse not rampant here: Survey. *Straits Times.* Retrieved January 27, 2004, from http://www.asianlabour.org/archives/000432.html

Ashcroft, B., Griffiths, G., & Tiffin, H. (1995). *Introduction, issues and debates. The postcolonial studies reader.* London: Routledge.

Ashton, D., & Sung, J. (1997). Education, skill formation and economic development: The Singaporean approach. In A. Halsey, H. Lauder, P. Brown, & A. Wells (Eds.), *Education: Culture, economy and society* (pp. 207–218). Oxford, England: Oxford University Press.

Asia's best universities. (2000). *Asiaweek.* Retrieved April 20, 2002, from http://www.asiaweek.com/asiaweek/features/universities2000/

Association of University Teachers. (2003). *The future of higher education: Response by the AUT to the government's white paper.*

Auletta, A. (2000). A retrospective view of the Colombo Plan: Government policy, departmental administration and overseas students. *Journal of Higher Education Policy and Management, 22,* 47–58.

AusEd. (1999). *When east meets west. Universe.* Melbourne, Australia: Author.

Austrade. (2000). *Market information for education services: Brazil.* Retrieved January 15, 2004, from http://www.austrade.gov.au/australia/layout/0,,0S2-1CLNTXD0019-2

Austrade. (2004). *Market entry strategies: Brazil.* Retrieved January 15, 2004, from http://www.austrade.gov.au/australia/layout/0,,0_S2-1_CLNTXID0019-2_-3_PWB155247-4_marketstrat-5_-6_-7_,00.html

Australian Education International. (2002). *Branding Project.* Canberra, Australia: Department of Education, Science, and Training.

Australian Parliament Joint Committee on Foreign Affairs and Defence. (1984). *The Jackson Report on Australia's Overseas Aid Program.* Canberra: Australian Government Publishing Service.

Australian Tourist Commission. (2001). *Australia.* Retrieved October 20, 2001, from http://www.australia.com/index.aust

Australian Vice-Chancellors Committee. (1998). *Provision of Education for International Students: Code of Practice and Guidelines for Australian Universities.* Retrieved June 20, 2002, from http://www.avcc.edu.au/news/public_statements/publications/AVCC_Code_2001final.pdf

Australian Vice-Chancellors Committee (AVCC). (2001). *Discussion paper on international education.* Retrieved February 2, 2002, from http://www.avcc.edu.au/policies_activities/international_relations/international_news/avcc_strategy_on_international_education1.pdf

Australian Vice-Chancellors Committee. (2002). *Positioning Australia's Universities for 2020.* Retrieved January 21, 2004, from www.avcc.edu.au/documents/policies_programs/statements/2020.pdf

AVCC (Australian Vice-Chancellors Committee). (2003). *AVCC appreciates support for internationalisation of education.* Media Release, October 14, 2003. Retrieved January 12, 2004, from www.avcc.edu.au/documents/news/media_releases/2003/avcc_media_54_03.pdf

Back, K., Davis, D., & Olsen, A. (1996). *Internationalisation and higher education.* Canberra: Australian Government Publishing Service.

Badley, G. (1998). The TQA and its impact on international education. *Innovations in Education and Training International, 35,* 133– .

Baker, M. (2002, July 24). *Hell's kitchen for Singapore's maids.* Retrieved January 27, 2004, from http://www.singapore-window.org/sw02/020724ag.htm

Baker, M., McCreedy, J., & Johnson, D. (1996). *Financing and effects of internationalisation in higher education: An Australian study (96/14): DEETYA.* Canberra: Australian Government Publishing Service.

Ball, S. (1994). *Education reform: A critical and post-structural approach.* Buckingham, England: Open University Press.

Ball, S. (1998). Big policies/small world: An introduction to international perspectives in education policy. *Comparative Education, 34,* 119–130.

Ball, S. (2000). Performativities and fabrications in the education economy: Towards the performative society. *Australian Educational Researcher, 27,* 1–23.

Ball, S. (2003). The teachers soul and the terrors of performativity. *Journal of Education Policy, 18*, 215–228.

Ballard, B. (1987). Academic adjustment: The other side of the export dollar. *Higher Education Research and Development, 6*, 109–119.

Ballard, B., & Clancy, J. (1984). *Study abroad: A manual for Asian students.* Kuala Lumpur, Malaysia: Longman.

Ballard, B., & Clancy, J. (1997). *Teaching international students: A brief guide for lecturers and supervisors.* Deakin: IDP Education Australia.

Barnett, R. (1999). The coming of the global village: A tale of two inquiries. *Oxford Review of Education, 25*, 293–306.

Barr, M. (1999). Lee Kuan Yew: Race, culture and genes. *Journal of Contemporary Asia, 29*(2), 145–156.

Barr, M. (2000). *Lee Kuan Yew: The beliefs behind the man.* Richmond, England: Curzon.

Barrow, C., Didou-Aupetit, S., & Mallea, J. (2003). *Globalisation, trade liberalisation and higher education in North America.* Dordrecht: Kluwer.

Bartelson, J. (2000). Three concepts of globalization. *International Sociology, 15*, 180–196.

Bassnett, S. (2004, March 25). Overseas students are being exploited. *Independent.* Retrieved March 20, 2004, from http://education.independent.co.uk/higher/story.jsp?story= 504598

Batty, D. (2004, March 27–April 2). A professional disservice to the South. *Guardian Weekly,* p. 24.

Baty, P. (1999, July 23). Derby dumbs down to gain Israeli cash. *Times Higher Education Supplement,* p. 1.

Bauman, Z. (1998). *Globalization: The human consequences.* Cambridge, England: Polity Press.

Bauman, Z. (2001). *The individualized society.* Cambridge, England: Polity Press.

Beazley, K. (1992). *International education in Australia through the 1990s, Ministerial statement.* Canberra: Australia Government Publishing Service.

Bechtel Corporation. (2002). *About Bechtel.* Retrieved March 20, 2002, from http:// www.bechtel.com/about.html

Bechtel International Center. (2000). *Orientation handbook for international graduate students.* Stanford, CA: Stanford University.

Bechtel International Center. (2001). *Statistics.* Retrieved August 15, 2001, from http:// www.stanford.edu/dept/icenter/GenInfo/stats/stats.html

Beck, L. (2002, August). Election dysfunction. *Brazil Politics.* Retrieved February 8, 2004, from http://www.brazil-brasil.com/pages/p20aug02html

Beckett, F. (2004, March 4–10). British universities ride in pursuit of high spending Russian students. *Guardian Weekly,* p. 7.

Beech, J. (2002). Latin American education: Perceptions of linearities and the construction of discursive space. *Comparative Education, 38*, 415–427.

The benefits of top-up fees. (2003, December 11). *Independent.*

Benesch, S. (1999). Rights analysis: Studying power relations in an academic setting. *English for Specific Purposes, 18*, 313–327.

Bennell, P., & Pearce, T. (2003). The internationalisation of higher education: Exporting education to developing and transitional economies. *International Journal of Educational Development, 23*, 215–232.

Bennett, P. (1997). The Dearing Report: Paving the way for the learning society. *Australian Universities Review, 40*(2).

Berdahl, R., & McConnell, T. (1999). Autonomy and accountability: Who controls academe. In R. Berdahl, P. Altbach, & P. Gumport (Eds.), *American higher education in the twenty-first century: Social, political and economic challenges* (pp. 70–88). Baltimore: Johns Hopkins University Press.

Berman, E. (1998). The entrepreneurial university: Macro and micro perspectives. In J. Currie & J. Newson (Eds.), *Universities and globalization* (pp. 213–233). Thousand Oaks, CA: Sage.

Berry, C. (1999). University league tables: Artefacts and inconsistencies in individual rankings. *Higher Education Review, 31*(2), 3–10.

Bhatt, A. (2003). Asian Indians and the model minority narrative: A neocolonial system. In E. Kramer (Ed.), *The emerging monoculture: Assimilation and the "model minority"* (pp. 203–220). Westport, CT: Praeger.

Biggs, J., & Watkins, D. (1996). *The Chinese learner: Cultural, psychological and contextual influences.* Melbourne: Australian Council for Educational Research.

Billig, M. (1995). *Banal nationalism.* London and Thousand Oaks, CA: Sage.

Birch, D. (1993). Staging crisis: Media and citizenship. In G. Rodan (Ed.), *Singapore changes guard* (pp. 72–83). New York: Longman.

Blair, T. (1998). *Foreword, Building the knowledge driven economy* (Competitiveness White Paper, Department of Trade and Industry). Retrieved June 19, 2002, from http://www.dti. gov.uk/comp/competitive/main.htm

Blair, T. (1999, June 18). *Attracting more international students.* Speech delivered at the London School of Economics. Retrieved March 29, 2001, from http://www.number10.gov.uk/ news.asap?NewsId=392

Blaxter, L., Hughes, C., & Tight, M. (1998). Telling it how it is: Accounts of academic life. *Higher Education Quarterly, 52,* 300–315.

Boehner, J. (2003, October 21). *International Studies in Higher Education Act: Bill summary.* Committee on Education and the Workforce. Retrieved January 14, 2004, from http://www. edworforce.house.gov/issues/108th/education/highereducation/intlbillsummary.html

Bosworth, S. (1992). Adaptation and survival in changing conditions: The international context. *Journal of Tertiary Education Administration, 12,* 105–139.

Boulger, D. (1897). *The life of Stamford Raffles.* London: Horace Marshall & Son.

Bourdieu, P. (2003). *Firing back: Against the tyranny of the market.* London: Verso.

Brandao, C. (1999). Young citizens: The landmark achievements of Brazil's social movement for children's rights. *New Designs for Youth Development, 15*(3). Retrieved January 12, 2005, from http://www.cydjournal.org/NewDesigns/ND_99Sum/Brandao/html

Branford, S. (2003, July 10). The bankers think they've tamed Lula. *Guardian Unlimited.* Retrieved December 20, 2004, from http://www.guardian.co.uk/comment/story/ 0,3604,995060,00.html

Brett, J. (1997). Competition and collegiality. *Australian Universities Review, 40*(2), 19–22.

Bright, M. (2004, August 13–19). Scramble for lucrative foreign students is corrupting universities, claims leading don. *Guardian Weekly,* p. 9.

British Council. (1995). *Code of Practice for Educational Institutions and Overseas Students.* London: Author.

British Council. (1999a). *The Brand Report.* London: Author.

British Council. (1999b). *The Brand Report.* Retrieved May 4, 2001, from http:// www.britishcouncil.org/ecs/brand/report1999909/summary.htm

British Council. (2000). *Realising our potential: A strategic framework for making UK education the first choice for international students* (ECS 0000255). Manchester, England: Author.

British Council. (2001a). *Education UK: The best you can be.* London: Author.

British Council. (2001b). *Prime minister's initiative.* Retrieved June 20, 2002, from http:// www.britishcouncil.org/promotion/pmi.htm

British Council. (2002). *Education Counseling Service: Review of the year.* Retrieved October 29, 2003, from http://www.britishcouncil.org/ecs/membership/services_review/index.html

British Council. (2003a). *Education UK: Positioning for success.* Retrieved January 9, 2004, from http://www.britishcouncil.org/ecs/pmi/positioning_for_success/consultationdocument. pdf

British Council. (2003b, November 23). *British Council invites students to discover the real UK* [Press release]. Retrieved January 11, 2004, from http://www.britishcouncil.org.hk/main/ pr36.asp

British Council Brazil. (2004). http://www.britishcouncil.org/br/brasil

British Council Singapore. (2001). *The speak good English inquiry.* Retrieved February 18, 2001, from http://www.britishcouncil.org/sg/english/sge.htm

Broadhead, L., & Howard, S. (1998). The art of punishing: The Research Assessment Exercise and the ritualisation of power in higher education. *Education Policy Analysis Archives, 6*(8). Retrieved April 11, 2002, from http://www.olam.asu.edu/epaa/v6n8.html

Brown, D. (1993). From aid to trade: Contradictions, contestations and complexities of Australia's policy to market education to Asia. In M. Bella, J. McCollow, & J. Knight (Eds.), *Working papers of the Higher Education Policy Project, Graduate School of Education* (pp. 124–138). Brisbane, Australia: University of Queensland.

Brown, R. (1998). Institutional responsibility: Reality or myth. *Higher Education Review, 30*(3), 7–22.

Brown, T. (1999). Challenging globalization as discourse and phenomenon. *International Journal of Lifelong Education, 18*(1), 3–17.

Bruch, T., & Barty, A. (1998). Internationalizing British higher education: Students and institutions. In P. Scott (Ed.), *The globalization of higher education* (pp. 18–31). Buckingham, England: Society for Research into Higher Education & Open University Press.

Budd, J. (2002, September 24). Land of expense. *Guardian Education,* pp. 14–15.

Buell, F. (1998). Nationalist postnationalism: Globalist discourse in contemporary American culture. *American Quarterly, 50,* 548–591.

Burbach, R., & Tarbell, J. (2004). *Imperial overstretch: George W. Bush and the hubris of empire.* Fernwood, Nova Scotia: Zed Books.

Burchell, G. (1993). Liberal government and techniques of the self. *Economy and Society, 22,* 267–281.

Burgess, R. (2003, November 13–19). Australia questions students' skills in learning English. *Guardian Weekly,* p. 1.

Cadman, K. (2000). "Voices in the air": Evaluations of the learning experiences of international postgraduates and their supervisors. *Teaching in Higher Education, 5,* 475–491.

Caldwell, K. (2001). Racialized boundaries: Women's studies and the question of difference. *Journal of Negro Education, 70,* 219–231.

Campaign Against Arms Trade. (2004). *Clean Investment Campaign 2004.* Retrieved December 20, 2004, from http://www.caat.org.uk/campaigns/clean-investment-2004/CIC04.php

Canclini, N. G. (2000). The state of war and the state of hybridisation. In P. Gilroy, L. Grossberg, & A. MacRobbie (Eds.), *Without guarantees: In honour of Stuart Hall* (pp. 38–62). London: Verso.

Carnevale, D. (2001, December 5). New York pulls plug online. *Australian,* p. 32.

Carroll, R. (2003, July 17–23). Mining giant threatens to scar island. *Guardian Weekly,* p. 23.

Carvel, J. (1999, June 19). Colleges rebranded for overseas appeal. *Guardian Unlimited.* Retrieved December 20, 2004, from http://www.guardian.co.uk/uk_news/story/0,,29276, 00.html

Cassidy, S. (2004, February 21). Academics fight back with week of action. *Independent.* Retrieved February 22, 2004, from http://education.independent.co.uk/news/story.jsp? story=493567

Castells, M. (1996). *The rise of the network society: The information age, economy, society and culture* (Vol. 1). Cambridge, England: Blackwell.

Castles, S., & Miller, M. (1998). *The age of migration: International population movements in the modern world.* Basingstoke, England: Macmillan.

Chagas, C. (2004). Brazil: Why hunger is absurd here. *Brazzil.* Retrieved February 7, 2004, from http://www.brazzil.com/2004/html/articles/feb04/p108feb04.html

Chan, H.-C. (1976). *The dynamics of one party dominance: The PAP at the grass-roots.* Singapore: Singapore University Press.

Chandler, A. (1999). Funding international education: Problems and prospects. *International Educator, 8*(2). Retrieved May 15, 2000, from http://www.nafsa.org/publications/ie/ spring99/chandler.html

Chang, H.-Y. (2000). Education in Singapore: A study of state values as cultural capital. *Education Research and Perspectives, 27*(2), 24–37.

Chapman, B., & Ryan, C. (2003). *Higher education financing and student access: A review of the literature.* Accessed December 29, 2003, from http://www.avcc.edu.au/policies_activities/education_review/Chapman_HECS_study_Oct03.pdf

Chen, Q. (1999, October). *The quality of Australian education: What do international students' experiences tell us?* Paper presented at the Australian International Education conference, Fremantle, Australia.

Chen, T.-M., & Barnett, G. (2000). Research on international student flows from a macro perspective: A network analysis of 1985, 1989 and 1995. *Higher Education, 39*, 435–453.

Cheung, W. L., & Sidhu, R. (2003). A tale of two cities: Education responds to globalisation in Hong Kong and Singapore in the aftermath of the Asian economic crisis. *Asia Pacific Journal of Education, 23*, 43–68.

Chin, J. (2000). *Who or what is a Singaporean.* Asean Focus Group. Australian National University. Retrieved December 20, 2004, from http://www.aseanfocus.com/asiananalysis/article.cfm?articleID=255

Chipman, L. (1998, August–September). *The changing face of transnational education: The future of higher education in a global context.* Paper presented at the third GATE (Global Alliance for Transnational Education) conference, Paris.

Chipman, L. (2000). Academic freedom and the well managed university. *Policy, 16*(1), 22–31.

Chitnis, S. (1999). The transformation of an imperial colony into an advanced nation. In P. Altbach & P. MacGill Peterson (Eds.), *Higher education in the twenty-first century: Global challenge and national response* (pp. 19–30). Boston: Institute of International Education.

Chua, B.-H. (1998). Racial Singaporeans, Absence after the hyphen. In J. Kahn (Ed.), *South East Asian identities: Culture and the politics of representation in Indonesia, Malaysia and Thailand* (pp. 28–50). Singapore: Institute of Southeast Asian Studies.

Chua, B.-H. (1999, August). *Living uncomfortably with capitalism in Asia.* Paper presented at School of Social Work and Social Policy, University of Queensland, Brisbane, Australia.

Chua, B.-H. (2000). Singaporeans ingesting McDonalds. In B.-H. Chua (Ed.), *Consumption in Asia: Lifestyles and identities* (pp. 183–201). London: Routledge.

Clinton, W. (2000). *White House memorandum: International education policy.* Washington, DC: U.S. Department of State. Retrieved March 16, 2002, from http://exchanges.state.gov/education/remarks/whstatement.htm

Clyne, F., Marginson, S., & Woock, R. (2001). International education in Australian universities: Concepts and definitions. *Melbourne Studies in Education, 42*, 111–127.

CNN. (2003, November 14). *Ten Commandments judge removed from office.* Retrieved January 15, 2004, from http://www.cnn.com

Coe, N., & Kelly, P. (2002). Languages of labour: Representational strategies in Singapore's labour control regime. *Political Geography, 21*, 341–371.

Cohen, D. (1997, September). Singapore wants its universities to encourage more creativity. *Chronicle of Higher Education,* pp. A71–A72.

Cohen, D. (2003, January 31). Australia has become the academic destination for much of Asia: Can it handle the influx? *Chronicle of Higher Education,* p. A40.

Cole, M. (1998). Globalisation, modernisation and competitiveness: A critique of the New Labour project in education. *International Studies in Sociology of Education, 8*, 315–333.

Cole, M. (2001, February 15). Unis fear Asian student backlash. *Courier Mail,* p. 22.

Colley, L. (2002, September 20). What Britannia taught Bush. *The Guardian.* Retrieved January 8, 2004, from http://www.guardian.co.uk/g2/story/0,,795386.00html

Colley, L. (2004, October 1–7). Hostages to history. *Guardian Weekly,* p. 15.

Collins Dictionary. (1991). Glasgow, Scotland: HarperCollins.

Committee on Education and the Workforce. (2003, September 25). *International Studies in Higher Education Bill ready for House consideration* [Media release]. Retrieved January 14, 2004, from http://www.edworkforce.house.gov/press108/09hied092503.html

Committee of Vice-Chancellors and Principals. (1992). *The management of higher degrees undertaken by overseas students.* London: Author.

Committee of Vice-Chancellors and Principals. (1995). *International students in the UK: Code of practice.* London: Author.

Cooper, S. (2002). Post-intellectuality: Universities and the knowledge industry. In S. Cooper, J. Hinkson, & G. Sharp (Eds.), *Scholars and entrepreneurs* (pp. 207–232). North Carlton, Australia: Arena Publications.

Court, S. (1999, March 9). Pay your money, take pot luck. *Guardian Unlimited.* http://www.guardian.co.uk/guardianeducation/story/0,,313488,00.html

Cox, H. (1999). The market as God. *Atlantic Monthly, 283*(3), 18–23.

Crow, J. (1992). *The epic of Latin America* (4th ed.). Los Angeles: University of California Press.

Cummings, D. (1991). Foreign students. In P. Altbach (Ed.), *International higher education: An encyclopedia* (Vol. 1, pp. 107–125). Chicago and London: St. James Press.

Currie, J. (1998a). Globalization practices and the professoriate in Anglo-Pacific and North American universities. *Comparative Education Review, 42*(1), 15–30.

Currie, J. (1998b). Globalization as an analytical concept and local policy responses. In J. Currie & J. Newson (Eds.), *Universities and globalization: Critical perspectives* (pp. 15–20). Thousand Oaks, CA: Sage.

Currie, J., & Newsom, J. (1998). *Universities and globalization: Critical perspectives* (1st ed.). Thousand Oaks, CA: Sage.

Curtis, P. (2004, December 22). *Sussex Sussex makes moves to cut £4m deficit.* Retrieved December 23, from http://www.education.guardian.co.uk/universitiesincrisis/story/0,12028,1378253,00.html

Dahrendorf, R. (1995). *LSE: A history of the London School of Economics and Political Science, 1895–1995.* Oxford, England: Oxford University Press.

Da Matta, R. (1999). Is Brazil hopelessly corrupt? In R. Levine & J. Crocitti (Eds.), *The Brazil reader: History, culture, politics* (pp. 295–301). Durham, NC: Duke University Press.

Danaher, G., Schirato, T., & Webb, J. (2000). *Understanding Foucault.* London: Sage.

Dash for cash or trade tactic? (1999, December 2). *Independent,* p. 113.

Da Silva, L. (2003, July 12). Political realism doesn't mean we ditch our dreams. *Guardian.* Retrieved from www.guardian.co.uk/brazil/story/0,12462,996918,00.html

Davie, S. (2002, June 9). Varsity changes controversy: Does Yankee do that dandy. *Straits Times Interactive.*

Davies, M., Nandy, A., & Sardar, Z. (1993). *Barbaric others: A manifesto on Western racism.* London: Pluto.

Davies, R. (2003, August 4). Brazil takes affirmative action in HE. *Guardian Unlimited.* Retrieved March 10, 2004, from http://education.guardian.co.uk/higher/worldwide/story/0,9959,1012157.html

Dean, M. (1999). *Governmentality: Power and rule in modern society.* London: Sage.

Dearing Report. (1997). *Higher education in the learning society: National Committee of Inquiry into Higher Education.* London: National Committee of Inquiry into Higher Education.

de Beer, P. (2004, January 15–21). Isolated Singapore girds against terror. *Guardian Weekly,* p. 29.

Deem, R. (2001). Globalisation, new managerialism, academic capitalism and entrepreneurialism and universities: Is the local dimension still important? *Comparative Education, 37,* 7–20.

Deem, R. (2003, April). A future for higher education? *Public Money and Management,* pp. 78–79.

de Jesus, C. (1999). Growing up Black in Minas Gerais. In R. Levine & J. Crocitti (Eds.), *The Brazil reader: History, culture, politics* (pp. 359–364). Durham, NC: Duke University Press.

Denny, C. (2004, April 1–7). Oil firms financing crooked regimes. *Guardian Weekly*, p. 23.

Department of Education and Science. (1985). *The development of higher education in the 1990s* (Green paper). London: Her Majesty's Stationery Office.

Department of Education and Science. (1991). *Higher education: A new framework* (White paper). London: Her Majesty's Stationery Office.

Department of Education and Skills. (2003). *The future of higher education* (White paper). Retrieved April 12, 2004, from http://www.dfes.gov.uk/hegateway/strategy/hestrategy/exec.shtml

Department of Education, Employment, and Training. (1990). *A fair chance for all* (DEET discussion paper). Canberra: Australian Government Publishing Service.

Department of Education, Science, and Training. (2000). *Backing Australia's ability*. Retrieved January 10, 2004, from http://www.dest.gov.au/science/analysis/pdf/backingAust,ability.pdf

Department of Education, Science, and Training. (2002). *Higher education at the crossroads*. Retrieved January 15, 2004, from http://www.backingaustraliasfuture.gov.au/publications/crossroads/default.htm

Department of Education, Science, and Training. (2003a). *Higher education review process*. Retrieved December 31, 2003, from http://www.backingaustraliasfuture.gov.au/pubs/html

Department of Education, Science, and Training. (2003b). *Backing Australia's future: Questions and answers*. Retrieved January, 2, 2004, from http://www.backingaustraliasfuture.gov.au/student_info/overview.html

Department of Education, Science, and Training. (2003c). *Higher education report for the 2004 to 2006 triennium*. Canberra: Australian Government Publishing Service.

Department of Education, Science, and Training. (2003d). *Engaging the world through education* (Ministerial statement on the internationalisation of Australian education and training). Commonwealth of Australia.

Department of Education, Training, and Youth Affairs. (1997). *Learning for life: Review of higher education financing and policy* (The West Report). Canberra: Australian Government Publishing Service.

Department of Education, Training, and Youth Affairs. (1999). *Knowledge and innovation: A policy statement on research and research training*. Canberra: Australian Government Publishing Service.

Department of Immigration and Multicultural and Indigenous Affairs. (2004). *Fact sheet: Abolition of White Australia policy*. Retrieved January 3, 2004, from http://www.immi.gov.au/facts/08abolition.htm

Department of Trade and Industry. (1998). *Our competitive future: Building the knowledge driven economy* (Competitiveness white paper). Retrieved June 10, 2002, from http://www.dti.gov.uk/comp/competitive/main.htm

de Wit, H. (Ed.). (1995). *Strategies for internationalisation of higher education: A comparative study of Australia, Canada, Europe and the United States of America*. Amsterdam: European Association for International Education and OECD.

de Wit, H. (1999, Spring). Changing rationales for the internationalization of higher education. *International Higher Education*. Retrieved June 18, 2002, from http://www.bc.edu/bc_org/avp/soe/cihe/newsletter/News15/text1.html

Dicken, P. (2004). Geographers and globalization: (Yet) another missed boat. *Transactions of the Institute of British Geographers, 29*(1), 5–26.

Dill, D. (1997). Higher education markets and public policy. *Higher Education Policy, 10*(3), 167–185.

Dill, D. (1999). Student learning and academic choice. In J. Brennan, J. Fedrowitz, M. Huber, & T. Shah (Eds.), *What kind of university* (pp. 56–70). Studies of Research in Higher Education: Balmoor, Bucks.

Dirlik, A. (1996). The global in the local. In R. Wilson & W. Dissanayake (Eds.), *Global/local: Cultural production and the transnational imagination* (pp. 21–46). Durham, NC: Duke University Press.

Dons bring in the dough. (2003, November 29). *Economist*, p. 53.

Drahos, P., & Braithwaite, J. (2002). *Information feudalism: Who owns the knowledge economy.* London: Earthscan.

Drier, P., & Fox-Piven, F. (2000, May 24). Student activism is back. *Miami Herald.* Retrieved August 31, 2003, from http://www.commondreams.org/views/052400-102.html

Duckett, S. (2004). Turning right at the crossroads: The Nelson Report's proposals to transform Australia's university. *Higher Education, 47,* 211–240.

Dunnett, S. (1998). International recruitment in the United States: A brief history. *International Education, 7*(4).

Dunstan, P. (2002, November 6). Foreign students: Who cares. *Australian,* p. 28.

Dunstan, P. (2003, July 28). Australia's universities must raise their standards before they raise students' fees. *The Age.* Retrieved December 10, 2004, from http://newstore.theage.com.au/apps/news.Search.ac?

EDB names second bond-breaker this year. (1999, November 26). *New Straits Times.*

Edge, J. (2004, April 15–21). English in a new age of empire. In *Learning English, Guardian Weekly,* p. 3.

Education Counselling Service, British Council. (2002). *Market information: Australia.* Retrieved May 5, 2002, from http://www.britishcouncil.org/ecs/market_information/australia/index.htm

Education gold in Japan. (1999, March 26). *Courier Mail,* p. 15.

Education Travel. (2003). *Brazil's uncertainty: Consultant's report.* Retrieved February 15, 2004, from http://www.hothousemedia.com/etm/etmbackissues/janetm03/janetm03cons report.htm

Ehrenberg, R. (2000). *Tuition rising.* Cambridge, MA: Harvard University Press.

Ehrenreich, B. (2001). *Nickel and dimed: On (not) getting by in America.* New York: Metropolitan Books.

Ehrenreich, B., & Hochschild, A. (2002). *Global women: Nannies, maids and sex workers in the new economy.* New York: Holt.

Ellingboe, B. (1997). *The most frequently asked questions about internationalization.* Minneapolis: University of Minnesota.

Elliott, L. (2003, July 17–23). Third way addicts in need of a new fix. *Guardian Weekly,* p. 12.

Emmerson, D. (1995). Singapore and the Asian values debate. *Journal of Democracy, 6*(4), 95–105.

Engel, M. (2003, November 6–11). Road to ruin. *Guardian Weekly,* p. 22.

Eshiwani, G. (1999). Higher education in Africa. In P. Altbach & P. MacGill Peterson (Eds.), *Higher education in the twenty-first century: Global challenge and national response* (pp. 31–38). Boston: Institute of International Education.

Fairweather, J. (2000). Diversification or homogenization: How markets and governments combine to shape American higher education. *Higher Education Policy, 13*(1), 79–98.

Farquhar, R. (1999). Integration or isolation: Internationalisation and the internet in Canadian higher education. *Journal of Higher Education Policy and Management, 21,* 5–15.

Fausto, B. (2002). *Concise history of Brazil.* Sao Paulo, Brazil: Editora da EDUSP.

Featherstone, M. (1996). Localism, globalism and cultural identity. In R. Wilson & W. Dissanayake (Eds.), *Global/local: Cultural production and the transnational imaginary* (pp. 46–75). Durham, NC: Duke University Press.

Ferguson, N. (2003, March 28). America: An empire in denial. *Chronicle of Higher Education, 49*(29), B7.

Figueirido-Cowen, M. (2002). Latin American universities, academic freedom and autonomy: A long term myth? *Comparative Education, 38,* 471–484.

Fisher, W., & Ponniah, T. (2003). *Another world is possible.* London: Zed Books.

Fiske, J., Hodge, B., & Turner, G. (1987). *Myths of Oz: Reading Australian popular culture.* Sydney, Australia: Allen & Unwin.

Flint, C. (Ed.). (2004). *Space of hate: Geographies of discrimination and intolerance in the USA.* New York: Routledge.

Flynn, P. (1999). Brazil: The politics of crisis. *Third World Quarterly, 20,* 287–317.

Foreign and Commonwealth Office. (2002). *Promoting the UK: Re-presenting the UK.* Retrieved June 11, 2002, from http://www.fco.gov.uk/servlet/Front?pagename=OpenMarket/Xcelerate/ShowPage&c=Page&cid=1007029395249

Foreign uni students lack English skills. (2002, October 23). *Australian,* p. 2.

Foucault, M. (1972). *Archaeology of knowledge.* London: Tavistock.

Foucault, M. (1977). *Discipline and punish.* London: Penguin.

Foucault, M. (1978). *The will to knowledge: The history of sexuality* (Vol. 1). London: Penguin.

Foucault, M. (1980a). Question on geography. In C. Gordon (Ed.), *Power/knowledge: Selected interviews and other writings, 1972–1977* (pp. 63–77). New York: Pantheon.

Foucault, M. (1980b). Two lectures: 1 January 1976. In C. Gordon (Ed.), *Power/knowledge: Selected interviews and other writings, 1972–1977* (pp. 78–108). New York: Pantheon.

Foucault, M. (1980c). Truth and power. Interview by A. Fontana & P. Pasquino. In C. Gordon (Ed.), *Power/knowledge: Selected interviews and other writings, 1972–1977* (pp. 109–134). New York: Pantheon.

Foucault, M. (1980d). Body/power. In C. Gordon (Ed.), *Power/knowledge: Selected interviews and other writings, 1972–1977* (pp. 55–62). New York: Pantheon.

Foucault, M. (1982). The subject and power. In H. Dreyfus & P. Rabinow (Eds.), *Michel Foucault: Beyond structuralism and hermeneutics* (pp. 208–226). Brighton, England: Harvester Press.

Foucault, M. (1984a). What is enlightenment? In P. Rabinow (Ed.), *The Foucault reader* (pp. 32–50). London: Penguin.

Foucault, M. (1984b). Truth and power. In P. Rabinow (Ed.), *The Foucault reader* (pp. 51–75). London: Penguin.

Foucault, M. (1988a). Truth, power, self: An interview with Michel Foucault. In L. Martin, H. Gutman, & P. Hutton (Eds.), *Technologies of the self: A seminar with Michel Foucault* (pp. 9–15). London: Tavistock.

Foucault, M. (1988b). Technologies of the self. In L. Martin, H. Gutman, & P. Hutton (Eds.), *Technologies of the self: A seminar with Michel Foucault* (pp. 16–49). Amherst: University of Massachusetts Press.

Foucault, M. (1991a). Governmentality. In G. Burchell, C. Gordon, & P. Miller (Eds.), *The Foucault effect: Studies in governmentality* (pp. 87–104). Chicago: University of Chicago Press.

Foucault, M. (1991b). Politics and the study of discourse. In G. Burchell, C. Gordon, & P. Miller (Eds.), *The Foucault effect: Studies in governmentality* (pp. 53–72). Chicago: University of Chicago Press.

Foucault, M. (1991c). The ethic of the care of the self as a practice of freedom: An interview. In J. Bernauer & D. Rasmussen (Eds.), *The final Foucault* (pp. 1–20). Cambridge, MA: MIT Press.

Foucault, M. (1994). Psychiatric power. In P. Rabinow (Ed.), *Ethics: Subjectivity and truth* (pp. 39–50). London: Penguin.

Foucault, M. (1996). The ethics of the concern for the self as a practice of freedom. In S. Lotringer (Ed.), *Foucault live (Interviews, 1961–1984)* (pp. 432–449). New York: Semiotexte.

Foucault, M. (2000). Truth and power. In J. Fabioun (Ed.), *Essential works of Michel Foucault, 1954–1984* (Vol. 3, pp. 111–133). London: Penguin.

Foucault, M. (2001). The word parrhesia. In *Fearless speech* (pp. 9–23). Los Angeles: Semiotexte.

Foundation for Economic Education. (2002). *What is FEE.* Retrieved March 25, 2002, from http://www.fee.org/vnews.php?sec=aboutfee

Francis, A. (1993). *Facing the future: The internationalization of post-secondary institutions in British Columbia: Task Force Report.* Vancouver, Canada: Centre for International Education.

Frank, T. (2002). *One market under God.* London: Random House.

Fraser, N. (2003). From discipline to flexibilization? Re-reading Foucault in shadow of globalization. *Constellations, 10*(2), 160–171.

Friedman, A. (1999). Hamada announces GSB campus in Singapore. *Chicago Business, 37*(2). Retrieved February 18, 2002, from http://gsbwww.uchicago.edu/student/chibus/articles/990125/990125042.html

Friedman, J. (2000). Americans again or the new age of imperial reason. *Theory, Culture and Society, 17,* 139–146.

Friedman, T. (2000). *The Lexus and the olive tree.* London: HarperCollins.

Friedman, T. (2004a, February 27). The silver lining of outsourcing overseas. *International Herald Tribune.* Retrieved March 15, 2004, from http://www.iht.com/articles/131494.html

Friedman, T. (2004b, March 16). Technology, terror supply chains being filled, but which will prevail? *Salt Lake Tribune.*

Fulbright, J. (1989). *The price of empire.* New York: Pantheon.

Gade, M. (1991). United States. In P. Altbach (Ed.), *International higher education: An encyclopedia* (Vol. 2, pp. 1081–1096). Chicago and London: St. James Press.

Gallagher, M. (2000). *The emergence of entrepreneurial universities in Australia.* Paper presented at the IMHE general conference, Paris.

Gallagher, M. (2001, July). *Modern university governance: A national perspective.* Paper presented at The Idea of a University: Enterprise or Academy, Australian National University, Canberra, Australia.

Gandin, L., & Apple, M. (2002). Can education challenge neoliberalism? The citizen school and the struggle for democracy in Porto Alegre. *Social Justice, 29*(4), 26–41.

Garner, R. (2003, December 7). Top-up fees: The educational problem. *Independent.* Retrieved February 18, 2004, from http://education.independent.co.uk/higher/story.jsp?story=470864

Garner, R. (2004, February 11). Universities face threat of zero ratings. *Independent.* Retrieved February 22, 2004, from http://education.independent.co.uk/news/story.jsp?story=489990

Gates, R. (2004, March 31). International relations 101. *New York Times,* p. 23.

George, A. (1985). *East Timor and the shaming of the West.* London: Tapol.

George, C. (2000). *Singapore: The air conditioned nation.* Singapore: Landmark Books.

Giddens, A. (1990). *The consequences of modernity.* Cambridge, England: Polity Press.

Giddens, A. (1998). *The Third Way: The renewal of social democracy.* Malden, MA: Polity Press.

Gilbert, A. (2000). The idea of a university: Beyond 2000. *Policy, 16,* 31–37.

Gillespie, H. (2001). Opening minds: The international liberal education movement. *World Policy Journal, 18*(4), 79–100.

Ginway, E. (1999). Literature under the dictatorship. In R. Levine & J. Crocitti (Eds.), *The Brazil reader: History, culture and politics* (pp. 248–253). Durham, NC: Duke University Press.

Gladieux, L., & King, J. (1999). The federal government and higher education. In R. Berdahl, P. Altbach, & P. Gumport (Eds.), *American higher education in the twenty-first century: Social, political and economic challenges* (pp. 151–181). Baltimore: Johns Hopkins University Press.

A global liberal arts education. (2000, November 1). *New York Times.*

Goh, C.-T. (1997). *Shaping our future: Thinking schools learning nation.* Ministry of Education (Singapore). Retrieved August 27, 2001, from http://www1.moe.edu.sg/press/1997/index.htm

Goh, C.-T. (1999). *Making globalisation work with social accountability.* Keynote address at the Commonwealth Business Forum. Retrieved November 22, 2001, from http://www4.gov.sg/sprinter/archives/99111101.html

Goldring, J. (1984). *Mutual Advantage: Report of the Committee of Review of Private Overseas Student Policy.* Canberra: Australian Government Publishing Service.

Gopinathan, S. (1997). Educational development in Singapore: Connecting the national, regional and the global. *Australian Educational Researcher, 24,* 1–26.

Gordon, C. (1980). *Michel Foucault: Power/knowledge.* New York: Harvester Wheatsheaf.

Gough, N. (2000). Globalization and curriculum inquiry: Locating, representing and performing a transnational imaginary. In N. Stromquist & K. Monkman (Eds.), *Globalization and education.* Rowman & Littlefield.

Gow, D. (2004, March 11–17). Business cries foul over UN rights code. *Guardian Weekly,* p. 12.

Green, M. (2002). Joining the world: The challenge of internationalizing American undergraduate education. *Change, 34*(13), 13–21.

Hage, G. (2003). *Against paranoid nationalism: Searching for hope in a shrinking society.* Annadale, Australia: Pluto Press.

Hall, M. (2003, December 2). New security plan in place, U.S. halts foreigner registry. *USA Today,* p. A03.

Hall, S. (1988). The toad in the garden: Thatcherism among the theorists. In L. Grossberg & C. Nelson (Eds.), *Marxism and the interpretation of culture* (pp. 35–73). Urbana: University of Illinois Press.

Hall, S. (1997). Old and new identities, old and new ethnicities. In A. King (Ed.), *Culture, globalization and the world system* (pp. 41–67). Minneapolis: University of Minnesota Press.

Halliday, F. (1999). The chimera of the "international university." *International Affairs, 75,* 99–120.

Halliday, F. (2000, October 11). *Globalisation: Good or bad?* Debate at London School of Economics. Retrieved June 28, 2002, from http://www.globaldimensions.net/articles/debate/hallidaytext.html

Hamilton, S. (1998, March). *Setting the foundations for the internationalisation of Australian higher education.* Paper presented at the Education 98: Industry Practitioners Forum, Sydney, Australia.

Hamlin, K. (2002, June 7). Remaking Singapore. *Institutional Investor.* Retrieved January 26, 2004, from http://www.sfdonline.org/Link%20Pages/Link%20Folders/02Pf/ii0602.html

Han, F.-K., Fernandez, W., & Tan, S. (1998). *Lee Kuan Yew: The man and his ideas.* Singapore: Singapore Press Holdings.

Harcleroad, F. (1999). The hidden hand: External constituencies and their impact. In R. Berdahl, P. Altbach, & P. Gumport (Eds.), *American higher education in the twenty-first century: Social, political and economic challenges* (pp. 241–269). Baltimore: Johns Hopkins University Press.

Hardt, M., & Negri, T. (2002). *Empire.* Cambridge, MA: Harvard University Press.

Harley, S. (2002). The impact of research selectivity on academic work and identity in UK universities. *Studies in Higher Education, 27,* 187–205.

Harvey, D. (1989). *The condition of postmodernity: An enquiry into the origins of cultural change.* Oxford, England and Cambridge, MA: Blackwell.

Harvey, D. (1993). From space to place and back again: Reflections on the condition of postmodernity. In J. Bird, B. Curtis, T. Putnam, G. Robertson, & L. Tickner (Eds.), *Mapping the futures: Local cultures, global change* (pp. 3–29). London: Routledge.

Hay, C., & Smith, N. (2005). Horses for courses? The political discourse of globalisation and European integration in the UK and Ireland. *West European Politics, 28*(1), 124–158.

Hay, C., & Watson, M. (1999). Globalisation: Sceptical notes on the 1999 Reith lectures. *Political Quarterly, 70,* 418–425.

Hay, C., & Watson, M. (2003). The discourse of globalisation and the logic of no alternative: Rendering the contingent necessary in the political economy. *New Labour, Policy and Politics, 31,* 289–305.

Heidhues, M. (1974). *South-east Asia's Chinese minorities.* Melbourne, Australia: Longman.

Held, D., McGrew, A., Goldblatt, D., & Perraton, J. (2000). Rethinking globalization. In D. Held & A. McGrew (Eds.), *The global transformations reader* (pp. 54–60). Cambridge, England: Polity Press.

Hellstein, M. (2002, November). *Students in transition: Needs and experiences of international students in Australia.* Paper presented at the Australian International Education conference, Hobart, Tasmania.

Help students not banks [Editorial]. (2004, April 25). *New York Times.* Retrieved April 26, 2004, from http://www.nytimes.com/2004/04/25/opinion/25SUN2.html?ex=1083928717&ei=1&en=95fb684321196ea3

Heng, G. (1997). "A great way to fly": Nationalism, the state and varieties of Third World feminism. In M. J. Alexander & C. T. Mohanty (Eds.), *Feminist genealogies, colonial legacies, democratic futures* (pp. 30–45). London: Routledge.

Henkel, M. (1999). The modernisation of research evaluation: The case of the UK. *Higher Education, 38,* 105–122.

Henry, M., Lingard, B., Rizvi, F., & Taylor, S. (1999). Working with/against globalization in education. *Journal of Education Policy, 14,* 85–97.

Henson, B. (2002, January 13). Who will speak up for voiceless maids. *Straits Times Interactive.* Retrieved April 10, 2003, from www.straitstimes.asialcom.sg/columnist/0,1886,1351-96277

Her Majesty's Government. (2003). *The future of higher education* (Cm. 5735). London: Her Majesty's Stationery Office.

Hertz, N. (2004). *IOU: The debt threat and why we must defuse it.* London: Fourth Estate.

Hesse, B. (1999). Reviewing the Western spectacle: Reflexive globalization through the black diaspora. In A. Brah, M. Hickman, & M. Macan Ghaill (Eds.), *Global futures: Migration, environment and globalization* (pp. 122–143). Houndsmill, England: Macmillan.

Hickling-Hudson, A., Matthews, J., & Woods, A. (2004). *Disrupting preconceptions: Postcolonialism and education.* Flaxton, Australia: Post Pressed.

Higher Education Funding Council. (2000). *Circular letter: E-University Project.* Retrieved May 5, 2002, from http://www.hefce.ac.uk/Pubs/CircLets/2000/cl04_00.htm

Higher Education Quality Council. (1995). *Code of practice for overseas collaboration provision in higher education.* London: Author.

Higher Education Statistics Agency. (2000/2001). *Student statistics.* Retrieved April 18, 2004, from http://www.hesa.ac.uk/holisdocs/pubinfo/student/Institution01.htm

Hira, A. (2003). The brave new world of international education. *World Economy, 26,* 911–931.

Hirst, P., & Thompson, G. (1999). *Globalization in question* (2nd ed.). Cambridge, England: Polity Press.

Hite, R., & Yearwood, A. (2001). A content analysis of college and university viewbooks (brochures). *College and University, 76*(3), 17–27.

Ho, W.-K. (2002). Still the kiasu Singaporean. *Nanyang Digital Chronicle.* Retrieved June 20, 2002, from http://www.ntu.edu.sg/studorgn/chronicle/stories/opinions.html

Hobsbawn, E. (1984). *Industry and empire.* Middlesex, England: Penguin.

Hobsbawn, E. (2003, June 4). America's imperial delusion. *Guardian Unlimited.* Accessed April 14, 2004, from www.guardian.co.uk/usa/story/0,12271,9774700.htm

Hodge, R., & Mishra, V. (1991). *Dark side of the dream: Australian literature and the postcolonial mind.* North Sydney, Australia: Allen & Unwin.

Hodges, L. (1999a, November 18). Overseas students bankroll colleges. *Independent.* Retrieved May 12, 2001, from http://education.independent.co.uk/news/story.jsp?story=12930

Hodges, L. (1999b, December 2). Dash for cash or trade tactic? *Independent.* Retrieved July 15, 2001, from http://education.independent.co.uk/news/story.jsp?story=12962

Hodgson, G. (Ed.). (1996). *The world turned right side up: A history of the conservative ascendancy in America.* Boston: Houghton Mifflin.

Hodgson, G. (2001). Can America go modest? Retrieved May 17, 2002, from http://www.opendemocracy.net/forum/document_details.asp?CatID=108&DocID=722

Hodson, P., & Thomas, H. (2001). Higher education as an international commodity. *Assessment & Evaluation in Higher Education, 26*(2), 101–112.

Holman, R. (2004). *Overseas students shun US universities.* Retrieved December 23 from http://education.guardian.co.uk/higher/worldwide/story/0,9959,1378786,00.html

Honan, J., & Teferra, D. (2001). The US academic profession: Key policy challenges. *Higher Education, 41,* 183–203.

Hong, L. (1999). Making the history of Singapore. In P.-E. Lam & K. Tan (Eds.), *Lee's lieutenants: Singapore's old guard* (pp. 96–115). St. Leonards, Australia: Allen & Unwin.

How to woo students from overseas. (2001, October 10). *Times Higher Education Supplement.* Retrieved March 15, 2002, from http://www.thes.co.uk/search/story.aspx?story_id=66439

Huffstutter, P., & Fields, P. (2000). A virtual revolution in teaching. *Los Angeles Times.* Retrieved March, 16, 2000, from http://www.latimes.com/business/updates/lat_online 000303.html

Huggins, M., & Mesquita, M. (2000). Civic invisibility, marginality and moral exclusion: The murders of street youth in Brazil. In R. Mickelson (Ed.), *Children on the streets of the Americas: Globalization, homelessness and education in the United States, Brazil, and Cuba* (pp. 257–270). London and New York: Routledge.

Humphreys, N. (2001). *Notes from an even smaller island.* Singapore: Times Books International.

Hyland, T. (2002). Third way values and post-school education policy. *Journal of Education Policy, 17,* 245–258.

IDP Brazil. (2004). *Bem-Vindo à IDP Brasil.* Retrieved March 15, 2004, from http://www.idp.com/brazil/default.asp

IDP Education Australia. (2001, September 28). *New scholarship to foster global peace and understanding.* Media Release. Retrieved February 21, 2002, from www.idp.edu.au/media/291001.asp

IDP Education Australia. (2004). *Fast facts: Higher education.* Retrieved March 5, 2004, from http://www.idp.edu.au/services/research_consult/fast_facts/higher_education.asp

Illing, D. (1998, March 4). Uni push to export courses. *Australian,* p. 33.

Illing, D. (1999a, April 1). Asian demand to endure. *Australian,* p. 40.

Illing, D. (1999b, June 23). British push for bigger share. *Australian,* p. 36.

Illing, D. (1999c, November 24). Chinese market ready for boom. *Australian,* p. 38.

Illing, D. (2001a, February 7). Marking inquiry leads to QUT inquiry. *Australian,* p. 37.

Illing, D. (2001b, June 20). Dark side to export boom. *Australian,* p. 34.

Industry benefits in virtual aid plan. (2001, August 3). *Australian,* p. 2.

INS arrests 10 in hunt for student-visa violators. (2001, December 13). *Wall Street Journal,* p. C13.

INSEAD. (2002). *Dean's welcome.* Retrieved February 16, 2002, from http://www.insead.edu/about/Singapore/Singf/index.htm

Institute of International Education. (2001). *Annual report.* Retrieved April 10, 2002, from http://www.iie.org/PDFs/AnnualReport2001/ar2001.pdf

Institute of International Education. (2002). *Opening minds to the world: Annual report.* Retrieved February 12, 2004, from http://www.iie.org/PDFs/AnnualReport2002

Institute of International Education. (2003). *Impact.* Retrieved January 23, 2004, from http://www.iie.org/PDFs/Publications/Brochures_April_28_2003.pdf

Institute of International Education. (2004). *Open doors.* Retrieved December 14, 2004, from http://www.opendoorsiienetwork.org/?p=49929

Inter-church Coalition for Africa. (2000). *Debt, structural adjustment & jubilee update.* Retrieved August 15, 2002, from http://www.web.net/~iccaf/debtsap/debtupdate5.html

Jacobsen, S. (2000, May 16). Nike's power game. *New York Times,* p. 23.

Jacobson, W., Sleicher, D., & Burke, M. (1999). Portfolio assessment of intercultural competence. *International Journal of Intercultural Competence, 23,* 467–492.

Jameson, F. (1989). *Post modernism: The cultural logic of late capitalism.* London: Verso.

Jary, D., & Jary, J. (1995). *Collins dictionary of sociology* (2nd ed.). Glasgow, Scotland: HarperCollins.

Jessop, B. (2000). The state and contradictions of the knowledge-based economy. In P. Daniels, J. Bryson, N. Henry, & J. Pollard (Eds.), *Knowledge, space, economy* (pp. 63–78). London: Routledge.

Johnson, R., & Deem, R. (2003). Talking of students: Tensions and contradictions for the manager-academic and the university in contemporary higher education. *Higher Education, 46*, 289–314.

Johnston, J., & Edelstein, R. (1993). *Beyond borders: Profiles in international education.* Washington, DC: Association of American Colleges and American Assembly of Collegiate Schools of Business.

Jones, P. (1986). *Australia's international relations in education.* Hawthorn, Australia: Australian Council for Educational Research.

Jones, P. (1997). On World Bank education financing. *Comparative Education, 33*(1), 117–129.

Kahn, J. (1998). *South-east Asian identities: Culture and the politics of representation in Indonesia, Malaysia, Singapore and Thailand* (1st ed.). Singapore: Institute of South-East Asian Studies.

Kaplan, A. (2004). Violent belongings and the question of empire. *American Quarterly, 56*, 1–18.

Karpin, D. (1995). *Enterprising nation: Renewing Australia's managers to meet the challenges of the Asia-Pacific century.* Canberra: Australian Government Publishing Service.

Kaufman, H., & Goodman, A. (2001). *Educational exchanges for a safer world.* Retrieved April 1, 2002, from http://www.iie.org/iie/educational_exchange.html

Kayatekin, S., & Ruccio, D. (1998). Global fragments: Subjectivity and class politics in discourses of globalization. *Economy and Society, 21*, 74–96.

Keen, B. (1992). *A history of Latin America.* Boston: Houghton Mifflin.

Keeping intellectual borders open. (2004, March 29). *New York Times*, p. 20.

Kelly, J. (2003, November 13). The future is uncertain. *Independent.*

Kelly, P. (1998). Internationalisation and post-development vision. *Futures, 30*, 739–744.

Kelly, P. (2000). Internationalizing the curriculum: For profit or planet. In S. Inyatullah & J. Gidley (Eds.), *The university in transformation* (pp. 161–172). Westport, CT: Bergin & Garvey.

Kempner, K. (1994). Constructing knowledge in Brazilian universities: Case studies of faculty research. *Studies in Higher Education, 19*, 281–293.

Kenway, J., & Bullen, E. (2003). Self-representations of international women postgraduate students in the global university "contact zone." *Gender and Education, 15*, 5–20.

Kenway, J., & Langmead, D. (1998). Governmentality, the "now" university and the future of knowledge work. *Australian Universities Review, 41*(1), 28–32.

Kingston, P. (2000, January 25). New UK brand is launched. *Guardian Unlimited.*

Klees, S., Rizzini, I., & Dewees, A. (2000). A new paradigm for social change: Social movements and the transformation of policy for street and working children in Brazil. In R. Mickelson (Ed.), *Children on the streets of the Americas: Globalization, homelessness and education in the United States, Brazil and Cuba* (pp. 79–98). London and New York: Routledge.

Klein, C. (2003). *Cold War orientalism: Asia in the middlebrow imagination, 1945–1961.* Berkeley: University of California Press.

Klein, N. (2001). *No logo.* London: Flamingo.

Klein, N. (2003, March 22). Outsourcing the Friedman. *The Nation.*

Knight, J., & de Wit, H. (1995). Strategies for internationalisation of higher education: Historical and conceptual perspectives. In H. de Wit (Ed.), *Strategies for internationalisation of higher education: A comparative study of Australia, Canada, Europe and the United States* (pp. 5–32). Amsterdam: European Association for International Education.

Koeller, D. (1998). *Treaty of Tordesillas.* Retrieved January 31, 2003, from http://campus.northpark.edu/history/WebChron/Americas/Tordesillas.html

Kong, L. (1999). Globalisation, transmigration and the renegotiation of ethnic identity. In K. Olds, P. Dicken, P. Kelly, L. Kong, & H. Yeung (Eds.), *Globalisation and the Asia-Pacific* (pp. 219–237). London: Routledge.

Kramer, E. (2003a). Assimilation and the model minority ideology. In E. Kramer (Ed.), *The emerging monoculture: Assimilation and the model minority* (pp. 1–32). Westport, CT: Praeger.

Kramer, E. (2003b). Cosmopoly: Occidentalism and the new world order. In E. Kramer (Ed.), *The emerging monoculture: Assimilation and the model minority* (pp. 234–292). Westport, CT: Praeger.

Kurtz, S. (2003, June 23). Hearing both sides of Title VI [Electronic version]. *National Review.* Retrieved January 20, 2004, from http://www.nationalreview.com/kurtz/kurtz062303.asp

Kwok, K.-W. (1999). The social architect. In P.-E. Lam & K. Tan (Eds.), *Lee's lieutenants: Singapore's old guard* (pp. 45–69). St. Leonards, Australia: Allen & Unwin.

Lam, P.-E. (1999). The organisational utility men. In P.-E. Lam & K. Tan (Eds.), *Lee's lieutenants: Singapore's old guard* (pp. 1–23). St. Leonards, Australia: Allen & Unwin.

Lam, P.-E., & Tan, K. (Eds.). (1999). *Lee's lieutenants: Singapore's old guard.* St. Leonards, Australia: Allen & Unwin.

Lambert Review of Business–University Collaboration. (2003). Retrieved February 15, 2004, from www.lambertreview.org.uk

Lapham, L. (1998). *The agony of mammon: The imperial world economy explains itself to the membership in Davos, Switzerland.* New York: Verso.

Larner, W., & Le Heron, R. (2002). The spaces and subjects of a globalising economy: A situated exploration of method. *Environment and Planning D—Society and Space, 20*(6), 753–774.

Larner, W., & Walters, W. (2002, July). *Globalisation as governmentality.* Paper presented at the Isa Panel, RC 18: Governing Society Today, International Sociological Association, World Congress of Sociology, Brisbane, Australia.

Larner, W., & Walters, W. (2004). Globalization as governmentality. *Alternatives, 29,* 5.

Law, J., & Hetherington, K. (2000). Materialities, spatialities, globalities. In J. Bryson, P. Daniels, N. Henry, & J. Pollard (Eds.), *Knowledge, space, economy* (pp. 34–49). London: Routledge.

Law, J., & Urry, J. (2004). Enacting the social. *Economy and Society, 33*(3), 390–410.

Lawnham, P. (2000, July 15). Joint degree opens door to China market. *Australian,* p. 39.

Lawnham, P. (2001a, April 28). Oz shopfront in the UK. *Australian,* p. 44.

Lawnham, P. (2001b, June 6). Marking inquiry exposes glitches. *Australian,* p. 23.

Lawnham, P. (2001c, September 12). Marks and sparks. *Australian,* p. 37.

Lawnham, P. (2001d, September 26). Nations plot to grab share. *Australian,* p. 36.

Lawnham, P. (2002, May 29). Unis warned of fiscal breaches. *Australian,* p. 33.

Lee, K.-Y. (2002, February). *An entrepreneurial culture for Singapore.* Ho Rih Hwa Leadership in Asia Public Lecture, Suntec, Singapore.

Lee, Y.-S. (2000). *Rennaisance City Report.* Singapore: Ministry of Information and the Arts.

Lemke, T. (2001). The birth of biopolitics. *Economy and Society, 30,* 190–207.

Leon, P. (2000, June 23). How to be sensitive to Chinese minds. *The Times Higher Education Supplement,* p. 30.

Leon, P. (2002, May 29). Ideas flow in a sellers' marketplace. *Australian,* p. 34.

Leonard, D. (2001). *A woman's guide to doctoral studies.* Buckingham, England; Philadelphia: Open University.

Leonhardt, D. (2004, April 22). As wealthy fill top colleges, new efforts to level the field. *New York Times.*

Levine, P., Sen, S., & Smith, R. (1999). *The political economy of the international arms trade: A framework for policy analysis.* Retrieved March 11, 2002, from http://www.regard.ac.uk/research_findings/R000235685/summary.pdf

Levine, R. (1999). How Brazil works. In R. Levine & J. Crocitti (Eds.), *The Brazil reader: History, culture, politics* (pp. 402–407). Durham, NC: Duke University Press.

Levine, R. (2003). *The history of Brazil.* New York: Palgrave McMillan.

Levine, R., & Crocitti, J. (Eds.). (1999). *The Brazil reader: History, culture and politics*. Durham, NC: Duke University Press.

Lingard, B., & Blackmore, J. (1997). Editorial—The "performative" state and the state of educational research. *Australian Educational Researcher, 24*(3), 1–20.

Lofgren, O. (2003). The new economy: A cultural history. *Global Networks, 3*, 239–254.

London School of Economics. (2000). *Profile*. London: Author.

London School of Economics. (2001a). *Undergraduate prospectus*. London: Author.

London School of Economics. (2001b). *The graduate school prospectus*. London: Author.

London School of Economics. (2002). *About the LSE: Introduction to the school*. Retrieved June 18, 2002, from http://www.lse.ac.uk/about/intro.htm

Longley, C. (2002). *The chosen people: The big idea that shapes England and America*. London: Hodder & Stoughton.

Loombia, A. (1998). *Colonialism/postcolonialism*. London: Routledge.

Lord, M. (2001, November 26). Student scrutiny: Universities cringe as foreign enrollees face a visa crackdown. *U.S. News and World Report*, p. 50.

Lyon, J. (2000, May 31). Conference showcases education as business. *Australian*, p. 34.

Lyon, J. (2001, May 30). There's profit in ideas. *Australian*, p. 43.

Lyotard, J.-F. (1984). *The postmodern condition: A report on knowledge*. Manchester: Manchester University Press.

MacLeod, D. (2004a, January 22). Overseas students in UK could top 1 m by 2025. *Guardian Unlimited*. Retrieved December 20, 2004, from http://education.guardian.co.uk/higher/news/story/0,,129030,00.html

MacLeod, D. (2004b, February 11). RAE overhaul to produce research "premier league" [Electronic version]. *Guardian Unlimited*. Retrieved February 24, 2004, from http://education.guardian.co.uk/higher/news/story/0,,1145159,00.html

MacLeod, D. (2004c, March 4). Hefce pulls the plug on UK e-university. *Guardian Unlimited*. Retrieved December 20, 2004, from http://education.guardian.co.uk/higher/news/story/0,,1162103,00.html

MacLeod, D., & Curtis, P. (2004). *Acid test*. Retrieved December 20, 2004, from http://education.guardian.co.uk/universitiesincrisis/story/0,12028,1367647,00.html

Madsen, D. (1998). *American exceptionalism*. Edinburgh and London: Edinburgh University Press.

Maguire, M., Ball, S., & MacCrae, S. (1999). Promotion, persuasion and class-taste. *British Journal of Sociology of Education, 20*, 291–308.

Maguire, M., Ball, S., & MacCrae, S. (2001). "In all our interests": Internal marketing in Northwark Park School. *British Journal of Sociology of Education, 22*, 35–50.

Maiden, S. (2004, July 21). Foreigners treated as "cash cows." *Australian*, p. 31.

Major, L. (1999, October 19). Dons blunt global push. *Guardian Unlimited*. Retrieved December 20, 2004, from http://education.guardian.co.uk/higher/story/0,,93538,00.html

Major, L. (2000a, February 15). A small degree of danger. *Guardian Unlimited*. Retrieved December 20, 2004, from http://education.guardian.co.uk/higher/story/0,,136677,00.html

Major, L. (2000b, August 15). Slipping abroad. *Guardian Unlimited*. Retrieved December 20, 2004, from http://education.guardian.co.uk/higher/story/0,,354120,00.html

Mamdani, M. (2001). *When victims become killers: Colonialism, nativism and the genocide in Rwanda*. Oxford, England: Curry.

Manne, R. (2004). The Howard years: A political interpretation. In R. Manne (Ed.), *The Howard years* (pp. 3–56). Melbourne, Australia: Black Inc Agenda.

Mansfield, N. (2000). *Theories of the self from Freud to Haraway*. St. Leonards, Australia: Allen & Unwin.

Marcuse, P. (2002). Really existing globalization after September 11. *Antipode, 34*, 633–641.

Marginson, S. (1997a). *Markets in education* (1st ed.). St. Leonards, Australia: Allen & Unwin.

Marginson, S. (1997b). *Educating Australia: Government, economy and citizen since 1960.* Cambridge, England: Cambridge University Press.

Marginson, S. (1997c). Competition and contestability in Australian higher education 1987–1997. *Australian Universities Review, 40*(1), 5–9.

Marginson, S. (2000). Research as a managed economy: The costs. In T. Coady (Ed.), *Why universities matter* (pp. 186–213). St. Leonards, Australia: Allen & Unwin.

Marginson, S. (2002). Nation-building universities in a global environment: The case of Australia. *Higher Education, 43,* 409–428.

Marginson, S. (2003a, November). *Markets in higher education: National and global competition.* Radford Lecture, Australian Association of Research in Education/New Zealand Association of Research in Education joint conference, Auckland, New Zealand.

Marginson, S. (2003b, September 24). Australian universities need public funding to be global players. *Online Opinion.* Retrieved January 2, 2004, from http://www.onlineopinion.com.au.asp?article=749

Marginson, S. (2004). Higher education policy (relaxed and comfortable). In R. Manne (Ed.), *The Howard years* (pp. 216–244). Melbourne, Australia: Black Inc Agenda.

Marginson, S., & Considine, M. (2000). *The enterprise university: Power, governance and reinvention in Australia.* Cambridge, England: Cambridge University Press.

Marginson, S., & McBurnie, G. (2004). Cross-border post-secondary education in the Asia-Pacific region. In *Internationalization and trade in higher education* (pp. 137–200). Paris: OECD.

Marginson, S., & Mollis, M. (2000). Comparing national education systems in the global era. *Australian Universities Review, 43*(1), 53–63.

Marginson, S., & Mollis, M. (2001). "The door opens and the tiger leaps": Theories and reflexivities of comparative education for a global millenium. *Comparative Education Review, 45,* 581–617.

Marginson, S., & Rhoades, G. (2002). Beyond national states, markets and systems of higher education: A glonacal agency heuristic. *Higher Education, 43,* 281–309.

Marklein, M. (2001, December 13). Knock, knock, the FBI's here: Interviews of Muslim students create tensions on campuses. *USA Today*, p. D9.

Marshall, J. (1995). Foucault and neoliberalism: Biopower and busno-power. *Philosophy of Education.* Retrieved April 1, 2002, from http://www.ed.uiuc.edu/EPS/PES-Yearbook/95_docs/marshall.html

Martinkus, J. (2001). *A dirty little war.* Milsons Point, Australia: Random House.

Mason, R. (1998). *Globalising education: Trends and applications.* London: Routledge.

Massey, D. (1994). *Space, place and gender.* Cambridge, England: Polity Press.

Massey, D. (1999). Imagining globalisation: Power geometries of time-space. In A. Brah, M. Hickman, & M. Macan Ghaill (Eds.), *Global futures: Migration, environment and globalization* (pp. 27–44). Houndsmill, England: Macmillan.

Massey, D. (2002). Time to think. *Transactions of the Institute of British Geographers, 27,* 259–261.

Mathiason, N. (2004, September 24–30). Handouts and tariffs still lock out the developing world. *Trade Justice, Guardian Weekly*, p. 2.

McCarthy, C., & Dimitriadis, G. (2000). Governmentality and the sociology of education: Media, educational policy and the politics of resentment. *British Journal of Sociology, 21,* 169–185.

McCarthy, R. (2002, February 9). Manhunt for public school kidnapper. *Guardian Unlimited.* Retrieved December 20, 2004, from http://www.guardian.co.uk/uk_news/story/0,,647467,00.html

McGuinness, A. (1999). The states and higher education. In R. Berdahl, P. Altbach, & P. Gumport (Eds.), *American higher education in the twenty-first century: Social, political and economic challenges* (pp. 183–214). Baltimore: Johns Hopkins University Press.

McLaren, P., & Farahmandpur, R. (2001). Teaching against globalization and the new imperialism. *Journal of Teacher Education, 52,* 136–150.

McNay, L. (1994). *Foucault: A critical introduction.* Cambridge, England: Polity Press.

Meadmore, D. (1998). Changing the culture: Governance of the Australian pre-millennial university. *International Studies in Sociology of Education, 8,* 27–45.

Meek, L., & Wood, F. (1997). The market as a new steering strategy for Australian higher education. *Higher Education Policy, 10*(3–4), 253–274.

Mestenhauser, J. (1998). International education on the verge: In search of a new paradigm. *International Educator, 7*(2–3), 1–17.

Middleton, C. (2000). Models of state and market in the modernisation of higher education. *British Journal of Sociology, 21,* 537–554.

Miles, T. (2003, December 15). Desperate colleges may turn to foreign students. *Evening Standard.*

Milito, C., & Silva, H. (1999). Voices from the pavement. In R. Levine & J. Crocitti (Eds.), *The Brazil reader: History, culture, politics* (pp. 420–422). Durham, NC: Duke University Press.

Miller, P., & Rose, N. (1990). Governing economic life. *Education and Society, 19,* 1–31.

Miller, P., & Rose, N. (1997). Mobilizing the consumer. *Theory, Culture and Society, 14,* 1–36.

Miller, R. (1999). *Major American higher education issues and challenges in the 21st century.* London: Jessica Kingsley.

Milmo, D. (2001, September 17). New York gets back to Brisbane. *Guardian Weekly.* Retrieved from http://www.media.guardian.co.uk

Milton-Smith, J. (2001, September). *International education, policy and marketing: The case of Singapore.* Paper presented at the Australian International Education conference, University of New South Wales, Sydney, Australia.

Ministry of Education (Singapore). (2002). *About national education.* Retrieved April 15, 2002, from http://www1.moe.edu.sg/ne/AboutNE/AboutNE.html

Mitchell, K. (1997). Different diasporas and the hype of hybridity. *Environment and Planning D (Society and Space), 15,* 533–553.

Mitchell, K. (2001). Transnationalism, neo-liberalism, and the rise of the shadow state. *Economy and Society, 30,* 165–189.

Mitchell, T. (1993, September). *Critical multiculturalism in textual studies.* Paper presented at the Cultural Diversity and Higher Education Conference, University of Technology, Sydney, Australia.

Mitton, R. (2000). Singapore: For richer or poorer. *Asiaweek.*

Monash University. (1999). Monash to reside with Kings in London. *Monash Newslines.* Retrieved January 20, 2002, from http://www-pso.adm.monash.edu.au/news/Story.asp?ID=162&SortType=12

Monash University. (2000a). *Leading the way: Monash 2020.* Retrieved February 13, 2002, from http://www.monash.edu.au/monashplan/

Monash University. (2000b). Monash University launches South African campus. *Monash Newslines.* Retrieved June 20, 2002, from http://www-pso.adm.monash.edu.au/news/Story.asp?ID=182&SortType=11

Monash University. (2000c). *Study abroad.* Retrieved March 18, 2000, from http://www.monash.edu.au/intoff/monashabroad/

Monash University. (2002). *Postgraduate course guide for international students.* Clayton, Australia: Monash International.

Monbiot, G. (2003a, August 7–13). America is a religion. *Guardian Weekly,* p. 13.

Monbiot, G. (2003b, October 4–10). The myth of morality. *Guardian Weekly.* Retrieved from http://www.guardian.co.uk/comment/story/0,3604,1092487,00.html

Monbiot, G. (2004, January 15–21). Standing on the edge of lunacy. *Guardian Weekly,* p. 24.

Moodie, G. (2002, January 9). Ups and downs in bottom line. *Australian,* p. 27.

Moreno, K. (2000, July 24). Wasted opportunity. *Forbes,* pp. 129–130.

Morris, S., & Hudson, W. (1995). International education and innovative approaches to university teaching. *Australian Universities Review, 38*(2), 70–74.

Morrow, R., & Torres, C. (1998). Education and the reproduction of class, gender and race: Responding to the postmodern challenge. In C. Torres & T. Mitchell (Eds.), *Sociology of education: Emerging perspectives* (pp. 19–45). Albany: State University of New York Press.

Morrow, R., & Torres, C. (2000). The state, globalization and educational policy. In N. Burbules & C. Torres (Eds.), *Globalization and education: Critical perspectives* (pp. 27–54). New York: Routledge.

Mosse, G. (1988). *The culture of Western Europe: The nineteenth and twentieth centuries*. Boulder, CO: Westview.

Moulin, N., & Pereira, V. (2000). Families, schools and the socialization of Brazilian children. In R. Mickelson (Ed.), *Children on the streets of the Americas: Globalization, homelessness and education in the United States, Brazil and Cuba* (pp. 43–54). London and New York: Routledge.

Mowery, D., Nelson, R., Sampat, B., & Ziedonis, A. (2001). The growth of patenting and licensing by the U.S. universities: An assessment of the effects of the Bay-Dole Act of 1980. *Research Policy, 30*, 99–119.

Munk, D. (2003, December 31). Lula's dreams for Brazil are delayed as the realities of power hit home. *Guardian Unlimited.* Retrieved December 20, 2004, from http://www.guardian.co.uk/international/story/0,1114175,00.html

NAFSA. (2000). *Toward an international education policy for the United States.* Retrieved October 20, 2001, from http://www.nafsa.org/content/PublicPolicy/USIntlEdPolicy/president.htm

NAFSA. (2003a). *In America's interest: Welcoming international students* (Report of the Strategic Task Force on International Student Access). New York: NAFSA.

NAFSA. (2003b). *Towards an international education policy for the United States: International education in an age of globalism and terrorism.* Retrieved January 13, 2004, from http://www.nafsa.org/content/PublicPolicy/USIntlEdPolicy/NIEP2003updateFINALwebversion.html

NAFSA. (2003c). *American leadership and security: The role of international education* (Issue brief). Retrieved January 13, 2004, http://www.nafsa

Nandy, A. (1983). *The intimate enemy: Loss and recovery of self under colonialism.* New Delhi, India: Oxford University Press.

Nandy, A. (2000). Recovery of indigenous knowledge and dissenting futures of the university. In S. Inayatullah & J. Gidley (Eds.), *The university in transformation* (pp. 115–124). Westport, CT: Bergin & Garvey.

Nascimento, A. (1999). The myth of racial democracy. In R. Levine & J. Crocitti (Eds.), *The Brazil reader: History, culture, politics* (pp. 379–381). Durham, NC: Duke University Press.

A new boom sweeps clean. (1999, April 28). *Australian*, pp. 38–39.

Niles, S. (1995). Cultural differences in learning motivation and learning strategies: A comparison of overseas and Australian students at an Australian university. *Journal of Intercultural Relations, 19*, 369–385.

Nines, P. (1999). Acculturation of international students in higher education. *Education and Society, 16*(2), 73–101.

Norton, A. (2002). The market for tradition. *Policy, 18*, 8–14.

Odih, P., & Knight, D. (2000). Just in time: The prevalence of representational time and space to marketing discourses of consumer buyer behaviour. In J. Bryson, P. Daniels, N. Henry, & J. Pollard (Eds.), *Knowledge, space and economy* (pp. 79–100). London: Routledge.

Oehlers, A. (1998). Youth in Singapore: Agents for social and political change. *Journal of Future Studies, 3*, 1–14.

O'Farrell, C. (1989). *Foucault: Historian or philosopher?* Basingstoke, England: Macmillan.

O'Farrell, C. (1996, January 18–24). Restoring the scholarly balance, Comment. *Campus Review*, p. 8.

O'Keefe, B. (2004, April 21). Asian toast with Singapore fling. *Australian Higher Education Supplement*, p. 23.

Olds, K., & Thrift, N. (2004). Cultures on the brink: Re-engineering the soul of capitalism on a global scale. In A. Ong & S. Collier (Eds.), *Global assemblages: Technology, politics, and ethics as anthropological problems* (pp.). New York: Blackwell.

Olds, K., & Yeung, W.-C. (2004). Pathways to global city formation: A view from the developmental city-state of Singapore. *Review of International Political Economy, 11*(3), 489–521.

On your bike, says Nike founder. (2000, May 3). *Australian*, p. 3.

Open Doors. (2001). Retrieved March 5, 2002, from http://www.opendoorsweb.org

Open Doors (2003). Retrieved January 20, 2004, from http://opendoors.iienetwork.org/

Organization for Economic Cooperation and Development. (2003). *Education at a glance.* Paris: Author.

O'Tuathail, G. (1999). *Borderless worlds: Problematizing discourses of deterritorialisation.* Retrieved February 15, 2003, from http://www.majbill.vt.edu/geog/faculty.toal/papers/Borderless.html

O'Tuathail, G., Herod, A., & Roberts, S. (1998). Negotiating unruly problematics. In G. O'Tuathail, A. Herod, & S. Roberts (Eds.), *Unruly world: Globalization, governance and geography* (pp. 1–24). London: Routledge.

Overseas students bankroll colleges. (1999, November 18). *Independent.*

Oxford Brookes University. (2001a). *International viewbook.* Oxford, England: Author.

Oxford Brookes University. (2001b). *Master of international management: Prospectus.* Oxford, England: Author.

Oxford Brookes University. (2001c). *University course finder.* Oxford, England: Author.

Ozga, J. (1998). The entrepreneurial researcher: Reformations of identity in the research marketplace. *International Studies in Sociology of Education, 8*, 143–152.

Paehlke, R. (2003). *Democracy's dilemma: Environment, social equity and the global economy.* Cambridge, MA: MIT Press.

Palatella, J. (2001, September 22). Making cents of a market. *Australian*, p. 34.

Parekh, B. (1995). Liberalism and colonialism: A critique of Locke and Mill. In N. Pieterse & B. Parekh (Eds.), *Decolonizing the imagination* (pp. 81–98). London: Zed Books.

Parekh, B. (2000). *Rethinking multiculturalism.* Basingstoke, England: Macmillan.

Parekh, B. (2003). Cosmopolitanism and global citizenship. *Review of International Studies, 29,* 3–17.

Parrenas, R. (2003). The care crisis in the Philippines: Children and transnational families in the new global economy. In B. Ehrenreich & A. Hochschild (Eds.), *Global woman. Nannies, maids and sex workers in the new economy* (pp. 39–54). New York: Metropolitan Owl Book.

Parry, B. (2002). Cultures of knowledge: Investigating intellectual property rights and relations in the Pacific. *Antipode, 34*, 679–706.

Parry, B. (2004). *Trading the genome: Investigating the commodification of bio-information.* New York: Columbia University Press.

Parsons, A. (1987). A history of international engagements. In S. Shotnes (Ed.), *The teaching and tutoring of overseas students* (pp. 4–15). London: United Kingdom Council on Overseas Students Affairs.

Patrick, K. (1997). *Internationalising the university: Implications for teaching and learning at RMIT Royal Melbourne Institute of Technology.* Retrieved May 21, 1999, from http://www.teaching.rmit.edu.au/resources/index.html

Pearson, C., & Beasley, C. (1996). Reducing learning barriers amongst international students: A longitudinal development study. *Australian Educational Researcher, 23*(2), 79–96.

Peck, J., & Tickell, A. (2002). Neoliberalizing space. *Antipode, 34*, 380–404.

Pegrum, M. (2004). Selling English: Advertising and the discourses of ELT. *English Today, 20,* 3–9.

Peters, M. (2004). Disciplinary knowledges of knowledge societies and knowledge economies. *New Zealand Sociology, 19*(1), 28–49.

Pettifor, A. (Ed.). (2003). *Real world economic outlook: The legacy of globalization.* London: Palgrave McMillan.

Pettifor, A., & Greenhill, R. (2003). Framework for economic justice and sustainability. In A. Pettifor (Ed.), *Real world economic outlook: The legacy of globalization* (pp. 211–218). London: Palgrave McMillan.

Philippines Bureau of Statistics. (2004). *Overseas Filipino workers remittances.* Retrieved January 25, 2004, from http://www.bsp.gov.ph/Statistics/sefi/ofw.htm

Pieterse, J. N. (2004). *Globalization or empire.* London: Routledge.

Pieterse, N. (2004). *Globalization and culture: Global melange.* Lanham, MD: Rowman & Littlefield.

Pieterse, N., & Parekh, B. (1995). Shifting imaginaries: Decolonization, internal decoloniza-tion, and postcoloniality. In J. Pieterse & B. Parekh (Eds.), *The decolonization of imagination* (pp. 1–20). London: Zed Books.

Plan to throw net over poverty. (2001, July 7). *Australian*, p. 3.

Polster, C., & Newson, J. (1998). Don't count your blessings: The social accomplishments of performance indicators. In J. Currie & J. Newson (Eds.), *Universities and globalization* (pp. 173–191). Thousand Oaks, CA: Sage.

Power, S., & Whitty, G. (1999). New Labour's education policy: First, second or third way? *Journal of Education Policy, 14*, 535–546.

Prasad, R. (2004, October 1–7). A passage from India. *Outlook, Guardian Weekly*, p. 33.

Pratt, G., & Poole, D. (2000). Global Corporations "R" Us. The impact of globalisation on Aus-tralian universities. *Australian Universities Review, 42*(2), 16–23.

Preston, D. (2001). Managerialism and the post-Enlightenment crisis of the British university. *Educational Philosophy and Theory, 33*, 333–363.

Prystay, C. (2004, January 21). Singapore encourages entrepreneurial grit. *The Asian Wall Street Journal.* Retrieved December 10, 2004, from www.sedb.com/edbcorp/sg/en_uk/index/in_the_news/news_articles.html

Puri, S., & Ritzema, T. (1999). *Migrant worker remittances, micro-finance and the informal economy: Prospects and issues* (Working Paper No. 21). International Labour Organisation. Retrieved March 29, 2002, from http://www.ilo.org/public/english/employment/ent/papers/wpap21.htm

Purushotam, N. (1998). Disciplining difference: "Race" in Singapore. In J. Kahn (Ed.), *South East Asian identities: Culture and the politics of representation in Indonesia, Malaysia, Singapore and Thailand* (pp. 51–94). Singapore: Institute of South-East Asian Studies.

Pusser, B. (2000). The role of the state in the provision of higher education in the United States. *Australian Universities Review, 42*(2), 24–35.

Quality Assurance Agency. (1997). *Code of practice.* London: Author.

Quality Assurance Agency. (1999). *Overseas audit report: Malaysia.* Retrieved December 20, 1999, from http://www.qaa.ac.uk/osea_idx.html

Quality Assurance Agency. (2001). *The agency's work overseas.* Retrieved May 15, 2002, from http://www.qaa.ac.uk

Quality Assurance Agency. (2002a). *Overseas quality audit report: Oxford Brookes University and In-formatics Holdings, Ltd.* Retrieved January 1, 2004, from http://www.qaa.ac.uk

Quality Assurance Agency. (2002b). *Overseas quality audit report: University of Bradford and the Management Development Institute of Singapore.* Retrieved February 2, 2004, from http://www.qaa.ac.uk

Queensland Government. (2001). *Study Queensland.* Brisbane, Australia: Author.

Queensland University of Technology. (2000, June 1–July 17). QUT staff reach out to preschools in India. *Inside QUT, 23*, 2.

Queensland University of Technology. (2001a). *International prospectus*. Brisbane, Australia: Author.

Queensland University of Technology. (2001b). PhD candidate urges disaster plan for Mozambique. *Links*.

Queensland University of Technology. (2001c). *Study abroad guide*. Brisbane, Australia: Author.

Queensland University of Technology. (2004, March 9). Students aid Fijians. *Inside QUT*, p. 8.

Rahman, T. (2000). Pakistani universities: Past, present and futures. In S. Inyatullah & J. Gidley (Eds.), *The university in transformation* (pp. 125–136). Westport, CT: Bergin & Garvey.

Rai, S. (2003, August 19). Indian companies are adding Western flavor. *New York Times*, p. W1.

Ramburuth, P., & McCormick, J. (2001). Learning diversity in higher education: A comparative study of Asian international and Australian students. *Higher Education, 42*, 333–350.

Rao, G. L. (1979). *Brain drain and foreign students*. St. Lucia, Australia: University of Queensland Press.

Reddy, M. (2004, February 8). Overseas uni students lured here with false promise. *The Age*.

Rhea, M. (2002). The economy of ideas: Colonial gift and post-colonial product. In T. Goldberg & A. Quayson (Eds.), *Relocating postcolonialism* (pp.). London: Blackwell.

Rhoades, G. (1998). *Market models, managerial institutions and managed professionals*. Retrieved April 15, 2002, from http://www.bc.edu/bc_org/avp/soe/cihe/direct1/news13/text2html

Ridley, D. (2004). Puzzling experiences in higher education: Critical moments for conversation. *Studies in Higher Education, 29*, 91–107.

Rizvi, F. (1997). Beyond the East–West divide: Education and the dynamics of Australia–Asia relations. *Australian Educational Researcher, 24*, 13–25.

Rizvi, F. (1998). Higher education and politics of difference. *Australian Universities Review, 41*(2), 5–6.

Rizvi, F. (2000). International education and the production of global imagination. In N. Burbules & C. Torres (Eds.), *Globalisation and education: Critical perspectives* (pp. 205–226). New York: Routledge.

Rizvi, F., & Walsh, L. (1998). Difference, globalisation and the internationalisation of the curriculum. *Australian Universities Review, 41*(2), 7–11.

Roberts, G. (2003). *Review of research assessment*. Retrieved February 3, 2004, from http://www.ra-review.ac.uk/reports/roberts.asp

Roberts, P. (1998). Extending literate horizons: Paolo Freire and the multidimensional word. *Educational Review, 50*, 105– .

Roberts, S. (2000). Realizing critical geographies of the university. *Antipode, 32*(3), 230–244.

Robertson, R. (1992). *Globalization: Social theory and global culture*. London: Sage.

Robertson, R., & Khondaker, H. (1998). Discourses of globalization. *International Sociology, 13*, 25–40.

Rodan, G. (1993). The growth of Singapore's middle class and its political significance. In G. Rodan (Ed.), *Singapore changes guard* (pp. 52–71). Melbourne, Australia: Longman Cheshire.

Rodan, G. (1996). The internationalisation of ideological conflict: Asia's new significance. *Pacific Review, 9*, 328–351.

Rodan, G. (2001). Globalisation and the politics of economic restructuring. In G. Rodan, K. Hewison, & R. Robison (Eds.), *The political economy of South-East Asia* (2nd ed., pp. 138–177). Oxford, England: Oxford University Press.

Rohter, L. (2003, August 10). Brazilians find a political cost for IMF help. *New York Times*, p. 3.

Rojas, C. (2004). Governing through the social: Representations of poverty and global governmentality. In W. Larner & W. Walters (Eds.), *Global governmentality* (pp. 97–114). London: Routledge.

Rose, N. (1993). Government, authority and expertise in advanced liberalism. *Economy and Society, 22,* 283–299.

Rose, N. (1999a). *Governing the soul: The shaping of the private self* (2nd ed.). London: Free Association Books.

Rose, N. (1999b). Inventiveness in politics. *Economy and Society, 28,* 467–493.

Rose, N., & Miller, P. (1992). Political power beyond the state: Problematics of government. *British Journal of Sociology, 43,* 173–205.

Rosemberg, F. (2000). From discourse to reality: A profile of the lives and an estimate of the number of street children and adolescents in Brazil. In R. Mickelson (Ed.), *Children on the streets of the Americas: Globalization, homelessness and education in the United States, Brazil and Cuba* (pp. 118–135). London and New York: Routledge.

Rosenfield, A. (1999). *An investment in education pays the best return.* Retrieved March 16, 2001, from http://www.cardean.com/Lotusphere.html

Rout, L. (1999). Brazil: Study in black, brown and beige. In R. Levine & J. Crocitti (Eds.), *The Brazil reader: History, culture, politics* (pp. 367–373). Durham, NC: Duke University Press.

Roy, A. (2001). *Power politics* (2nd ed.). Cambridge, MA: Southend Press.

Ryan, J. (2004). Views in a warm climate. *Singapore Journal of Tropical Geography, 25*(1), 18–22.

Ryn, C. (2003). *America the virtuous: The crisis of democracy and the quest for empire.* New Brunswick, NJ: Transaction.

Sadiki, L. (2001). *Internationalising the curriculum in the 21st century.* Centre for Educational Development and Academic Methods (CEDAM), Australian National University. Retrieved May 18, 2002, from http://www.anu.edu.au/CEDAM/internationalc.html

Sai, S.-M., & Huang, J.-L. (1999). The "Chinese educated" political vanguards. In P.-E. Lam & K. Tan (Eds.), *Lee's lieutenants: Singapore's old guard* (pp. 132–168). St. Leonards, Australia: Allen & Unwin.

Said, E. (1981). *The world, the text and the critic.* Cambridge: Harvard University Press.

Said, E. (1993). *Culture and imperialism.* London: Chatto Windus.

Salter, B., & Tapper, T. (2000). The politics of governance in higher education: The case of quality assurance. *Political Studies, 48,* 66–87.

Samoff, J. (1999). Institutionalizing international influences. In R. Arnove & C. Torres (Eds.), *Comparative education: The dialectic of the global and local* (pp.). Lanham, MD: Rowman & Littlefield.

Samuels, D. (2003). Fiscal straightjacket: The politics of macroeconomic reform in Brazil. *Journal of Latin American Studies, 35*(3), 543–569.

Sarup, M. (1993). *An introductory guide to postmodernism and poststructuralism.* Athens, GA: University of Georgia Press.

Sassen, S. (2001). Spatialities and temporalities of the global: Elements for a theorization. In A. Appadurai (Ed.), *Globalization* (pp. 260–278). Durham, NC and London: Duke University Press.

Saunders, F. (1999). *Who paid the piper: The CIA and the cultural cold war.* London: Granta.

Schein, E. (1996). *Strategic pragmatism.* Cambridge, MA: MIT Press.

Schemo, D. (2001, November 18). Eager for foreign students, universities persuade senator to drop plan to limit visas. *New York Times,* pp. B1, B7.

Scheyvens, R., Wild, K., & Overton, J. (2003). International students pursuing postgraduate study in geography: Impediments to their learning experiences. *Journal of Geography in Higher Education, 27*(3), 309–323.

Schirato, T., & Webb, J. (2003). *Understanding globalization.* London: Sage.

Scholte, J. (1996). Globalisation and collective identities. In J. Krause & N. Renwick (Eds.), *Identities in international relations* (pp. 38–78). London: Macmillan.

Scholte, J. (2000). *Globalization: A critical introduction.* London: Macmillan.

Schwartzman, S. (2002). *Higher education in Brazil: The stakeholders.* Washington, DC: World Bank.

Scott, P. (1995). *The meanings of mass higher education.* Buckingham, England: Open University Press.

Scott, P. (1998). Massification, globalization and internationalization. In P. Scott (Ed.), *The globalization of higher education* (pp. 108–129). Buckingham, England: Open University Press.

Seah, C.-N. (2004, February 15). Schools shaping elitist mindset. *Star.* Retrieved February 18, 2004, from http://www.singaporewindow.org/sw04/040215st.htm

Senate Employment, Workplace Relations, Small Business and Education Committee. (2001). *Universities in crisis.* Commonwealth of Australia. Retrieved March 18, 2002, from http://www.aph.gov.au/senate/committee/eet_ctte/public%20uni/report/index.htm

Seneviratne, K. (2002, December 27). Recession in Singapore puts dependence on foreign workers in peril. *Karachi Dawn.* Retrieved February 18, 2004, from http://www.singapore-window.org/sw03/021227da.htm

Sennett, R. (2003). *Respect: The formation of character in a world of inequality.* London: Allen Lane.

Sevier, R. (2000). Building an effective recruitment funnel. *Journal of College Admission, 169,* 10– .

Shanmugaratnam, T. (2004, March 26). Speech given at the closing ceremony of the NUS-Motorola Technopreneurship Challenge. Retrieved August 10, 2004, from http://www.moe.gov.sg:80/speeches/2004/sp20040326a.htm

Shapper, J., & Mayson, S. (2004). Internationalisation of curricula: An alternative to the Taylorisation of academic work. *Journal of Higher Education Policy and Management, 26*(2), 189–200.

Shephard, E. (2002). The spaces and times of globalisation: Place, scale, networks and positionality. *Economic Geography, 78,* 307– .

Shore, C., & Wright, S. (2000). Coercive accountability. In M. Strathern (Ed.), *Audit cultures* (pp. 56–89). London and New York: Routledge.

Sidhu, R. (2004). Governing international education in Australia. *Globalisation, Societies and Education, 2*(1), 48–66.

Sidley, P. (2003). Competition body rules that drug companies "abused" their position. *British Medical Journal, 327,* 946.

Singapore Economic Development Board. (1998). *The competitive advantage: Chairman's message* (Annual report. Singapore Economic Development Board). Retrieved March 15, 2000, from http://www.sedb.com/edb_corp/annual/an 1997

Singapore Education. (2003). *Why study in Singapore.* Retrieved January 20, 2004, from http://www.singaporeedu.gov.sg/htm/index.htm

Singapore International Foundation. (2002a). *Corporate profile.* Retrieved March 18, 2002, from http://www.sif.org.sg/index1.htm

Singapore International Foundation. (2002b). *About Singapore.* Retrieved January 27, 2004, from http://www.sif.org.sg

Singapore Management University. (2002). *Who we are and president's welcome.* Retrieved June 20, 2002, from http://www.smu.edu.sg/

Singapore 21 Committee. (2002). *What is Singapore 21?* Retrieved June 10, 2002, from http://www.sif.org.sg/yep_doc/singapore_21.doc

Singh, M. (1998). Globalism, cultural diversity and tertiary education. *Australian Universities Review, 41*(2), 12–17.

Singh, N. P. (1998). Culture/wars: Recoding empire in an age of democracy. *American Quarterly, 50,* 471–522.

Slater, D. (1998). Postcolonial questions for global times. *Review of International Political Economy, 5*(4), 647–678.

Slater, D. (2002). Other domains of democratic theory: Space, power, and the politics of democratisation. *Environment and Planning D (Society and Space), 20,* 255–276.

Slater, D. (2003). Geopolitical themes and postmodern thought. In J. Agnew, K. Mitchell, & G. O'Tuathail (Eds.), *A companion to political geography* (pp. 75–91). Malden, MA: Blackwell.

Slaughter, S. (1998). National higher education policies in a global economy. In J. Currie & J. Newson (Eds.), *Universities and globalization: Critical perspectives* (pp. 45–70). Thousand Oaks, CA: Sage.

Slaughter, S. (2001a). Problems in comparative higher education: Political economy, political sociology and postmodernism. *Higher Education, 41,* 389–412.

Slaughter, S. (2001b). Professional values and the allure of the market. *Academe, 87*(5), 22–26.

Slaughter, S., & Leslie, L. (1997). *Academic capitalism: Politics, policies and the entrepreneurial university.* Baltimore: Johns Hopkins University Press.

Smart, D., & Ang, G. (1993). Exporting education. *IPA Review, 46*(1), 31–33.

Smart, D., Volet, S., & Ang, G. (2000). *Fostering social cohesion in universities: Bridging the cultural divide.* Canberra: Australian Education International.

Sparke, M., & Lawson, V. (2003). Entrepreneurial geographies of global–local governance. In J. Agnew, K. Mitchell, & G. O'Tuathail (Eds.), *A companion to political geography* (pp. 315–334). Malden, MA: Blackwell.

Spring, J. (1998). *Education and the rise of the global economy.* Mahwah, NJ: Lawrence Erlbaum Associates.

Stanford Graduate Business School. (2003). *Prospective students.* Retrieved March 25, 2004, from http://www.gsb.stanford.edu/academics/students.html

Stanford University. (2000a). *Stanford Bulletin.*

Stanford University. (2000b). *Orientation handbook for international graduate students.*

Stanford University. (2002). *Stanford University: History.* Retrieved March 18, 2002, from http://www.stanford.edu/home/stanford/index.html

Stanford University. (2003). *Introduction to Stanford University.* Retrieved January 20, 2004, from http://www.stanford.edu/home/html

Stanford University. (2004). *People.* Retrieved from http://www.stanford.edu/home/welcome/students/people.html

Stanford University School of Education. (2002). *Mission statement.* Retrieved March 20, 2002, from http://ed.stanford.edu/suse/home09-01.html

Stanley, A. (2004, April 29). Understanding the president and his God. *New York Times.* Retrieved April 29, 2004, from http://www.nytimes.com

Starr, M. (2004). Reading the economist on globalization: Knowledge, identity and power. *Global Society, 18*(4), 373–395.

State University of New York Stony Brook. (2000). *International student services.* Retrieved May 18, 2002, from http://www.grad.sunysb.edu/International/

State University of New York Stony Brook. (2001a). *Biomedical engineering graduate school programs.* Stony Brook: Author.

State University of New York Stony Brook. (2001b). *Expand your universe.* Stony Brook: Author.

State University of New York Stony Brook. (2001c). *Facts and figures.* Retrieved October 20, 2002, from http://naples.cc.sunysb.edu/Prov/ubinfo.nsf/pages/intro

State University of New York Stony Brook. (2001d). *Graduate bulletin.* Stony Brook: Author.

State University of New York Stony Brook. (2002). *Claims to fame.* Retrieved July 2, 2002, from http://www.stonybrook.edu/sb/claims/

State University of New York Stony Brook.(2004a). *About Stony Brook.* Retrieved January 23, 2004, from http://www.stonybrook.edu/ugadmissions/about/

State University of New York Stony Brook. (2004b). *Superb faculty.* Retrieved January 23, 2004, http://www.stonybrook.edu/ugadmissions/facultyquotes.shtml

State University of New York Stony Brook. (2004c). *At the front of the class.* Retrieved January 23, 2004, from http://www.stonybrook.edu/ugadmissions/forms/outstandingfaculty.pdf

State University of New York Stony Brook. (2004d). *Undergraduate admissions* [Online tour/ slideshow]. Retrieved January 23, 2004, from http://www.stonybrook.edu/ugadmissions/ tour/slideshow/

Steele, J. (2002, October 28). The triumph of Lula lite. *Guardian Unlimited.*

Stewart, C. (2004, March 28). Outsourcing joins the MBA curriculum. *New York Times.*

Stiglitz, J. (2002a, August 14). A second chance for Brazil and the IMF. *New York Times.* Retrieved February 10, 2004, from http://lists.essential.org/pipermail/stor-imf/2002q3/000686.html

Stiglitz, J. (2000b). *Globalization and its discontents.* London: Allen Lane.

Stiglitz, J. (2003a, September 11–17). Trade debate. *Guardian Weekly*, p. 3.

Stiglitz, J. (2003b, August 15). Trade imbalances [Electronic version]. *Guardian.* Retrieved February 8, 2004, from

Strathern, M. (2000). The tyranny of transparency. *British Educational Research Journal, 26,* 309–321.

Stromquist, N., & Monkman, K. (2000). Defining globalization and assessing its implications on knowledge and education. In N. Stromquist & K. Monkman (Eds.), *Globalization and education: Integration and contestation across cultures.* Lanham, MD: Rowman & Littlefield.

Students attracted to dot com degrees. (2000, March 22). *Australian.*

Study in Australia. (2004). *Why study in Australia?* Retrieved December 20, 2004, from http://studyinaustralia.gov.au/Sia/en/WhyAustralia/WhyAustralia.htm

Sum, N.-L. (1999). New orientalisms, global capitalism, and the politics of synergetic differences: Discursive construction of trade relations between the USA, Japan and the East Asian NICs. In A. Brah, M. Hickman, & M. Macan Ghaill (Eds.), *Global futures: Migration, environment and globalization* (pp. 99–121). Houndsmill, England: Macmillan.

Sutherland, J. (2003, September 4–10). Keep your talented. *Guardian Weekly*, p. 11.

Swarns, R. (2004, April 3). U.S. to mandate fingerprinting and photos of more foreigners. *New York Times.*

Tan, J. (2003). Reflections on Singapore's education policies in an age of globalization. In K.-H. Mok & A. Welch (Eds.), *Globalization and educational restructuring in the Asia-Pacific region* (pp. 32–57). Houndmills, England: Palgrave McMillan.

Tan, T. (2001, February). *Tertiary education in Singapore.* Speech delivered at the NUS Political Association, Ministry of Information and the Arts (Singapore). Retrieved February 10, 2002, from http://app.internet.gov.sg/data/sprinter/pr/archives/2001021602.htm

Tan, T. (2002, March). Speech at the Graduation Ceremony of the University of Chicago Graduate School of Business, Singapore. Retrieved March 20, 2002, from http://www.sg.news.yahoo.com/0202028/57/2hcla.html

Tavora, A. (1999). Rehearsal for the coup. In R. Levine & J. Crociti (Eds.), *The Brazil reader: History, culture and politics* (pp. 231–235). Durham, NC: Duke University Press.

Taylor, S., Rizvi, F., Lingard, B., & Henry, M. (1997). *Educational policy and the politics of change.* London: Routledge.

Teather, D. (2004, April 15–21). Two thirds of US corporations paid no tax during the boom. *Guardian Weekly*, p. 15.

Teo, C.-H. (1999). *Principals: Leaders, entrepreneurs and innovators for the new millennium.* Ministry of Information and the Arts. Retrieved August 27, 2000, from http://www4.gov.sg/sprinter/archives/99123001.html

Teo, C.-H. (2002, January). *Making NIE an international leader in professional teacher training and educational research by 2010.* Speech at the National Institute of Education. Retrieved June 20, 2002, from http://www1.moe.edu.sg/speeches/2002/sp28012002.htm

Teo, L. (2001, February 20). "I want to be proud of Singapore . . . but what about?" *Straits Times Interactive.*

Tester, K. (2001). *Conversations with Zygmunt Bauman.* Cambridge, England: Polity Press.

Thaman, K. (2002). Shifting sights: The cultural challenge of sustainability. *International Journal of Sustainability in Higher Education, 3,* 233–242.

Therborn, G. (2000). Globalizations. *International Sociology, 15,* 152–179.

There's gold in them commercial arms. (2000, February 9). *Australian,* p. 37.

Thrift, N. (1998). The rise of soft capitalism. In G. O'Tuathail, A. Herod, & S. Roberts (Eds.), *Unruly world: Globalization, governance and geography* (pp. 25–71). London: Routledge.

Thrift, N. (1999). The place of complexity. *Theory, Culture and Society, 16*(3), 31–69.

Thrift, N. (2001). "Its the romance, not the finance, that makes the business worth pursuing": Disclosing a new market culture. *Economy and Society, 30,* 412–432.

Throsby, C. D. (1985). *Trade and aid in Australian post-secondary education.* Canberra: Australian National University, Development Studies Centre.

Tierney, W. (2001). The autonomy of knowledge and the decline of the subject: Postmodernism and the formulation of the university. *Higher Education, 41,* 353–372.

Tikly, L. (1999). Postcolonialism and comparative education. In C. Soudien, P. Kallaway, & M. Breier (Eds.), *Education, equity and transformation* (pp. 603–621). Dordrecht, The Netherlands: Kluwer Academic.

Tikly, L. (2001). Globalisation and education in the postcolonial world: Towards a conceptual framework. *Comparative Education, 37,* 152–171.

Tikly, L. (2004). Globalisation and education in sub-Saharan Africa: A postcolonial analysis. In A. Hickling-Hudson, J. Matthews, & A. Woods (Eds.), *Disrupting preconceptions: Postcolonialism and education* (pp. 109–126). Flaxton, Australia: Post Pressed.

Tomasevski, K. (2003). *Education denied: Costs and remedies.* London and New York: Zed Books.

Tomlinson, J. (1999). *Globalization and culture.* Cambridge, England: Blackwell.

Tootell, K. (1999). *International students in Australia: What do we know about the quality of their education.* Paper presented at the Australian Association for Research in Education (AARE), November 29–December 2, Melbourne. Retrieved April 15, 2002, from http://www.aare.edu.au/99pap/too99642.html

Torres, C. (2002). The state, privatization and educational policy: A critique of neoliberalism in Latin America and some ethical and political implications. *Comparative Education, 38,* 365–385.

Torres, C. (2003). *Music and social dissent in Brazil.* Unpublished paper.

Tota, A. (1999). The military regime. In R. Levine & J. Crocitti (Eds.), *The Brazil reader: History, culture and politics* (pp. 235–237). Durham, NC: Duke University Press.

Transparency International. (2003). *Global corruption report.* Retrieved April 18, 2004, from http://www.transparency.org

Trow, M. (1994). Managerialism and the academic profession: The case of England. *Higher Education Policy, 7*(2), 11–18.

Trowler, P. (1998). What managerialists forget. Higher education credit frameworks and managerialist ideologies. *International Studies in Sociology of Education, 81*(1), 91–110.

Tsoukas, H. (1997). The tyranny of light: The temptations and paradoxes of the information society. *Futures, 29,* 827–843.

Tuhiwai-Smith, L. (1999). *Decolonizing methodologies.* London: Zed Books.

Tully, J. (2003). *Civic freedom in a globalising age.* Retrieved April 15, 2004, from http://www.trudeaufoundation.ca/pdf/TullyCahiersEN.pdf

Turner, G. (1994). *Making it national: Nationalism and Australian popular culture.* St. Leonards, Australia: Allen & Unwin.

Turpin, T., Iredale, R., & Crinnion, P. (2002). The internationalization of higher education: Implications for Australia and its education "clients." *Minerva, 40,* 327–340.

Tysome, T. (2000, April 7). Britain must fight to keep foreign trade. *Times Higher Education Supplement,* p. 1.

Tysome, T. (2003, December 19). UK must keep grip on market. *Times Higher Education Supplement.*

United Kingdom Council for International Education. (1987). *Responsible recruitment: A model for a code of practice for institutions involved in the education of students from overseas.* London: Author.

Universities in crisis. (2001). Report into the capacity of public universities to meet Australia's higher education needs. Senate Employment, Workplace Relations, Small Business and Education References Committee, Commonwealth Government of Australia. Retrieved March 18, 2002, from http://www.aph.gov.au/senate/committee/eet_ctte/public%20 uni/report/index.htm

Urry, J. (1995). *Consuming places.* London: Routledge.

Urry, J. (1998). Contemporary transformations of time and space. In P. Scott (Ed.), *The globalization of higher education* (pp. 1–17). Ballmoor, England: Open University Press and Society for Research into Higher Education.

U.S. Department of Education. (2003). *Amendments to Higher Education Act of 1965.* Retrieved January 18, 2004, from http://www.ed.gov/policy/highered/leg/hea98/sec601.html

U.S. Department of State. (2003). *Fulbright Program.* Retrieved April 12, 2004, from http://exchanges.state.gov/education/fulbright/

Van Damme, D. (2001). Quality issues in the internationalisation of higher education. *Higher Education, 41,* 415–441.

van de Wende, M. (1999). Quality assurance in higher education and the link to internationalisation. OECD/IMHE (pp. 225–237).

van de Wende, M. (2000). Internationalisation policies: About new trends and contrasting paradigms. *Higher Education Policy, 14*(3), 249–259.

Vargas, G. (1999). New Year's address. In R. Levine & J. Crocitti (Eds.), *The Brazil reader: History, culture and politics* (pp. 186–189). Durham, NC: Duke University Press.

Venn, C. (2002). Altered states: Post Enlightenment cosmopolitanism and transmodern socialities. *Theory, Culture, and Society, 19*(1–2), 65–80.

Vianna, O. (1999). Why the Estado Nouvo. In R. Levine & J. Crocitti (Eds.), *The Brazil reader: History, culture and politics* (pp. 184–186). Durham, NC: Duke University Press.

Vidal, J. (2003, October 30–November 5). Oil giant in dock over Amazon waste. *Guardian Weekly,* p. 4.

Vidal, J. (2004, April 8–14). Demand for beef speeds destruction of Amazon forest. *Guardian Weekly.*

Vidovich, L., & Currie, J. (1998). Changing accountability and autonomy at the "coalface" of academic work in Australia. In J. Currie & J. Newson (Eds.), *Universities and globalization* (pp. 193–211). Thousand Oaks, CA: Sage.

Vidovich, L., & Slee, R. (2001). Bringing universities to account? Exploring some global and local policy tensions. *Journal of Education Policy, 16,* 431–453.

Volet, S., & Ang, G. (1998). Culturally mixed groups on international campuses: An opportunity for intercultural learning. *Higher Education Research and Development, 17,* 5–23.

Volet, S., & Renshaw, P. (1995). Cross cultural differences in university students' goals and perceptions of study settings for achieving their goals. *Higher Education, 30,* 407–433.

Volet, S., Renshaw, P., & Tietzel, K. (1994). A short-term longitudinal investigation of cross cultural differences in study approaches using Biggs' SPQ questionnaire. *British Journal of Educational Psychology, 64,* 301–318.

Volet, S., Smart, D., & Ang, G. (2000). *Fostering social cohesion on campuses.* : Australia Education International.

Wachter, B. (2000). Internationalisation at home. In P. Crowther, M. Joris, M. Olsen, B. Nilsson, H. Teekens, & B. Wachter (Eds.), *Internationalisation.* Amsterdam: European Association for International Education.

Wallis, R. (1999, December 2). UK universities are"exploiting" overseas students. *Independent.* http://education.independent.co.uk/news/story.jsp?story=12949

Walters, J. (2003, October 9–15). Sky-high money for campus stars. *Guardian Weekly,* p. 25.

Walters, J. (2004, April 1–7). Sorry seems to be the hardest word. *Guardian Weekly,* p. 27.

Warwick, D. (1999, March). *Globalisation: The challenges and opportunities for UK higher education.* Paper presented at the Association of University Administrators, London. Retrieved July 2, 2002, from http://www.universitiesuk.ac.uk/speeches/show.asp?sp=23

Waters, M. (2001). *Globalization.* London: Routledge.

Watson, D., & Bowden, R. (1999). Why did they do it? The Conservatives and mass higher education, 1979–1997. *Journal of Education Policy, 14,* 243–256.

Wee, C. J. W.-L. (2001). The end of disciplinary modernization: The Asian economic crisis and the ongoing reinvention of Singapore. *Third World Quarterly, 22*(6), 987–1002.

Wee, H.-T. (1998). *In time for the future: The role of education.* National Institute of Education. Retrieved August 27, 2000, from http://www.nie.ac.sg:8000/~wwwnie/KeySpeeches/Convo98/DGE.html

Wei, T.-D. (2000). The five Cs and the good life. In *Singapore* (pp. 16–20). Singapore: Singapore International Foundation.

Weiss, K. (2003). *States in the global economy: Bringing domestic institutions back.* Cambridge, England: Cambridge University Press.

Weiss, L. (1997, September). Globalization and the myth of the powerless state. *New Left Review, 225,* 3–27.

West, R. (1998). *Learning for life: Reviews of higher education financing and policy.* Canberra: Department of Education, Training, and Youth Affairs.

Western Governors University. (2002). *About WGU.* Retrieved June 20, 2002, from http://www.wgu.edu/wgu/about/

Westheimer, J. (2002). Tenure denied: Anti-unionism and anti-intellectualism in the academy. *Social Text, 20*(4), 47–64.

Whalley, T. (1997). *Best practice guidelines for internationalisation of the curriculum.* Ministry of Education, Skills and Training and the Centre for Curriculum Transfer and Technology. Province of British Columbia.

Wicks, P. (1972). Diplomatic perspectives. In S. Bochner & P. Wicks (Eds.), *Overseas students in Australia* (pp. 10–21). Randwick, Australia: University of New South Wales.

Wilkin, P. (2003). Revising the democratic revolution—Into the Americas. *Third World Quarterly, 24,* 655–669.

Williams, G. (1997). The market route to mass higher education: British experience 1979–1996. *Higher Education Policy, 10*(3), 275–289.

Williams, W. A. (1988). *The tragedy of American diplomacy.* New York: Norton.

Willinsky, J. (1998). *Learning to divide the world: Education at empire's end.* Minneapolis: University of Minnesota Press.

Willmott, H. (2003). Commercialising higher education: The state, industry and peer review. *Studies in Higher Education, 28,* 129–141.

Wong, K.-S. (2003, August). Speech by Minister for Home Affairs Wong Kan Seng at the Convocation of Singapore Management University.

Wong, P., & Balestino, R. (2001). Prioritizing the education of marginalised young people in Brazil: A collaborative approach. *Journal of Education Policy, 16,* 597–618.

Woods, R. (1987, May). Fulbright internationalism. *American Academy of Political and Social Science, 491,* 22–35.

Work experience. (2003, November 13). *Independent.*

Yee, A., & Lim, T. (1995). Educational supply and demand in East Asia: Private higher education. In A. Yee (Ed.), *East Asian higher education: Traditions and transformations* (pp. 179–191). Oxford, England: Pergamon/IAU Press.

Yeo, G. (2003, August). *Singapore: The global schoolhouse.* Speech by Minister for Trade and Industry. Retrieved January 20, 2004, from http://www.sedb.com/edbcorp/sg/en_uk/index/in_the_news/2003/20030/singapore_-_the_global.html

Yerbury, D. (2001, September). *Developing global capacity through international education.* Opening Plenary Session, Australian Education International Conference, University of New South Wales, Sydney, Australia.

Yerbury, D. (2004, September 15). Nurturing peace, love and understanding. *Higher Education Supplement, The Australian,* p. 32.

Younge, G. (2003, August 28–September 3). God help America. *Guardian Weekly,* p. 11.

Zhao, Y. (2004, January 18). The visa trap. *New York Times,* pp. A4, A32.

Zusman, A. (1999). Issues facing higher education in the twenty-first century. In R. Berdahl, P. Altbach, & P. Gumport (Eds.), *American higher education in the twenty-first century: Social, political and economic challenges* (pp. 109–147). Baltimore: Johns Hopkins University Press.

Index

A

AAUP (American Association of University Professors), 65, 80
Academic capitalism, 66–69, 122, 189
ACE (American Council of Education), 62, 65, 70, 79
AEI (Australian Education International), 191
Africa News Service, 113
Agence France Press, 234
Aglionby, J., 254
Agnew, J., 166
"Ah Beng," 88, 236, 259
Ahier, J., 123
Ahmad, A., 50
"Air conditioned nation," 238
Alai-Amlatina, A., 274
Alexander, D., 10, 11, 184, 190
Almeida, A., 283
Altbach, P., 12, 28, 66, 78, 127, 250
Altenberg, I., 90
America
    foreign policy & educational aid, 6, 7, 8, 9, 76, 80–82
American exceptionalism, 9, 71, 73, 76, 97, 98, 99, 117
    and Manifest Destiny, 9, 72, 98, 114, 297
Amin, A., 133, 240, 241
Amman, E., 279, 294
Andrews, C., 278

Ang, G., 33, 185, 193
Angelova, M., 33
Anglo-Globalization, 6, 285
Anthias, F., 48, 50
Appadurai, A., 16, 44, 47, 50, 52, 53, 60, 100, 294
Apple, M., 85, 285
Archibugi, D., 314
Ardolino, K., 66
Armitage, C., 198
Arshad, A., 319
Ashcroft, B., 208
Ashton, D., 244
Asiaweek, 40
Auletta, A., 184
Australian higher education
    international education, 183–194
        branding of, 190–191
        marketization, 179, 185, 188–190, 194–196
        policies, 178–185
AUT (Association of University Teachers), 125
AVCC (Australian Vice-Chancellors Committee), 2, 187, 188, 189

B

Back, K., 184, 185
Badley, G., 122
Baer, W., 279, 294

Baker, M., 16, 233, 234
Balestino, R., 282
Ball, S., 13, 38, 122, 129, 141, 178
Ballard, B., 33, 34, 35
Barnett, G., 22, 23
Barnett, R., 124
Barr, M., 237, 239
Barrow, C., 64, 66, 70, 79
Bartelson, J., 42
Barty, A., 140
Basnett, S., 145
Batty, D., 139
Baty, P., 146
Bauman, Z., 53, 60, 303, 311, 312, 313, 314
Bechtel Corporation, 88
Bechtel International Centre, 88, 90, 95, 96
Beck, L., 280
Beckett, F., 145
Beech, J., 284
Benesch, S., 37
Bennell, P., 2, 143
Bennett, P., 124
Berdahl, R., 64, 65
Berman, E., 39
Berry, C., 40
Bhatt, A., 50, 65, 83
Biggs, J., 36
Billig, M., 58
Birch, D., 237, 238
Blackmore, J., 39
Blair, T., 125, 128
Blaxter, L., 121
Boehner, J., 80
Borderlands, 86
Borders, 53, 54, 59, 112, 190
Bosworth, S., 122
Boulger, D., 234
Bourdieu, P., 17, 311
Bowden, R., 119
Brain drain, 10
Braithwaite, J., 113
Brand Report, 129-130
Brandao, C., 278
Branding, 92, 101–104, 129–137, 150, 152,
        159–161, 190–192, 200–206,
        214–217, 250–253, 299–300, 308
Branford, S., 280
Brazil
    governing technologies, 274–277
    higher education, 281–285
    history, 271–273
    internationalization, 285–291

power and politics, 273–275
racial democracy, 277
Brett, J., 180
Bright, M., 145
British Council, 128, 129, 130, 132, 136,
        137, 138, 139, 261, 289–291
    Education Counselling Service, 129, 133,
        136
Broadhead, L., 38, 119
Brown, D., 10, 193
Bruch, T., 140
Budd, J., 69, 70
Buell, F., 73, 74
Bullen, E., 33
Burbach, R., 86
Burchell, D., 32
Burgess, R., 193
Burke, M., 33
Business technologies of the self, 98,
        201–203, 302, 304, 305

C

Cadman, K., 37
Caldwell, K., 278
Canclini, N., 148
Cardean University, 67
Carroll, R., 114
Carvel, J., 146
Cassidy, S., 126
Castells, M., 44
Castles, S., 11, 190
Chagas, C., 278
Chan, H.-C., 237
Chandler, A., 78
Chang, H.-Y., 244
Chapman, B., 180
Chen, Q., 193
Chen, T.-M., 22, 23, 193
Cheung, W.-L., 59
Chin, J., 240
Chipman, L., 65, 195
Chitnis, S., 28
Chua, B.-H., 49, 235, 237, 238, 239, 240,
        242, 243, 253, 260, 261
Clancy, J., 34, 35
Clinton, W., 78
Clyne, F., 2, 193
Coe, N., 59, 237, 240, 243, 259
Cohen, D., 193, 246, 256, 259

Cold War, xxiii, xxiv, 3, 7, 11, 80
Cole, M., 124, 198
Colley, L., 56, 79, 127
Colombo Plan, 10–12
Colonial power, 3–6, 56, 127, 130, 132
Committee on Education & Workforce, 80, 81
Considine, M., 39, 179, 193, 214, 220, 222
Cooper, S., 105
Corporate university, 13–15, 66–67, 142–144, 195–196, 200, 215–219, 221, 222, 245
Cosmopolitanism, 72, 162, 306
Cox, H., 10
Crinnion, P., 194
Crocitti, J., 277, 273, 274, 275
Crow, J., 272
Cultural circuit of capital, 51, 68, 69, 250
Cultural diversity, 74, 106–108, 154–156, 167–168, 174–175, 211–214, 225, 227, 229, 238–239, 306–308
Cummings, D., 24
Currie, J., 38, 180
Curtis, P., 126

D

Da Matta, R., 277
Da Silva, L., 282
Dahrendorf, R., 148, 149
Davie, S., 246, 256
Davies, M., 5
Davies, R., 284
Davis, D., 184, 16, 185
Dean, M., 31
De Beer, P., 240
Deem, R., 123, 125, 126, 305
DEET (Dept of Education, Employment & Training), 180
Defensive fundamentalism, 74
De Jesus, C., 278
Denny, C., 114
DES (Dept of Education & Skills), 119
DEST (Dept of Education, Science & Training), 183, 186, 188, 189, 190, 193
Deterritorialization, 54, 55
DETYA (Dept of Education, Training & Youth Affairs), 181
De Wit, H., 2, 63

Dicken, P., 42, 61, 305
Didou-Aupetit, S., 64, 66, 70, 79
Dill, D., 63, 66, 182
Dimitriades, G., 59
Dirlik, A., 50
Discourse, 27–29
    and disciplines, 28, 29, 31–37
    and globalization, 42, 43
Discursive practices, 27
Disjunctures of living, 50, 54
Dispositif, 45
DoFES (Dept of Education & Skills), 125
Drahos, P., 113
Drier, P., 220
DTI (Dept of Trade & Industry), 125
Duckett, S., 183
Dunstan, P., 197, 198, 199

E

Edelstein, R., 79
Edge, J., 291
Education
    Empire building, 3–6, 76, 127
    Enterprise, 92, 94
Education Counselling Service (ECS), 137
Education Travel, 286
Education UK brand, 130–136
Educational aid, 6–8, 10–12, 76
    Colombo Plan, 10–12
    Fulbright Program, 6–8, 11
Educational instrumentalism, 79, 103, 201, 203, 255
Educational tourism, 150, 210–212, 222–227
E-education, 14, 68
Ehrenberg, R., 39, 66, 69, 103
Ehrenreich, B., 85
Ellingobe, B., 79
Elliot, L., 124
Emmerson, D., 237
Empire, 3, 4, 6, 56, 76, 79, 234
Engel, M., 114
Eshiwani, G., 28
ESOS (Education Services for Overseas Students), 187
Ethnocultural identity, 238–240
"Exposure," 262–263

F

Fairweather, J., 67
Farahmandpur, R., 69
Farquhar, R., 2
Fausto, B., 273
FCO (Foreign & Commonwealth Office),
    136
Featherstone, M., 47
Ferguson, N., 76
Fernandez, W., 235, 261
Fields, P., 68
Figueirido-Cowen, M., 5, 282
Fisher, W., 58, 113, 279
Fisk, R., 81
Fiske, J., 11, 190
Flint, C., 53
Flynn, P., 280
Foucault, M., 27, 28, 29, 30, 31, 45, 46,
    176, 203, 315, 316
Fox-Piven, F., 220
Francis, A., 3, 315
Frank, T., 9, 74, 75
Fraser, N., 303
Friedman, J., 48, 49
Friedman, T., 83
Fulbright, J., 7
Fulbright Program, 7

G

Gade, M., 63
Gallagher, M., 182
Gandin, L., 285
Garner, R., 125
Gates, R., 77, 78, 80
George, A., 113
George, C., 237, 238, 239, 253, 262
Giddens, A., 44, 53, 123
Gilbert, A., 195
Gillespie, H., 71, 77
Ginway, E., 276
Gladieux, L., 63, 64
Global peace, 1, 2
Global public good, 308
Global Schoolhouse, 245–250, 256
Global talent race, 82–84, 102–103, 297
Global trade in education, 13, 18–25, 138,
    142, 166–167
Globalization, 42–47, 238, 243
    and nation-states, 55–57

and the social imagination, 157–158
deterritorialization, 54–55
discourse, 43–45, 52, 53
genealogy of, 43, 45
globalization-from-below, 294, 295
"Globalization," 48
metaphors, 44
neoliberal, 130
postcolonial, 12, 145
reterritorialization, 58–60
scapes, 48, 52
uneven, 53–55, 58, 232–233
Goh, C.-T., 238
Goldblatt, D., 44
Goldring Review, 184
Goodman, A., 1
Gopinathan, S., 244
Gordon, C., 32
Gough, N., 315
Governmentality, 30–32
    and globalization, 43–45
    Singapore, 236–238
Green, M., 22, 71
Greenhill, R., 57
Griffiths, G., 208
Guantanamo Bay, 86

H

Hage, G., 58, 307
Hall, M., 84
Hall, S., 28, 53
Halliday, F., 53, 105, 149
Hamilton, S., 2
Hamlin, K., 255, 257, 259
Han, F.-K., 235, 261
Harcleroad, F., 62
Hardt, M., 297
Harley, S., 119, 120, 121, 122
Harvey, D., 44, 240
Hay, C., 42, 46, 49, 51, 53, 61, 124, 305
Heartlanders, 236, 259
Heidhues, M., 234
Held, D., 44
Hellstein, M., 33
Heng, G., 231, 233, 262
Henkel, M., 120, 122
Henry, M., 13
Henson, B., 234
Herod, A., 310

Hesse, B., 45, 46, 53
Heterotopia, 159
Hetherington, K., 27, 178
Hickling-Hudson, A., 127
Hira, A., 67
Hirst, P., 44
Hite, R., 66, 67, 92
Ho, W.-K., 253
Hobsbawn, E., 56, 72, 76, 127
Hochschild, A., 85
Hodge, B., 11, 190
Hodges, L., 145, 146
Hodgson, G., 81
Hodson, P., 141
Holman, R., 76
Honan, J., 70
Hong, L., 239
Howard, S., 38, 119
Huang, J.-L., 235
Hudson, W., 37, 194
Huffstutter, P., 68
Huggins, M., 277, 278
Hughes, C., 121
Humphreys, N., 253, 262
Hybridity, 44, 47–50, 51–52, 227, 229,
    261–262, 266–268, 310–311
Hybridization, 47, 48, 49, 50, 260, 261,
    262
Hyland, T., 123

I

ICCAF (Inter-Church Coalition for Africa),
    209
IDP Education, 11, 287–289
IIE (Institute of International Education),
    81, 110–117, 286
Illing, D., 196, 198
Individualization, 153
Individualism, 130, 153, 203–206, 260, 238
INSEAD, 257
Intellectual property, 113
Intercultural brokers, 306
International education
    definitions, 2–3
    demand, 18–25
    push & pull factors, 20, 22–25
International student
    learning issues, 33–37
    mobility, 18–25

Internationalization, 2, 3
    and the OECD, 2
    in Australia, 183–194
    in United States, 76–82, 84–86
    in UK, 127–136, 144–145
Iredale, R., 194

J

Jackson Review, 184
Jacobsen, S., 220
Jacobsen, W., 33
Jameson, F., 44
Jessop, B., 14, 55
Johnson, D., 16
Johnson, R., 126
Johnston, J., 79
Jones, P., 24, 179, 185

K

Kahn, J., 238
Kaplan, A., 8, 73, 74, 76, 81, 86
Karpin, D., 186
Kaufman, J., 1
Kayatekin, S., 43
Keen, B., 271, 272, 273, 274, 276
Kelly, J., 125
Kelly, Patricia, 37, 206,
Kelly, Phillip, 59, 237, 240, 243, 259
Kempner, K., 283, 286
Kenway, J., 33, 179
Khondaker, H., 42
Kiasu/kiasu-ism, 253–255
King, J., 63, 64
Kingston, P., 146
Klees, S., 277
Klein, C., 6, 7,8, 72, 73, 297, 298, 307
Klein, N., 83, 84
Knight, D., 191
Knight, J., 2
Knowledge based economy (*see also* New
    Economy), 125, 243–244, 247,
    255–257
Knowledge goods, 101–104
Koeller, D., 271
Kramer, E., 50, 65, 130, 193
Kurtz, S., 81
Kwok, K.-W., 237, 239

L

Lam, P.-E., 237, 261
Langmead, D., 179
Lapham, L., 117, 236, 243, 281
Larner, W., 14, 43, 45, 46, 47, 48, 54, 57
Law, J., 27, 61, 178
Lawnham, P., 182, 196
Lawson, V., 240
Le Heron, R., 14, 45
League Tables, 39–40, 104, 122–123, 166
Lee, Kuan Yew, 235, 258, 259
Lee, Y.-S., 242
Lemke, T., 32, 38
Leon, P., 197
Leonard, D., 70
Leonhardt, D., 69, 70
Leslie, L., 38, 63, 66, 68, 70, 77, 122,
Levine, P., 60, 271, 272, 273, 274, 275, 276,
    277, 278, 279, 280
Libidinal capitalism, 240, 250
Lim, T., 77
Lingard, R., 13, 39
Lofgren, O., 14, 15, 68, 309
Longley, C., 9
Loombia, A., 4, 6, 11, 208
LSE (London School of Economics),
    148–162, 152
Lyon, J., 68, 196
Lyotard, J.-F., 122

M

Ma Rhea, Z., 4
MacCrae, S., 129
MacCreedy, J., 16
MacGill-Peterson, P., 78
MacLeod, D., 20, 121, 124, 126
Madsen, D., 81
Maguire, M., 129
Maiden, S., 199
Major, L., 146
Mallea, J., 64, 66, 70, 79
Manichean logic, xxiii, xxiv
Manne, R., 307
Mansfield, N., 32
Marcuse, P., 57
Marginson, S., 2, 13, 16, 17, 38, 39, 63,
    102, 123, 177, 178, 179, 180, 183,
    184, 185, 193, 194, 195, 214, 220,
    222, 287, 301, 302, 305, 308, 311,
    313
Market populism, 74–75
Marketing education (*see also* branding),
    91–94, 101–105, 129–139, 150–156,
    159–162, 164–172, 250–253,
    190–194, 200–206, 221–228,
    286–291, 308–309
  "Arm chair" marketing, 102
  elite marketing, 91, 92, 159–161
Markets
  discourse, 1, 12, 17
  international education, 14, 18–25,
    128–139, 142–143
Marklein, M., 84
Marshall, J., 32
Martinkus, J., 113
Mason, R., 50
Massey, D., 33, 45, 46, 53, 302, 303
Mathiason, N., 58
Matthews, J., 127
McBurnie, G., 185, 195
McCarthy, C., 59
McCarthy, R., 159
McConnell, T., 64, 65
McCormick, J., 33
McDonald's, 49
McGrew, A., 44
McGuiness, A., 64, 66, 70
McLaren, P., 69
McNay, L., 27
Meadmore, D., 18
Media discourse, 82–85, 126, 145–147,
    196–199
Meek, L., 39, 180, 185
Mesquita, M., 277, 278
Mestenhauser, J., 78
Middleton, R., 122, 123
Miles, T., 145
Milito, C., 278
Miller, M., 11, 190
Miller, P., 27, 30, 32, 38
Miller, R., 77
Milmo, D., 9
Milton-Smith, J., 249
Mishra, V., 11, 190
Mitchell, K., 48
Mitton, R., 239
Model minorities, 50, 83, 88, 115
Modernization, xxiii, 6, 10–11, 114–115,
    123, 132, 291
Mollis, M., 38, 177, 313

Monash University, 214–228
Monbiot, G., 9, 81, 86, 136
Monkman, K., 53
Monroe Doctrine, 8
Moreno, K., 82
Morris, S., 37, 194
Morrow, R., 77, 79
Mosse, G., 56
Moulin, N., 278, 282
Mowery, D., 64
Munk, D., 278, 281

N

NAFSA (North American Foreign Students
    Association), 72, 77, 80, 81, 82
Nandy, A., 4, 5, 6, 11, 12, 312
Nascimento, A., 278
Negri, T., 297
Nelson, R., 64
Neoliberal personhood, 305
Neoliberal state, 57, 61
Neoliberal vision, 92
Neoliberalism, 56, 74–76, 119, 310
    roll out neoliberalism, 58, 250
    roll back neoliberalism, 238
New Economy, 14–15, 75, 240–241,
    309–310
'New World Order', 75–76
    and international education, 78–82
Newson, J., 39
Niles, S., 36
Nines, P., 36, 37
Norton, A., 195

O

Odih, P., 191
OECD, 18
Oehlers, A., 253
O'Farrell, C., 16, 27, 316
O'Keefe, B., 248
Olds, K., 240, 241, 243, 245, 246, 250, 252,
    256, 257, 259
Oliver, A., 85
Olsen, A., 184, 185
Open Doors, 18, 101
O'Tuathail, G., 52, 54, 55, 310
Outsourcing, 82, 83, 84
Overton, J., 33

Oxford Brookes University, 163–175
Ozga, J., 38

P

Paehlke, R., 58
Palatella, J., 67
Papademetriou, D., 310
Parekh, B., 5, 6, 11, 58, 133
Parrenas, R., 233
Parrhesia (fearless speech), 315–317
Parry, B., 113
Parsons, A., 127
Patrick, K., 3, 315
Pearce, T., 2, 143, 144, 145
Peck, J., 58, 250
Pegrum, M., 23, 130, 132
Pereira, V., 278, 282
Perraton, J., 44
Peters, M., 14, 61
Pettifor, A., 57
Pieterse, J., 5, 6, 11, 48, 49, 50, 72, 76, 81,
    307
Place-branding, 103, 150, 164, 210–212,
    223–228, 308
Polster, C., 39
Ponniah, T., 58, 113, 279
Poole, D., 179
Positional goods, 17, 100, 150, 221–223, 263
Positioning for Success, 136–139
Postmodern colony, 231–236
Postmodern imperialism, 236
Power, 29–31
    and government, 30–32
    capillary power, 30
    descending analysis, 29
    soft, 73, 297
Power, S., 123, 124
Power-knowledge, ix, 27, 31–33, 42–43,
    51–54, 61, 92–94, 112–113, 143–145,
    194–196, 286–289
    calculative technologies, 37–40, 104–105,
    120–123
    expert systems, 33–41, 92
Prasad, R., 138
Pratt, G., 179
Preston, D., 39, 119, 122
Prime Minister's Initiative (PMI), 127–129
Productive Diversity, 186, 189
'Promising Practices', 79, 80

Prystay, C., 256
Puri, S., 233
Purushotam, N., 237
Pusser, B., 63

Q

QAA (Quality Assurance Agency), 140, 141
Quality assurance, 37–39, 139–141
Queensland Government, 212
QUT (Queensland University of Technology), 200–214, 203, 206, 208, 209, 210

R

Rahman, T., 5, 312
Rai, S., 50
Ramburuth, P., 33
Rao, G., 10
Reddy, M., 197, 199
Religion, 9–10, 85–86, 159, 240
Remittances, 233, 310
Renaissance City (see Singapore), 240–243
Renshaw, P., 36
Reterritorialization, 58, 60, 99, 147
Rewarded acculturation, 50, 65, 82, 83
Rhoades, G., 38, 63, 66, 70, 79, 123, 305
Riazantseva, A., 33
Ridley, D., 33
Ritzema, T., 233
Rizvi, F., 10, 11, 13, 184, 186, 190, 194, 195
Rizzini, L., 277
Robber Barons, 90
Roberts, G., 121
Roberts, P., 285
Roberts, S., 302, 310
Robertson, R., 42, 53
Rodan, G., 235, 237, 238, 239
Rojas, C., 7
Rose, N., 27, 30, 31, 32, 38, 39, 124, 178
Rosemberg, F., 278
Rosenfield, A., 69
Rout, L., 277, 278
Roy, A., 59, 84
Ruccio, D., 43
Ryan, J., 252
Ryan, L., 180
Ryn, C., 86

S

Sadiki, L., 3, 194, 315
Sai, S.-M., 235
Said, E., 4, 52, 152
Salter, B., 119, 120
Samoff, J., 284, 294
Sampat, B., 64
Samuels, D., 279, 280
Sardar, Z., 5
Sarup, M., 5
Sassen, S., 46, 232
Saunders, F., 8, 72
Schapper, J., 284
Schein, E., 259
Schemo, D., 84
Scheyvens, R., 33
Schirato, T., 43
Scholte, J., 42, 299, 313
Schwartzman, S., 283, 284
Scott, P., 12, 118, 119, 122, 145, 311
Self goods, 17, 106–110
Self–Other relations, 34–36, 85–86, 94–100, 105, 154–156, 206–209, 265–268, 298–299
Sen, S., 60
Seneviratne, K., 232
Sennett, R., 306, 307, 311
Sevier, R., 66, 67, 92
Shephard, E., 45, 46, 51
Shore, C., 39, 120, 123
Sidhu, R., 59, 192
Sidley, P., 113
Silva, H., 278
Singapore
    "Culture building," 238–240
    "Exposure," 262
    Global Schoolhouse, 245–250, 256, 269
    governing discourse, 235–240
    history, 234–236
    "Intelligent Island," 243–245
    productive absence, 240
Singapore 21 Committee, 94, 242
Singapore Education Brand, 250–253
Singapore girl, 231
Singapore Education, 251, 252
Singapore International Foundation, 243, 259
Singh, M., 194
Singh, N., 6, 73, 74, 307

Slaughter, S., 38, 63, 66, 68, 70, 77, 120, 122
Slee, R., 38, 180
Sleicher, D., 33
Smart, D., 33, 185, 193
Smith, N., 42, 61, 124, 305
Smith, R., 60
Socrates, 34
Sparke, M., 240
Spatial scripts, 28
Speak Good English Movement, 260
Spring, J., 127, 244
Stanford University, 90–100
Stanford University Graduate School of Business, 92, 94
Stanley, A., 85
Starr, M., 55
Steele, J., 281
Stewart, C., 83
Stiglitz, J., 113, 280, 281
Strathern, M., 205
Stromquist, N., 53
Study in Australia, 192
Subject positions, 26–27, 29, 33–37, 51, 113, 142, 153, 253–255
   cosmopolitan, 154–155
   entrepreneurial, 255, 287, 302
   global, 60–61
   international student, 100, 114, 138
Sum, N.-L., 53
Sung, J., 244
SUNY (State University of New York), Stony Brook, 101–110
Sutherland, J., 80
Swarns, R., 24, 84

T

Tan, J., 240
Tan, S., 235, 261
Tan, T., 244, 250, 258, 259
Tapper, T., 119, 120
Tarbell, J., 86
Tavora, A., 276
Taylor, S., 13
Teather, D., 75
Technologies of spin, 311
Technologies of the self, 31, 32, 253–255, 291, 301, 305, 315–316
Teferra, D., 70

Teo, C.-H., 244, 254
Terrorist attacks, 1
Tester, K., 307, 311, 314, 316
Thamon, K., 228
Therborn, G., 42
Third Way, 123
Thomas, H., 141
Thompson, G., 44
Thorsby, C., 179
Thrift, N., 14, 51, 52, 68, 69, 75, 240, 241, 243, 245, 246, 250, 252, 256, 257, 259, 269, 302, 304, 305
Thrift, Nigel, 52, 69, 252, 305
Tickell, A., 58, 250
Tierney, W., 79
Tietzel, K., 36
Tiffin, H., 208
Tight, M., 121
Tikly, L., 6, 11, 45, 46, 52, 53, 127, 313
Tomasevski, K., 24
Tomlinson, J., 147
Tootell, K., 183
Torres, Carlos, 77, 79, 282, 284, 294
Torres, Cecilia, 276
Tota, A., 275, 276
Trade in Education, 13–17
Transnational exchanges, 52, 149
Transparency International, 114
Trow, M., 119, 120, 121
Trowler, P., 122
Tsoukas, H., 205
Tuhiwai-Smith, L., 6, 152
Tully, J., 279, 315, 316
Turner, G., 11, 190
Turpin, T., 194
Tysome, T., 145, 146

U

United Kingdom higher education
   and globalization, 142
   and internationalization, 143–145
   history, 118
   policies, 119–126
United States higher education
   internationalization, 78–82
   Stanford University, 91–94
   state–market relations, 62–68
   SUNY Stony Brook, 101–105

Universities
    cosmopolitan scholarship, 314–315
    social imagination, 311–317
Urry, J., 42, 48, 61
U.S. Dept of Education, 81

V

Van Damme, D., 18, 22
Vargas, G., 275
Venn, C., 6, 11, 312
Vianna, O., 275
Vidal, J., 291
Vidovich, L., 38, 180
Volet, S., 33, 36, 193

W

Wachter, B., 3
Wallis, R., 146
Walsh, L., 194
Walters, J., 66, 68, 69
Walters, W., 43, 45, 46, 47, 48, 54, 57
Warwick, D., 142, 143
Waters, M., 53, 97
Watkins, D., 136
Watson, D., 119
Watson, M., 46, 49, 51, 53
Webb, Beatrice and Sidney, 148
Webb, J., 43
Wee, C.-J., 242

Weiss, L., 57
Westheimer, J., 70
Whalley, T., 315
Whitty, G., 123, 124
Wicks, P., 10
Wild, K., 33
Wilkin, P., 281
Williams, G., 119, 120, 121, 122, 127
Williams, W. A., 9, 81
Willinsky, J., 4, 6, 127
Willmott, H., 121
Wong, K.-S., 245
Wong, P., 282
Woock, R., 2
Wood, F., 39, 180, 185
Woods, A., 127
World Class Universities (WCU), 245–248
Wright, S., 39, 120, 123

Y

Yearwood, A., 66, 67
Yee, A., 77
Yeo, G., 245, 256
Yerbury, D., 2
Yeung, H. W.-C., 240, 243
Younge, G., 9, 85, 86

Z

Zhao, Y., 24, 84
Ziedonis, A., 64
Zusman, A., 70